November, 2012

A Poet's Mind

Dear Kristian,

You, too, have a poet's mind.
This book is connected to your
two professors. Dennis wrote his
doctorate on Duncan & Duncan,
when he visited St. John's College,
is the only thinker I've ever met
who could - & did - outtalk David.
It was a sight to behold!

Love,
Dad.

A Poet's Mind

COLLECTED INTERVIEWS WITH
Robert Duncan, 1960–1985

EDITED BY
CHRISTOPHER WAGSTAFF

Foreword by Gerrit Lansing

North Atlantic Books
Berkeley, California

Published by
North Atlantic Books
P.O. Box 12327
Berkeley, California 94712

Jacket photo by Harry Redl
Jacket and book design by Brad Greene
Frontispiece: Robert Duncan, Stony Brook, New York, 1969
Copyright acknowledgments are listed on pages 463–64.
Printed in the United States of America

A Poet's Mind: Collected Interviews with Robert Duncan, 1960–1985 is sponsored by the Society for the Study of Native Arts and Sciences, a nonprofit educational corporation whose goals are to develop an educational and cross-cultural perspective linking various scientific, social, and artistic fields; to nurture a holistic view of arts, sciences, humanities, and healing; and to publish and distribute literature on the relationship of mind, body, and nature.

North Atlantic Books' publications are available through most bookstores. For further information, visit our website at www.northatlanticbooks.com or call 800-733-3000.

Library of Congress Cataloging-in-Publication Data

Duncan, Robert, 1919–1988.
  A poet's mind : collected interviews with Robert Duncan, 1960–1985 / edited by Christopher Wagstaff.
      p. cm.
  Summary: "*A Poet's Mind* gives an excellent introduction to a major American poet in his own thoughtful, engaging, and often funny words"—Provided by publisher
  ISBN 978-1-58394-454-7 (hardback)
  1. Duncan, Robert, 1919–1988—Interviews. 2. Poets, American—20th century—Interviews. I. Wagstaff, Christopher, 1943– II. Title.
  PS3507.U629Z48 2012
  813'.54—dc23

                                                                    2011046948

1 2 3 4 5 6 7 8 9 SHERIDAN 17 16 15 14 13 12

Contents

Part V. In an Order of Orders ... 343

PHOTOGRAPHS

Unless indicated, all photographs are of Robert Duncan.

FOREWORD: ROBERT DUNCAN AND THE SLIPSTREAM OF MEMORY

When in 1962 Robert Duncan and I shared a bedroom one night in Robert Kelly's apartments at Bard College, we had our first long conversation. In the course of it I felt a happy shock of recognition: both of us had read and delighted in certain writers of fiction who were at that time somewhat obscure, Mary Butts, Algernon Blackwood, Charles Williams, and George MacDonald.

The affinity was not totally unexpected. In New York, in the 1950s, when I first read Duncan's early work I was immediately attracted to his poetic vision. At the Gotham Book Mart I had stumbled onto a copy of his book of poems *Caesar's Gate*. In those days, fresh out of college, I took as anthem Kurt Weill's "Alabama Song" as sung by Lotte Lenya. In Robert's poem "Goodbye to Youth" I found a line quoted, "Show me the way to the next whiskey bar."

Before our encounter at Bard I had met Robert once in Manhattan. He was giving a reading at Diane di Prima's Poets' Theater. I attended with friends Ruth Yorck and Frederick Kiesler. Kiesler, architect and theorist of an older avant-garde, friend of Marcel Duchamp, and admirer of John Cage, dismissed Duncan's poetry as old-fashioned, outdated Romanticism.

I was rapt however by Robert's presence, spellbound by his carefully controlled hand gestures and modulated voice. And I felt he was, as Helen Adam put it, "akin to the mighty tribe of cats."

Afterwards I was told that the anthropologist Jaime de Angulo said Robert, because of his abundant furry body hair, would be classified by Native Americans as belonging to the Great Bear clan.

Much later, when I gave him the manuscript of my serial poem "The Soluble Forest . . ." for his critical scrutiny, my anxiety was assuaged when he gave it his approval. He read me his own unpublished "The Regulators." I was bowled over. By that time I had published his great poem "Osiris and Set" as the opening poem in the first issue of my poetry magazine *SET*.

The last time I was with him, only a couple of years before his death, was again in Manhattan. He was staying at a luxurious Park Avenue apartment belonging to international art dealers who were agents for the work of his lifetime companion Jess Collins. Robert was much weakened by kidney disease and on a dialysis machine, but his old feline sinuosity was unabated as he spoke with vehemence about the East Coast poetry scene of unappreciative cliques.

In spite of physical disability his mental state was of excited joyfulness. He celebrated the slipstream of memory, recombining images from his past and his multifarious reading, subliming them in the athanor of his imagination.

It was the faculty of Imagination he exalted. Unlike William Blake, Duncan did not oppose the Muses of Memory to the Muses of Inspiration.

In calling himself a "derivative poet" he accepted others' influence without anxiety. He had no desire to found a school of poets like him.

His view both of himself and his work was multiphasic; he refused to deny the shifts and transformations of his psyche or his bewildering sleights of tongue in favor of a monolithic identity.

In one interview he says, "Rightly viewed, my voice is theosophical, the lore of the gods or the lore of the divine." Another time he terms himself "a devout gestaltist" and a "vitalist," and, another twist, "a Judeo-Christian poet." (Certainly he was no more an orthodox Christian than Charles Williams, whose terminology of Permission, Obedience, and Courtesy he often used both in poetry and prose.) His aunt Fayette had combined pantheism and vitalism in her privately printed "The New Hypothesis."

A drawing by the British visionary artist Austin Osman Spare, "Slipstream of Memory," graphite and charcoal, shows the artist beholding faces and masks of his past as they arise in turbulent slipstream of memory. And in Robert's self-awareness of the poetic myth he created and was created by, entwining his living and writing, he witnessed the conjunction of time's opposites, vortex of present and past, memory and desire.

— *Gerrit Lansing*
Gloucester, Massachusetts, 2012

Acknowledgments

I'm grateful to Richard Grossinger, publisher of North Atlantic Books, for his immediately saying he wanted to issue this book when I first mentioned it and then his following through on the project so well. Two editors at North Atlantic, Lindy Hough and Elizabeth Kennedy, were most supportive, and my current editor, Jessica Moll, has been a great pleasure to work with and has given valuable guidance throughout the volume's final stages. Barbara O'Brien offered assistance throughout the preparation and lent her editorial expertise to the introduction and the head notes. Poet Evan Karp patiently keyboarded the entire text. Adrienne Armstrong provided meticulous copyediting (partly defrayed by Barbara O'Brien), and Karin McPhail helped in numerous ways, including sending and answering emails. James Maynard of the Poetry Collection of the University Libraries, University at Buffalo, the State University of New York, generously provided copies of transcripts of various interviews from Robert Duncan's files and several of the photographs used here, as well as information and answers to many queries. Steve Dickison, director of the Poetry Center in San Francisco, tracked down the two photographs of Charles Olson and Robert Duncan, which are apparently the only ones of the poets together. In addition, Gui Mayo kindly lent the rare photograph she took of her father, Jaime de Angulo, and Becky Brockway unearthed two photos of Robert Duncan from the 1940s. I am especially thankful to Gerrit Lansing for his beautiful foreword, which affords a glimpse of his great heart and erudition, two of many qualities he shares with Robert Duncan. Of course, this book owes everything to Robert Duncan, whose spirit and mind can be felt in vital and tangible ways on every page.

A mention should be made of a few interviews that regrettably could not be published here because of their length or other reasons, including conversations with Bobbie Creeley (Bobbie Louise Hawkins), Robert Creeley, Lewis Ellingham, Richard O. Moore, the *New York Quarterly*, John Taggart, Eloyde Tovey, two anonymous questioners, and possibly others the editor is unaware of. Finally, I appreciate all the painstaking effort the interviewers originally put into preparing these discussions—in some cases many years ago—which now may be enjoyed in a fresh context and perhaps by a new generation of readers.

A note: Ellipses in the text indicate pauses in Duncan's or the interviewer's speech or omitted material.

INTRODUCTION

These interviews with Robert Duncan are one of the most extensive and illuminating series of conversations with any major poet of the twentieth century, and they constitute a significant component of the poet's *oeuvre*. In all, Duncan gave about thirty-eight interviews, and the twenty-eight collected here took place over a twenty-five-year period. They include biographical information not found elsewhere in his writings, along with extensive discussions of poetics and other subjects that shed light on his thought and work as a whole as well as on the meaning and impetus of post–World War II American poetry. Thus, they offer an invaluable companion to *The Collected Writings of Robert Duncan*, issued by the University of California Press.

The ten interviews not included in this volume either require extensive editing and clarification not possible at this time or present material already covered in the other conversations. The editor especially regrets the omission of the 148-page discussion with Eloyde Tovey of The Bancroft Library in 1978, containing much about the poetry scene in the San Francisco Bay Area, and also of the interview of equal length with Richard O. Moore in 1974, both as yet unpublished. A few interviews are not given in their entirety because of length, and the editor apologizes for the omission of any interview a reader looks for here and cannot find. Most of the discussions originally appeared in little magazines or college newspapers, now out-of-print and difficult to find. Seven of the interviews are transcripts from Duncan's own files and, along with David Melnick's, are published here for the first time.

In reading these conversations, it seems apparent that they were for Duncan opportunities to teach, which he loved to do, if by that we understand occasions to let new ideas appear. Although he spoke of interviews as necessarily lacking in "care and design," he granted many and invariably gave himself totally to these interactions, even during his last five years when he was unwell. What may initially impress one is the amazing breadth and depth of his interests and knowledge, whether he is talking about anthropology, shamanism, linguistics, contemporary biology, enjambment, post–World War II painting, Darwin, Kenneth Rexroth, Spenser, the Beats, or what he calls the American love of "polyglot assemblage." Equally evident and undergirding this intelligence is his great humanity, which shows in an almost complete absence of self-consciousness and in a disarming honesty about his ignorance of a subject he isn't familiar with or remembers little about. Thus, he is here an ever-curious participant rather than an authority. In these discussions, as in every aspect of his work, he sought a mind content with what Keats called "half-knowledge," that could be intellectual and yet not saturated with the known. Like Gertrude Stein, who remarked, "I wouldn't know what I knew," Duncan loved stumbling onto new insights and connections in the dark, or accidentally, as it were. He reminds one of that educated person Gerald Heard says can entertain himself, entertain a stranger, and entertain a new idea.

This kind of engagement is central to the imagination, a recurring subject in these interchanges. An early provisional title of this collection was "A Visionary Imagination," because this phrase so well describes Duncan's mind and work. He states, "Finally, imagination is my ground, and I hold to it," adding that there are no boundaries or limits for what remains a final ground for him. In his view, the imagination is a capacity everyone has (although poets and artists seem to have it in special abundance) to participate emotionally and over time and space in what is larger and beyond oneself. For example, if one is studying the Middle Ages, one can, through an empathy of the mind, feel that one is *in* these Ages, rather than being *outside* them as an observer learning about them. Likewise, both the writer and the reader can lose themselves in the poem. The opposite of such participation is Conventionalism, Duncan believes. As a living matrix of "What Is," the imagination continually unfolds what is unanticipated and at times even inscrutable. Duncan admits to an appetite for "writing to be strange" and observes, "and that's what the imagination produces, and it's absolutely expected." To Robert Peters he comments, "I loved adventure beyond my being able to understand it. I've always wanted to be inside an unexplained poem, a poem that was an adventure that you couldn't sum up."

No doubt, other editors would arrange the material here differently and in their own way. To me, these conversations seemed to fall into five general subject areas, and although these interrelate and overlap, I hope the presentation in five parts makes it easier to chart a course through them and to appreciate some of Duncan's most dearly held beliefs and convictions.

Part I, "Derivation and Obedience," explores what it means to be a "derivative poet," which is how Robert Duncan describes himself to Deborah Digges and to others with whom he speaks. He says he early gave up the struggle to be "original," as he knew it was really impossible to be so entirely distinctive, and he wanted his writing to openly express his love and appreciation for other poets' work. Being "derivative" in part means that all the ideas and inspiration don't have to come from *oneself*, but from the language and the world that flood a writer's being. He feels that most of our language and even our emotions derive from "the condition of Man," and mentions to Digges that in writing, a poet is obeying a *law*—another key concept for him—that guides him or her, thus letting the genius of the language direct one rather than moving words and phrases around in a poem. "It's what comes to me that I go along with, not what I seem to initiate myself," he tells Eugene Vance; and to Anne Waldman he says that a poem has "a commanding presence," obedience to which must be pursued in a volunteerist, Vanzetti-like fashion rather than imposed by the will or from without.

Part II, "A Poetry of Unevenness," continues to explore a poetics that involves a transcendence of the poet's personality and feelings and moves unbounded in a field or cosmos. He remarks to George Bowering and Robert Hogg, "You will find throughout my poetry the idea of an individuality that has absolute freedom and is a law to itself, that has its being in a larger being [which] is the cosmos finally." Cosmos as a "field" is a metaphor for what has a capacity to extend beyond itself and invites one to move freely within it and not according to prescription. It requires a surrender of the "me" and a participation in "a world of forms," as he says to L. S. Dembo: "We don't make up language ourselves, and we don't think it." Rather, Duncan sees himself as bringing out the qualities that are there, instead of "giving the quality to the language. Now I don't *put* the meaning in." He probably would concur with the composer Morton Feldman, who once said to Karlheinz Stockhausen, "Let the sounds alone, Karlheinz—don't push them," to which the German composer replied, "Not even a little bit?"

The interviews in Part III, "Toward the Liberation of Human Love," present Duncan's subtle, complex views of homosexuality. He reveals intimate aspects of his personal experience not found elsewhere in such detail or told with such candidness. Perhaps, above all, a reader will be struck with his rejection of labels and dislike of categories in relation to sexuality, as in other areas. He several times observes that he is not a gay or homosexual poet. To David Quarles he describes himself as "an intellectual poet with pantheistic and anarchistic leanings." Homosexuality he feels can include "conviviality" as well as explicit sexuality and needn't isolate one into a special group. Eventually he feels we will all accept our differences and just be. He notes his work is in essence a record of human love. At last, "I am a poet of emotions," he says.

Part IV, "Surrounded by Love's Company," focuses on those poets and other figures who have been Duncan's enduring companions and who have had a lasting impact on him, whose work and thought have been generative and without whom he wouldn't have survived. Their part in the emergence of his own work is beyond calculation. Although many are not discussed here, this company includes Dante, Coleridge, Blake, Rumi, Freud, H.D., Saint-John Perse, James Joyce, Mary Butts, L. Frank Baum, D.H. Lawrence, Virginia Woolf, Gertrude Stein, Baudelaire, and others. Chief among his own loved contemporaries are Ezra Pound and William Carlos Williams, along with Charles Olson, Robert Creeley, Jack Spicer, Louis Zukofsky, and Denise Levertov. One often feels their momentous presence as Duncan speaks of them in these conversations. After H.D., Ezra Pound was the first major modern poet who ushered Duncan into a new world of thought and feeling. He twice movingly describes picking up *XXX Cantos* for the first time in a

Berkeley bookstore when he was seventeen and being overwhelmed by the opening line, surely one of the determining moments in his poetic destiny. "Stein and Pound I stayed with from my adolescence and never swerved," he declares, and to James Laughlin, L. S. Dembo, and Michael André Bernstein and Burton Hatlen, he gives some of the most profound and stirring readings of *The Cantos* to be found anywhere.

Unlike Pound, who despaired over the failed form of his poem and his inability to bring his materials under the discipline of a "preplan," Duncan feels the greatness of *The Cantos* is that it broke the mold of such a plan, remaining close to Whitman's idea of "an ensemble," a conglomerate without a controlling center. Williams's *Paterson,* also, though it looked as if it were under the poet's control, was like *The Cantos,* constantly opening out in surprising ways. Duncan remarks, "In Williams's case everything appears as an epiphany to him. That's where we have our tie to Williams. He realized that the crucial experience in art is coming upon something, which is why the preplanned won't do at all."

Charles Olson is mentioned in almost every conversation. Once, when asked if he cared being sometimes placed in Olson's shadow, Duncan replied that he didn't mind and was happy to just fit in and play his part. Duncan was perhaps the only person who could hold his own in a conversation with the author of *The Maximus Poems.* The late poet and naturalist Linda Parker (later Linda Crane) once described to the editor Robert Duncan's arriving for dinner and an overnight stay at Olson's Fort Square house in Gloucester. The two had not seen each other for some time and immediately fell into an intense conversation, with barely a pause between each one's torrent of ideas and words. After dinner, Linda excused herself, and upon awakening the next morning heard voices in the kitchen. Olson and Duncan were still talking energetically at the kitchen table, the discussion continuing through breakfast until each fell asleep midmorning. Shortly before his death in 1970 in a New York City hospital, Olson whispered to Duncan, "We've been on a great adventure," and to a degree the interviews articulate that immense quest these two embarked on in language and cosmology.

Part V, "In an Order of Orders," consists of five interviews that are some of Duncan's last published thoughts on the nature of poetry. He speaks of a love of enigma for its own sake, those areas where things are "not understood," congenial to him from his earliest years, which he compares to the spirit of modern poetry, which is "to have maybe no guarantee and maybe no mastery" in the poem. The *Zohar*, the great Kabbalistic Jewish text that is discussed in depth with poet and professor Rodger Kamenetz, concerns such mystery, and like *The Divine Comedy*, is a universalizing rather than sectarian text, which opens one up to what he calls "an order of orders." Responding to such an "order," a writer encounters what Rudolf Otto calls "das numinose Gefühl," a numinous feeling taking one away from oneself and facing one toward what is other and timeless. Finally, to Michael Bernstein and Burton Hatlen in 1985, Duncan says he is not interested in being current or a part of literariness, which has a danger of lacking soul. He mentions his "ideal reader," whom he depicts in five pencil drawings in his volume *Letters* (1958), as a plump woman in a big hat who sits reading a book by a stream, or holds a cat on her lap, or stands without a book watering her plants, "not in the literary world at all."

Anyone who spent time with Robert Duncan witnessed his own such reading of things as his conversation explored several ideas almost simultaneously, following one direction of thought and then going off in another, pointing to the signals and signposts of an "order of orders" and ever inviting one to become along with him that "ideal reader" and join the dance. In one of the interviews in this volume Duncan mentions that for him poetry was often "a visitation" and that he was frequently in a trance-like state when he wrote. In another, he gives an account of his visit one night to Jackson Pollock's studio, where he watched the artist moving around in the *middle* of the canvas, painting on and on until a light and radiance appeared. This description could be of Duncan's own mind in all its multiphasic brilliance, ever at work within a poem or in such talk as we are privileged to overhear in these conversations.

In his beautiful tribute written after the poet's death in 1988, which begins, "Robert Duncan was everything we believed him to be,"

Michael McClure evokes the tangible presence of this imagination at work: "On going to visit Duncan there was the feeling that one was meeting Yeats or Joyce or Nerval or Villon—one felt that just before entering, Duncan might have been communing with the troubadour Peire Vidal or Emily Dickinson. There was a luminosity about Robert, and it grew with each decade as he lived in the aura—not really seeking it—and he always lit it up with his unexpected smile and his spontaneous, merry laugh." Reading these interviews, we can sense that smile, hear that laughter, and observe this communion of the poet's mind as it discovers more about itself and the world.

    — *Christopher Wagstaff*
      Berkeley, California, 2012

PART I

Derivation and Obedience

Circa early 1970s

Meeting with a College Student

(with Deborah Digges, 1974)

At the time of this interview in 1974, in which Robert Duncan refers to his beginnings as a poet, Deborah Digges was a junior majoring in English at the University of California at Riverside. She later earned an MFA in Poetry from the Iowa Writers' Workshop and taught at Tufts. Sadly and tragically, she passed on in 2009. In this interview Duncan describes himself as a "derivative poet" and states, "I have a term 'obedience' and that is obedience to the poem I hear." Poets are involved with language "in a way that it floods them with being." He also sheds light on the term "projective verse." This discussion was in typescript in Duncan's files, and there is no evidence that it had been published.

—Ed.

"I think for any young writer the important thing to remember is that there is only one person who is actually going to be himself. That's the one, no matter what you're doing with it."

DEBORAH DIGGES: Mr. Duncan, I think it would be interesting to know how you began as a poet.

ROBERT DUNCAN: I began as a poet when I was sixteen or seventeen. Before that I was going to be an architect like my father. He died when I was sixteen so I was seventeen when I considered being a poet. I also had a remarkable English teacher in high school and she had us write poems. We read Chaucer, and wrote either in prose or poetry, prologues of our own if we wanted to and dramatic monologues like Robert Browning. It was Robert Browning who made me determined to be a poet.

It took me a long time before I wrote well enough for anything to be published in a collected work by me today. Unfortunately as a college freshman and sophomore I had poems printed in a college magazine. That's a great misfortune.

DD: Why do you say that?

RD: Well, I mean they are hopeless, but there they are. However, it took me some time to find a language that I would be able to speak fully.

DD: As you found the language, did imitating other writers seem to be of value? Were there specific writers you imitated in the evolution of your own language?

RD: Yes, I imitated. I still imitate today. If I read Yeats, I'm soon "Yeats-ing," and Wallace Stevens is another poet whom I think, in quotes, like Henry James turns us on, end of quotes. I've called volumes derivations, and I've described myself as a derivative poet. I think that's a particular kind of poet.

DD: This isn't an individual voice, then?

RD: No, I'm speaking of the language I use. Going to college in '36 and '37, that was the grand period of Auden and Spender and MacNeice, and I tried writing that way; it didn't talk for me. I loved Pound's *Cantos* from the very beginning. I would still be a Poundian. It took me a long time to discover what that derivation might mean, but my early poems, the ones I like best, are heavily Pound and Eliot. I would still show signs in my work, I would think, of Pound and Eliot.

Part of what poetic language is about can be compared to having a mode in music. If you think about the long period of Baroque music, there were so many who could write well in it. I discovered through Pound and Eliot, and later Wallace Stevens, and very much later as I began to understand William Carlos Williams, a power of speech for my own language. I'm not interested in whether or not I'm original. My view about that is I do happen to be the only Robert Duncan, after all. I think for any young writer the important thing to remember is that there is only one person who is actually going to be himself. That's the one, no matter what you're doing with it. I mean, one could imitate and it would prove, lo and behold, to be his or her imitation. Of course I worried for a long time about the imitative and derivative character of my work.

DD: Yes, it does tend to be a factor in a writing sensibility, or maybe, development. If you become a part of, say, Eliot's language, you identify with the sound of it. But there is an internal pressure to be an original.

RD: But if you look at Renaissance literature for instance, how original was Shakespeare? There was a language of the stage and all of them wrote gloriously in it. We can tell the individuality but sometimes we become confused even about that. We say, did Shakespeare write this or did someone else? Shakespeare himself loved to write Marlowian passages. So do I, by the way, love to write Marlowian passages, so it isn't even just Moderns that I still relish in imitating.

DD: Do you see a separation between the poet and the poem?

RD: The poet I think of as being the person in the poem, a person created in the poetry. I have a term "obedience" and that is obedience to the poem I hear. This would be clear as I pose myself as a derivative poet, derivative not only from the poetry I've heard and read, but also derivative from the world I'm in. I think we're all ultimately derivative; we're oddly derivative from the DNA coding, so I think of the language as a germinal ground for the poem.

However, the writer and the poem are separate. There is a thesis about Whitman creating himself as a poet, that is using himself. He does what a painter does when painting a self-portrait; he's creating the person we're looking at, but we're mistaken if we think it's Whitman, if you see what I mean. People writing a diary often have this confusion. Are they the person in the diary? What is it that you address? Well, actually a character forms. Even when you sit down to write a letter to someone you create something you call "you," and this is what interests me, the creative thing. In that it is creative, it is not ourselves. It's been made up.

I have a strong feeling that if we give ourselves over to the feeling and love the language itself, well, this is what all poets have even though they may have different ways of disposing of themselves in it. They have in some sense a love-hate relationship, a deep involvement with the language in a way that it floods them with being. How come you have or seem to have more fullness of being in the poem? That's because the language has started, and we listen there.

DD: In relationship to the reader, Mr. Duncan, the question of the social or public character in poetry comes to mind. How do you see your reader? Has this any bearing on your writing of the poetry?

RD: I'm a reader as well as a writer, and I think the position of the reader is entirely voluntary. The best thing for me is I don't have to know my readers. There is a kind of reader I'm concerned with and that makes for the particular character of my work. I myself read deeply, and I read over and over again, so I give a gift back to the same world in which I read. My imaginary reader is one who reads more times than I do, and who reads deeper than I, so everything I could possibly put over in a poem is wanted.

DD: Charles Olson's articles on "the projective verse" are said to be an influence in your poetry. Is this more than simply projecting the poet into the image?

RD: As Olson uses it, the term "projective" probably owes a great deal to the Jungian ideas of projection. That is, when I write a poem, the things that appear in it are projections of my psyche; they are going to tell about me. The other meaning of the word that was important to Olson was that he wanted a poem to project its own self.

In a conventional poem, for instance, you propose certain rules. The first line is going to have ten syllables and five stresses, and your second line is going to then follow the conventions of the first line. Now that one is not projected, it is prescribed, or it is prescription.

Another meaning of projection is like a project you're going to do. Whereas the conventional poem proposes a theme and then illustrates it, the projective verse begins as a kind of mystery to the person who is writing it, and in this he projects the poem. Eliot, in his very late essay on poetry and the poet, says there's a new kind of poem, one that is hard for him to understand; nevertheless, it seems to him to be a new form, a poem which is "creating itself," as he writes, and that's exactly the poem that interests me.

In the projective poem everything is active, so you must pay attention all the time. Either it's on its way or it's not quite there yet. In music, you know, Mozart is conventional. You hear a part of a sentence in Mozart and you can finish the sentence because the Baroque conventions are so compelling. There are five or six ways you can go, but they're all true finishes. Along with the proposition about the projective verse, Olson was talking about "composition by field," and that means timewise it's not significant that there is a beginning, a middle, and an end of the poem. The total poem is viewed as a field, and everything in it is active; you're reimagining all the time in projective verse, this totality.

DD: My final question you have really answered for me, Mr. Duncan, and that is: Do you find poetry to be, then, a serious event?

RD: Well, yes, I guess I do. I am a serious poet, but the other kind, occasional poetry, can be quite serious too. It's serious and occasional, isn't it? Funny poetry isn't always funny, really. It can be quite serious. *Alice in Wonderland* is serious. Do you know the real meaning of serious? It means "series," something that follows through and has consequences. Yes, I think that's exactly what it is.

For *The Sullen Art*
(with David Ossman, 1960)

This interview with poet, actor, and teacher David Ossman may be Robert Duncan's first formal interview. It was part of a series of radio interviews with modern American poets on WBAI in New York City beginning in 1960, although it was not included in the published discussions in Ossman's The Sullen Art *(Corinth Books, 1963). In this conversation Duncan clarifies his stance on personality, saying he cultivates "a multiphasic possibility" or "just being." He describes meeting the creator of the Watts Towers and discusses writing "A Poem Beginning with a Line by Pindar" and working for meanings rather than self-expression. This interview was also unpublished.*

—Ed.

DAVID OSSMAN: Does keeping a notebook on varied subjects, such as was published in the Donald Allen anthology, aid you in writing poetry?

ROBERT DUNCAN: No. I don't keep notebooks all the time, although I do exercises in notebooks, and write poems in notebooks in order to avoid the oppressive duty of writing an important poem all the time, or any time. Also, because I tend to have different phases and different moods or modes from which a poem will come, I can take a notebook that has a blank space in it along for a train journey or write in it in the evening or morning—whenever I feel like writing. Certainly, a notebook doesn't have much to do with helping me write a poem. There is some preparation. I'm a reader as well as a writer, and I like to think about poetry as well as write it. I don't think it's necessary to think about poetry as well as write it, or to read it as well as write it, however.

DO: Is there a general base or subject matter from which your poetry grows?

RD: No, not at all. I'm the only general base from which it grows. Since I'm quite the opposite of what would be called an integrated personality (I dislike personality and I dislike integration), I tend to cultivate—not a disintegration, because that's part of the same subject as integration—call it a multiphasic possibility. To cultivate, or try, just being, instead of having a personality.

I had a good deal to do with the selection of my poems which appear in the [Don] Allen anthology, and I tried to present at least some picture of the variety of impetus toward writing poetry. I only write poetry when I'm in a certain kind of body tone, and that body tone is probably the ground. I don't have any particular mental bents that are specifically poetry—whatever coincides with the time one is to write.

DO: Are you affected more by exterior experiences, or by things which happen directly to you?

RD: I don't know much about any exterior experiences that don't happen directly to me. Though I would put one thing—I wonder if you were talking about the inside person and the outside world? I don't think that there's any me I know except what I see in the world. You know, my eyes look out and I get some news—if I have a pain inside or a disorder of some kind—but the outside world is where I find the thing I call myself. So, your exterior events, if I see them at all, are always part of me.

DO: What prompted you to write the poem about the Watts Towers?

RD: I'd gone and actually met the old man before he left those Towers, and then there was an immediate occasion for the poem—a news item that the City Council had met and was going to tear the Towers down. Well, the Towers are among those few monuments that I consider great works of art in this century, so, for one thing, Rodia was a great artist—a hero of THE Art. Just as we can talk about some painting and some architecture as having a poetry, having something to do with making, we can think of poetry itself as having something to do with THE Art: bringing meaning and feeling together as part of life. So, those Towers were that, but then I found, once I was starting on the poem, other things that had attracted me to them. If you remember in that poem: "He had told us proudly that his Towers were taller than the Holy Roman Catholic Church"—it has seemed to me I'm part of the cult of art, and that Christian religion had some strange transfer over into the arts of the seventeenth century, so that the nineteenth century begins to feel a strain. In the twentieth century, the living thing is in the arts.

DO: In reference to your "Poem Beginning with a Line by Pindar": was the first line by Pindar the actual inspiration for the entire poem?

RD: That was the beginning line! It was the fact that I couldn't quite understand what that line was saying that set me off to begin a poem with that title. I took that first line and tried to unfold it. "The light foot . . ."—I don't know, I can't remember now the Pindaric Ode that came from, but it was the first line in the Ode, too [*Robert Duncan added the following footnote:* March 1962: This line is actually the third line of "Pythian 1," *Pythian Odes of Pindar,* translated by H. T. Wade-Gery and C. M. Bowra in the beautiful little Nonesuch Press edition of 1928.]

Literally, it's tied to Pindar along only two lines. One, it begins with a line by Pindar, but the other thing is that I've always liked Pindar, because, like me, he could touch upon so many different things in the course of a poem, and he didn't have that modern worry about whether it was "integrated." He could simply compose a poem, like you might compose a piece of music, with a musical integration. We don't have to worry about why he started out writing an Ode to a winner of an Olympic race, and why he soon was talking about politics, and why he then went on to a bit of myth, and then wound up again at the end saluting the victor of the day. That's the typical pattern, as I remember, in a Pindaric. One thing I knew, and that was somewhat of a challenge to me, as my politics is very simple indeed, was that, since Pindar always laments the politics of his day, I would have to have a section on politics. I've never voted, and I'm an anarchist and find politics one of the saddest departments—sad, particularly, because it results in the death of millions and is run by mediocrities. But it would seem more terrible if it were run by inspired men—that always results really in the death of millions—aboveboard, or whatever.

But I found myself recalling Whitman, and writing the section on the presidents. What led into the section on the presidents was that I started picturing a stroke—a brain stroke. I was thinking of William Carlos Williams, and the poem had just led along to where it says:

> It is toward the old poets
> we go, to their faltering,
> to their unfaltering wrongness that has style,
> their variable truth.

(I'm interested in truth and variety.) Then, suddenly, while my own root and the person I return to always is Pound, at this point in the poem the great American poet seemed to me Williams. No sooner had I started on the business of the stroke and aphasia, than I saw that the President himself had had a stroke and aphasia. I've even collected, wherever they print them, actual paragraphs of his speech or his writing, because it's disorganized, as Miss Stein would have liked to have been, and I have them nicely pasted away in volumes of Gertrude Stein for ultimate pleasure in language departing from sense.

That led in directly then to the picture: "If presidents are as Whitman felt them to be—emblems or dream figures of what the whole nation is—then we know what the United States was from the time of Lincoln to the present." And then, if we are also a little cell of that (which begins to happen in the poem), then we must also have our own part of our being which is an Eisenhower, a Roosevelt, or a Hoover, or all the rest of them.

DO: What was it you said disturbed you? A "departure from the ordered"?

RD: It sure wasn't! In the first place, there's nothing in this world you experience if it isn't an order. If it were really not an order, you wouldn't see it or hear it or know it or anything. The reason you see this ashtray is because it's an order; all the elements that might be there, that you have not yourself brought into order, you don't see. I'm a devout gestaltist. I believe that you only see patterns, and those are already orders. So the disordered is literally impossible. What you can have, though, is a bringing more and more into conscious order. I think that what people call disorder is not in the world but stands for their very low tolerance of mixed orders. Some people are dependent on actual symmetry before they're ordered or balanced. I'm interested in harmony, more than in balance, and in harmony in relation to expanding scales, to include more and more things and more and more tones, with the other happy thing that can never be achieved or even conceived, which is total order. I mean the total scale, in which the sound of my voice and the shape of the table are all one, have all at last been united so that you understand what tone each one has.

DO: Is this an ultimate attempt...?

RD: I don't make ultimate attempts. I just mean that I could imagine such, about like I could imagine disorder. Although the most staggering thing human beings imagine is chaos and which has not come into being at all. Would you be specific about what you think is disordered?

DO: Well, *Howl* seems to me a disorder, which [Allen] Ginsberg has attempted to order, and which has not been ordered with complete success.

RD: Well, I don't know. *Howl* seems to be very definitely restricted in the things and the attitudes that it includes. Certainly, it's related to classical orders, and it's highly conventional, which I would hope my work wasn't. It stems from Christopher Smart and certain Jewish ideas. I think maybe I grasp a little of what you mean in relation to *Howl*, but I don't call that a disorder. That is the whole Hebrew teaching about poetry—that it should not be made, but spoken from an inspired voice. I think that Ginsberg is trying to recover the Jewish heritage—the spiritual convention—and that means speaking as a God-voice. There is a Jewish teaching that the law is that you shouldn't make graven images—that you shouldn't make what we call "poem"—a made thing like the Greeks talked about, but that you should speak from inner inspiration and pour forth. If *Howl* is a disorder, then so is the Song of Songs of Solomon or Ecclesiastes. The thing about *Howl* is that there's an exuberance of emotion in back of the poem. That's why it has such strength in front of Academic poetry, where there's none at all. But its experience is not ripened, and we can either posit a later poetry of Allen Ginsberg's with riper experience, or we might posit Allen Ginsberg continually trying to write *Howl*. But he seems to do all kinds of things.

No, I wouldn't call that disorder. One thing, however, that I work for (and I could contrast my poetry with Ginsberg's in this) is meaning. Ginsberg is a poet of expression, and the important thing communicated in a poem like *Howl* is the expressionist force. Now, I'm a poet almost entirely of meaning. When I start that poem with a line by Pindar, I follow the line by Pindar, and unwind the meanings in the language. Then, to unwind the meanings, or course, I have to say, "Where did I know this?" My experience feeds back to feed my own particular contact with meanings. For instance, even "foot" in "The light foot hears you and the brightness begins"—what the poem does is supply you with particulars to "foot." There's one place in the poem where "the footfall of snow falls from a roof around a house in Maverick Road," and you can see there what I tend to do. But it's meanings I'm after, not expression. I'm anti-expressionist. But I don't think expressionism is disorder. I'm anti-expressionist because I dislike personality and I dislike integration. And in general, I have a double play between meaning and feeling, which keeps me quite busy. Were I an expressionist, I would be sadly equipped, indeed.

DO: The word I had forgotten was not "disorder," but "integration." What is it you dislike about integration?

RD: Disintegration means you think you're a single thing, flying apart. But I believe that I'm part of an event, a total event. In a poem, what one is doing in one's activity in language is trying to open up that event. And that, of course, means opening up, or bringing together in order to open up, meaning and feeling—your own two areas in relation to this event that you're part of. This is very different from feeling that you're a person. Then, as a person, you may have a kind of progress! You can have integrity and integration. In which case, the poem's aims are quite different from the ones that I have. I feel that whatever integrity you've got is sort of naturally given by the fact that you've got two feet and two eyes. You've got your boundaries of exactly what you are—an individual creature. They're so definitely given that the struggle for integration seems an odd thing. However, I do know that there are people for whom integration is of great importance.

I had a talk last week with Charles Olson about Psyche and Eros—both of them terms which show in the Pindar poem. The whole center of the poem is about Psyche and Eros, and that, of course, is pretty close to what I'm talking about when I talk about integration. I have a feeling that we suffer a great deal today (and naturally, because that's the story of the soul) from belonging to a psychological period. Ginsberg and Robert Lowell believe that the core is that they're a Psyche. I have a good deal of that in the Pindar poem. It's an almost pure poem of Psyche and suffering, of life seen as that. It's a poem of life. The alternative to Psyche is Cosmos, which enters later in my work as a particular interest. This is the business of being an event. At the time I wrote the Pindar poem, while, let's say, I believed I was an event, I didn't quite feel it. But I don't match up with myself—tomorrow I'm likely to be a Psyche again.

Yale Reports: On Poetry

(with Eugene Vance, 1964)

The transcription of this three-way discussion in May 1964 with Eugene Vance and David Schaff, broadcast over WTIC in Hartford, Connecticut, was found in Robert Duncan's files and had not been published. Here Duncan talks about "the Berkeley Renaissance," the demands of Louis Zukofsky and Charles Olson for "a certain kind of clarity," and his efforts to "write by trust or by faith." He strives to follow the integrity of the poem, which rises "within the poem as it is being written" and to keep with that process wherever it leads. His attraction to Greek, medieval, and Renaissance literature came from the fairytales, myths, and Bible stories he heard and read in his childhood. Such stories include "rumors of the divine world." This interview is an excellent introduction to Robert Duncan and to how he approaches and views the poem.

    —Ed.

ANNOUNCER: *To extend knowledge far and wide is one of the purposes of a university. To educate and inform as well as to entertain is the task of enlightened broadcasting. To achieve these goals WTIC in cooperation with Yale University brings you each week* Yale Reports.

Good evening, ladies and gentlemen, and welcome to the 328th edition of Yale Reports. *Tonight you'll hear a program about poetry, and our special guest is San Francisco poet Robert Duncan. Numerous collections of his verse have been published, most recently* The Opening of the Field, *brought out in 1960. Mr. Duncan was recently on the Yale campus to give a series of readings from his own works. During the discussion this evening, you'll also hear a young poet, David Schaff, an undergraduate at Yale majoring in English. Tonight's program will be moderated by Mr. Eugene Vance, a poet and an instructor in Yale's English Department.*

Here now is Mr. Vance to begin the discussion:

15

Berkeley, 1948

EUGENE VANCE: Mr. Duncan, I know that you are a longtime resident and perhaps even a native of San Francisco, and I'm interested to know whether in your opinion there was ever a moment when one could point to a group of writers in San Francisco who really had common ideals and values in their art, and who were conscious of forming a "school."

ROBERT DUNCAN: Yes, several times. One time, when the group was not so very well known but was important for me was in 1946 in Berkeley, when we thought of ourselves as the Berkeley Renaissance. Appropriately, to use the term "renaissance," we were concerned with our own revival of Greek mythology, the pagan world, and also with ideas of magic—this group included Jack Spicer and Robin Blaser. A short time after the group was formed, we met at a house where a group of students ate every day at dinnertime. We formed a table, a round table in our own minds, as though we were knights and ladies of a round table, and I drew on this when I was writing my *Medieval Scenes.* In the background of that group at that time was the great medievalist, Ernst Kantorowicz, who was teaching at the University of California, and eventually we all were lured to return to the University and take up medieval studies. I think on the part of Spicer and Blaser and myself this was entirely a romantic and poetic adventure. It led none of us into history, and especially in my case it was a pure extension of my own poetry.

Of course, the next big thing that happened in San Francisco was the "Beat" movement in 1955, and unfortunately that year I was in Majorca. As a matter of fact, no sooner did I get away from home than everything happened. I began getting letters about this terrific scene, and I was not in on it. I felt really like Majorca was off the map and nothing ever happened in Europe, so I was ready to come home the next year for the tail end of the Beat scene.

DAVID SCHAFF: This is the Allen Ginsberg–Lawrence Ferlinghetti period you are talking about. I picked up in one of your phrases the idea of extension, a romantic, poetic type of return to Renaissance figures. I noticed in your work that you are particularly concerned with Renaissance and then with modern themes, making somewhat of a correlation between Renaissance figures of one kind or another (in the

"Apprehensions" poems) and modern figures—for example, Pound and H.D. Do you follow a definite pattern in this kind of association?

RD: I think my attraction to the Renaissance and my attraction also to *The Cantos* of Ezra Pound, or to the later poetry of H.D., all goes back to something more in early childhood than it does to the later period in University circles. When we keep talking about the Renaissance, we sound like we're in some department of higher education. As a child, I was raised on Greek myths and Germanic fairytales and Bible stories, and this formed a background of things that seemed to me very true. You had the feeling, or your parents had the feeling, that certain fairytales were true, more true as a matter of fact than daily life—and life, like dreams, had to come true in some way to even resemble these stories. My first attraction to someone like Ficino or Pico della Mirandola is that they really brought this old lore back into the Western world and formed a mixing pot in the Renaissance—the revival of not just pagan religion, but they were fascinated by what I would really prefer to call lore rather than religion. They also felt that there was something most true in the ancient world and that they would bring it into our world. So that it has a double role.

All this interested me at later times—and I'm interested in whatever period, whenever there were let's say rumors of the divine world, and this is why I'm interested in religions. I mean presence of gods or spirits is much more exciting to me, or opens up to me in daily life a life that's more exciting than life would be if they didn't exist—if we weren't going to admit them, let them in—admit they are there.

EV: Mr. Duncan, as you write your poems are you writing to some kind of audience? Do you feel as you compose, presences of people whom you admire or love, people who are witnessing, so to speak, each aesthetic choice that you make?

RD: Sometimes I do. I have certain people, mainly Louis Zukofsky and Charles Olson, whose temperaments are so different from mine and they often appear to me, or I feel them when I'm writing, as a form of discipline. They would demand something of me, demand that I take a firmer view of the area of the poem I'm in than I would ordinarily take.

So I have two poets whose work I love and at the same time whose work I feel as a restraining—no, it's a demanding, more than a restraining influence. An absolute demand for a certain kind of clarity, clarity I wouldn't always practice unless I borrowed some such mentors that I also have affection for. So you're right there.

I don't know about the other way around. When I'm really happily myself, I don't worry very much about whether all the people that I like are going to like the poem. I forget about it all. But I do, along the line of the demand for more attention in the writing, borrow such mentors, and Pound has always been a mentor of that kind for me. I have to aim higher, for instance. I have still the definite feeling both Zukofsky and Olson are superior to me in writing, and this would also be of course why I feel them as mentors. In other words, their work demands something of me, not their persons, and then I love them for their superiority.

EV: But do you feel that when you're best, you're free even of these mentors?

RD: Oh yes. I don't care about superiority when I'm best. At my own best, I mean when I'm happy in the poem, I'm perfectly glad to be way down at the very bottom playing around. I have no such aspirations. But then I'm not entirely unhappy when I have aspirations. It just means, I think, I look a little more strange while I'm writing a poem, and I don't know whether I'm climbing upward and onward. I'm not clear about it. But you *are* right in what you're hinting at. For much of the time in poetry even mentors won't sidetrack me from the fact that I'm just "with it."

EV: Mr. Duncan, your poems might appear formless to some of your readers, because you seem to avoid imposing extrinsic classical poetic forms of line and stanza when you work. And I'm wondering if in your opinion each of your poems has its own individual form—something arising from within the poem.

RD: Yes, I feel that each poem has its individual form while I'm working on it, and at the same time I've got a good deal of patience about what that form is going to finally relate to. I think that all the poems that one writes, even the very bad early poems, as a matter of fact, belong to a kind of mosaic of statement, in which you eventually sketch out a much larger thing. In other words, I do feel I'm working on a very large poetic and that it never gets stated. It is always being stated in any immediate poem, and any of these immediate poems would be like a cell of some body that I don't yet know. I mean, that a cell will have a very definite stance. No cell of your body is without its own very definite internal order, and we can look at the individual cell itself and find the signature of what you are, and we can also learn a great deal about the body from the cell itself, that it does have its absolute internal integrity. Now that integrity of the poem I think you feel just as definitely as you would the integrity of a cell.

Usually people want to talk about good and bad poems, and they mean in the first place that they like or dislike a poem. But that liking or disliking a poem may be like being allergic to something or not being allergic. I'm thinking again of cells which do not mix but go by kind, so that you get all the confusion that we see when a group of intelligent people will not agree at all about the poems they like and dislike and end up staring in utter amazement across the table because they've come to one of these contradictions.

Now there is another sense in which a poem could be good or bad, and this can also be compared to the cell. Something could go wrong in the cell—the cell can be disordered and lose its internal integrity. It can be invaded by an outside virus, a whole series of things. It can be a sick cell. A "crisis" as a critical term does hold for doctoring. The doctor is the one who attends you at the moment of crisis in an illness and tells you this is the crisis. Now you have the volition yourself in this crisis, and the doctor attends that volition of whether you're going to go toward life or whether you're going to go toward death. So a poem holds—its integrity is its life; it also holds its possible dissolution. It can lose form. I would say that I always try to follow the integrity of the poem, not its possible dissolution.

I think of the poem's integrity as rising within the poem as it is being written; by my coming to know it as the poem comes into existence, not as if it had preexisted. Some people think of human beings as models of a primary model, and we are all thought of as bad or good copies of this model. The best way to account gracefully for this school of thought is that we must have fallen, or something must have happened for us to be so poor an example of the paradigm that existed before. So that for many poets this is what they are doing—they think of a paradigm preexisting before the poem they write, and then they have a struggle toward the perfection of that poem. They are trying to perfect the copy to an imaginary paradigm. They feel as if this is what they were aware of when they started writing the poem.

Now I don't feel that. I feel that a process is started, that if I keep with the integrity of the process, the poem will be alive. If I mess it up—there's where I thought of a virus—if I bring in something extraneous to what's going on. I often think of my own emotions as possibly messing up the poem, or my own ideas as messing it up. I've got all sorts of pet opinions I could get off on. Does that give you some idea?

EV: Yes, that's exactly what I wanted to know.

DS: On that basis you might mention thematic composition, and how one at times gets trapped by it. Could you clarify this somewhat? In your own style, as you indicated yesterday during your reading, you are letting the syllables govern—or progressing by tone leading from word to word. Could you explain this matter of thematic composition and how you want to keep with the process?

RD: Let me explain first that what I call the process of the poem is the feeling that I have that I am ready to write the poem, that I am ready to work with language as a material. This must be some counterpart of what is generally held in great scorn—waiting for the muse. Well, obviously, when you're going to college you can't wait for the muse. The thing is due Tuesday morning and the muse won't arrive, believe me, until the Monday following. But when you're not one of those people trying to write the poem by Tuesday, but you are actually obedient to the language, you have to wait for a physical condition and also for some condition of your own mentality: a readiness to deal this way with language. Now given that readiness, you can begin working; and with an intuition of this, you can go beyond what you know and trust what comes to you.

It's what comes to me that I go along with, not what I seem to initiate myself, think up as a way out. Now frequently I find that what does come to me organizes itself along thematic lines. For one thing, poem after poem has ended in a coda in which there is dancing. And I can recognize the whole dancing motif early in a poem and hope it doesn't take over before something has happened—I know that I'm a goner if the dancing motif takes over completely, because I'm a compulsive dancer as far as that goes. Now there's nothing wrong with dancing in the poem but—this is where you are sometimes influenced by others—some people say, Well, Duncan always rescues himself at the end of a poem and we know that dance is going to come in here. I want to break up such things because I do not believe that only one track is the integrity of the poem. I've had a lot of dancing going on in those poems and I don't have to have more—if I can forestall the dance, I may find out what is behind it. If you are not able to dance, what do you do? becomes the question. I mean how will the form assert its integrity if it can't go in this direction?

Again, words become almost habitual for me, responses like "light" or the idea of Man. They are overwhelming ideas. If I do not permit them to come in at some point in the poem, then I have forced the poem to find a new course. You see, again, I think of the poem as a process, something impending that will find a new course, that doesn't need the word "light" or "Man," and will find another direction to go in. It would give me more of the mosaic, you see. I already know quite a bit about light and Man, and the same message will come back again if I go in that direction.

DS: Yes, definitely.

RD: . . . that's what I mean about change. You could change the form. I've worked a lot with long lines—lines beyond my conscious measure—alternating with short lines that are consciously measured as far as stress and syllables go. And this gives me a sort of dance. Then if I recognize that this has happened—that I began in that habitual way of dancing—in order to find out what would happen, I will prevent myself from having those short lines, and see what will happen if I dare have a sequence of four and five long lines, longer than I can consciously measure. Then how will this go? What will I find out? Because it is finding out something.

DS: Discovery and search . . .

RD: . . . but back of that is trust. I write by trust or by faith, and believe me you can lose the trust. That's why it's very hard to do something you haven't done before, because you don't have that much trust; you keep wanting to go back, to yield to something.

DS: Mr. Duncan, your audience at your readings noticed that you have a manner of suddenly breaking off the articulation of a word or a line, and one cryptic listener suggested to me that you're simply making a good thing of a speech defect. Well, of course anyone can hear now that you don't have a speech defect. Once you mentioned to me that you were actually delighted at one point when you thought you were learning to stutter. Now what function does this sudden interruption of syntax or thought serve in your poetry, and do you have a name for it?

RD: Well, let me not find a name right away. Interruption was one of the first things I thought of doing. That is, if I start talking here and I can see what I'm saying right ahead of me, I would interrupt it with something else. This is, after all, the essence of the actual disability of the stutterer. The stutter happens because the person becomes stuck, not wanting to say something or not being able to see what is about to be said. Now both in talking and whenever I think about poetry, I try to prevent going along the lines that I am perfectly familiar with, because these seem to me to be clichés. To some people I would be much more articulate were I to have in my mind the things I have said in the past. But when I talk and when I write I do try, in relation to poetry—I don't do it in prose—to prevent the formation of a previous conception in order to force some other thing I haven't seen yet, so that I can be entertained while I'm talking. Something will come to me that I didn't even realize was possible.

Again to come back to my speech—I do interrupt myself. Sometimes I wonder since I like to talk all the time, how do I ever hear anything? I must only hear something when people interrupt me. And I can only hear what is going on if I interrupt me. Maybe this is a glib explanation for this interruption. Certainly now after ten years or so I've got some form of stutter—I can observe that myself. Whenever I try to think, I stutter-think, hoping that something will come in there.

DS: I'd like to propose an example—would you read something for us to illustrate it?

RD: Let me read "The Dance," and that will give the whole thing— the long lines and the short syllables and some of the stutter break. At Wesleyan University I had a reading some years ago, and I opened by reading "The Dance." The student reporter who covered the reading said, "Mr. Duncan began with a serious speech impediment which disappeared later. He was probably scared of us." That's the opinion I left him with!

THE DANCE
from its dancers circulates among the other
                  dancers. This
would-have-been feverish cool excess of
                  movement makes
each man   hit the pitch   co-
                  ordinate.

Lovely their feet pound the green solid meadow.
                  The dancers
mimic flowers—root stem stamen and petal
                  our words are,
our articulations,   our
                  measures.

It is the joy that exceeds pleasure.

      You have passed the count, she said

or I understood from her eyes. Now
old Friedl has grown so lovely in my years,

      I remember only the truth.
      I swear by my yearning.

      You have conquerd the yearning, she said
      The numbers have enterd your feet

          turn   turn   turn

When you're real gone, boy, sweet boy . .

Where have I gone, Beloved?

Into the Waltz, Dancer.

Lovely our circulations sweeten the meadow.
In Ruben's riotous scene the May dancers teach us our learning
    seeks abandon!

Maximus calld us to dance the Man.
We calld *him*   to call
    season   out of season-
d mind!

        Lovely
join we to dance green to the meadow.

Whitman was right.   Our names are left
    like leaves of grass,
likeness and liking,   the human greenness

tough as grass that survives cruelest seasons.

        I see now a radiance.
        The dancers are gone.
        They lie in heaps, exhausted,
        dead tired we say.
        They'll sleep until noon.

        But I returnd early
        for the silence,
        for the lovely pang that is
        a flower,
        returnd to the silent dance-ground.

(That was my job that summer. I'd dance until three, then up to
get the hall swept before nine—beer bottles, cigarette butts, paper
mementos of the night before. Writing it down now, it is the after-
math, the silence, I remember, part of the dance too, an articulation
of the time of dancing . . like the almost dead sleeping is a step. I've

got it in a poem, about Friedl, moaning in the depths of. But that was another room that summer. Part of my description. What I see is a meadow . .

I'll slip away before they're up . .

and see the dew shining.*

DS: I've noticed a great deal of progression, for example, from *Letters* to *The Opening of the Field,* to material you read from *Roots and Branches.* There is a progression of form the poems seem to take and of the tremendous concentration of material inside them. You mentioned that you might plan some kind of long narrative poem. Do you have any ideas or any plans for the immediate future—what you are going to do?

RD: I think I've already said that although I sometimes throw hints out for myself, just exactly at the point I intend to do something, I blank out. If I tell you now about a long narrative poem, I bet you I won't be writing it. I write with a sense of discovery about the thing that is ahead, and perhaps the reason I've never done that long narrative poem is because I had ideas about it. And felt, wow, what a thing that would be! Again that's different from something that comes to you when you start working. Although I've written a short narrative poem, "Cyparissus," I really have to do what is at hand when I sit down to work on a poem.

EV: We're all very grateful to you, not only for your readings, but for this chance to ask questions which I'm sure have been on the minds of many of us. I hope you'll come back and talk some more with us and give us more readings. Thank you, Mr. Duncan.

---

* From *The Opening of the Field,* New York, NY: Grove Press, copyright 1960 by Robert Duncan. [This volume is now issued by New Directions Publishing Corporation. —Ed.]

"Wonder Tales"

(with Michael Auping, 1983)

This interview conducted in 1983 by Michael Auping, now the Curator of the Modern Art Museum of Fort Worth, is from his 30 Years: Interviews and Outtakes *(2007). In this disarming dialogue Robert Duncan touches on the role of myth that permeated the household he shared with the artist Jess. He says that the many books by Romantic poets, writers, and artists in their home concern "the romance of remembering the mysteries that we've lost."*

—Ed.

MICHAEL AUPING: Where does your language or your imagery come from in the most basic sense—even just finding a place to begin?

ROBERT DUNCAN: I understand a need, a desire, to ask that question, but who could answer it—what artist, poet, doesn't ask it themselves? We never get an answer. We can never really provide ourselves an answer. It would indeed seem odd if we could give one to you. Think of it. If we knew where to begin, we would probably know where to end, and that would be the end of the imaginative construct. You can't have the answers and still connect to the imagination.

MA: I know it's a stupid question, but it seems like it always needs to be asked. So it has been asked. Let me ask another stupid question. Do you have a . . . a routine, a way of working up to starting your work?

RD: Now that's more available as a point of discussion. We [Duncan and his life partner, the artist Jess Collins] read. We read to each other as a routine. Right here in this kitchen—often in the morning. We have our morning discussions. We try to connect a text or myth to things in the household. We project ourselves out to engage the imagination from the microcosm of this household—this domestic cosmos.

MA: I can understand that—even envisioning you here in the mornings, like we are now. This house is like a giant book. There are bookcases everywhere. It's a literary playground. All kinds of stuff—gothic novels, Greek literature, science fiction, children's books. Do you read children's books to each other?

RD: Jess has a great collection of children's books. We love them.

MA: The innocence of childhood?

RD: No. That's the Modernist conceit—the supposed intellectually advanced modern mind seeking some simple, indivisible reverie—the myth of a simple truth hidden in the imagination of the child. We're interested in the wicked complexity of the childhood imagination—the prismatic ironies and opposites that are presented in any given moment, experience, or story. . . . Our household is partly about that—children's books, fairytales, nursery rhymes, Mary Butts, puzzles. . . . Jess has an immense collection of puzzles. It's the perfect metaphor for how we view the imagination. Rather than using the metaphor of the book for this house, I would use the image of the puzzle. We surround ourselves with a puzzle of myths. You can't take a piss in this house without being hit with a myth.

MA: The third floor where I'm staying is really spooky. You need to get some more lights for those rooms. I hope there aren't too many myths flying around up there. All the books on those shelves are pretty strange.

RD: That's the science fiction and Surrealism floor for the most part. There are some wonderfully off-center stories and poems from the '20s, '30s, and '40s up there. There are a fair number of goblins up there.

MA: That's what I was afraid of. It's where the Mary Butts novels are.

RD: Yes, I think so. They are wonderful stories published in the '20s and filled with a rich field of symbols—remarkably visionary. She moved in and out of circles with Eliot and Woolf, but she was very unique. You might think of them as surreal fairytales, if that is not redundant. You should read *Armed with Madness*. It's like Eliot's *Waste Land* but in a magical natural world with goddesses ascending and descending through layers of mythic realms. It's a puzzling-together of fragments of the stories and myths that make up our present reality.

MA: This puzzling-together of realities—I can see how that feeds into Jess's fragmented collages and the sectionalized surfaces of his Translations. But how do they feed into your poetry?

RD: For me, it's about lost romance or rediscovering romance . . . Shelley, Blake—the whole construct of Romance—the Romance of remembering the mysteries that we've lost.

MA: Romance. I'm not sure exactly how you mean that. When someone starts talking about "romance" I cringe at the whole sentimental—

RD: Well, that's it! Of course, it's a cynical time. Anything that is not cynical is marginalized. We've lost sentiment. . . . There are no models for falling in love. The romance novel of a high order, the fairytale, may be the highest form of romance we have today. . . .

MA: You were associated with the Beat poets. That doesn't seem so romantic, or maybe it was and I am misreading it.

RD: I was never a Beat poet. You have misread that. They had no Romance, or at least not the high level I am speaking of. . . . What I am talking about are the stories, the myths that lead you there—to that unexplainable precipice of human love—no matter how spooky or strange the story may be—the communal fairytales that we share, and that connect all of us.

MA: Like the circle of children holding hands on the cover of your book?

RD: *The Opening of the Field.* That is a viable image for the construct we're talking about—wonder tales, which is what fairytales used to be called. We think art needs more wonder tales.

Australian Radio Interview

(with Ian W. Reid, 1976, excerpts)

In 1976 Robert Duncan spent two months in Australia, where he gave readings, taught classes, and met with younger poets. In this excerpt from an unpublished radio interview with the poet and scholar Ian Reid, Duncan speaks of "a world style" of poetry "not of the nation," and of the community of poets and the tradition outside of the formal canon of "literature" Milton proposed. He also addresses the critique of his own work as "bookish."

—Ed.

IAN REID: I'm going to be talking here to Robert Duncan, who is visiting Australia at present. His poetry is well known in many parts of Australia and in particular in Sydney, where the magazine *New Poetry* has adopted him as something of a patron saint. His influence has also been very evident in recent years in Canada and parts of Britain as well as in the States.

ROBERT DUNCAN: In this decade your poetry is rising, about ten years later than the period in which Canada's poetry was on an upswing, and all of this is the New Poetry. The characteristic of our poetry in the 1950s is for the first time we weren't writing American poetry although we had very definite rules—Olson laid down a whole logic of how we would be proceeding from [Herman] Melville, from certain critiques of the nineteenth century; it's still quite clear that we were sailing out into world poetry. The sky for instance is important, and I thought of your sky right away first, but the one thing we understand about the sky we stand under is that it is not restricted to one country. Earth and sky, earth is your country, and we took hold on locality on earth, but the main thing that it is is that we again looked at the heavens and that erases any possibility of nation.

IR: And you see the uprising in Australian poetry now as being directly related to its transcendence of nationalistic concerns?

RD: Well, it didn't have to transcend nationalism; it's simply that nationalism had become antiquated. I think it shows that a whole educated class is contemporary with ideas of physics and especially ideas of anthropology that were not fully mature till after the Second World War. Before the Second World War anthropologists still considered some men to be primitives and other men to be civilized, and after the Second World War more and more anthropologists referred to ways of being man, and that is a significant change. Poetry then will inherit it, any place that someone comes in contact with it. In Fiji the New Zealand–raised Samoan poet Albert Wendt had a room full of students and they were identical with—they were talking about the poem we all write, they weren't talking about some strange poem. Some of them came from Tonga, which is an anthropological curiosity, but *they* weren't anthropological curiosities, because they were an English-speaking community of the world, not of the nation, so their poetry was writing into the concerns that we recognize. We have a world style, is what I'm saying. And the world style is stronger than any national style because the national style cannot entertain major ideas that we have about physics or the nature of the earth or the species especially.

IR: You've mentioned the ideas of community, and it seems to me that in your own poetry not only is this communal sense *spatially* limitless but also your community as a poet extends temporarily back to the point where you're able to say (as I think you have said, in almost so many words) that people like Heraclitus and [Jacob] Boehme and Dante are your spiritual contemporaries. So you feel yourself to be not so much a part of a particular American poetry scene in a given place or time as a member of a community of poets that extends in various directions.

RD: Well, I was related very closely to a community of American poets, but they weren't a community in the sense that they were living in the same place. The group that I was closest to as a writer. . . . You take Charles Olson and Robert Creeley and Denise Levertov: when we began

Australia, 1976

to correspond together I was in San Francisco on the Pacific Coast, Charles Olson was at Black Mountain College on the East Coast, Robert Creeley was in Majorca, and Denise Levertov at that early time was in Mexico. So it wasn't the business of being in the same place. What related us was just the fact that our poetry had its main sources in the late poetry of William Carlos Williams and that it had a very strong allegiance to the poetics and vitalism of D. H. Lawrence.

IR: Your mention of Williams prompts a different kind of question. I think it was Williams who said, in effect, that [T. S.] Eliot's *Waste Land* had set poetry back many years by giving it to the academies. My impression is that a supposed basis of some criticism of your work that has appeared from time to time is the notion that you are an excessively bookish poet, and that in a manner that is imagined to be very similar to Eliot's, you're giving poetry to the academies instead of giving it to "the people." How do you react to that?

RD: Well, their sense of the crisis I think would be quite accurate. In the first place I'm bookish: I read everything that's in front of me, including cereal boxes if put in front of me. I have been bookish since the beginning of time. I'm certainly more likely to be reading a book than to be reading a leaf, or an oceanfront or a mountain, although I *read* them, and that tells you something. Other people look at them; I read them. If I'm going to look at nature I don't look, I read. So I'm a reader in the very first ground. One of my first rounds of contact is to read a face or read hands or read the way they're sitting. Okay. But the other aspect of the critique about being bookish does not have to do with books at all, and this is where we get back at [Robert] Adamson's recognition of my spirit, and that is I'm a traditionalist. So is Charles Olson. But even to recognize that you come in a tradition, something handed down from William Carlos Williams's and Lawrence's traditionalism—but traditionalism goes back to a Hermetic tradition in poetry that's verifiable through Shelley and Blake and Milton and Shakespeare and certainly Spenser; and I think I can go back to the first command in English poetry, that Bede tells us of, when Caedmon is commanded to sing of a world of made-up things. . . . The word "academy" is a little difficult here, but those who had proposed an English literature, one thing they don't believe is there's such a tradition. Because the literature qualifies by having certain literary qualities and being judged, and it's Milton who proposes a literature, I think, in order to sell it to a Protestant parliament, and he realizes, "Gee, the poets can't sing at the bottom of the King's table anymore or make out with the Duchess and get their dinners; we've got to have our dinners someplace else." So he tells a new parliament that one of the things they're going to want to have in England is a glory known as "literature." And having sold them on literature, and that *that* will be a real commodity like they need great buildings, they really want to be in a period of glory, well, judge it by the paintings and the literature. Well, that's not *the* tradition, of course; the tradition is talking about the world of spirit, and the fact that it writes—it's not incidental but of an entirely different nature. Poets of the tradition tend in ways to *hide* the tradition and so I've got other aspects, but I don't mean to . . . I want to make it difficult enough so that it won't look like you can rip it off. I think you can see. I want my readers to be involved and enmeshed in the experience because the tradition is not just something handed down but a transforming perspective, at least, of life. And yet where a poet is drawn entirely into that, and that was our problem with Adamson, I have trouble treading my own water, the flood of my own thought or feeling, and so that tradition is not easy with me. I think my poetry shows signs of fear within the tradition.

IR: So when you read a poem in public you won't be at all concerned if you feel your audience is not immediately responsive to . . .

RD: Oh, I'd flip out if they weren't responsive. I try to command them, and one of the features of my reading I guess is that I advance a fairly hypnotic style. That's in order to keep an audience from flipping me by not making it.

IR: I want to put the emphasis on "immediately responsive," and I was going to add "in their intellectual comprehension of what is happening." That's to say, you'd be quite happy if you felt the audience was struggling with the process by which a poem takes its shape rather than simply ingesting, as consumers, a poem-product.

RD: Yes, I think of a poem being read, re-read, and the meaning of it found in different ways over a lifetime. That's the way I find my poems, read my poems. In current poetry we do sort it out with different opinions and get certain leads or shapes, but when I talk about the poets in Australia that have interested me (one of them is Millet, by the way, John Millet) it's because they contain some promise of my own subject matter. I think when I was in my twenties I would have been much more widely excited by *things happening.* But at fifty-seven I don't look forward to participating in some revolution; it wouldn't have even begun by the time I would be kind of getting more tired and crawling into a corner.

IR: So the allusiveness, the bookish allusiveness in many of your poems is something that you would like your readers to *work at,* and not to feel that they need to follow all references in a scholarly manner. They should allow elements of the poem to play in their imagination, through a series of readings and re-readings.

RD: If you take the art of Boehme (or Behmen, as it's sometimes translated into Tudor English): that's not just an allusion; I really do want to insist that my readers get involved in Behmen so that they are understanding my entire poetry from an involvement there. Or as I sometimes put it . . . certainly I don't make "allusions" to Dante. I think if you haven't read Dante you'd better read it first and get to Duncan later. And sometimes there are allusions that have to do with affection, but they would be perfectly apparent; I'm very, very *fond* of George Herbert, but I'm not sure that I insist that my readers read George Herbert in order to cope with a poem.

Let's get back to what we were saying. My poetry is also a proposition of a kind of education, and the only reason it *has* to be that is that we have quite a contrary education going on. You can hear the sound of that when I sound off how I feel about English literature or American literature. The fact that it is fundamentally hostile to the tradition. By the way, for a tradition, of course, you only have to read the prefaces and papers of [W. B.] Yeats to find a poet in the tradition who knows that they aren't being educated that way in schools. So my poetry is filled with elements that I know very well are not at all part of Western education. A question I often ask is: Everybody knows Dante's *Divine Comedy* (I'm not talking about whether they've read it but they know of its existence), but there was a work of equal greatness and spiritual greatness written in the same century. And very few know that. It's the so-called Kabbalah, the *Zohar* of Moses of Leon. Because we have a Christian Western education that does not countenance at all the existence of a high Jewish civilization in Europe at the same time.

IR: Robert, would you like to read a poem that might exemplify some of the things that you've been talking about? Perhaps from one of your early works—say, the "Poem Beginning with a Line by Pindar" would illustrate, for one thing, the kind of allusiveness that often initiates your poems.

RD: Yes, I guess this *is* truly allusive. Where I read allusion is that the poem itself, when I was writing it, was unfolding before me, so I became a kind of detective. You'll hear in this poem when I read it a lot of "What is there?" Because as the poem is unwinding I'm trying to get with and find out where I did see that before, and so of course it's going to turn out to be allusive and I'm following a series of allusions. It started with a line that I was reading late at night: *"The light foot hears you and the brightness begins."* That's quoted from a translation of Pindar. It had separated from the poem it was in and a set of puns had come up. "Light"—I couldn't decide whether that meant that the foot didn't *weigh* very much, or whether it was made of light in a dark area, and especially "hears you" was very strange; then "light foot" must be the name of someone, someone called "the light foot" hears you. Well, I realize that a foot can't hear you, but there was a pun about poetry because we have feet moving through a line, and when I write I'm not really that certain that I am not listening to feet that move through the language, and not putting them there, and that whatever is treading through there may really hear me right. I follow it and it sounds like me, if that could get across. And "the brightness begins": brightness means that you're a hyperactive intellectual kid, doesn't it? "That's a real bright kid," they say. "Shut up!" And so you know the poem's going to be overloaded if all *that's* started, and I should never have begun with such a line, but there it was, a poem beginning with a line from Pindar.

I don't have to explicate it any further; you *know* you're in for trouble, *I* knew I was in for trouble, and so the whole poem is trying to figure out what the trouble is, like you would if you went into a dream. In *Alice in Wonderland* you don't worry, but gee in poetry today they want you to straighten it out when it's a dream of this kind.

. . .

"Then You Live in the Spirit"
(with David Melnick, 1985)

At the time of this unpublished discussion with San Francisco poet David Melnick in Robert Duncan's home in 1985, Duncan was preparing a collection of his essays for New Directions. The biography referred to is Ekbert Faas's Young Robert Duncan: portrait of the poet as homosexual in society *(Black Sparrow Press, 1983). In this conversation Duncan mentions the "exploratory" nature of his work in the early 1950s. He describes writers whom he calls "vitalists" who view "life" and "not themselves" as the significant thing. He discusses the influence of Yeats and Blake, who are "both rich sources of the lore of the divine," which is being lost by "the drive to suppress all words for the divine or the invisible world."*

—Ed.

ROBERT DUNCAN: The title, "Fictive Certainties," is I think a little hedgy, but when it came to me I was rather won by it. I've never decided how to handle a theory of fictions, since everything we contact is incorporated right away as facts, and facts are things that belong to fictions, and we're the origin of the fictions that we ourselves project. But at the same time, "Fictive Certainties" combines the fact that they're certain, and that really means they're external to me. Since that title—since thinking of that title even—I more and more question the doctrine of fictions, because it's a stage in a metamorphosis, but the important thing in the metamorphosis is *the world* itself and how it goes through something in order to be incorporated and become experience, become our selves, each, individualized.

The book of essays—they're not all my essays. There are some literary essays: the one on *Maximus* by Charles Olson is in there, for instance. But the core of it is the condition of Man. That was very much on my mind all the time in relation to writing the essays. When I wrote *The Truth and Life of Myth,* I thought of it as belonging to the condition of

Man. The subtitle of *The Truth and Life of Myth* was *An Essay in Essential Autobiography,* because it seems to me, as my biography shows, the biography is never essential. The autobiography can be, but mostly it's not. It's gossip and things, trying to remember what happened. What merely happens is not the core of experience, which has gone through a creative process, and that's the one that concerns me.

. . .

The following volume of *Ground Work,* the second volume of *Ground Work,* which is called *In the Dark,* will appear in my seventieth year, which is 1989. That's the date. I may have finished it before then. I'll know when the volume is finished. But the date has its own significance for me. For one thing, I sort of declare that once I'm seventy—I've threatened a title called "Senilities," "Later Senilities," "Last Senilities." I've always loved that title of Rossini's "Follies of My Old Age." If I *could* commit follies, it would be very elegant. If I have a critique of my own work, it is that it is not exactly frivolous. It was for a while, in the period when I was writing *Faust Foutu.* And problems that come up in the composition of the new volumes? Do I include *Faust Foutu* in a volume of poems? What do I do?

(And that is not completely frivolous.)

No! But completely frivolous? Who wants to be completely frivolous? We've got several who take care of complete frivolity!

In the early '50s there was more exploration. *Letters* is the one book that belongs to the '50s. It was finished in '56. In that period I thought in general of books. *Letters* was conceived of as having the title "Letters," but the poems were still fairly independent coming in to contribute to that. I wasn't haunted by "the book" all the way through. It was when I put it together I thought, my goodness, this is a book. Then I knew that I was going to start, when I started *The Opening of the Field,* it was started as a book.

That's the mid-'50s. That's the period in which I was actually associated at all with Black Mountain College. In the early years I was in correspondence with Olson and with [Robert] Creeley and with Denise Levertov, and consequently was part of the *Black Mountain Review.* By that time, then, the title "Black Mountain Poets" got stuck on us. And yet, at the time of the *Black Mountain Review,* Creeley had been very briefly at Black Mountain College, but didn't fill out any term. It was the Black

Mountain College funds that were used for the *Black Mountain Review* that gave this name "Black Mountain" to the whole thing. And yet it *was* a kind of center. Olson thought of it as a center, and Black Mountain itself, with its ideas of education, has gone forward into my ideas and the ideas of the core faculty in the Poetics Program at New College, of what it is we're doing.

Olson was distinctively a vitalist. There is a subterranean war in American letters, of alarm at times, about vitalists. I remember *Partisan Review* had a symposium about the danger of even poor Henry James, who is a vitalist. And they divided writers into vitalists and—I've forgotten what the others were—the others I guess were "Solid Citizens." It was again one of those divisions of sheep from goats. I still think the term "vitalist" tells quite a lot. Essentially, the vitalist believes there is a living flame, and they can pursue—they don't have—I have no trouble with materialism because I think it's all alive. It does come down to a belief, it comes down to one of those watersheds where there are people who believe and live as if life is the significant thing and people who live as if their self is the significant thing. That sounds rather like I'm putting it down, and in a way I do mean to put it down; it's a real division from life, because the vitalist thinks trees speak, and so forth.

Olson had *Process and Reality* that he fed on. He didn't accept Bergson—he had a prejudice about him, although he had read him. It would be a perfect example. Darwinian evolution is something that was an illumination for me, and yet it never canceled out the flame of the Bergsonian evolution, which almost has a purpose.

DAVID MELNICK: Was Michael McClure exposed to this through you?

RD: He was, but he also had an appetite for it, so it was very easy to feed Michael McClure things to read. What he never accepted was the thing we haven't talked about, my preoccupation with form, in which it seems to me that form is the primary. Now there, Bergson would be form, and for [Alfred] Whitehead it's form. But I notice that in this last year Michael McClure has been doing a lot of deep reading in Whitehead, and coming up with great hunks of it, so he still follows the paternal path. Which leads to divisions, because there's nothing like reading the same text and having an entirely different take on it. Olson is the one who brought *Process and Reality* into my world, and as he was lecturing on it—there was a series of lectures in 1957 here in San Francisco—I began reading it and absolutely taking it as if it were my text and at the same time recognizing that it wasn't the same book he was talking about. So that was the difference of, the times when I've had to have the shock of recognition—between Charles and myself there could have been plenty of shocks of recognition, but it becomes vivid when you both have a key book. The more so that he, of course, was the one who glowingly converted my mind to the Whitehead, and at the same time I found, yes, that I was most unorthodox in the way I read it.

DM: Do you think Pound learned from you and Olson toward the end, in the composition of the last Cantos?

RD: No, I don't. Because Pound, really, at the end, I think, found continued work painful. Pound was a great source for us, but the main part of the Pound story is that he didn't read toward the end of his life himself. Responsibility, in an early, maybe too jazzy, line, I said was to keep the ability to respond. And Pound toward the end kept talking about this ability to respond, but for such a long time he had "reacted" rather than "responded." Response should be vividly kept, because it is the only cure to reaction. Reactionary responses we usually stick with the extreme right, but they're really all those responses that we have that simply bounce off of things and don't go into them. A response means if it offends, you go in to find out what it is. It is investigatory. Then, the imagination comes into action in response. In a reaction, imagination doesn't have to come in. Old habits govern. In politics and many things, I would say I would be "reactionary," because I have a blind "reactionary" fury and hatred at what goes on in politics, which is hardly known as a response!

In poetics, if you're concerned with poetics, you're concerned with what is happening, and there's no down and up to that. You can see that if you're concerned with what is happening in something, and that includes a text, you're not in a value system, because the minute a value system enters it, you're no longer actually looking at what was in the text. In the sciences and so forth, the value system comes after the fact of having to do with—the first very great big question is, what is happening here? And, as a matter of fact, the final one, for the valuable things in science, the final one is, what is happening here? That is what we turn to science for, ourselves, for a picture of what is happening. In that I think science and poetry are identical as pictures of what is happening.

Poetry is in an area that we can't put out on a table even for ourselves, so in a sense the poem, and the writing of the poem, the construction, *is* the putting out on the table of, the materialization, and once it's material-ized there, now we can ask what is happening. Otherwise it's in an area of the fugitive, there is no register at all of anything happening. But once it's a word right before us, then the word is happening. We don't go fuss-ing around with saying, "but, but, but, but," or "should have been," and "ought to have been," all of those crowding in. And most of our criticism is "ought to have been" instead of asking what is happening and what is the significance of it.

So in a sense poetics doesn't have to do with poetry! Because right away we think about poetry: "Is my poem good?" "Is this a good poem?"—a million questions. "Do I like this poem?" "Would I like to take it home and live with it?" All of these things are not questions that have to do with what is happening.

And so I would say that I have a great deal of curiosity about what goes on in poems. At the present time, in the Pound course, I'm using Robert Frost, and reading every single poem—I've finished *North of Bos-ton*—and observing what happens. It doesn't leave me at all complaining about what happens, or saying, "Oh, Robert Frost," or something. There are things going on there, and a gradual accumulation.

Now, what happens: Responsibility is not a total kind of thing, because there is a point at which reaction will set in and we see why reaction exists, because otherwise we'd be exhausted by responsibility. Our imagination has to extend even beyond its intelligible limits in order to imagine the existence of some things, and I think we naturally let them go. They're uninteresting, so we can't start thinking about what is happening in them. My more characteristic reaction when a reaction is called up is not to be interested.

That's the one actually that's used in the world at large in relation

41

to my work. The Eastern critics, for instance, aren't interested. They're not antagonistic; they haven't come out with their hatchets in the wind. They're just not interested. I have a stronger and stronger alliance with the most doubted of all vitalists, like Yeats. The alliance I've always had with Pound probably has the same course. The best of Pound is the son of Yeats. My mind does not balk at Yeats's mind. It's not only fascinated with it but loves it.

Anaïs Nin's cousin, Eduardo Sanchez, had a theory of trying to link me with Yeats and Blake, but at the time it just meant that I didn't want to read any late Yeats and Blake. I've always felt that my own link with Blake and Yeats is how close their thought—and religion—about the nature of the universe is to the kind of, it's loosely called mystical thinking. I can clear up why I mean mystical. Mystical ought to mean that there's a direct connection and a different mode for the voice. Rightly viewed, my voice is theosophical, the lore of the gods or the lore of the divine. Blake and Yeats are both rich sources of the lore of the divine.

If there's a disastrous blind spot in the whole contemporary civilization—it's not simply a blind spot—it's since the eighteenth century a deliberate drive to suppress all the words, for instance, that lead us to think at all in terms of the presence of the divine or the invisible world: as [Jack] Spicer always insisted, Do you obey the invisible world?

While we've uncovered the prejudice in which Freud was translated: "psyche" and not "soul," when he was a soul doctor, but the word "spirit" really gets left out, entirely, and in the eighteenth century in France it comes to mean the same thing as "mind," and then becomes confused with mind. So that it's very hard for twentieth-century French writers to insist upon spirit again. They're up against the word *esprit*, which has been built into a common resistance to any spiritualism. Spiritualism does not—well, it would only interest me like a circus thing—it doesn't thrill me, as we would say. But what we call spiritualism is also limited in that box of what we've let the word "spirit" mean.

DM: Spiritualism as a religion?

RD: Spiritualism is one of the forms in which people are trying to live in the spiritual world. When mankind has an idea, and spirit takes over, when something takes over their ideas like that, then you live in the spirit. That can result in spiritualism, and it can result in the kind of life Blake had. Your interpretation of your life throughout is that it is a life of spirit. And that's comparable to the way in which the person in a Freudian analysis or a Jungian analysis lives in the life of psyche. Everything is psyche then, and that becomes the perspective. So that for the spiritual life—and I keep wondering, yes, I tend, I do tend indeed to live a spiritual life.

Spicer was antagonistic to the visible world, and more than that, it was feared. The Spicer question is one of a very personal, I think it can be described as a dementia. Even he in the famous last remark describes it as a dementia. If you take his remark, it comes from Robin Blaser's hearing, and so in part it's relayed by Blaser—this is the one: because of my language, I'm dying because of my language—the force of that is, I think, true, that one can indeed, that the whole civilization is boxed because of its language. It has destroyed key parts of its structure by destroying the words, by ridiculing the words and by outlawing them and then making them ruthlessly mean something other. The sign always is that one aspect is scorned, as are spiritualist séances and so forth, and the other side is transferred, where spirit means, at best, just that you have vim or vigor, or something—a person of spirit.

And yet, of course, that spiritual world is as much a puzzle as death. Since we have no answers at all for it, it is a pure realm in which the imagination is the only thing that we can indeed come from and go to, and so the part of what it is that has been disowned and mistrusted is the imagination in our civilization. It isn't just incidental that we can't think our way out of the deadly problems we get into. The fact that the imagination can only think of bombs or poisonings via the atomic split, nothing else, shows that there is a real bent to the imagination. Something is blocked. And the imagination can think of nothing very clearly, not even simple, clear, evident things can the imagination think of when it comes to the economy. For the imagination-to-advance has almost been defined at every place as communism.

I have a sense that twentieth-century music is based on sensationalism more and more from an absence of imagination. But then our perspectives on the contemporary are—music is a notorious place for a litmus paper to show how inaccurate our perspectives are, how colored they are. But composers like Boulez seem to be centered on—and listening more to Ligeti—they're centered on an aspect, and intellectually centered on it, which means that it doesn't have the full risk of the imagination. I'm thinking of the tonalities and so forth. So that we get a great professionalism in the music, and we begin to miss—with many people commenting on it—miss the furor of what it came from.

A perfect example is the modern playing of [Richard] Strauss. When Strauss's music was composed it was experienced by the audiences and undoubtedly experienced by the orchestras, too, as a disturbing and furious sort of roar, uproar. And now it is meticulously registered note by note, and it seems to be an extension of Mozart or something. There is a certain area that is constantly cleaned up in the contemporary production of music, in our professionalism. Our professionalism has transferred Beethoven and Schubert and so forth, that were not composed for geniuses or virtuosi into virtuoso pieces. And we have many benefits from that, we have many that are awesome that come out of that, minute interpretations, but it still is removed from the hearty life of the music.

Music suffered almost at root. I'm a record listener who can barely pick out a little baby Bartok on the piano, and consequently a victim of a civilization that went away from playing music in the home, went away from the individual playing music to individuals going to hear great players and being very impatient about hearing any other kind of music.

And if we were dependent on great readers of poetry! When I think about what people think are great readers of poetry! The general attitude is that a poet's a bad reader, and there *are* poets who read badly. We can put that all together. But in the experience of poetry it doesn't consist any more than experience does in sorting out good and bad. What is going on in a bad reading is highly educational, and that poetry can be bad shows what a wide extent it has. So that again if we went back to, if we were actually listening—now we're in a different experience when we're collecting ways we've heard something read. The ones that otherwise we would be calling bad are one of the varieties, and the varieties fit in to give shape to the very best, that we like. It gives it body that it belongs to.

I certainly feel that living in San Francisco, with hundreds of poets, that the hundreds of poets are what enable me to write. I'm ruthless about that, it's as if, as far as I'm concerned, they make the environment, they make the place. Not that they're listening to me, or even that I'm listening to them, but as we lift a paper and see almost every day, in *Poetry Flash*, see that you've got four or five different readings that you could be at, that's a very different world from the one where once a month you had a reading or something.

[In 1946–48] when we started, as a matter of fact, we weren't interested in printing, because we had an audience. At the very best, we had an audience of about two hundred, when everybody got together. It was a wider distribution of audience. At that time, poets as various as, from Academic poets like Thomas Parkinson and Leonard Wolf, were reading, and it wasn't even a sense of mixing—they were distinct in one way, they weren't part of the bohemian world, as Spicer and myself and Philip Lamantia would be, but there were only about ten or twelve of us. The audience was prepared to think of about ten or twelve poets without starting to discard any. They were interested in all twelve. One of the results of having hundreds of poets is that that no longer is true. No audience is going to think, including myself—tolerance won't get you there—is going to listen to all hundred and know, have the shape. But it is amazing what a San Francisco audience will, indeed, listen to. They'll listen to an evening of thirty poets. And they will have opinions about all of them. In the great period of poetry readings, which I think is past in a way—they were messy events, whatever they were—but they don't happen as often as they did. It was the Beats who really made a scene that grew out of our little audience. Suddenly overnight it was a big audience. And for Ferlinghetti, for instance—a wide, popular audience.

The thing that is most thrilling about San Francisco is that it does rally. It rallied in marches against the Vietnamese War, and it rallied in gay liberation marches. And are there any other rallies? I think those are the rallies. The worst of our attitude toward El Salvador and so forth is that none of those rallies are like the ones—of course, "we" weren't drafted, so that's when it comes home. But meanwhile, it's wildly encouraging that 250,000 people will march in the streets. But that same

250,000 people won't appear in voting. And we'll have a Nixon for president in the next round.

We're mistaken to go by presidents anyway. The whole eighteenth-century frame of what a government would be seems wrong in almost every direction. Wrong to be represented by somebody politically, instead of speaking and moving and doing it yourself. And wrong indeed to have a leader or somebody, to have a shape in which government is solved by a little gang, a little gang of operators, is no virtue. If they were a little virtuous gang, we would be suffering from their virtues. As it is we suffer from their stupidity in the present regime and suffer from their crookedness in the previous regimes. Although none of us suffer what the victims of our framework suffer: it's Grenada that's a victim, or Vietnam that was a victim, or it's El Salvador.

My fury rose indeed in those years in those poems, when presented with the lie. The lie really is an enemy of poetry, because of the very subtle area of fictions that poetry is always struggling not to prove finally false and to find the good of, when you've got the realm of the lie in which they're finding the wickedness of it, it is appalling. You know very well the power of the world is going in the other direction.

And you know also the crippling of words. The fullest extent of the destruction of words has taken place, a major extent has taken place in the American governmental use of words. You know that certain things that are absolutely necessary for you to use, and you go ahead and use them, have been so destroyed, and so blocked away, that it seems as if that other use of the very same word is more powerful.

One word, of course, that shows the political distortion of words is the word "gay." The word "gay" has been destroyed by its being a particular political meaning. And it's a very key word in poetry. I came across it in reading Pound, as a matter of fact, and realized that there you were at one of the places where this word has been so misused that we smirk when we come across it in its serious use. All because they didn't want to say "homosexual." Now all we see is a Castro bird on a Castro bough! Is that bird really gay, you ask?

My maternal family is having a family convention in July of this year in Yosemite. I rather resent that in the biography [Ekbert] Faas refers to my "natural" mother, when I was—I was six months old when I was adopted: I was never in a foster home. Those comments are not only incorrect but insulting in some way. For my parents, as Hermeticists and believing in reincarnation, adoption was a serious religious rite as well as a legal rite—r-i-t-e.

Always there are the bad days when you are curbed in something, and so forth, and you have a spat or so. But the real point of division was quite clear, because my tie, particularly to my mother, was so intense. My father died when I was sixteen and my family mind and tie were still absolute in that period: I was going to be an architect, I was concerned with mathematics, my family values I hadn't even begun, well, I'd begun perhaps to question them. But in the following year, when I was seventeen, I saw a show at the Legion of Honor of French painting, through the ages of French painting. And when we came to the modern rooms, I saw the Picassos at the end of the hall. I'd never seen anything like this at all, and I ran toward them, came back and ran toward Mother. I think it must be, it might have even been before my father's death; I never introduced an aesthetic battle with my father; it would have come up because of the architecture; I was on the bridge of it at the time he died. But with my mother, my mother's response to the French modern painting was, that they did it to insult us because of the war debts, that they had sent demented paintings by demented people over, and then that they should be castrated. I heard more and more expression that they should have concentration camps, which both my father and mother believed in. Republican concentration camps: They should be isolated. Especially my mother immediately thought "genetic damage" and all sorts of things.

So I saw, then, there was a real break, and yet there was a break before that time, because I was beginning to read things that my mother wouldn't—where we read everything together before—when I came to read *Ulysses* and came to read Virginia Woolf's work, and Lawrence, my mother was not going to read those books, and, more than that, would be very hostile to my reading them, and hostile toward the English teacher who was introducing "bad" reading to me.

So this is the break in adolescence, and it came for me around painting, since books you read all by yourself anyway. However, it was an

47

acute pain that I could not talk about or share any longer in reading. I realized my sister wasn't going to. So that the close relationship—my sister was only a year younger than I was—but by the time I was sixteen and seventeen, the absolute, continuous relationship I'd had with my sister was broken because she was not sharing these things that were immediately important to me. They were a new me really being born and not being born out of anything that the family wanted to happen.

Music would have been in question, too, except that, sitting in Bakersfield we weren't subjected to it. I was reading about the *Sacre,* and didn't hear it really until I came to college and discovered it was on records—the first records I got.

That did make a break with the family. Then the other thing that made a break is that at the same time we went into the Second World War, and I was violently against it and my sister was a recruiting officer. My mother was just as violently for it, always for it, always "Your country right or wrong," which I heard as "Your mother right or wrong." And I had no doubt about it, it was wrong, wrong, wrong. Of course, at that age I was likely to be drafted and I experienced it as a personal threat. The threat was not coming from Hitler; it was coming from the government. And that's kept alive all my life, though I've not been threatened by the government drafting me for a good many ages.

I had certain models that I've kept all my life. One of them was [Gertrude] Stein, and the other was James Joyce's *Ulysses.* In the period when I was an acolyte, a camp follower of Anaïs Nin's and [Kenneth] Patchen's, I really turned against them as I had turned against my parents, because they did not measure their writing against Stein and Joyce. They scoffed at superior writing that they didn't take up the discipline of, the recognition of. Still, *Ulysses* is awesome to me, and Stein all the way through, awesome. So I had a sense of where I am. But their writing [Nin's and Patchen's] was self-indulgent. Self-indulgent is when you supply your *own* redundant—and then it can only be redundant—definition of what you're doing.

Naropa Institute Interview

(with Anne Waldman et al., 1978, excerpts)

The following are excerpts from an interview taped on July 21, 1978, in Robert Duncan's guest apartment at the Naropa Institute in Boulder, Colorado, where he was teaching numerous classes. The interviewers were Anne Waldman, John Oughton, and Rob Fromme. The entire dis-cussion was published as a little endarkenment and in my poetry you find me *(Buffalo, NY: Poetry/Rare Books Collection; Rodent Press; Erudite Fangs Editions, 1997). Among many subjects, Duncan explores the importance of a voluntary obedience that includes "listen-ing to the sound and giving voice to the sound" the poet hears. He men-tions the destructive results of building a personality, so encouraged in our time, which denies "the completeness of what we are."*

—Ed.

ANNE WALDMAN: I missed the first part of your class this morning but I gather you were talking, and extending some of the things you were talking about earlier . . . such as obedience.

ROBERT DUNCAN: Oh yes, this morning I was moving out from our talking about what was the nature of obedience—because obedience is very important to me—as what's involved in the art. One of the feelings—a poem has a commanding presence. I talked about two things cooperating as it emerged and the earlier ideas of obedience. Were you there when I talked about Martha Graham, whom I called the Hitler of Dance?

AW: Yes, the Hitler of Dance—but she didn't have an oven backstage.

RD: Right, right. Well, that was just an example of the kind of obedience. You learned a lot, a lot of dance developed in it, but it was all in the place where *she* was the dance. If we thought about it, the people who were in it were obedient to her, were not really suffering the deformation that she was.

AW: And what was her deformation?

RD: Oh, she was just a deformed, warped creature doing nothing but Martha Graham at the end. Remember that Roberta Lefkowitz asked me about her voice, and then she hears these poets' voices that are so specific, where the personality is up front? That sort of strikes me too. It's not at all to be identified with what we were talking about, which is listening to the sound and giving voice to the sound. And certainly we could turn further than we do when we give voice to the sound. And certainly we could turn further than we do when we voice our poems. Well, in a play, it would be clear, wouldn't it? In a play we don't imagine that Shakespeare had a Shakespeare personality out front. We used the example earlier of Bette Davis . . ., [who's] not an actress at all, because she's always Bette Davis. And it's Bette Davis who goes out front, not the role she plays. So it's a series of costumes. We all suffer from this warp, but if we want to go back to it, I started with obedience—tried to give the positive picture that I would have of obedience . . . and it's volunteered. We talked this morning before class, Anne and I, about "volunteered," and I brought the term forward again and related it to Vanzetti. After Kirpal Singh, and that was a marvelous presentation. [Kirpal briefly explained some ideas from Indian religion about holy sounds in Sanskrit, and the image of the mouth as sexual, productive.] I knew when he came up and told me about that, if he were to tell the class he would tell more. You see, he wanted to come up and tell me because he felt attuned to me because of what I was saying. But actually we're all attuned, that's something I feel about that class, it's beautifully attuned. I won't be able to go to all parts of the class. Bobbie Louise Hawkins can have her own way of tuning in on it then, but I'm sure a whole thing is there. So it's magic for me in that way. And Kirpal's presentation to the class went further than it was for me. He then started talking about a thing that is very valuable: the *lingam-yoni* mouth-tongue relationship and sounding all the centers so that they sounded together and this is what's projected in sound. Now as you even think of that, certainly one of the places we lose our personality front is in sexuality. I mean we got a lot of front about sex, and it's supposedly what cashes in our personality, and we got a lot of strutters and so forth, but if any of us tried to put our heads together with it, that they were still strutting when they were actually in embrace, that's impossible to believe. I mean they must be out the window. And the poem has that way of dissolving it—it does it—I mean we disappear in the poem.

. . .

JOHN OUGHTON: You can't hit the reader over the head with a stick at some point.

RD: Well, the nice thing about poetry is that it's in a book and a reader gets to close it when a reader doesn't want to read it. That's our one great noble courtesy and since we read, now we read in big auditoriums. I'm certainly never bugged if someone gets up and moves out. But Charles [Olson], for instance, was coming on [at the Berkeley Poetry Conference in 1965] like he was a superpower. First Borregaard—this is that long spiel of Charles's—and first Borregaard gets up after the fourth or fifth time Charles has . . .

AW: Ebbe Borregaard.

RD: Ebbe Borregaard. About the fourth or fifth time that Charles says, "We've had enough of beauty." And I'm muttering, "Cripes, you've never seen anything beautiful in your whole life, you silly old man." In a world that hasn't got any beauty around he's saying "NO MORE BEAUTY," and we're sitting in the ugliest auditorium you could ever *see*, with *ugly* chairs all around and *ugly* everything and an *ugly* occasion, and I'm mainly thinking like, like, like the monkey in the tree, how do I get out of it when this king of the beasts is calling us all into order. When Ebbe gets up and walks out, Charles doesn't dare say a thing. Here's this big, tall, blond, cool cat walking out. If he'd called on Ebbe, Ebbe would just have turned around and said "Oh shit" and walked out the door, and he didn't want to hear that. And then a little old lady who thinks "Oh God" there's going to be a space for her to get out. Unfortunately, Ebbe is already out the door and she starts out and Charles turns and roars at her. Then I thought this is not a test of powers, because I don't believe in a test of powers at all, 'cause I thought "Will I bring a big whammy?" Charles felt my flunking out as if I'd brought a whammy. Then I realized, it's not a whammy, we all have to pee, so I said, "Charles, can we have our break to go pee?" And then I just never came back from the break to go pee. He felt like it was a whammy, but the alternative in my mind, that's another thing. So we're just talking about poetry orders here.

. . .

RD: There are people who love the poem no matter what comes, what's going on, almost. But when we begin to be aware of where the poem goes, in its disorder, when it starts being as if it ought to be there for everybody. Someone like Jonathan Williams blaming America for not supporting the poet, and finally you end up picketing the football stadium because they're not at McClure's play. I mean, if you can see the absurdity—or the other way around, picketing McClure's play because they're not at the football game.

JO: For the work and dedication that you've put in as a poet, do you not feel that society owes you anything, even if it's reading you occasionally?

RD: I rip off everything that they have ever extended to me, but I sure don't feel they owe me a thing. Not at all. I'd love to cash in on my readers, but they don't owe something. Remember, remember the work, *work* is something you do and more than that. If you thought about payment! Well, we just had today the real source that it's all coming from and going back to is that sound up there that was put at the top of the board [Om] . . . Now, that's the circuit. What the poet does rightly have to aim at is how to make the time and space in which they can work. And since the society doesn't offer it—it offers it in peculiar ways, if you can find a way to find that space and time. Poets are very cunning about it. Shakespeare. In Shakespeare's day the stage was there and they all wrote for the stage. Then they're all Protestant ministers, for almost the next two centuries. They could always get a little parish someplace and give their sermons. And in our period, the thing they buy at all for the arts is terribly destructive because what they buy is a personality up front. You make it in the movies or TV just as far as you're a personality, so poets build personalities all over the place out front in order to move around and buy, that way, the space and time. That's our star system. Well, it's very destructive of our energies, and especially it can be destructive of the person we are. I think personality is sort of a growth out from, and uses some of, the central person energies in order to make this front thing. When I extend my personality and the imaginary me, I build in prefaces, and legends, associations. And that's in general the way we do it. So that our readers for instance begin to have us as stars just about the time they're reading us. And yet that's very hard on the reader. My real imaginary reader is someone who knows nothing of all that.

AW: Ideal reader.

RD: Ideal reader, who picks up the book anonymous in a secondhand shelf and starts reading poetry, poems of whom he knows not. Because the one who suffers most under this is the reader [who] is drawn into a glamour and hardly gets a real experience of reading a poem, which is how much it means to ourselves. So I try in my prefaces to sort of build in a picture in which the reader knows, begins to know that I am handing it across. But the money thing is not "owes." No, no, we use our cunning, we do what anybody else does, we try to make that space for it to happen.

JO: As a matter of fact I'm used to seeing on the back of poets' slim volumes, you know, where they have a biography, at least twelve different professions. It's sort of a mark of honor.

RD: Washing dishes, milking cows.

JO: Someone like Wallace Stevens or Raymond Souster [a Canadian poet who published many of the Black Mountain writers in his magazine *Combustion*] who works in a bank all his life—you wonder what's going on.

RD: No, they made a real space—or William Carlos Williams, a doctor, that's even more a call. He had to interrupt a poem in a flash, and get in his car and answer a midnight appointment.

JO: Is the story true that he kept a typewriter in his desk and he'd whip off a few lines between patients?

RD: Well, that might have been true. I don't know about that one, but lots of times of course he was working at home and he'd get a call in the middle of the night. He did lots of writing driving in his car to different calls. But he himself didn't like that. In *Voyage to Pagany* he expresses a great deal of resentment that he had to go through that and his poetry really blossoms once he retires, [when] he isn't on call.

   . . .

AW: Well, there are levels of practice.

RD: Levels of practice, okay, that would be similar.

JO: And vows you take.

AW: Vows you take, through the Hinayana, Mahayana, Vajrayana.

RD: All right, then, yes, [my parents] had this. They had vows and they had initiations. And my father was a high-degree Mason and so everywhere was this business of hierarchies. Actually after I graduated from high school I didn't want to graduate from nothing, and if I could have figured out earlier than high school I would have failed. I would have gotten out from graduating [from] high school. So I really read life, "I'm not going to graduate, I'm not going to be . . ." So I immediately turn away if someone says, "I'm going to spiritually improve you, here's a little enlightenment." I say, "No, no, I'll take a little endarkenment and in my poetry you find me." I'm very different from Blake in my poetry, absolutely the antithesis of Blake, who wants it light. You find me no, *sfumato,* mixture, color. I love Blake but I'm not phobic toward the light kids, you know. I love Rembrandt with his dark, deep study of the dark. Of course Freud was lovely because not only do we finally have an asshole but finally shit. And so is Joyce, and not only was it part of life, it was a meaningful part of life. That was one of the things I think we most importantly bring forward today, is the completeness of existence, admitting the completeness of what we are. My parents' religion, like Neoplatonist religions, was all to sublimate, to move up, and I love sublimation. I have no trouble when the Freudians say, "That's just sublimated." I say, "Hooey, I mean I just told you I have an asshole and I also have a sublimation so don't tell me I borrowed for one from the other." No way. There are many things I carried forward from that family. As above, so below, obviously. I mean the Freudian as above, so below fascinates me, carried forward there. There were also Christian Kabbalists because both Masonry and Hermeticism . . . Hellenistic Hermeticism had already got shades of the fact that very early stages of the Kabbalah are developing. But once you've come past the Renaissance, there everything's together, one great big melting pot. And I tend to bring forward all the things that I find fascinating and try to find a way of having them so that they don't form subscriptions.

. . .

RD: Yes, and yet in poetry I obviously have trance states. You see, I entered—poetry we enter. We choose our own masters, by the way, in poetry, because we don't meet them personally. We choose them in texts, although I had sessions with Ezra Pound and sessions with H.D. They weren't these kind of sessions we're having today. And that's the only kind of sessions. Mostly poets don't study with masters; painters do. They go to their studio, they grind the paints. Painting has a whole order which would be exactly like the acolyte-master-discipline thing. That's what Renaissance painting came from, but even Renaissance poets had no poets. Dante met with Cavalcanti and met with Ficino and so forth. They were a group, like we are, sitting around, and they talked about love. There was no doctrine. And they imagined what do those poems mean and poems, I think—the characteristics of poetry—it would be very hard to get a doctrine from it. My last session with Charles, I said, "Isn't it wonderful that from the beginning you would think that you were laying down a dogma. Maybe only *you and I* are interested in what composition by field is. All the time you must have realized one thing you didn't need was a secondhand Charles Olson." He beamed, he said, "We've been on a great adventure." And that's something . . . That's like Robin Hood Duncan. And this, of course, in the imagination all these things can be reposited. And in the meantime this was a man who was not on a great adventure when he was standing up on a platform trying to say, "Well, here we are. We're a big power and we're going to have some poetry politics." His fantasy is imagination, and suddenly he wanted to make it realer than imagination. That's what I mean about that imagination, in that essay on "Occult Matters" on Blavatsky [in *The H.D. Book*], I talk about the fact that although she could work marvelous tricks and produce all sorts of magic effects, she wanted it to be *real*. She wanted to come down on things. Her head was more marvelous than anything she could have done. She writes to, I think it's Sinnett [Alfred Percy Sinnett, 1840–1921, Anglo-Indian Theosophist], "Can you bring back a real magician from Egypt?" and while we can hear rumors of real magicians in Egypt, I'm sure they couldn't have brought anything that compared with Madame Blavatsky when she was going on. Not at all. But she wanted it real. When religions don't want to be real, in that sense they're doing all right. They're doing fine, because it's a whole realm, like theater and everything else. And yet it's not theater; you go into it in a different way. But we're still talking about the coexistence of a poetry and the misunderstandings between a poetry and a religion. Burckhardt [Jacob Burckhardt, nineteenth-century German historian, who wrote *The Civilization of the Renaissance in Italy* (1860)] says there's a fundamental misunderstanding between poetry and religion. Poets think that religion gives them a great subject matter, wonderful. And religion thinks, "Gee, they're really a jazzy way to get our message across."

AW: Right.

RD: And so between these two people there must be a larger misunderstanding than you could imagine, of any kind, between the two groups.

AW: But poets don't come here for the subject matter, I don't think.

RD: Yeah, I know. But they could. When I say that Christendom enters the imagination in Dante, the whole subject matter is there.

AW: Of course.

RD: Aquinas is sitting there, and meanwhile I'm not reading Aquinas. Aquinas has written, wait a minute now, I'm blabbering on in philosophy. But Aquinas is where it has to be real, in medieval law. There are no laws in poetry.

AW: No laws.

RD: Well, are there? Can you think of a law?

JO: I was just wondering if anyone has asked Anne to write a Buddhist poem, you know, to say, "If you could get a little Vajra into that poem it would really help the movement." Does anyone do that?

AW: Not quite. [*laughs*] Not yet.

RD: There's no reason why certain terms couldn't be there. I'm disturbed by Joanne Kyger, for instance. Actually the Buddhism isn't part of the poem, it isn't part of the imagination. And so you get a little homily in the middle of the thing. And poets have homilies of different kinds. I just call, I call this whole . . .

AW: Speeches.

RD: I call this whole department Mother's Day messages, you know. How many poets write "To My Wife" and you wonder, what did they do to her that day, that they want to give a guarantee again in a poem, or Mother's Day cards, or "My Country, 'Tis of Thee." I mean it's all of that level. . . . Certainly we can have powerful feelings of country, powerful feelings of religion, and so forth. In my poetry the religions that appear, like the Christ and so forth, are because I don't have a subscription, so I get to move them around.

JO: How do you feel about your place in the Whitman–Pound lineage, tradition of poetry? I'm thinking mostly in terms of anyone who's carrying on from your discoveries, who's sort of forging ahead in terms of new technique from your work specifically.

RD: I think of myself as close in spirit to Whitman and Pound, and so their language speaks for me and I tend to write like that frequently. I really don't think of myself, nor do I think of them, as "forging ahead" or something.

JO: Well, yeah . . .

RD: My experience about poets is discovering a company. Growing up in that WASP family, I really didn't have much company, I felt insane much of the time. And then, a teacher in high school, ah, Miss Edna Keogh, I still know and see, opened up to me Lawrence and Pound, not Pound, no, D. H. Lawrence and Virginia Woolf, and suddenly there were spirits I could really commune with, feel I had a company with. I didn't care that I wouldn't know them. I understood that, yes, probably I will never meet these people but I understood. I love to read, anyway. But it never dawned on me that what I loved in reading was that all the time I felt suddenly companied. I didn't have to talk to them but they were making it clear that I could have, because they were extensions. So I feel them as extensions, is my feeling. Sometimes poets have written poems . . . Well, LeRoi Jones [Amiri Baraka] is coming here, and he wrote a poem on dancing responsive to my poem "The Dance." I almost burst into tears because I didn't know him. I had never met him. It was so close to me and I felt, "Oh my . . ." I mean I'd found a like soul. A very early thing, I said I write for those alike in soul.

JO: Yeah.

RD: Yes, I feel close to Whitman and to, ah, Pound as if there was some kind of spiritual company in that. And with Emily Dickinson, she seems awesome. I mean, I tremble. I spoke of some other poems and things where I found myself trembling. In Wordsworth, I'm not sure. I don't feel the kind of company with Wordsworth because it is awesome, because it seems too grand. Shakespeare I love more and more. But Shakespeare seems to have so indwelt on imagining who any of us readers were going to be that we all discover ourselves in him. That's why everybody thinks someone else wrote him. Because almost anyone who gets into him finds that he was really writing for *you*, whoever you are. That's way out. That's unbelievable. I felt, "Yeah, well, okay then, what are we answering to? I also would like to be that open, I also would like to be for everybody." Then you don't have to feel that they have to pay you, do you? I mean, Shakespeare doesn't feel "Lorenzoni has to pay me for the misery I went through." God, even Macbeth, if he could have read, could have read it and not been insulted at all, by the play. We would all try to injure Hitler. We'd all try to. That doesn't even signify. We'd all try to injure Nixon. Shakespeare does not try to injure Macbeth. I think this is a miracle of displaying what it can mean, that you can see what a person is and not want to injure them. And not want to add a little kick.

JO: Just portray them as they are?

RD: Well, when Dante's going through Hell with Virgil, when they get to the circle of the lawyers and the ones who lie, and Dante suddenly wants to give one of them a shove back into the shit they're in, and Virgil says, "Look, ah, you're now taking on the character of this place." Everywhere else Dante also doesn't injure. And suddenly he wants to injure, and he embodies it in the poem and tells us something wonderful at that point. Because his guide, the spirit guide, Virgil, says, "All right, Buddy, if you want to injure, this is your circle, and I will leave you. You're not making the trip you said you were in." Okay.

AW: What about the younger poets?

RD: Younger poets? I've had several times when surprising books have seemed very close to me. One recent one is Michael Davidson's, who I actually wrote on. Oh, Jess wanted to do a cover. How did we contrive it? Yes, Jess was thrilled by the book too, and very close to it, and so he did a cover. Then they printed it, and the printer printed it in colors when it should have been black and white. So I said, "Fine, the solution is we'll make a jacket for it and I will write on the jacket." I was thrilled by the book. But it was also because the book was very close. The things that, ah, where I feel close indeed to poetry I guess is to a poetry that embodies a very human and personal love situation, in a very immediate way. I think that's the thing that's most essential to me. To make me feel close to it. I understand Whitman that way although his kind of love is not mine at all. Since he was one person after another after another, so it isn't even that, it's the person . . . the immediacy, personal immediacy, that kind of present time.

Well, of my contemporaries, Denise Levertov—and I have terrible quarrels with other poems of hers—she's written poems that I gaze into over and over again. Immense closeness is felt, and a puzzling one. Because she's a moralist, and I don't like moralism. And so forth, lots of things. So, so, it isn't that you get along with them all the time, that's the story on that. There's such a richness but I'll take your one going back to the ones that mean something *very* personal to me. And that would mean some poems of Denise's. H.D.'s poems were a great revelation and the *late* poems of William Carlos Williams; I cannot separate them at all from the human condition. I can't think of them as whether they're great poetry or what kind of poetry because they seem to be just purely, just immediately the voice.

JO: Do you still read Yeats?

RD: Oh yes, I read Yeats. But Yeats seems to me an artist, and I understand Yeats most on artists and mysteries. And I love arts and mysteries. I read Yeats over and over and over again. And his prose I love. I don't feel the closeness to Yeats. I feel close to Pound because I'm a mixed-up person like Pound, perhaps. I mean, this is a personal thing.

AW: What about Stein?

RD: [Fake Southern accent] You're referring to my mother. Yes, there are times when Stein is certainly in. The "Valentine for Sherwood Anderson" is a lovely little love poem to Alice, and "Lifting Belly" I love. It's just a glorious, glorious poem. Yeah, she would be one of those. Not only is she a writer that is absolutely liberating to go to and learn to let language move that way, and get the sort of thing we were doing where you let "turbine" talk, instead of you trying to move it around. That's just great. But she does have also the crossover where I feel the same. I'm not a person with only ten poets to mention, so we've got too long a list to be going to. I could only take the poets that came immediately to mind.

JO: That's my list [of questions].

AW: Okay, thank you, Robert.

Transcribed and edited by John Oughton
July/August 1978

PART II

"A Poetry of Unevenness"

Late 1950s. Photo by Wallace Berman.

Beat Scene Interview

(with Colin Sanders, 1980)

This engrossing interview gives a clear picture of the poetry scene Robert Duncan was part of in the 1940s in New York and California and the flavor of his conversation, which often explores numerous ideas and subjects rapid-fire and almost simultaneously. He talks about the little magazines he issued, his early contacts with Kenneth Rexroth and William Everson, his complex relationship with Jack Spicer, and his association with the writers in the anarchist circle around Rexroth in San Francisco. This interview was conducted by Colin Sanders in 1980 and was published in the magazine Beat Scene *in the United Kingdom in 1980.*

—Ed.

COLIN SANDERS: What was your initial contact with William Everson and Kenneth Rexroth?

ROBERT DUNCAN: My first contact with Everson and Rexroth came at exactly the same point which—my first work that was published outside of campus magazines was published in a magazine called *Phoenix,* edited by James Peter Cooney and Henry Miller in Europe. It's through that— through reading *Phoenix,* which was a Lawrencian-anarchist-pacifist magazine before the Second World War, anti-industrialist, anti-city magazine, but what interested me was that it was Lawrencian. And it's there that I found Anaïs Nin's writing. Miller had already appeared in *New Directions.* This would be around '38. So I sent poems to *Phoenix,* and was printed by *Phoenix,* and then started what was eventually *Experimental Review* myself in Berkeley in '38, I guess it would be. And by '38 and '40 was printing Nin and Lawrence Durrell, in other words, as a very junior tagalong of what was essentially a Miller/Nin circle. The war broke out, and almost all the Surrealists were over in New York, so it was on the fringes of the Surrealist scene. Sanders Russell is the first poet that I met outside of the ones that were my own peers at college like Mary Fabilli. So when I started a magazine I wrote to Russell and asked him to come be co-editor. Russell didn't have a job or—well, he came and we were living on an allowance I had until I was twenty-one, up until 1940. And it was at that point that *Phoenix*—that Blanche and Peter Cooney went south to Georgia to a utopian sort of commune, and I bought the press from Cooney and started printing the first issues of *Experimental Review,* the first ones that were printed instead of mimeographed with Sanders helping. And in the office of *Phoenix,* in the leftover papers that had been sent to *Phoenix,* were poems of Rexroth, I think, perhaps, and of Everson, and I wrote to both of them, but Everson had been printed in *Phoenix.* His closeness, at that point, to [Robinson] Jeffers interested me and, as our correspondence will show, I printed Everson then in *Experimental Review.* Although I think that petered out, largely because we became more and more concerned with—Sanders was very concerned with metaphysical qualities in a poem. There was conflict all the time between Sanders and myself over Mary Fabilli and Anaïs Nin. And so that things he didn't really want to print—we would have gotten into print "A Cross Portion's Pastoral" by Thomas Merton. *Experimental Review* printed one of the first poems of Merton that was published. Of the little freelance work sent in, Merton was about the only person we didn't know.

CS: Was Merton living at Gethsemani in the monastery, at this point?

RD: No, no. He was in the process of going into a monastery and so he was corresponding.

CS: He was still studying at Columbia?

RD: Yes, he was at Columbia when he was first sending poems and then he was in retreat at the monastery but not even entered—was not certain about it—and the "Cross Portion's Pastoral" would have been fascinating, because it was Joycean and would certainly bring into question was he or was he not going into a monastery. So, I wrote to Kenneth Rexroth, and we didn't like anything he sent us. So that was my first contact with Kenneth, 1940. When I came back to San Francisco in

1942—but this was not just because he had some manuscripts at *Phoenix*. It was that he had marvelous and very, very crotchety and funny letters that he sent into *Partisan Review* and *View* magazine and so forth, so that by the time I came out to San Francisco in 1942 I wanted very much to meet Kenneth Rexroth and went to—wrote to him beforehand and almost the first week I was here. I was here for about four or five months, I think it is, during '42—Rexroth was living in South San Francisco. It was a period of the incarceration of the Japanese in concentration camps and both Maria and Kenneth Rexroth were working sort of underground to get Japanese out of this area—east, where they could be free once you could get them across. And they were also working in the camps, volunteer working in the camps, taking messages back and forth. So the first Kenneth I met was in his thirties, about thirty-eight, and he was a marvelous man. And also, in Rexroth, I found for the first time here somebody older who was really an avid—who knew about *transition* and *Little Review* and so forth. And in the circle around Kenneth at that time he had known Philip Lamantia, before Philip went to New York. In the war years Philip was in New York, where I had already met him. At the time, around Rexroth, I was the only other poet. There were really only a handful of us directed by Rexroth at that time. In those years Kenneth was—well, all his life he had a great regard for Yvor Winters and he was absolutely fascinated with him.

Partly, Yvor Winters was a case of rejection that was quite constant, and Kenneth tried to win his way through. But it was the first time I had met anybody in writing where the poet was an intellectual. And I think poets are rather—it's very rare for poets to be intellectual, but that was my disposition. And there wasn't going to be another one until Charles [Olson]. Neither Robin [Blaser] nor Jack [Spicer] is truly intellectual. I'm never asleep. I'm fascinated by everything. They can learn, but that's very different. There's a learned tradition that came out of Kantorowicz, but that's different from Kenneth Rexroth's disposition.

CS: In one of Rexroth's essays it seems he wishes to create an argument against Everson's fascination with Jeffers.

RD: Well, even some of the writing about Rexroth makes it seem as if

65

Jack Spicer, 1960s

he came to know Everson in that original circle, but I'm the one who brought—when Everson was at Waldport and when Everson got out of Waldport after the war in '46, he came to Treesbank, to the Tylers's, and I'd already introduced Rexroth to the Tylers, so it's in that context that Kenneth came to know Everson. He would have come to know him anyway but—and Everson himself was never really, as I was, for instance, an acolyte, I mean, really learning from Kenneth. And by 1945 when I came back and Kenneth began coming up to Treesbank, already the Tylers had gathered around Richard Moore, who did the NET film on me, for instance. Richard did both of the two films done by the NET and [Tom] Parkinson, who was at that time thinking of himself as possibly a poet and at the same time working for his degree at Cal. And Philip

Lamantia was back from New York and he came up to Treesbank. Even Spicer did at one point, oddly enough, later. Well, he came up and scared the baby—made faces, but didn't really scare the baby, delighted the baby! [*laughter*]

CS: In reading through Spicer's books, he at various stages makes reference to you, then doesn't. When did your friendship with him disintegrate?

RD: There are various stages. The first break came when I moved in with Jerry Ackerman, which is the beginning of "The Venice Poem" period. That's late 1947, in November of '47, and Jack was already living in that building; we shared the same shower, and so forth. And Jack was not speaking to me at all nor looking at me, which was—I have a whole collection of signs that I made at that time. Well, that was in part because he'd made Robin and me promise we wouldn't go over there and we of course did that right away but Robin didn't get not forgiven. I'm the one. The reason that he didn't want us to go over there was exactly because of what happened. And that made the first real rift. And then over "The Venice Poem" reception, there was a real controversy about the poem—Jack fighting it and fighting the last harlot. But on the other hand, it was much stronger then that I didn't forgive him for the period of his rejection because his correspondence shows that he was asking me why had he not got the last of "The Venice Poem" and so forth, and I was not just going to let him, even if he'd written that. I was astounded when I went back over the correspondence and I was the one who actually was refusing to let—it was much more important to me to have Jack in opposition than it was to have Jack possibly enter in on discussion of points. And it was in that period that Robin became very important because he was the only one person who was responsive to "The Venice Poem" and who actually expounded reasons and so forth for "The Venice Poem" reception. Although they weren't exactly like mine would be but they still were—he was for it. And the ones who had been following me at all before I lost almost all my readers over "The Venice Poem," the academic ones right off. Well, a complex of things with "The Venice Poem" would be ... that "The Venice Poem" made homosexuality clear, which was after all covert in anybody else's poetry and that was horrifying to Parkinson. Not that I minded that point, but the major trouble I had though had nothing to do with that. It had to do with the fact that it was a formalist poem so that I couldn't get Rexroth to understand at all. I went to Rexroth wanting to talk about the problems I faced after "The Venice Poem." Those are ones that I was alone in, and it's a period that Jack and Robin and everyone went through, the one of "An Essay at War" and then my Stein imitation period. Which would look like my trying to become essentially Modernist, because I would take Stein on her own terms to be what we're talking about when we talk about Modernism. But it was not because [of] "An Essay at War" and the Stein thing—I read Stein and Williams, as I'd already never experienced Pound as anything other than continuous with Romantics and Pre-Raphaelites. Just temperament differences but still Romantic, and Stein uses magic and so forth.

CS: Had you already become acquainted with Charles Olson?

RD: Oh yes, Charles and I met during the same period. When Charles came out—I met Charles first in the year of the *Medieval Scenes*, which is 1947. Wait a minute, it might be, even the manuscript might be the fall of '46 or '47, I'm not sure. But Charles's own dates would check that in, it was when he was out here doing the work on the Donner Party. Charles had gone to see Rexroth and he'd gone to see Everson. Evidently, Everson and Mary Fabilli took a very bad reaction to Charles.

Well, in the first place, Charles would take a bad reaction to them because Mary Fabilli would blow up as an ex-Catholic; that's getting pretty objectionable! Anyway, I know that Everson's references to Charles seem to be very negative. And Everson's sense of how abrasive I was for Everson comes from how merciless I was in needling and, as a matter of fact, this is the period of my real break with Mary Fabilli, is this conversion thing. It isn't that they were Catholic but that I was embarrassed because I felt that there wasn't anything genuine about Everson's conversion, that it was purely theatrical, and I still do. So it's a profound embarrassment since to him it's necessary. It's necessary that he be in a quandary like in [Georges] Bernanos. How can he settle in his soul that it's theatrical and that it's also real, but it never looked like nothing but theatrical to me. So that is what really makes for a real break with Bill. In the first place I find the theatrical idiotic. And I really had broken with Nin and [Kenneth] Patchen over the fact that they were in that sense "personalities" and they had used their poetry to be the front of a personality. And Everson, of course, is a just grotesque—

CS: Patchen, too, was a "personality" by then for you?

RD: Yes, Patchen was a personality cult. Yes, indeed. Yeah. "*Are you on the side of the angels?*" and so forth and the whole thing! You couldn't sit there and just talk, because there you were right next door—I'm sure an actual saint like St. Francis of Assisi could talk to you if he could talk to fish or he could talk to a donkey, but they were graduating rapidly. And people undergo a kind of conversion to Patchen or Nin, and also the symptoms.

The other thing is, of course, that their writing is self-indulgent unless they're in a very charged situation. And there could be nothing very wrong with self-indulgent writing if that were only it, but they were real writers essentially—so that they had ruined—they were essentially ruining something that was really quite fine.

CS: Did you feel that toward Everson—that he was ruining his writing?

RD: I feel the same way about Everson. Oh yes. Late Everson I find very lax indeed. All the Everson I did prefaces for is that Everson I read with any happiness, and after that it isn't just what it's about. But I think that the alliterations begin to be habitual and the rhymes are falling apart. So the negative part can be found in correspondence, letters. I haven't looked to see if my letters to Everson reflect this, but at one point they did. Bill sent me books all the time and I just wrote analyzing the first couple of pages of a narrative poem. I think this is probably an early poem which is a horrid thing of grotesque—a poem of a rape, a medieval one of rape. So, by that point I'm really drifting away apart from them and from Kenneth—I come to loggerheads with Kenneth's doctrine of the poem as personal experience. Not the loggerheads that Spicer [had]— Spicer and Blaser had absolutely no use for Kenneth and some of that was personal.

Their own teacher had been Josephine Miles. And I was always negative towards the whole Miles influence because it was fundamentally non-Romantic. It was I think some of the complex superego that prevents Robin from really writing generously in relation to himself comes from this, this sense of—the idea of a perfection of a poem.

CS: Blaser isn't very prolific.

RD: Well, yeah. The Milesean thing was the poem cut back and in Jack's case, I see now—there's a period when I have quite an influence of blasting Jack—his conversations with God elegies are all attempts at writing a larger, open form, but I think Jack's temperament was closed. The actual one in which—when you come to the actual books of Jack Spicer, in which his genius is fully realized, it was quite akin to Josephine Miles. They both had some kind of crippling. Hers is quite evident and whatever the crippling in Jack is which makes him feel cursed so profoundly that language itself becomes a form of curse, he had in key with her. And he was very appreciative of poems of seizure. So, Jack may very well have had seizures of some kind.

CS: What was your appreciation of *After Lorca*?

RD: Oh, that's a magnificent book, but it's the flower and the fruit of the whole thing of what follows, and that's where we found out what the essential poetry was going to be. But if you compare *After Lorca* with a book that must have opened up a lot for Jack in that period, which is George Stanley's *Flowers*. George Stanley arrived here and came into my workshop or into Jack's. I think he came into Jack's. And George had already written *Flowers,* so his reading was the poems in *Flowers*. My own feeling is they had a lot to do with Jack, with something else opening up much more immediately for Jack. Complex sympathy back and forth between George's poetry and Jack. Jack, when he came back in 1956, went through that whole Magic Workshop unable to write a poem and didn't really start—then it all came flooding forward, but he was *miserable.* He was in a terrible state because—it's fascinating, he always suffered in between because it was already clear before *After Lorca* that his life now would be entirely devoted to the poem, and obsessively so that when a poem wasn't on, he was sick. And then essentially feeding himself, and also believing the poem came from the sickness sickening himself from the poem. I mean, there's a complex pattern. But back to Kenneth. The problem with Kenneth Rexroth [and] Everson I find [is] self-dramatization. That's not what—Kenneth does that outside of the poems! [*laughs*] Unfortunately, Bill does that outside [?] of the poems. Bill's very sweet. He's different as a person, by the way. The sort of sweet Bill is Bill standing around. I mean, his affections are still there, but so much baloney goes with them that I can't—well, I've known poets who dramatize themselves! Laura Riding was a self-dramatizing poet, and there are a whole series—I'm going to do a little thing on self-dramatizing poets!

CS: Spicer wasn't a "dramatizing" poet.

RD: Yeah, Jack was absolutely not. Robin's not a self-dramatizing poet. I'm not. A self-dramatizing poet makes you feel you've got a poet around! [*laughs*]

CS: In that respect, is Ginsberg a self-dramatizing poet where you're concerned?

RD: No, Allen seems to be just Allen! I don't like it entirely, but I don't know—right at the present time he's a guru! He's a self-dramatizing guru! Who also, once in a while, writes a poem! He *does* once in a while write a poem, which is amazing. But as guru he wants to be Buddhist. The rotten fruit on that tree is the Buddhism. The poetry is so seldom. I don't think it's rotten or anything. I think it's incidental.

CS: Could you describe the anarchist circles operating in the '40s and '50s in which you were involved?

RD: Oh, yes. In New York in the last years of the war, which would be '44, I guess, there were the Covens, David and Sally, Audrey Goodfriend and Mel Greek, though he's Michael Greek now. Those are the four from New York who came out to San Francisco, and are still here. Audrey Goodfriend had known Emma Goldman very well. They came out. I came back to San Francisco after the war in 1945, around Thanksgiving time. The others arrived after the fact of the anarchist group starting in San Francisco. When I did come back in '45, Kenneth Rexroth and Philip Lamantia and I went to an anarchist meeting, sometime in the winter of '45. There weren't regular meetings; this was a Sacco and Vanzetti memorial—sort of like a church picnic. As we were coming home on the streetcar, going back to Kenneth's, Philip said—and Philip had not attended the anarchist meetings in New York, but he knew about them and so did Kenneth. Philip said, "Why couldn't we have them here?" And I said, "Yes, all you have to do is find a place and we can meet." There were six of us. There were the four I mentioned, and then there was an Italian diva, and myself. Within four meetings, Paul Goodman and Jackson Mac Low and a whole score of people were attending. Toward the end there were a hundred people or so. Actually, there were other anarchist circles, more than we ever knew. The toughness of the Second World War—these were people who were against the Second World War. Also, there were a great number of Jews against the war. Most people would think it's impossible! It's a war against Hitler! [*laughs*]

CS: In an essay, Rexroth has mentioned your personal courage in refusing to remain in the US Army. What were the circumstances surrounding your decision?

RD: I was in the first draft. I never enlisted in anything. I was in the first draft, which was in the period of the *Experimental Review.* After one month in the army, a month and a half or so, I guess it was, I declared myself homosexual. I went through a grueling enough experience, not as bad as it could have been, and then got a discharge. That was the extent of—the war wasn't even on at the time I was discharged.

CS: Could you talk about the pacifism and activism of those writers with whom you were involved throughout the period of the war, and following?

RD: In '42, Kenneth Rexroth, Kenneth Patchen, and almost all of us had great alarm about Stalinists. There were Stalinist murders everywhere. [Carlo] Tresca had just been murdered, and the attack on Trotsky comes in those years. So it's a great period of Stalinist murders. Kenneth

Rexroth had spoken out . . ., and Kenneth Patchen, just that much older than I, really did think that the Stalinists—they were both beginning open attacks on the Stalinists—writing out in all directions. Both the Kenneths thought they were going to be shot down themselves. So meeting Kenneth (Rexroth) you didn't—you wrote a letter, then he wrote a letter back. I didn't phone him. Then he met me in his car and drove me off into—way off to where he was hiding. He *was* in hiding! [*laughs*]

CS: It was that serious a situation?

RD: Oh yes, it was serious. Yeah, sure. In 1939 I was in Philadelphia, '38 or '39, late '38, perhaps, and I joined the Young People's Socialist (YPS), to keep up socialist activities. Just the week before I started going to meetings, they had been raided by Nazis and then two weeks before that they had been raided by Stalinists. So it was your choice as to what was going to happen.

A catch, by the way, you should notice is that Rexroth, Patchen, and I are all highly politicized. When I make my list of tyrants it will include Stalin and Hitler for sure and Roosevelt and the whole works. And Roosevelt pretty much—the way you saw Roosevelt. And any president of the United States having a draft. This, by the way, is not Bill's (Everson's) position at all. As a pacifist, he's entirely different. When we come to some of the splits and difficulties between Kenneth and Bill—there is no difficulty at all, but the other side of Kenneth is the one that wants a sacred poem—a sacramental poem, not a sacred poem. That would be an atrocity. A sacramental poem. But a poem that relates to the sacraments of the Church. In Kenneth's case, the Anglo-Catholic Church. But what is absolutely missing from any part of Everson is any interest in the politics at all. None at all. And absolutely no interest in the history of the war. He was a pacifist in relation to the war as a matter of conscience, and the conscience is entirely personal and has no political intelligence, and so forth. And then, what was atrocious when you come to the Korean War or—he didn't know about that or he didn't know about the Vietnam War. So this is where I would begin to—you can hear—he had a well-trained Catholic conscience by that time and if you started to bring up—like, why would I sometimes be annoying?—because I would inevitably bring up the Inquisition and half a dozen—and call attention to Protestants killing Catholics, Catholics killing Protestants, and run the whole row of religions. [*laughter*]

Well, Kenneth Rexroth, he could give a greater story there. So that's what I mean by intellectual. Rexroth's was a mind constantly at work. He could gossip about Stalinists and Trotskyites and so forth, but he also had an actual political cast.

CS: Was Rexroth a Catholic convert?

RD: No, he was Anglo-Catholic all the time. He always maintained he was, in '42 and '45. I presume he still is. Kenneth's fascinated by Buddhism, but Buddhism can ride double saddle. It has no trouble at all. You would have free election of what gods and churches you'd want under it, I presume. But I think that was one of his difficulties. The total lack of—the naïveté, actually, the studied naïveté of Everson—the "I don't know and don't want to know"—*that* would drive Kenneth up the wall!

Kenneth's letters at UCLA will show that, at the same time he's promoting Everson, he would write to the same people demoting him, and so forth. So he seems to have had a real split feeling of a kind that he couldn't even keep track of himself. But it is Kenneth who got Everson his book with New Directions. Of course, Kenneth was also trying to get New Directions to do Philip Lamantia, which they never did. So it isn't Kenneth all alone. It had to be Jay [Laughlin] saying yes.

CS: Yes, speaking of Jay Laughlin and his New Directions, I understand he's to publish a collection of your essays soon.

RD: Well, yes, they would have been out two years ago if I hadn't taken two of them back.

CS: For revision?

RD: Yeah, one of them to be revised, but the other one had to be retyped because the xeroxes from *Caterpillar* pages are too poor. That was such poor print! [*laughs*]

CS: And *Caterpillar* pages so small!

RD: Yeah, right. So the essays are held up. Little term papers I haven't done.

CS: Would you describe the "Berkeley Renaissance"?

RD: Well, that's what we called it. In 1946 I left the Tylers's farm, which was around the Russian River area, and came down to Berkeley. And it's in that period that first—through the summer I was moving around from place to place and finally found a room in a co-op house called "Throckmorton Manor" on Telegraph Avenue, and then I put up signs everywhere and started a whole series of off-campus courses. I started an off-campus seminar on *Finnegans Wake*. I also started an off-campus seminar and a series of contemporary masters, and poetry readings. And it's gathering around those seminars that Jack (Spicer) was there right away. However, Jack had come to an anarchist meeting some time before that. But I didn't meet him at that time. He was a very strange-looking person. His intensity was upsetting, or whatever. He was not a person you wanted to know. He looked like trouble.

CS: Was he loud?

RD: No, he made faces at us.

CS: Made faces?!

RD: Yes. Also, he didn't wear a mask in those days. There was a little nest of us, a little circle of people—around the Whitnahs—one of them, anyway. The Whitnahs's circle is the one Jack really comes into focus around. One of the misunderstandings that comes from the way Robin (Blaser) writes about it is that it seems I've even got an account of—now for a *Contemporary Poetry* thing written by Butterick in which he has drawn, I guess, from reading Robin and not reading me carefully, that Robin was somehow in the group that was at Hearst Avenue when the *Medieval Scenes* were written. Well, Robin wasn't. I mean, Robin was a person that you read poems to or something and came to visit at times, but he never ate in that group and the group of people around Hugh

With *(left to right)* Landis Everson, Jerry Ackerman, George Haimsohn,
and Lyn Brown (later Brockway), circa early 1948

O'Neill, who is still living, I understand, around the Carmel or the Big Sur area. Jack, all his life, had a *series* of friends, and they were kept fairly apart and discrete. While he took me around to meet Robin, he really didn't bring Robin into the context of the writing of *Heavenly City, Earthly City*. He attended that himself. And then he moved me to the O'Neills, and that brought Hugh O'Neill and Janie O'Neill and the Fredmans (Fred and Jo) together at the table where Jack ate and where Jack wanted to get magic going. And the immediate product of that magic was *Medieval Scenes*. And it is in that period because—now, while *Medieval Scenes* refers a lot to things medieval, they are the most common things medieval, because it would be a whole year before I would start medieval studies. And Jack, however, I think, might very well have already been studying with Kantorowicz at that time. I'm not sure.

CS: Where does Robin figure at this time, in relation to Jack?

RD: Jack and Robin took Kantorowicz courses together, although Robin, it seems, never was in a Kantorowicz seminar. Jack was, because I actually inherited the paper Jack was working on. I mean, we were working on a manuscript that hadn't been published, and so it was preedited and the first couple of sentences are Jack's before mine. I can recognize the handwriting! [*laughs*] But both Jack and Robin were in English studies, not history. I went back to school in the spring of '48.

CS: Did you ever graduate?

RD: No, oh no, I never did. When Kantorowicz left Berkeley, I had about twelve units to finish and I said, "Why?" The adviser I had to go through every time said, "But you only have these units," and I said, "What purpose has a poet got in—" If I were to go in history, I'd have to go to Germany. I was sort of preparing, would I go to Germany and so forth and so that was—it was more complex than that. By the time I actually dropped out I had met Jess, and I was not minded to go to Germany to become a historian. So that was a decisive point for me. I was for a while almost geared that I'd do the two together.

CS: That was in 1950?

RD: That would be 1950. Well, actually '51. I was still going to school in '51, because I remember, I mean, I really came close to—I never finished that semester. I moved from Berkeley in '51, moved in with Jess on New Year's Day, so I did enroll in that Spring semester and didn't finish it.

CS: Where did Whalen, Snyder, and Welch fit into your poetic chronology?

RD: Oh, they came much later. As a matter of fact, I don't even—Phil Whalen and [Gary] Snyder and Lew Welch all relate—well, especially, of course, Snyder relates very directly to Rexroth. Snyder would be the straight descendant of Rexroth. Whalen's a mixture of other impulses. There's a good deal of Rexroth, but Snyder's on a straight line with Rexroth. Does the same things. And Rexroth and Snyder both model themselves after Waley, and Waley models himself after *Cathay,* which even Pound didn't do when he did the *Odes* a second time! But the real trouble with Rexroth—Rexroth is the origin of what's persuasive to Gary and that is that the poem is—there is no such thing as poetry for Rexroth as a *domain*—even a consciousness and domain in itself. And I think the first ones that I met at all, the first one believing that along with me was Jack. That's why Jack was so important for me. Olson did and it's impenetrable in a way because Olson put psychology—I mean, the Jungian psychology comes in as a primary; this is the difficulty I have with Jungianism. It *poses* itself as a primary like philosophy does, as if it had primary knowledge instead of the poem having primary knowledge, and so it will actually turn to the *Theogony* of Hesiod. It just happens to be a poetic theogony and behaves as if it were a psychological theogony or as if it were religious, which it isn't. Hesiod does not pose at all that he's a priest or that he's anything else. He tells you right away that he's writing fiction. That the muses are creatures of fiction and this is how the gods appear in fiction.

Jack really stood out in my life, along with Charles Olson, as two people who have been primaries for me to find myself as *radical to, not in agreement at all with.* For both of them, poetry was a primary knowledge, and not, for instance, a vocation or avocation or whatever. I tend to be professional in my attitude toward the poem, I think, by imitation of my father. So there's, you know, an architectured poem still holds for me. But underlying that is the idea that there is a thing, there is some primary, well, that there's no previous reality to poetry for poetry, right? Poetry doesn't have to go to a philosophy class to have its truth weighed!

Interview with George Bowering
and Robert Hogg
(1969, excerpts)

This brief excerpt from an extensive, illuminating discussion with Canadian poets George Bowering and Robert Hogg was first published in 1969 in a Beaver Kosmos folio. Robert Duncan tells about sending poems to William Carlos Williams, who said "there was no American language in there." Duncan articulates his sense of language, pointing out that both he and Charles Olson see language and individuality having their "being in a larger being," which is "the cosmos finally."

—Ed.

INTERVIEWER: Did you ever get any word from [W. C.] Williams about the rhetoric [in your poetry]?

ROBERT DUNCAN: Oh boy, did I get a word! I really got some blast-off letters and I think they gave me some indication of the naïveté or earnestness or mistakenness of any young poet. When I wrote "Domestic Scenes" I kept making these poems I could send to Williams as a little homage or something; they were filled with domestic scenes, filled with things around like buses and paraphernalia of the contemporary world. I sent them off to Williams, and oh, what a blast back I got about it; there was no American language in there. Of course I have never written in American language, nor did I ever in my whole life. But that letter was in itself an inspiration, because then with vengeance I wrote *Medieval Scenes*. I mean I just decided to write: Okay, no American language! I wrote it straight on, so those two sequences were a funny play around Williams. When I was later publishing the *Berkeley Miscellany*, which I printed at my own expense in order to get into print Mary Fabilli (Aurora Bligh) and Jack Spicer, Williams went wild about Mary Fabilli's writing and wrote at great length and so forth. He did not go wild about my writing at "The Venice Poem" stage either, and I think the last real correspondence came then. Williams wrote back: Couldn't tell male from female and so forth. Well, since the poem is mixed with both male and female in it, you can tell them all right, but you're really messed up with a sort of mixed-up scene—making it with that fat woman and making it with those boys, that was not his kind of whatever.

But he also suspected that the poetics had somehow allowed for this, and so there was an offensive difference and distance between what Williams made possible and what us kiddies did with it. The other thing about Williams is that the few times I met Williams, I met him in conjunction with young ladies that he himself had quite hot ideas about. They were always very ardently wanting him to appreciate me, which had quite the opposite effect. The first time I met him was at a Gotham Book Mart party—it would have been 1940, I guess, or '39—and at that time I was with Virginia Admiral. And he had obviously at this party landed on that blonde head of hair and complexion, and was moving in, and suddenly was presented with a young poet who didn't look very appetizing at all to be courting this young lady. I don't know that he made any connections from any one of these times with my existence really as a person. The last time, Denise Levertov wanted to say I was the other person in the world that she loved, and he didn't want any other person in the world that she loved in that scene. Pound tried to persuade me to go up and see Bill Williams, and when I spoke to Pound about Williams's letters, Pound said, "Oh, he comes in just mad after all that doctoring he hates, and he hits the typewriter, has to throw it at somebody." Of course this is Pound sitting in St. Elizabeths, where he has got some very angry letters indeed. What Pound is talking about in part, though, was that Williams had all his life a kind of hostility, and you find it in the autobiography, find shots of it. Denise wrote me that she felt that it was unfair to turn to the autobiography, because Williams was ill and the autobiography belonged to that kind of illness. But this was a character throughout; you can read his letters and you find this increasing part, but as an artist in the autobiography he composes it. We are not interested in the justice of an emotion in a poet or the creative artist; it's how he composes it, its ratio to other things, and its restoration to reality; and that's certainly there in the autobiography. He sees the creative complex that he belongs to, so even these irritations, that sometimes are extremely petty and personal, reappear in that autobiography related to a larger scene and a larger thing to say.

. . .

INT: I was just wondering, remembering when you said in "Ideas on the Meaning of Form" that you were looking for cooperation beyond the necessity of government, and this immediately brought up [William] Godwin to me, the whole Shelleyan Godwin thing; I was just wondering, you know, the perfectability thing, and the same thing is in *Democratic Vistas*, where Whitman says that sometime in the future we won't have to have any kind of government at all.

RD: But Whitman said that each man was a law to himself. And in the beehive, by the way—the atrocity that people do in making the beehive similar to the corporate state, although the cream of the corporate state would be like this—but neither Russia, nor Nazi Germany, nor Rooseveltian America (which didn't get there for being corporate states)—none of those has for instance a queen bee at the center. Or another great figure, of course, is the termite, the social termite colony with its vast, vast queen termite who is enormous, like a huge, huge thing, and all the working termites seem to be psychic extensions of her, they have their being in her. And you will find throughout my poetry the idea of an individuality that has absolute freedom and is a law to itself, that has its being in a larger being, but of course for me that's not just the state, that's the cosmos finally. And there I would be like Charles [Olson], I think, although my cosmos is different, very clearly, by having a being in the cosmos; and absolutely like Charles in that language is cosmos; and certainly like Charles in that I'm interested in the divine. Take those three great big things that will be so important that if we have the slightest disagreement, men have, before they burned each other happily, extinguished the lamp forever because of the heresy that's involved at such level of disagreement. Charles lays down dogma. I can't read him without knowing myself almost at every turn as your favorite adversary or heretical little—but at the same time of course the drama for me, since my parents—well, in relation to Charles—why did Charles lay down dogma, and also Robin Blaser for instance? They are Roman Catholics, and as for us Romanticists and Theosophists, our whole tradition was to identify with heretics throughout the world, and as a matter of fact, my parents believed that they (although there is no such claim that can be founded either) believed that they were identical with the DeMolays, the Knights Templars, and identical with the Albigenses. So they had this long business—we have been exterminated over and over again by the dogmatists (actually exterminated) but we were perennial, so I find the perennial doctrine instead of the established central doctrine. You find a cosmos that's perennial and that's destroyed—the law constantly *destroys* the law, which is not a dogma but a thing devouring itself and undoing itself, and you will find that in my poetry I undo my propositions. Now Charles actually contradicts, which gives him the same swing. He has to be the proposition of the poet since he is a poet and not a mere dogmatist, so his dogma was to contradict his dogma, and he does this because he is also Heraclitean. But, my God, when I read Heraclitus, which is all the time, and Charles has had it all the time, and Hesiod we share—how in the world do we do it? I mean, I know he gasps with horror and I gasp with horror as we turn around, because we were reading right close to the letter the same thing.

INT: He concentrates on the dogma. I don't get the sense that he concentrates so much on the ritual or the dances. I always had the sense if Olson sees a round dance he puts it into what this means in terms of the tradition of the place that it's in over the last three hundred years or something like that, but he doesn't express it as something that goes as a kind of an emblem of the entire universe or something like that; he concentrates on what it means.

RD: But we can also *see*, that's how close we get, because it's really—it almost turns into a negative-positive. If you find a position in Charles, you are very likely to find its antithesis in my work. The areas that had already been presumed, before we met— Well, your question about meeting Charles. Let's say certainly that the breakthrough into Charles's writing (and definitely the breakthrough, because just clearly, just across the board, this was on the same level all of a sudden as Pound was, when I was nineteen, or eighteen, and I had no expectancy)—it's hard to recapture now, to tell you about what it was like in 1950 to have something actually happening in poetry, because nothing, nothing, nothing, nothing had been happening in poetry in America, nothing at all. It had been a period dominated by vast and inert mediocrities. It's appalling that Randall Jarrell was read as a poet, absolutely appalling. But mainly because the propositions were so demeaning. [Karl] Shapiro would be an example also, of course, of the poetry in the *Partisan Review.* They had poetic sensibility in Robert Lowell, but one is absolutely shocked at how the level of the information is crippled, massively crippled by the culture to which he belongs.

INT: You talk about Eliot a lot more than anybody else does—

RD: But Eliot is like my early rhetoric that I was ashamed of. I came as near as to reciting "The Hollow Men" or the very Poe-esque sections of *The Waste Land,* with all the women coming out in purple hair or whatever, all that stuff; Eliot and I like mermaids and Siren Calls for sure. Charles may look like a sea cow, but that proves that that ain't a Siren. (Not that I look like a Siren. They are supposed to be hideous though, but with sweet voices.)

. . .

Unmuzzled OX Discussion

(with Howard Mesch, 1974)

This conversation with Howard Mesch appeared in the Unmuzzled
OX, *edited by Michael Andre, in 1976. Robert Duncan discusses many
issues relating to his work, including style, the presence of contradic-
tions, Darwinian intention, myth, and open form. He says his work
involves a "weaving process" like a tapestry and that "polyglot assem-
blage" describes much American art and poetry. He talks about his
interest in science and religion, the conjoining of faith and imagination,
the origin of poetry in "the order of orders," and symbolism.*

　　—Ed.

HOWARD MESCH: Your earlier poetry, I think, was symbolistic. Later,
in *Writing, Writing* and *Imitations of Stein,* you were not. In what terms
would you describe these apparent contradictions?

ROBERT DUNCAN: I never worry about contradictions in my seeming
development. I don't develop in the sense of growing up. There were
only three poems in my earliest work that were indicative of what I
was going to have to deal with, and they contradict each other, so I
was in 1942 realizing I wasn't going to have any style, observably, at
all. I ceased to have anxiety about "Did I have a style? Was there going
to be a Duncan style?" The test point would be "Passages," in which,
theoretically, everything can coexist. It doesn't have any boundaries
supposedly. Contradictions are dramatic propositions, and interesting
in a poem to get range, to be active throughout.

I had begun through the war to know the beginning of American
painting: painting was beginning to be thought of as an art and a process.
Medieval Scenes was a serial poem. "The Venice Poem" was composed
with symphonic form. I had to borrow a form, so it's not process at that
level; but it has a glimmer. The poem that followed—and the poem that
proposed pretty much the process of my later poetry—was the "Essay
at War." That was striking off from *Paterson.* And it picks up the Stein

thing and projects itself. Projective verse had even been named at that point, and the theories of projection I knew already because in the 1930s, we read Wolfgang Köhler and the American lectures on what is form in art. They have the terms like "vector" that Olson picked up. *Place of Value in a World of Facts* is the book, and those lectures have a chapter, one solid chapter, on the Gestalt theory of form in art and it proves to be a projection.

HM: *Letters* and even *Writing, Writing* come closer to the idea of the poem as process.

RD: Than the later books, which are a weaving process. Yes, I would say so, yes. *Letters* reflects the impact of what's called Black Mountain, and it addresses itself throughout to the idea of process.

HM: Were *Letters* actually written to someone?

RD: No, letters in that meant the letters of the alphabet. In taking the title I was myself a little concerned that its pun was not that valuable.

HM: I see.

RD: I remain in field theory and process only in the sense of Whiteheadian process. I'm a creationist; that is, everything is a creation for me. I would be Darwinian in relation to the evolution of forms; I think they're entirely produced by natural selection, and so intention changes its meaning.

Intention was one of the central questions in 1956 at Black Mountain. A poem without intent is not a poem, and so if you move from one concept of creation to another, you find yourself puzzling over an entirely new meaning given to intention. I'm Darwinian and not Lamarckian, because intention is more marvelous in Darwin than in Lamarck. In Lamarck, it's the kind of intention a professor would have in filling out a design. That doesn't interest me. In Darwin the intention is entirely what's going on.

HM: You don't go so far as to say process implies nonintention.

RD: I don't concede that there is nonintention anywhere.

HM: Well, John Cage says—

RD: Oh, I know, but I don't concede that there is nonintention—metals evolve—no, he's simply taking old-fashioned intention like Lamarck, as if intention were merely, "I mean to do so-and-so," whereas intention that has to find itself is very different. Intent is going in a direction; it's simply that the direction doesn't precede itself.

HM: Is it that—when you say you're a Darwinian—is it that, with Darwin, everything that grows, everything that becomes, is determined by its surroundings?

RD: Totally! Survival is determined by how something fits in with everything in space, everything that happens. Most of it is local to the earth, but if we had a change in the sun, that would change a very serious survival term.

But let's go back to the poem, because we're really talking about form in a poem. A poem for me is a language event, and is a primary experience in language. It doesn't refer to experience outside the self. Any event within the poem—the word "cat" in the poem—survives as meaning to everything else. There is no—and I see this also in Darwin—there is no significant push towards a future. It's total composition throughout the poem. Intention in Darwin is present; the intention we can find taken today, and looking backward as well as going forward.

HM: You would still agree that you get causal connection.

RD: You don't need a cause, because you've got a total condition where everything is constantly changing. But, yes, in simple, immediate events, you could find a reason and, consequently, a cause and a result of some particular survival.

Cage is a Buddhist and has in mind total unreality in the universe, and this is seriously different from my world. [laughs] I mean, and as a matter of fact, Cage has left art. A happening in Cage is very different from a happening in—from what happens in my mind. Williams was the first person who said "The End" and realized it isn't significant formally and found himself with a fifth book. Pound never theoretically could face what he was actually doing in *The Cantos;* they didn't have what he understood to be form. I mean, he wanted to manage *The Cantos* as a totalitarian poem; they didn't prove to be totalitarian so he was as distressed by them as by the democracy from which he came. We couldn't have a more extreme example of democratic composition than we had out of that man who kept hoping he'd rescue himself by having totalitarian order.

Williams said "The End" and found there was more to the poem, a fifth book, and there's even part of a sixth. He had already written a couple of poems called "Pendants." Denise [Levertov] asked me at the very beginning of my "Passages": "Don't you feel this part is a pendant?" And I wrote back, "What in the world is in your head? How can you have a pendant when you've got a poem with actually no boundaries?" It's within a given proposition that a given passage could be a sonnet, it could be anything, it could be a waltz. It could be a borrowed piece of furniture. But one thing it couldn't be is a mere appendix.

It also means—the weakness of a poem without boundaries—that time and space are almost in Buddhaland: time and space are really occasional to the existence of "Passages."

HM: To return to *Letters*. I can't remember which of the *Letters* speaks of spring and running water, but I thought that was working against the poem as a process; that was such a stable reference.

RD: Again, I'm not interested in "Am I uniform throughout?" I certainly don't think of the proposition of the poem as totally devoted to process. In the course of *Letters*—and letters refers to the *Zohar* with its new picture of language—I found that there were processes going on in language, not just a process of language. In Freudian terms, if the process is psychological, then all of language is symbolic. Or, if it refers to some other experience, and it does, it's symbolic in that role. But if language is seen as a process in itself, it ceases to be symbolic. I don't prune the other levels of interest away. The language will always and everywhere be symbolic, if you're interested in mountains or psychology; but that's providing you're not interested in the language itself. We're way back in "What was it like in the late 1940s if you were concerned about language?" And there you found that language itself was a process, in

Whorf and Sapir. And along with this, Olson wanted to reject the symbolic role of language. I was also interested in [Ernst] Cassirer's approach to language as a total system of symbols. But it's a process, you see; it's not a system.

HM: Yes.

RD: And so a poem is an event in language which may or may not survive in its meaning. For instance, you come from outside the English community, and you pick up some meanings specific to your reading; my survivals of meaning are as specific in your reading as my survivals in my human being are in my walk outdoors.

There's no total book in process in *Letters*—a difference between *Letters* and *Opening of the Field*. I started out from the very first poem in *Opening of the Field* to compose a book, so process is at work in the whole book. Now that process may call for a sonnet at one point. It might call for anything.

Of course, again, that's why I don't have any style. This room has no style. If we were to have a style, we would carry the wicker of the couch throughout the room. But, no, not at all. It's just an assemblage. *The Cantos* have no style. Observably: compare them to the Brancusi that Pound admired, and you find that Pound and the American style is polyglot assemblage. Ives was a polyglot assemblage; and Stravinsky, who was doing pastiches, was never really able to arrive at a polyglot assemblage.

Americans have no history. Their continent is a polyglot assembly— and now an empire. So our real art form is an "empire." Cubism, which started collage, is not assemblage. In a collage, everything is specific in its sentiments, everything in Schwitters is specific, and so are nineteenth-century American assemblages; but when it comes to ours, everything goes in there. Field changes. Unity is really posited someplace else. Unity is the energy; Charles [Olson] puts it in the energy.

But of "Passages" I can't quite bring myself to say "anything" goes. I immediately go into a very specific, narrow-ranged voice for that. *Letters* has greater range.

HM: But since there are no causal connections, what makes you think of "Passages" as a work in process?

RD: Well, when I return to "Passages" I find out what's going on in it. The poem's dependent, in the first place, on a particular tone from which I recognize that "Passages" is "on." I don't sit down and say, "Now I'm going to write a Passage." Anymore than I do in "Structures of Rime"! They can be part of another poem. I'm not sure if part of "Passages" has appeared as part of another poem, but "Structures of Rime" has appeared as part of "Passages," and as a part of a poem, "Apprehensions."

So these open forms can also appear within other forms. I have at the present time *A Seventeenth Century Suite,* and "Passages 37" is part of that suite. Oh, and there also: Passages are numbered up to 37 in sequence, but there's no point to a sequence in this, so after that there are no more numbers. But I leave the earlier numbers as possibly an incidental statistical happening within a posed field that doesn't have any boundaries at all. So a chronology like that isn't a chronology. It's an ordination—one, two, three, four—that can go on simply because we presume so many numbers that it's only incidental that they're called one, two, three, four to thirty-seven.

We're not, for instance, talking about dialectical process. No, no; not on your life—this poem doesn't lead forward to some consequences. *Maximus* leads to social consequences. I mean, it begins with social consequences and it's a powerfully dialectical poem. But, while Charles starts with Heraclitus and I start with Heraclitus, Heraclitus does not propose dialectics to me. Heraclitus proposes coexistence in a field of contrasting elements.

HM: I had the idea that you had actually discontinued writing "Structures of Rime" and that you continued that in "Passages."

RD: Oh, no, they are thought of as two different areas. And, oh, by the way, of course, they both are constantly deriving from the other poetry. People are always saying, "Well, why don't you print 'Structures of Rime' consecutively in a book of their own or 'Passages' in a book of their own?" But they're not in a book of their own anymore than I'm in a world of my own. And so the "Structures of Rime" will take its beginning rhyme from a preceding poem that's not "Structures of Rime" at all. You will even pick up and explain a figure which is two poems earlier in a book and not its own. And more than that, any figure in "Structures of Rime" is liable to be developed in some other poem.

And the same is true of "Passages." I can find passages that are really talking about poems that are not "Passages." So, in this sense, they're not part of a great poem at all. They're part of a tapestry. I am a craftsman. The figure of weaving, which is very early in "Passages," is really very much where I rapidly went after *Letters.* And so what I aimed at is a weaving that would be at the same time loose enough; indeed, I'm dissatisfied with how little I am able to break up my close weave.

When I am in the state to write a poem, I am so fascinated by rhyming and volume, and this includes rhyming of images, of content, that when I get through it's just overcomposed. I'd love to have more decomposition, and *Letters,* of course, does propose that; that's the shawl falling apart and the things with holes. Maybe getting a better income and better clothes—that didn't have holes in them—has got me back to my parents' bourgeois "We don't want no holey things around here." Like a hole in my argument. [*laughs*]

HM: Are you and Olson mythical poets?

RD: No. Olson had quite a powerful myth, I think. I'm concerned with myth. But I'm not at all certain that there's a myth that I make. I draw on myths. I don't think I'm primarily a mythical poet. I'm not sure that's what *The Truth and Life of Myth* says. And I'm certainly not a religious poet, or mystical; I have had an experience or two interesting from that angle, but that's not what things are built around. Olson is very squarely Jungian in his position, that myth is a primary intuition on some psychological level. Okay, I'll give that. But I think myth is made up. I believe the unconscious is unconscious and we have no access to it. Those things that are called myth or, in Jung, archetypes, I think, are imagined by the conscious mind to fill in the whole thing; we're constantly imagining what's in the unconscious. But we have no access to it. By the time anything appears to us in dreams, it's consciousness. If we can see it, it's conscious.

Consciousness is creative. The greatest difficulty with the question of truth is the fact that we're creative throughout, and so we have to battle all the time, not only in science, but in the arts, because we want to arrive at something sufficiently real. And art's engagement in reality I take seriously. And the foreground of reality is the reality of language, the thing it's working in. If it hasn't got that reality, then the rest of it would be like weaving without knowing the wool. The myth, I think, is in the weave.

But I'm not a mythmaker. I tend to be a theosophist; theosophists are concerned with the meaning of myth. Hesiod's not interested in the meaning of what's going on; that's theogony. Theogony interested Charles, but I'm a theosophist in relation to theogony. I get turned on to finding the meanings of myth, and I can't think of one case where I was turned on to finding the myth. I don't think Olson's a mythmaker at all, by the way; he also is a theosophist, though he hated the idea. Our theogony now is our science. I'm reading that all the time. It must be a myth. I mean, it again is a proposition that goes towards reality. Our mythical imagination is in our Einsteins and our physicists. Sure. It proves to be a myth. They have to redo it all the time; science no sooner proposes one framework within which things are real than it loses that reality, and has to find another one, because other facts, other factors enter.

HM: You mean myth is opposed to science?

RD: No, not opposed. I think science is contemporary mythmaking. You asked me if I was interested in myth? Gee, yes, the same way I am in science, and I read science as myth. I don't read Pound as myth. I read Pound for gossip about myth. Pound also uses myth. A mythmaker and a maker with myths are different.

HM: You have said that the poet distances myth.

RD: It interested me that in order to picture the world you're in, you picture its beginnings. That's the distance. And myth of course is posited as beginnings before you can know them—by any other means, by the way, than telling a story. Science today is myth, because science can't go and check how it did begin. The Big Bang—that's pure myth.

HM: You often speak of theology in terms of science. But I wonder about theology as a poetics. How far can you press that analogy?

RD: Let me make something straight. Poetics means making something up. Not only to make something, but to make something up. A theologian is not very happy if you explain to him he's talking about something he made up. The poet thinks that religion is a great subject matter. The religious person thinks poetry is a great way to carry the religious message. They're never going to know one another; and yet there have been poets who were saints—I take St. Francis and St. John of the Cross as poets. It's my own confession that I don't have a total religious observance. My religious disposition would be what I was raised in, which has reincarnation as its base; it doesn't even resemble Christianity. And that shows up, of course, in my disposition of Christ, where I put him.

HM: But still you write of Father, Son, and Spirit, and if one looks at that, at the surface, one really gets the idea that you're religious.

RD: Religion is present. I'm looking at religion. But then if you look at me like a theologian you find yourself worse off than if you tried to look at me as a philosophical poet and figure out whether there was a "system." I don't think you can find a system in my work at all, because I am so attracted to various systems, and build various systems in as if I were orchestrating, going from one system to another as if I were going from major to minor key. [A. N.] Whitehead and [Ludwig] Wittgenstein fascinate me, because they become a language. Whitehead has a constantly generated language. Any passage is enormously suggestive. It's like in Hesiod the actual events turn out to be language events, not any other kind at all. Every one of those gods is an event of a word. Every one of those families are families in constellations of words.

Charles is different. He's an historian reforming history and finding that poetry is more true than history. He then thought of myth as counter to history, as intuitions about what was going on in history. Charles's mind tended to be different from mine in another way. He thought the beginning was more authentic. And this I just don't understand. I don't bite on the Golden Age. All points in time are the same, and have the same quality of authenticity.

HM: You write in *The Truth and Life of Myth:* "A music of sounds and of meanings awakens the mythological reality in the actual." Do you think mythological reality is contained in the actual?

RD: No. Awakened. But, remember, if it's asleep, it's contained in the actual. Aristotle points out that the soul awake and asleep must be the same thing. That's really my sense of the actual. Let's say you have a fantasy about murdering someone. You'd never do it. Okay. And so it's not actual that a murder took place, but it is actual that you had a fantasy. You see you need only arrive at the where and the how of this thing and you find it's perfectly actual.

HM: Blake speaks of Newton falling asleep. How would you connect his science to the actual?

RD: I don't know that much about Newton. But I do know that we're really talking about Blake's Newton here. Yes, this image of falling asleep attracts me. Now we're opening up the department of mysticism in talking about awake and asleep; and ultimately this seems like Paul's asleep and awake: the Christians have very specific things they mean by asleep and awake. But we all mean very much the same thing, and that is to be thoroughly conscious of the meaning of your action; that's the opposite of having a compulsion. What the Christian really means is that you're awake to thoroughly Christian meanings that penetrate everything. My only departure from that is that there are other sets of meanings; I want a multiphasic consciousness. Also, I have no ultimate awakeness, because I have no conversion in mind. You could get as close as you could to reality but that'd be no guarantee you'd be anywhere the next minute. If it were a conversion, there would be no process. On the other hand, it may not be a dialectical materialist process; Hegel would guarantee what's going to happen next. But, you see, I view myself as deriving myself in our present situation. I don't think a recipe is the food that comes at the end of the recipe. [*laughs*]

HM: There's another thing which struck me. You also say in *The Truth and Life of Myth* that, "Indeed, philosophy like poetry stops in its tracks where belief and disbelief enter in." That is puzzling for me because isn't actually poetry a matter of belief or disbelief?

RD: No, I think imagination is quite different. If I believe or disbelieve something, it's of no imaginative order at all. My imagination is not in operation by the time I'm talking about do I believe or disbelieve. Let's ask, do I believe in you? or do I believe in myself as a person? Do I exist? I can't sit in Bishop Berkeleyland and worry about believing or disbelieving. I have no such disposition. But imagine—that's a very different thing. Then it's perfectly part of my concern that you may be vivid to me or not vivid to me. And you're vivid to me as I increasingly imagine your possible existence.

Pressed on my world of belief, I would say we must be an event of particles. And when I grew up in the '30s, I thought we were an event of atoms, and those were the only things really going on.

HM: Let me give you just one more quotation. [*laughs*] "All orders have their justification finally in an order of orders only our faith as we work addresses."

RD: Faith is different from belief or disbelief, totally different. Faith goes with imagination for me. Faith is so large because there's no guarantee. I have faith that I'm in a poem when I'm in a poem, and I certainly don't believe it or disbelieve it. When I'm working on a poem, I can be absolutely engrossed, enthralled—working in absolute faith. A poem that I'm absolutely with, at another time I may not be with: "Oh, gee, I'm not sure it feels right." I found out very early that, if there was something like a critical ability to tell if a poem were good or bad, I didn't have it, because I would make a different selection every time.

Faith is a property of work for me. In other words, yes, I can imagine something, and I don't have to worry about any aspect of faith in that. But if I am making something I have to have considerable faith to work in it. Well, if Shakespeare can afford to talk about grace in relation to his art, I guess it would be perfectly clear why it would be very, very apparent to me that you need faith to write a sentence.

HM: So if you do something, you don't worry about whether you believe or disbelieve it.

RD: Yes, well, the world's too concrete for me to believe or disbelieve. And I don't believe or disbelieve in Father, Son, and Holy Ghost, because I cannot conceive anything that any human being has given testimony to that doesn't somehow, somewhere exist. Now my faith is that if you can find the where and the how, its reality would be intensified.

In our imagination, we have to know that there are people who believe or disbelieve. Not only do we have to imagine *things*—like the Holy Ghost—but also *people* in states of belief or disbelief. But I don't imagine them at all as people who imagine. Madame Blavatsky would have found it intolerable that she imagined anything. She could believe and disbelieve and she wanted to believe very much, and she did believe. But she excluded the possibility of imagination.

At the age of ten I found myself guilty because I did not believe anything that anyone ever proposed to me, and also I couldn't honestly disbelieve it. I just didn't have this quality.

HM: What about the order of orders?

RD: Everything is continuous and orderly. There must be an order in which we understand the coexistence of Schopenhauer and Whitehead; all of these are absolutely compelling presentations of the world, and I'm not about to discard any of them. In a sense, there's a poetry of all poetry—and my poetry, by the way, surely isn't that poetry of all poetry. As a philosopher proceeds because he wants a corrected system in relation to the other systems, my poetry is demonstrably posited, for one thing, on its coexistence with Olson's and Creeley's very vivid facts. I feel it as a small mosaic existing within a vast mosaic.

The order of orders I would posit in the order of the universe, where the nuclear warheads are posited. The atomic structure resembles the Neoplatonic hierarchical powers. It must have been amazing to arrive at a world of matter that exactly resembles the kind of world of angelic powers that they were thinking about in the first century. The planets weren't arranged that way but lo and behold the atoms were. And that's what, when I was going to school in the '30s, we were taught. They were making pictures up of the atom as a little universe.

Another thing that sends me—a couple of Nobel Prize winners ago —is that particles are now considered unique. We were giving them names like proton, neutron. These things are unique happenings. How can we even suspect there's a unique happening when we're so crude we couldn't even come in contact with a unique happening—except we happen to be compounded of them? Language is an immensely gross happening. You can't even get interested in language now without finding growing in your imagination the existence of a single human language, something like DNA. There's a huge reservoir of meanings but none of them can be individual. No event in language is remotely as unique as the event of a particle. But language feels that way to us, and it's fitting that it does, like a jigsaw. I love rhyme, which must be the most crude fitting in the language. But the other strange thing is how the whole audience will feel a poem's there when it isn't behaving like a conventional poem. At one time, poems had to be even more conventional than the atom's rule.

HM: You mentioned rhyme just now and it appears in very different situations in your work.

RD: Oh well, in the very first "Structure of Rime," I've got a theoretical proposition. It comes out of Schoenberg's observation about harmony. Rime, or meter, which is the same word in English, is simply a sense of measure being present. And while measure may be like a ruler—twelve marks, and all of them equal—a measure actually means you're feeling something did happen before or did not happen before. Any sense of resemblance or any sense of disresemblance indicates the presence of rime. It was taken before, of course, to mean that you have *moon, June*. "Okay, I heard that sound before, so a measure is going on." But actually in many of those poems where you'd only hear the *moon, June,* there was no measure anyplace else.

My composition is dependent on how much I feel I am knowing whether something has occurred within an area before. It's as if we're back with "Structures of Rime," at talking about universal experience—

was it a unique experience? did it happen before? and how many times before? is it happening now in an ordination run? did it happen a long time before or close before? We won't guarantee when it's going to happen. A conventional poem guarantees when it's going to happen, and that's its most important guarantee.

When we are no longer centered on convention, you have to be aware all the time. If you go to a Mozart piece, you can fall asleep. And you can wake up. And, as a matter of fact, the contour of any melody is so specific, you could have completed it yourself. But if you go to a Cage concert and fall asleep, you've missed what wasn't there when you were asleep, because it's always happening. In other words, it has absolutely no prediction of what's going to go on ahead of itself.

HM: There is actually no way of really measuring anything; at least, I get that idea when I think of the continuous field in modern physics.

RD: It has, in that same way, been viewed as impossible that Apollo and T'ao might coexist. Or they were made to coexist, as the Jesuits manfully did by trying to put one in counterpoint with the other in order to find a common measure, which is the picture you may have had of an order of orders. That order of orders, by the way, is a common preoccupation of theosophy, meaning that all religions can be brought under one order. Well, actually, comparative religion shows that there is such an order. But that wasn't on my mind when we came to the order of orders.

HM: I connect measuring with metaphor, since if you experience something right now and you're trying to assess what you really experience, you will measure your experience by another experience. So there is always an attempt to measure. That's the language as I see it.

RD: But distancing would mean that you measure, too, wouldn't it?

HM: Yes. Now there is another question. Olson speaks of the poem as an energy, and the poet has got to put that energy across directly and immediately.

RD: I quote that passage, as a matter of fact, in one poem, and refer to him as The Poet. I certainly have no view that an energy gets put from point A to point B. Charles's view is in "Against Wisdom as Such"; this is an invaluable essay to me, it's the only one written on me, at least so far, that seems to give me a lever on my own situation. What he sees me as doing, of course, is losing energy by being concerned about meaning and wisdom. I don't know how I'm concerned with wisdom, just as I'm not concerned with belief or disbelief. He, like Allen Ginsberg, *Maximus*, like all of Allen's poems, really wants a qualitative change in what is. His poems have a qualitative resolve to them. They want a New Man.

So when they talk about awake and asleep, it's awake versus asleep. It's a conversion they're talking about, and it's got to be a conversion in depth. And the question of conversion gives me anxiety: I don't want to be converted. [*laughs*] Interestingly, Charles is talking about conversion of energy in me. He saw a thing in physics and he began to worry: if something is converted, will there be a gain on one side and a loss on the other? He sees the writer converting experience into language. Well, I wouldn't dream that you could put energy out of one place into another. Language as far as I'm concerned has stupendous energies. My head is practically blasted open with the energies that are present in the language. I would think the drain would come the other way around. I couldn't possibly put an experience into language; the big powerhouse is the language.

Of course, I can't imagine why Olson thought he needed more energies. The man has tremendous energy. Terribly power-starved, when he was one of the most powerful people I've known.

HM: This connects with what he says about metaphor and symbol.

RD: Oh yes, he's just undone by the fact that metaphor carries something over from somewhere else. When I wrote "Song of the Borderguard" in 1950, [Cid] Corman wanted to eliminate all the similes. And I said, "Well, when I say 'like' I mean 'like.'" I know a metaphor is supposed to be higher, or whatever, but actually this is what's going on.

I'm not a symbolist, though I play with symbols. They're all over the place. [*laughs*] The symbol, it seems to me, draws its power from the thing, not the other way around. The symbol, tree, derives its meaning from what a tree said to a man, from what a man saw in a tree. A tree can give birth to a million symbolic systems, but no symbolic system can give birth to a tree. Symbol is, I think, a message from a thing. And language is a primary thing. But mostly we talk with it and are very disturbed when its thingness appears—certainly disturbed in speech if its thingness appears—so we keep at a symbolic level throughout; that is, we refer to things we're thinking of.

Now poems force us to get words as things in and of themselves. It does it by making them puzzling. Symbol does it, by the way, by taking a thing and making it impossible for us to make the reference. And yet it can be a very simple one. It can practically be a rebus; it can look like a tree, it can be a symbol of a tree, and we'll fail to grasp the tree. The things that act as symbols in my poems are all word happenings, so they're always in the system of the poem. They don't symbolize something outside.

"Flooded by the World"

(with Jack R. Cohn and Thomas J. O'Donnell, 1980)

This first portion of an extensive two-part interview with Professors Jack R. Cohn and Thomas J. O'Donnell was published in Contemporary Literature *in its Autumn 1980 issue and republished by L. S. Dembo in his* Interviews with Contemporary Writers *(Madison: University of Wisconsin Press, 1983). (The second half appeared in* Credences *in its Spring 1985 issue, and was titled "The Poetry of Unevenness.") In this exploration of the poet's relation to the world, Robert Duncan examines the role of intellect in protecting him from being overwhelmed by "the seizure of the poem itself" as well as poetry itself being "a protective form." He says he is "constantly in study and recognition" as he writes, adding that he does not impose an order: "Oh, no. The order is there and I bring it out." He discusses at length his poems "Often I Am Permitted to Return to a Meadow," "Structures of Rime," and "The Dance."*

—Ed.

Robert Duncan is conventionally associated with the Black Mountain Movement and the experimentalism of postwar American poetry, and is specifically linked with Charles Olson. In this interview Duncan recalls that at the end of his life Olson saw that "we'd been on a great twenty-five-year adventure, and he also saw that I was excused and was at the end of that adventure." Despite his sense that the "Movement is no longer current," Duncan holds that its "spiritual imperative is one that even today will be felt." The following pages suggest the poet's own literary program, his place in his poetic generation, and make clear the romantic and spontaneous character of Duncan's temperament. He analyzes the relationship between his homosexuality and his choice of poetry as a career, emphasizes that he "read Freud straight across," offers his unique view of Olson and the Black Mountain Movement as well as his general conception of the development of American poetry in the last fifty years, and explains his theory of the collage (and conglomerate).

As revealing as the substance of Duncan's responses was his entire manner of participating in the interview. It was begun at the University of Kansas, where Duncan was serving as poet-in-residence for a week. Wearing a black cape against the early spring air, he looked the part of the poet and seemed to enjoy his various activities immensely: meeting with classes, lecturing on Yeats and Whitman, reading from his own work, and conferring with students. His extraordinary energy was apparent during the interview; in answering a question he would speak until interrupted or redirected. The range of his conversation and the intensity of his expression were often exhausting to the interviewers, if not to Duncan himself. In a single response he might mention and interrelate Dante, Milton, Pound, Olson, Williams, Eliot, Pindar, and Krazy Kat.

Duncan's talk was equally compelling and intense when he completed the interview in San Francisco a few months later. He shares an impressive four-story nineteenth-century house in the Mission District with the painter Jess Collins. Duncan met us at the locked, ornate iron grille before the door of the house and led us immediately into a library just beyond the entryway. Here his most valuable books are stored, and he stopped to show us rare editions of William Morris. The interior decoration of the house Duncan aptly characterized as a collage and said the house was "always making presentations, like a lyrebird." During the actual interview sessions Duncan seemed completely unaware of being recorded; whether the machine was on or not, he spoke with the same intensity and rapidity. He would circle around a subject, start a sentence, break it off, backtrack, begin another sentence, then digress suddenly to an arcane subject—which he would again begin to circle. No topic was taboo, including the death of his mother in childbirth, his adoption by an architect's family, and his homosexuality. Duncan seemed to respond to the questions spontaneously, as if he were considering them for the first time, or genuinely reconsidering all these matters. Not only was he generous with his time during the sessions, but the house as well seemed to open easily to his friends and to people making pilgrimages.

Toward the end of the interview Robert Duncan declares that "there'd be a hole if I disappeared, a small one." Most readers of postwar American poetry would find that hole much more significant than Duncan acknowledges. Although the difficulty of his poetry and the learning it displays evoke the image of the genius, the exceptional man, Duncan himself argues that he does not give *feeling and meaning to the object of his poetry. Rather, "it gives me passion, it gives me the identity of my passion." In the best of Duncan's work, the reader experiences this passion and renews his own faith in poetry as a way of knowing and being.*

INTERVIEWER: What do you see as the relationship between an individual poet and poetic movements or groups?

ROBERT DUNCAN: Well, I think there are some things I'd like to use an interview to clear up a bit. One of the larger ones is, what was the Black Mountain Movement that I've been identified with? What do groups mean to me, and what do movements mean? Particularly since the death of Charles Olson I feel I'm not a part of "current literature"—and don't have to be. I feel that somebody concerned about the "current," in exactly that historical sense, doesn't have to bother about my work at all, because I don't write as if there are any more movements, and that's a decision that I know many poets of the past would have recognized. In my case it's made deliberately—not with an antagonism to history, but with a much more deliberate sense of what's really going on. I'm a little puzzled by the fact that we have such rapid changes and such rapid dialectic going on in poetry, but I know that while I may use it or not, I am very happy to have the sense of timing back in my hands and not have to be out there. And so I feel my readers are off the beat when they land on me and ask, Where is the H.D. Book, or where is this or that? That book's going to come in its own time. I'm not writing a *Finnegans Wake* in the H.D. Book, but I am writing something; and it does have a plan, and I'll know when it's finished. Why are they breathing down my neck? History's not breathing down my neck; if history were breathing down my neck, the book would be there.

INT: When Olson was alive did you feel that you were a part of "current literature"?

RD: Oh, yes, yes, absolutely in the current. Olson called us to order. Previous to that I felt I had full permission not to be. I could do anything; I could ransack it; I could play in my little kindergarten all I wanted. But Charles called everything to order with *Projective Verse* in 1950. I had met him before, in 1947–48, but I didn't even know he was a poet. We talked about history and the clear emergence of what Charles would have called the sciences of man, and that is the coordination from which you approach history as a question about how you live. You're not paying attention to national history any longer. It's a history of cities and countrysides. Well, our first conversation was about them, because I was wound up in my thought at that time about how in every pattern, of either the Russian Revolution or that of the United States, the cities are ripping off the countryside because they have to have the food; but the countryside doesn't have anything, so you civilize them so they need the refrigerator that you're making. You make a lot of junk to sell to them, but the junk has to be ingenious, because it has to be something that makes them dependent. Well, that was what we talked about the first day, although he had looked me up because Muriel Rukeyser told him about a poet who had done something with medieval scenes—that meant history in it—and so he was already thinking of me as a poet, and I didn't return that interest. Consequently, when he sent me *y&x* in his first correspondence (and now you know you'd have a fortune if you had it) I was outraged. I mean, here's this guy in history, and why does he load his poetry off on me? I threw it into the wastepaper basket.

INT: But from 1950 to 1970 were you influenced greatly by Olson?

RD: I'm wondering if we would even call it influence. Well, no; I played heretic often to Olson's position, and he had a position in which heresy would sharpen my own sense of things. This is a familiar role; I've never been able to have a single figure, and Jack Spicer also was, for some time, an entertaining, an instructive person to play heretic to. I might have been more confused in the area of Manicheanism—about the glamour of Manicheanism and Calvinism—if I hadn't had somebody who was really very solidly *that* to disagree with. What I needed very much was someone who was serious about what the thing meant, and whom you wanted to be able to reach the final line of difference with. In Charles's case, the aftermath of my study in the Renaissance and medieval periods was an enormous sense of the intellectual excitement and power of Roman Catholic thought; and Charles really behaves in poetry as the pope. I don't mean that his thought is all orthodox, but it is charged through and through with analyzable Catholic origins, transvaluation of Catholic content. This vivified my own activity, which is always to transvalue the things in my parents' religion that I wanted to take with me because they made life vivid. And they can only be transvalued by being questioned and kept, arriving at a place not where they're acceptable, but where they're actually alive and not deadened by the terms and governance they are given when they're in the religion; and Charles was in the same process in relation to his Catholic content. He found a synthesis because Jungianism—he and Denise Levertov were both Jungian—allowed him to preserve his Catholic content and be at the same time current.

INT: But you're Freudian?

RD: Yes, I'm a Freudian, and Jungianism drove me up the wall with a good deal of fury; but it would have been an abstract fury had I not met a mind that I was always going to contend with as really being there and, moreover, a mind that would have to contend with me. And so when Olson wrote "Against Wisdom as Such," some people thought this was an attack and we must not be speaking to each other; but everything is absolutely accurate to me. We had been in conversation for some time; as a matter of fact, in the original that's a letter to me, he doesn't *not* know how I'm going to read every line, and then I can return and stretch my imagination and imagine how he's writing every line. I think you see part of what this is.

Eventually [Jack] Spicer's Calvinism and Manicheanism became a drunken obsession. (I sometimes wonder if alcohol causes such breakdown and damage in the brain circuits that they become locked in a kind of stupor in which our activity that keeps ideas vivid and moving fails.) Eventually Spicer's propositions that had been *méchant* originally of demons of outer space became no longer propositional; they became necessary to believe, so that he couldn't move the idea around. (And, by the way, there were possibilities *I* entertained; I keep alive the notion that angels and demons might possibly exist.) It's no fun to play heretic to a fanatic. I play heretic so that ideas are moving, and I'm entertaining their ideas, and I know they're entertaining mine. My correspondence with Spicer dropped off when I realized that he wasn't entertaining my ideas; and while I could picture his, they no longer would move around. There was no play left.

INT: You have spoken of a sense of freedom now that Olson's dead and a sense of freedom before you met him.

RD: I said freedom from history. Toward the end Charles saw where it was, but initially he wanted to be like Ezra Pound, a mover; and he was a mover, of course. He came charging in; and also he saw his man Melville as a mover of his mind and was really sort of shaking his poor old head as to how come Melville didn't move anything else. I mean how come Melville didn't move his own time? Well, maybe one of the explanations would be that Melville didn't get out there and do it. Charles was going to get out there and do it, no matter what, but he had a lot of reasons to do it. He did do it; "projective verse" really called us. We might have had a hazy memory about a lot of what Köhler was saying about composition by field and vector and so forth. But "projective verse" landed in our world and made a proposition that you have to start doing something. And, of course, it didn't come in nakedly: it came as a second proposition. Pound had not made a proposition that came into our world since the somewhat scattered proposition of the ideogram, at the stage of culture in 1936, and the real propositions were back in 1910. All this intrigued me as far as history is concerned; I knew I came out of the Pound propositions of 1910, and I knew that I was waiting at the bookstore door when that book *Kulchur* was going to appear. And the way that it was put together was through the ideogram, and the ideogram was the last stage that I had to think about and maybe incorporate. But incorporating something that's a proposition is not the same as what happened in "projective verse." It was supposed to be a change.

INT: Did you discuss these views with Olson?

RD: When I had one of the very last sessions with Charles at the hospital, one of the first things that I said to him was, "Well, Charles, we felt like we were moving the world, but maybe only you and I ever were interested in composition by field, although *Pieces* was written. And Dorn's doing something different." Well, that really hurt Charles. By the time he got to Buffalo and was thinking of dying, his graduate students there were very different from those at Black Mountain. At Black Mountain he had genius as a teacher, but that isn't going to be carrying Olson's program. When he got to Buffalo, he wanted young men who would do his work. Well, they are now lost young men, because there doesn't exist any "his work"—except what Olson did. And his first remark was that we'd been on a great twenty-five-year adventure, and he also saw that I was excused and was at the end of that adventure. It was a quest.

INT: Do you conceive of poetic movements as a series of quests?

RD: For a very good reason poetry has had the matter of King Arthur as very central to it, because it's *quests.* Britain may try it on and think it's calling for a new Britain; but one thing we know it calls for is something about the way a poem goes. You go on a quest, and when you complete the quest—and it can be a failure—you bring back the bloody head, or you follow the maiden with the bloody head, and you don't have a good time. But when you come back, you come back to that round table of poets sitting, and from no other round table do any of the Arthurian things start. Poetry wasn't written by kings or actual knights; even when people were playing their actual little jousts, poets weren't there. You come back, but you can still be writing poetry. You've done your quest, and that's what I mean.

INT: But it was a great quest?

RD: Yes, I think that was a tremendous experience, and so I have an Age of Charles Olson. The ones who were in the Age of Auden (and for much of the time that I was in the Age of Olson, the Age of Auden was still going on) did not read that as a quest; that was something else. I don't know what it was, but it makes for such a division of poets that they glare at each other as if one came from cannibal Africa and the other one from the Victorian parlor; and only two gentlemen went down to discover the source of the Nile. You can look through *Projective Verse* and look all the way through Charles; he always wanted to unlock a code. I don't go along with those projects; that was *his* quest; I don't think it was put on us. He did put it on the students. Charles Doria, for instance, who had just gotten out, finding his assignment, had gone on to a thing called *Origin,* where we've got very active translations of the key creation texts—not the myths, but the texts themselves, trying to get the direct feel of what it's like to be right in the Hittite. Well, what Charles wanted at Buffalo was for his young men to get the Hittite or to get the Mycenaean Greek and then get all the Lattimore stuff thrown out so that you're actually looking at the way it feels when you read it.

INT: Did your homosexuality affect your work? Were there aesthetic effects?

RD: Aesthetic effects? No, well, originally when you take *Medieval Scenes,* Spicer was very concerned about building up and reproducing something like a George Circle [from Stefan George (1868–1933)], which he knew about when I first met him. It was probably 1946, so I was about twenty-seven, and I guess Spicer would have been about twenty-one. He could also have been in his teens; he had come to Cal from one of those Quaker colleges. I'm not sure what college he came from, but he was a strange-looking kid. And he would want to sit during the entire day and learn everything I knew, so I know what it was he wanted to know right away—had I ever heard of the Maximin cult of George? And I had indeed. I had a very strange lead to that because just in 1945 I had had an affair with a German poet who was about ten years older than I was, and who felt he should initiate me into the inner ideas of what the George cult was. His mother had been in the George group; as a very young boy he had, then, been quite familiar with the George Circle. He had just gotten his degree in Mallarmé, and he eventually became the official German translator and editor of Yeats. I had a very personal, and actually still to me strange, initiation into the cult and was then very much in correspondence with it. Well, Spicer had a good deal of feeling about me all the way through this. And you find that even at the end, when I had not seen Spicer for two years or so (and in Vancouver he was trying to propose that his serial poem would supplant my work),

I was occupying the position of a master to him, though I was only six years older. But I had been writing, of course, and I was the first poet he ever met that was an actual poet. More than that, I was certainly an odd animal because I wasn't teaching and I was entirely a poet, only a poet. I'd wash dishes or do anything.

INT: Did your homosexuality determine your being "only a poet"?

RD: As a matter of fact, the reason I really was only a poet (it was clear even in high school that I wouldn't have a second profession, and that I would be just a poet, which was very distressing to my family) was that I was incapable, absolutely incapable, of living in the double standard. I would just blabber too much; I'm not talking about some great moral courage or something. I was literally incapable, and I didn't read myself wrong. So, without thinking about it, I understood that no one cares who or what is washing dishes—but by the time you're a busboy they care, and they're patting your bottom or whatever—and nobody cares who's typing his manuscript, and that's where I was and never asking myself. But if you would try to get an office job! I would take a Civil Service examination and would be A-1 or whatever is the top bracket; but when you'd go to get the job that's at the other end of that, they simply read you out, in no time at all. You never got the job and, more than that, they'd ask you to tell them why. And you'd meet a hostility that couldn't be described; so no wonder I didn't, luckily, remotely believe that I might grow up and be a teacher, maybe, as well as a poet. Well, I could already see when I was a freshman in college, no, you don't grow up and be a teacher. I was living with a French professor who lived in absolute terror. Three years later he was a French professor at the Naval Academy in Annapolis, and I could go out, providing it was after ten, and walk the dog. I got a lot of reading done; I read all the way through Proust and Trollope, but I couldn't go out of doors. And I had to exist as if I didn't exist. And then the hysterical other side of this is—because that's the backswing of absolutely abnormal double lives—people were just losing their minds at parties. Again they had to be very wealthy, where you had eight walls and whatever. Smoking pot was nothing compared with the simple sex lives in those days.

INT: Yet despite this legal and social pressure your poems are at times openly homosexual.

RD: The fact that I didn't have inbuilt any religious or negative formulation about homosexuality meant that my poetry didn't have to be covert. It's perfectly apparent from the start and, more than that, I had some models; I loved Marlowe and very soon found *Edward II*, but could also read what was going on in *Tamburlaine* and several other places. In the late 1930s there were key texts like that. Long before an English course would bring it up, I'd be starting out reading my Melville that way. *Moby-Dick* was always a little key text given to kiddies, because if you could read straight at the beginning of *Moby-Dick*, you could learn quite a lot—I mean the little bedroom scene. There were such key scenes in literature that gave you something straight on mores and human responses, something not distorted by your having to read faggots. If you read the scene with Queequeg and Ishmael in their first night in that hotel as written, it tells you as much as *Edward II*, because it's decent and straightforward and presents certain areas of feeling that you can inherit without being an ugly, distorted human being. Whereas if you read novels of the 1920s for your information, you'd think you'd come on like a freak in a parking lot.

INT: How do you think this enforced separation from the conventional affected your poetry or your ideas?

RD: Only in the fact that my education then was very much my own and that my formulations in poetry, of course, were completely free from the formulations I would have had if I had been teaching English, although later, if I thought of teaching, it would have been history. Ernst Kantorowicz at Cal had very much wanted me to go on; at the point that I met Jess, as a matter of fact, I had got my mother to back my going to Germany, and Kantorowicz had it charted out. So it was by a very slim margin of a month or two that I met Jess; otherwise I would have been off to Germany, where I would have chugged through to be an historian in medieval history. I was not unconvinced that I couldn't have been both an historian and a poet. I mean, I was a poet, but I had done papers and certain work in seminars. Things got straightened out; I am an artist. But it was so entrancing a prospect; this is again the George tradition: one of the closest ones to George was the great historian Friedrich Gundolf, who was Kantorowicz's immediate mentor. And that whole transformation of German history was a transformation that could have taken place in American history. When I met Charles Olson, by the way, what I didn't know about him was that he also was on the verge of a similar development; he had been in American studies that, under F. O. Matthiessen, were increasingly history and "science of man" centered. And Charles, reading Melville, began to realize, "Melville has all of this and is transforming the novel; I can transform the poem, and I get to be a poet; I am a poet, and my long training and history-centered mind do not disqualify me." I think you realize that the entire tenor of having an English department was that history was an extraneous concern of the poem, as, for instance, God was extraneous.

INT: How did this attitude toward God affect you?

RD: I remember, when I was a freshman at Cal, that they didn't have classes in poetry, but poets, the ones who felt they were poets, met and talked about poems in an evening session. And Jo Miles came to a session and rebuked me for having stars in a poem, because they were too big, for having the universe in it. She's a funny kind of objectivist; she relates to Williams's poetry in the early stage. And everybody objected to the fact that I was God-headed; I had gotten it off Marlowe. I hadn't really stumbled on Shelley; that would have been even worse. Shelley was a really bad name there.

INT: To return to homosexuality, when did you first publicly declare it?

RD: There was a battle sense at Cal; and partly out of that I wrote, in 1942, the first article on homosexuality in which it isn't just apparent; I state that I'm a homosexual. I was twenty-three and it was published in Dwight Macdonald's *Politics*; it's called "The Homosexual in Society." James Agee had just written an article on blacks and the fact that their form of comedy, and their only area of social acceptance, was one in which they made it amusing to whites that they, the blacks, were hostile,

and that their blues were, as a matter of fact, amusing to the whites—
that they were blue and were sold as such. And Agee rightly found this
a very dangerous social symbol. One of my contemporaries that I've
known the longest, Pauline Kael, was very interested in political writing;
one of the reasons I came to know her so well is that arguing back and
forth with Pauline, who was very sharp on Marxism and who strongly
questioned the anarchism that I was proposing as a political position,
gave me a challenge to build ideas around. That article was very much
written with a sense that I had people who would judge what I was
saying there. Agee was recognizing a symptom, and it struck me that I
could talk about another symptom of another hostility that is perfectly
acceptable and absolutely amusing to everybody, providing it presents
itself in the way that it does, and everybody in the whole society likes
it. One thing I knew about our friendly University—of course, I mean
the set of people that I've seen crippled by it, such people as I was in
love with in the early period—when that was their environment, I saw
them absolutely done in by it. It was always known that the whole
department would love its pet queer; what they didn't like was the
challenge that demanded intellectual respect and not on the grounds of
this. If it was always on the grounds of *this*, that was fine; but it would
really alarm them if it was pointed out in ways that didn't ask for some
special social position, or didn't say I'm hurt over here, or didn't excite
a sympathy.

INT: What did you achieve with this article?

RD: One of the immediate results was that I also escaped from being
acclaimed at that point. John Crowe Ransom accepted effusively a poem
of mine called "An African Elegy" and then wrote that because a major
poem by Stevens was coming out in the fall issue, he's transferring me
to the spring; he wanted this poem by a poet who had not appeared
before to be a lead poem and it would not otherwise be a lead poem.
The article on "The Homosexual in Society" came out and I got a letter
from Ransom, saying that he had not realized that this was a covert
advertisement for homosexuality; *Kenyon Review* was not a journal
accepting this sort of thing. And then I wrote back, "Would you prefer

113

an *overt* one?" And then I got a letter, and he said he did not know what the law provided, but he believed that homosexuals should be castrated so that they wouldn't breed more homosexuals. Among our many odd versions of what [was] likely to happen, I think the castration document is strange indeed. So scratch a Southern gentleman and you'll find something awfully interesting. So I was *out*, just read out, out, out, at a point when I would have been *in* at the wrong place. When the issue came out, I would have been *in:* Auden, Paul Goodman, Parker Tyler; I mean the place looked like it was a coffee klatch. I'm glad I wasn't in there; I would have been read not as an advertisement but a conformist of the first water.

INT: You said that you "escaped from being acclaimed."

RD: Well, let's call it "claimed," because I very much wanted to be in the current when I was young. I did understand that there was an immense impetus that would be important to me in the sense of having contemporaries—I wouldn't have to cover everything in my own writing. I could be increasingly on my own, providing there was a Creeley also writing and people would be reading us together. Let me give an example, a concrete one, of the opposite of this. I began to run across a few poems of Bill Merwin's that looked something like "Structures of Rime," but they seemed awfully fake to me, and I couldn't find any verifications when I was reading them that the poet had actually had visitations. I think you can begin to see what a difference it must make. Does the poet dispose of these visitations as poetic fancies and as an ambience in which something poetic happens? Or is he having (and I think he was, but not ready to put his mind there) something like a Master of Rime appearing and talking directly, and certain figures as would be in a dream, but others as persons of Poetry? We would have no questions with Stevens, would we? We don't have to run around and ask him; the poem makes it very clear. But something was unclear with Merwin. While I actually find some of them pleasurable to listen to, they also make me angry because it will be possible for someone who is reading in the Merwin sense to turn to "Structures of Rime" and get them wrong. Mostly I make it impossible for somebody to get it wrong. If you don't pick it up right, you can't go anywhere. This is the way I read lots of things that happen in *The Cantos;* as a matter of fact, scholars were beginning to observe that the modern poem is making it impossible for somebody to read it wrong. And so my first question was that in Merwin nothing was forcing me to read it in some particular way; it was beautifully available; and I began to wonder, "Can this possibly be?" And he can still produce poems; they simply remain back there where the English gradually taught themselves a poem should be: it's a form that a gentleman writes. Disastrously it happened to [Richard] Wilbur; Wilbur's first book comes with an amazing force. And my first book—not only was Ezra Pound embarrassed when he had to read it, but he said, "Why are you doing this?" when he knew from correspondence. But Wilbur's first book is truly a first book, and from there on he erases it, and he's writing those poems as you're told to write; maybe only a war gave him the context of the straight stuff. So this was one of the meanings of the Black Mountain Movement: you don't get mixed up. Think how important it was to Coleridge and Wordsworth that they weed out and that they not get mixed up with Southey.

INT: What you've said, then, suggests that the Black Mountain Movement is over for you personally.

RD: That's not quite what I said. I think that the Black Mountain Movement is no longer current; consequently, I'm not current, because it's very much what I do. But I think the Movement took place; its beginnings are 1947 to 1949, and clearly by 1960, when Don Allen's anthology appears, it's there. What my life work will be is entirely there at the point when I begin *The Opening of the Field.* You find its content and its propositions are in the preceding period, from 1952 to 1956, and it takes place in the book *Letters;* and from there on I have a work assigned, and it's, as Charles would say, a vector. When I say I'm not current, I don't mean my work might not be of influence, but the influence will not be the vital one going on in *Letters.* However, our spiritual imperative is one that even today will be felt as the continuing spiritual imperative of the 1950s.

INT: You've spoken about visitations and your interest in occultism. Have you ever participated in a séance?

RD: Oh, I did very early; in the period when I left college—that would have been 1937–38 or so—and was living in Woodstock, we had séances during the winter. We had no mediums; I think I have references in poems to a "fireman" I saw at that time. After we had been meeting for about three months, and only at the beginning of any kind of manifestation, I felt the muscles in my lower leg going in a whole series of pulsations, rising clear up, and I got quite alarmed. As it was happening, I saw sitting by the fireplace a man entirely of fire, and I reasoned it and reassured myself, well, that's Sanders Russell, and I'm seeing him in the glow of the firelight. Then I began to realize that I was talking and the talking was getting remote, and I didn't want to lose consciousness, so I lurched up (like lurching up from sleep) and put on the light. And there was no Sanders there at all, so that would be an example of seeing. Another example of seeing: Michael McClure was taking drugs, and wanted me to take LSD, because he was very excited about what had happened. I was sitting in their dining room, and they have a big plane tree in the back. And I said it was not a plane tree. And Mike said, you'll see this great flowing something or other. And I was going to say, Mike, you don't realize that it's too easy for me to let go, and every leaf on that tree was a crawling, faintly hostile animal kind of thing, as I looked right past him at the tree. And I said, in reference to LSD, Mike, if I'm going to go to hell on a visit, I want to be sure I'm on a visit and not on a trip. None of those drugs; it's only too easy for my chemistry to shift.

INT: How does your poetry relate to such states?

RD: Actually, I think poetry may also have been, very clearly, a protective way for me. Why is the poem surrounded and why does the intellect happen to be so much present in my poetry? This may be an enormous protection against the seizure of the poem itself. My sense of my poetry is that it's extremely anxious. Large portions of it will be in a rhythm that's built up of almost machine-gun-like stutters, all of them keyed as highly intellectual propositions, before it starts to flow. The flow would be very dangerous for me. I don't have any psychotic periods, and I have very few hallucinatory periods that I can remember, and yet in "Passages" there were disturbing dreams. The one in the Victor Hugo poem is a reference to pillars of light (moonlight) that came in the night; Jess woke up and I was whimpering, and he realized that this was not just a dream to be wakened from, because I might have been frightened, and that he had to sit through it and I had to go through it. And it was experienced as a visitation of angels, mothering angels, and one was actually my adopted mother, and one was H.D., who was adoptive, because I had come to know H.D. in correspondence. But it was an experience I didn't doubt. Everybody thought when I wrote "The Carpenter" it was perfectly apparent that I say, you came in a dream and I knew I was to write to you, not pose like I'd made you up. And actually that was another dream visitation. I was never sure who the Carpenter was; in the dream, or in the visitation, I raise the question myself, "Is it Christ?" But it could also have been Christ because it was huge and I was little. I clearly was running from God, as in "The Hound of Heaven," which would be exactly where I would be today. So the intellectuality we're talking about is also the form of running from God.

INT: Do these poems seem to come from inside or outside?

RD: When lines come to me, frequently it's not clear that they aren't outside my head. Now that would be a psychotic symptom, but I never experience it as such, nor do I quarrel. I don't set up something about this is "inside my head"; I will work with it as if it did come from "outside." I'd work with things that come from somebody talking, reading. Learning that [James] Joyce had gone to bars and used conversations was one of the encouraging things that we knew. As a matter of fact [Henry] James is getting whole novels out of a little sentence or two in a newspaper and calling them a "germ." We read that when we were little and understood what it was; I mean James's germinal theory of the novel is one of the origins, lo and behold, of how Duncan proceeds in poetry. And while Pound doesn't reflect on it in his essay on the poem, probably it's prevalent. [D. H.] Lawrence proceeds as if people who belong to the novel came to him, and then he says, once he started them, he can barely write it down as fast as *they* do it. So all of that would be in the territory you're talking about; and, consequently, when I read testimony of saints, I take that as testimony, and certainly it's a little more dependable than Nixon.

INT: You say you write only when you have to?

RD: Well, as a matter of fact, yeah; actually, it's quite compelling.

INT: You mean an internal compulsion.

RD: Well, no, it's almost always an external one. Many of my leads toward writing come from applied Freudianism out of *The Psychopathology of Everyday Life.* I go by a series of omens, these leading to the point where you have to deal with them in the poem.

INT: A series of what?

RD: Omens—of compelling directions that certain things are no longer. Things that you would ordinarily take, in a Freudian context, to be parts of your psyche I take to be parts of my poetic projection. For instance, I am not in my derivation from Freud; I have not been psychoanalyzed; I am not remotely interested in my psyche. It's not an interest in psyche when I speculate upon the primal scene. The primal scene is exactly like the primal scene if you're dealing with the Fall; and the way I read my *Paradise Lost,* Milton's angels instructing his Adam and Eve on the nature of the Fall are way over there where my Freud is. If you were in the course of a psychoanalysis instead of in the course of a poetics, then if something happened you would recognize the dream was telling you to do certain things, and you had, for instance, a thing called the dreamwork. In the first Freud I ever read, *The Interpretation of Dreams,* he's already talking about a thing called dreamwork. That is, he sees his patients as if they're in the course of an analysis; immediately I took that over. That poetry-work was like dreamwork was premise number one when I was seventeen and started reading my Freud. And it went along to things that had been in my family's occultist tradition, because if they talked about their alchemy, they had work to do. They taught me that dreams told you things you had to do. Freud produced in his psychology analogous structures to the ones that had been present in the whole Jewish mystical tradition. But it was a tradition of things you had to do, of ways you read things of being significant of more than they said. And I grew up in an atmosphere where anything written always meant more than it said. And the dream is certainly polysemous. I'm not building a psyche; I'm building a poetry. I find myself in profound aversion when faced with close friends who were in Jungian or Freudian analysis and doing things with their psyche. I feel as Joyce does: they're playing with their icky, or something. Little games, psychodramas—and yet what is a poem?

INT: But how does the process of writing compel you?

RD: You don't initiate themes; the themes are there all the time, but you recognize that they're leading and drawing. One thing is certain, that my internal chemistry changes, because I feel a body change. Well, I would not need a poem at all in order to be involved with mythology, in order to be involved with most of what you take to be the content of a poem, but a poem has an entirely different thing going on in it that is proper to it, and so that is its poetry. The fact that you're working with language and making something with it is far different from the pursuit of ideas or the study, and yet all my poetry incorporates, tries to incorporate, the ranges of my personality in its work. That is, it's study—study is *au naturel* for me—so my poetry also will show it. At the point when I take up a work I find frequently I'm in study, within the poem. But they're conceived of now as building; I think we talked about this one thing from my father.

INT: Your adoptive father was an architect?

RD: Certainly it's my judgment, then, that he was not a true architect. Then I had to ask, okay, am I a true poet? No, I wouldn't want to have to be, so I decided I was going to make up poetry the same way I would make up love. If I'm incapable of loving, as my mother told me once, then I'll make it up; I would prefer to make it up than be real me. No wonder I don't want to go into psychology. I read Freud straight across. I also discovered in Jacob Boehme, a philosopher, the idea that the whole universe is grounded in wrath, and love has only one root, which is wrath (it's a transformation of wrath and not the other way around). Or now I'm attracted to Heidegger, because he says *Dasein* is rooted not in its possibility but in its impossibility, so all of life is rooted in death. Isn't this for our whole period our apprehension of what's involved in the third thermodynamic law? Our entire energy world is rooted in zero energy and ordered by it throughout, and coming to it, *not yet*, so we live in what Heidegger called the *not yet*. These are not things that influenced my poetry, but recognitions so like what I felt was the nature of the poem, rooted in its not being true. So the poetry seems true to me, whereas I would be as abashed to say I was a true poet, and abashed if somebody made that announcement, as I would to say, "I love you," which is also an announcement I can't make. And essential. So there are essential points when the dread of language leaves you in such an abyss as what the Lie is. Much of my poetry's gone into all those areas in which we learn that the word "poem" means "to make it up, make up what is not true." And fiction, then, means to me something more severe than Wallace Stevens proposes to us, although I think, since he has roots in Hawthorne, he's not so jolly as Whitman, from whom he also stems. Wallace Stevens doesn't have the confidence in language he sometimes proposes. Whitman has a confidence in language which I'm certain I don't have. It's the one place I am not like Whitman.

INT: You take the idea of *making* quite seriously, then?

RD: I'm making buildings and architectures frequently. So I go back to build something, and my intuition of when it's time for me to work is when the whole language proposition appears to me as intuitions of building a building. A poem to me is a building of this kind: it's got very specific properties and it can be intricate; but it always has a suite or a number of rooms; it always has a current that goes through. As a child I was making floor plans with choreographies. And I had very elaborate floor plans and choreographies that move from my head as well as ideas; and they can never come into activity, except when I'm making poems. Now all the rest of the so-called verbal area, the so-called content, constantly comes into conversation, but the floor-plan aspect of it comes in only in the art, so again it's the architectonics of the poem that seems to me one of the crucial things. The minute that comes forward, then I'm writing, feel a call to it (doesn't mean I can do it). I'm as often stranded in impossible architectures as anybody else, I would presume.

INT: Would you discuss a specific poem? Perhaps "Often I Am Permitted to Return to a Meadow." How did you write that?

RD: I had for some years told the story that "Often I Am Permitted to Return to a Meadow" was a poem in which I recognized the beginning of the book it belongs to, *The Opening of the Field*. And so *The Opening of the Field*'s got a plan. It is continuously illustrating itself throughout, and, more than that, it has thematic propositions moving out of the idea of "field," which is constantly found and refound, and has a drama that moves through it. But initially I didn't have any such proposition of what was going to be—just a determination that the initial poem would be nuclear to be a book, and it would contain themes and I would be called to them. Well, I had two poems, and what I remembered in the legend, then, was that my first two poems that came were poems in which angels were present, and I wanted to be sure that I didn't have any involvement with angels.

INT: Why the prohibition against angels?

RD: Rilke's *Duino Elegies* had been an overwhelming conversion for me, and I dreaded, and still dread, any angelic invasion—I'm not talking about angels as they invade religion, but angels as Rilke found them invading poetry. And I would say the same thing: my difficulty with the proposition of angels is that they are so much a proposition of poetry; they must be the same danger there that they would be anywhere else. They're not a proposition about do I or do I not believe in them, and would it be disturbing if one walked into the room? All those doctrines of angels, about how they move our lives, are beside the question I'm entertaining here. I did know that if they come into a realm of poetry we're in very heavy trouble, analogous to what happens in the *Duino Elegies*. I actually did pray that I'd be excused, in other words, be permitted to. And so, when I wrote the opening line, "Often

I am permitted to return to a meadow," I recognized that this was my permission, and that this meadow, which I had not yet identified, would be the thematic center of the book. In other words, what's back of that opening proposition I understood immediately: twice *you* wanted to compel me to have a book that would have angels at the center, but *now* I am permitted, often you have permitted me, to return to a mere meadow. But I was also flooded with meadows from childhood, and I also knew immediately that I was permitted to return to a dream, a dream which appears in this poem and also appears in the Pindar poem. Typically, the dream is an absolute experience for me—that is, it is not illustrative of something—so when [M. L.] Rosenthal, who wants to make a confessional poem out of it and to find a personal psychological extension of that dream, comes to it, it's merely those children dancing in the circle on the hill. But to me it is a generative symbol, and revelatory in the sense it throws me forward to a question, not to an answer, and it is not relevant to a psyche.

INT: The opening sentence contains meanings, then, that are far from apparent.

RD: And if we take just that opening sentence, "Often I am permitted to return to a meadow," at the same time that I recognized it meant you have permitted me now to return to this meadow (I will be safe from angels) that is not what happened by the time I'd done an "eternal pasture folded in all thought." I knew the idea of a "folded pasture" or a "folded field" as a proposition given in the *Zohar* for the Cave of Machpelah, so my field was identified initially in this poem, in its very first version, with the cave that Abraham sees, and he recognizes before he buys it that it is the center of the universe, and also that the forefathers are gathered there, are buried there, of whom he is going to be the fourth. You find in the same period in my writing to Olson, I was building a picture of the quartet; I had kept trying to picture what was happening in the generation of Pound and Williams and Lawrence. The quartet, as I finally designed it, was Williams and Lawrence and Pound, and then Olson became both an ancestral figure and a fellow figure, and I got to be the son. In other words, l am re-creating a father and fathering myself. In the H.D. Book I talk about poets mothering themselves in the language, in the loss of their mother, and frequently I have father constructs, just as I construct an architect almost immediately.

INT: The "first version" you mention is a manuscript version of "Often I Am Permitted to Return to a Meadow"?

RD: The manuscript version and the press publication are only a couple of weeks apart, so you can read the first version. What I did that made for a second version is that when I began to see the theme of the woman appearing (which may have been as late as "The Maiden"), I redid the first poem so that it included "Queen Under The Hill." I'd also begun to see that the theme in the matter was going to make a union of the Judaic, the classical, and the Celto-Germanic. In medieval studies I'd had a seminar in Celto-Germanic art, and I'd had—back of the medieval studies—quite a lot of delving into a picture of what parts of European consciousness were really Celto-Germanic. I put the two together; there's a negative feeling about the Germanic I want in there. And so this book develops—by the time it comes to the end—the idea that there's a kind of rope in which these are thoroughly entwined, and consequently it is the growth of a single vine. In time it comes to be the whole Semitic, because I make a union between the Moslem and the Judaic and then the Semitic back of that; and if that's broken at all, you have catastrophe, which is how I read what happened in Nazi Germany.

INT: What specifically is added?

RD: It is the "She it is Queen Under The Hill / whose hosts are a disturbance of words within words / that is a field folded," and it makes most intolerable to both parties a union in which the Celtic and the Judaic are combined. And the queen then becomes a Shekinah. But I already knew, of course, from the *Zohar* that there was such a queen folded in the fold of God and that while we pose this father—right into the center of this poem which has its hidden reference to that Cave at Machpelah, which is fathering yourself again—you pose inside the queen who becomes the queen of the whole hive. Well, that's all I had to do to have enough. Once that was there I saw I had everything that I was going to unwind/

wind in the book. The field very rapidly is identified with another source of the field I knew, and that is in Fustel de Coulanges's *Ancient City* (his description of Rome and the Roman field), so that in the midst of the Beat movement, by lovely synchronicity, while they're talking about squares, I am dealing with a *square:* my field is square. It gave me great elation to be building a fourfold square field, but the thing that haunts the book is that at the center, I knew, of that where the hearth is built, something has to be lost. What it was is the cat and the death of the cat. As I came toward the end of the book I became more and more apprehensive about the death of someone, and at one point I asked what had happened to my closest friend in the Second World War. I was told he had died, and you have a poem which really addresses his death; and when it was printed in a magazine in Chicago, it turns up he wasn't dead, so I came to know him again. But "A Storm of White," the death of that cat (of the cat Pumpkin, who was very close to us indeed) produced a paroxysm of grief, because it was a necessary sacrifice to this field.

INT: There's another connection with the idea of the field a bit later, isn't there?

RD: Oh, you mean where the title of the book comes in. Well, that's actually in "The Structure of Rime II." That's where I recognized the title of the book: "He brings his young / to the opening of the field. Does he so fear beautiful compulsion?" My poetry is a process of opening. Of opening meanings out of meanings out of meanings, with a confidence that there's closure. In the question of closure—you know at the present time physics has still not decided whether we are an endlessly opening universe with no possible proposition of closure at all—I'm sure about life that death can't be experienced as closure. There are no terminal experiences. So I think of it as altering; that's all I can think of it as. I don't mean the eternal: it does not interest me in the least. I was raised in reincarnation, and I tend in crisis situations to behave as if that's where it was. But when I'm talking about death's being an opening, I mean it can't possibly be a closure. It is not a terminus, because experience itself has closure, whereas a coma is not experience.

INT: In "The Structure of Rime II" you attribute observations to a lion who appears in several guises. What does the lion symbolize?

RD: Well, "lion" and "line" are always analogous to me; my puns are not puns, because they're entirely in the world of language. And it is presumed within the world of language that language is always specific. A difficulty I notice is that if we talk about speech, then we don't have to talk about English or French or any other kind of speech. And under speech we've got many kinds of languages. Speaking is a very great activity and, in the English speech, that is a real limitation on my poetry: that it inhabits the English language as if it were speech. Translators have to give up on a word like "sentence," because it is crucial in the whole structure of my world that a "sentence" in a law court and a "sentence" in grammar are identical. That's not true in German; it's not true in French. God gives his sentence upon the earth but not in any other language but ours, I think. So here "line" and "lion" are at every point. Sometimes I wonder, "That again?" But my artistic feeling about it—I'm not sure at all where my aesthetic's going to be—is that if I am continuously intrigued with "line" and "lion" I can do it as often as Mondrian's intrigued with his propositions of light and dark, and so forth. I don't save myself with "line" and "lion," but I'm surprised how often new terms enter in the pattern. And we don't have to talk about hierarchies, because often my own perception of the poem, when I'm working on it, is very close to putting together a patchwork quilt. And I refer to myself as a jackdaw in some [places]— and frequently ask, "How do we lyrebirds build nests continually on top of themselves?" My house, for instance, is frustrating because you fill it and you get into certain sets and you keep wanting to add house on top of house because you're always making presentations, like a lyrebird. So a poem to me is a lyrebird's presentation to an imaginary reader. A "lyre" is one I run [into?] all the time. I never write "lyre" without the other "liar" around.

INT: I understand your approach to writing "Often I Am Permitted to Return to a Meadow," but I'm interested as well in your general practice. When you're working on a poem, do you do several manuscript versions?

RD: No. Manuscript versions are in notebooks, and by the time I'm working on passages I have a method of composition so that when I'm typing them I make new developments; but I don't write them twice in order to arrive at these. At the present time, in working on a complex recital from a translation from Pindar, I am actually having to work the recital. Now the recital is written in one notebook, and then in preparing it to be typed for publication, for being part of a composition, I have to use the material of the recital. The recital is a series of mistakes, and I did not want to worry at all about whether this is unwieldy. So the first writing is a sketch. In the middle of the poem it's lyrical; it's a long essay recital of the translation of the Pindar passage, making all the possible mistakes that can be along the line of "line" and "lion" in order to find extensions. Okay. Now, that becomes material which I now have to work, also still in the notebook, in order to shape it in relation to the suite it belongs to. And then, once that's there at the typing point, I call that almost like orchestration—more and more, as I listen to music and learn how composers and music proceed, I'm to a good degree composing. It's themes that enter that poem to change it, not improvements, and I understand what I'm doing with those themes, because they make possible the large structure of the book. The recital has long held up this particular poem from being finished, because the last two lyrics can't possibly come into existence until I have got the complex web of this recital to where I've got the gist of what it is that's in that poem. I mean the lyrical passages would certainly not be the maze that the essays are.

INT: We've tried to relate you to the Romantic notion of the artist, the artist drenching what he sees with feeling and meaning. In "Dejection: An Ode" Coleridge looks out and sees nature, sees the green light and the storm, and says, "I may not hope from outward forms to win / The passion and the life, whose fountains are within."

RD: I see it the other way around: *it* gives me passion, *it* gives me the identity of my passion. I used to feel, "Am I not maybe empty or have no identity at all because I'm all out there?" I was mentally excited when I started Whitehead, which is the same time as *The Opening of the Field* begins. Olson came in the spring of 1957, and he was just reading Whitehead, so I began not so long after him reading *Process and Reality.* And I had that feeling that the world illustrates *us,* that we were the *tabula rasa.* I had always been baffled by the [Bishop] Berkeley proposition. Are we going to worry about, "Is it there when we're not looking?" My question is, "Am I there when I'm not looking?" And I vote for Aristotle's view that a soul is simply the life experience of a lifetime. It is the shape of the lifetime. Now that means, "Am I there when it isn't there?" No. The "I" can be the universe, because there it is out there. And then we get, "What about this world?" Every imagination of the universe extends this universe for me, so none of that is unreal. I make no choices among it, so science forms a more generative idea; a perfect one, where I really do know my center, is strict, straight-line Darwinism—which is *no purpose.* And there damn well better not be a purpose, because you're lost if there is. You find Darwin entering early in *The Opening of the Field* and in *Letters,* where I'm trying to propose, "Okay, if the biggest generative process is *no purpose,* how do I remove purpose from a poem when I'm working at it? How do I actually evolve as I begin to understand what life does?" Because my model of how a body is most viable—how its life is most going to survive—no longer resembles the one you have if you are a paradigm that might be extinguished. When the DNA appeared you'd have thought you'd written it yourself!

INT: Could you explain the symbolic significance of that discovery for you?

RD: DNA is a biological analogy derived from the very linguists we were reading. Cybernetics is the birth ground of the DNA—of seeing biology as if it could be a code which they then assumed language was. And it's my generation who got it for the very first time—could even imagine language as a code. The watershed by which I am not at all the same species of poet as Robert Lowell is that Lowell knoweth nothing of cybernetics—knoweth nothing of a language which is a code. Language doesn't behave that way; that's not the world of language that his mind addresses or from which he comes. Pound himself couldn't address it. He also knew nothing of a cybernetics, so he feels that *The Cantos* have a logic, but his mind isn't going to go to their logic; his mind rushes to fascism in order to boss that big form. So he feels it's formless at the last, at the very time when it's actually significant. For how do we think language behaves? He thinks it's falling apart and he can't use it; but actually being entirely contemporaneous with Norbert Wiener and the people who are all in the language field (but not reading them), he has no idea. He could have gone to [Arnold] Schoenberg to find out what was happening in music, but he couldn't because of his anti-Semitism; he could have gone to Freud to find out what was happening in a new psychology, but he couldn't; so he behaves as if he were a wandering Voltaire writing the wrong thing and inherits all the anti-Semitism of the eighteenth-century mind trying to get itself clean.

INT: Where would the world that's mediated by your poetry be if your poetry didn't exist to represent it?

RD: I'm a locality of what's happening in poetry, as I am personally a locality in the universe. Well, if I weren't here, we wouldn't worry about that locality's being missing. I do understand there'd be a hole if I disappeared, a small one. No, I'm a development in a language, but I certainly didn't develop the language, so I refer to myself as derivative entirely. And at the same time I am the only place where that derivation can happen, so I don't resemble what I derive from, couldn't possibly because there's only one locality for something going on. Where would the language be? The language is the source of all the possible poetries. It's like asking where the DNA would be if your own local sperm hadn't connected with this local egg. Well, there's millions of sperms that don't connect, and there are lots of eggs that don't connect, and we could build whole imaginary worlds about the missing bodies. No, I don't think it's a jigsaw puzzle like that. I'm sure that the field of language is as destructive of its individual occasions as literature clearly is of its. But I do build myself large enough that I might leave a fossil, if only a bone somewhere in the debris.

INT: In "A Letter," addressed to a carpenter, you speak of working with wood, planing it down. In your poetry are you trying to expose the grain of that wood, the grain that is in the external world, the pattern or form that's out there?

RD: Yes, I bring out a content as you would bring out a grain, that's true. Frequently you'll find me taking a quotation because there's a promising grain in it. Marquetry is referred to often in my work; it also bears a relation to carpentry, and you're not just bringing out the grain but relating it to contradictory grains. The place where I've seen it as being impressive is in the marquetry of the eighteenth century, or the seventeenth century, where it's really elaborate. And the elaboration fascinates me; but again, though it's fitting and contrasting, you bring out what's there in the text. And I'm always bringing out possibilities of language, even in that initial poem in *The Opening of the Field,* and eliminating other things, in order to bring out a promise toward things that will happen later. But you're bringing out the qualities that are there: I don't think of myself as giving the quality to the language.

INT: To take it one step further back, you're not, as a Romantic would be, imposing that order?

RD: Oh, no. The order is there and I bring it out. I have an aesthetic about the composition of the poem; this would not describe what I think a poem arrives at, but what governs its coming into shape. Specifically, it was a decision made—I don't know why I made it, because I'm not sure I had a talent for what I thought I was rejecting—against the kind of artful, orchestral coloring that goes on in Hart Crane's use of the language. It sounds poetic because it's not located. And then there were things described in the 1930s and talked about as being ambiguities, where they really meant not double locations or triple or polysemous, but simply that it was so vague that we could do almost anything with it. Certainly by the time I came to *Letters,* I began to articulate the line into even, short phrases; I determined that every part of the poem would be active at the conscious, meaningful, directed level, and that my business would be to recognize how many meanings were present, like "line" and "lion" and so forth. And so I became a recognizer. This is the grain of the language: you *recognized* all the activities that you'd ever known that would tell you. And, of course, the phrases became much smaller. Why the articulation of a line into a series of smaller elements? So the caesuras widen, and there's no longer a punctuation within a syntax. It calls attention to the fact that the mind is in full attention on the minutiae of the poem. In the formula of the poem it meant that the poem was finished when every part of the poem was significantly related to every other part. And in "The Dance," for instance, where I explore these propositions, inner lines, like dance that the "movement makes co-/ordinate" and even the division of "co-" from "ordinate," are meaningful, so I insist that there are not terms of the poem that are not meaningful. Now I don't *put* the meaning in. There was a rumor at one time that Spicer, because he was trained in linguistics, had poems in which there would be whole areas that were front vowels and whole areas that would be rear vowels and so forth. Well, actually, every time I've tried to teach the feel of where the vowels are in the mouth, I've got very strong prohibition, and yet I feel it's essential that they be felt. But I could not *put* a vowel somewhere in a poem, because I'm bringing out a grain; I'm not *putting* a grain into the wood.

INT: Could you illustrate how you bring out this grain in a particular instance or word?

RD: In "The Dance" I get a line right away: "The Dance / from its dancers circulates among the other / dancers." I'm not putting anything in there, but I've got, as fast as I write it, to recognize everything that's potentially in that. I'm not going to be able to recognize more that's in "circulates" than I have. So what do I do when I'm not writing a poem? I am constantly in study and recognition, not only of what's going on in other poems, but I know that *circ* means "circle" and a million such things about the word "circulates." I acquire language lore. What I am supplying is something like grammar of ornament, I mean grammar of design, or of the possibilities of design. I'm not going to produce everything that circulates, but I'm not going to be caught out of court with some activity of that word "circulates" that I don't want to recognize. We're talking about the negative possibility—if you're unhanded because you refuse to recognize how words work. But my ideal of the poem is that every word be viewed as polysemous, and it can only be governed then by its rhymes and the structure in which it happens; and if you don't recognize all of its polysemous activity it's going to break down the structure. So one of my ideas, then, of the structure of the poem is that it's a constant closing down of an absolutely protean situation until finally you have only one identity. If I'm strictly there, absolutely, not directing but bringing every attention upon every happening within the poem, then I know that everything will bear (what we otherwise would assume) a signature. The reader is also going to be attending to all these phrases; he's forced to attend to the phrases more and more in my poetry because he can't even hit the rhythm unless he is. And it moves faster. It's amazing when Charles talked about "instanter" as he did, because he had some of the same drive toward this insistence. I think all finely articulated poems have this insistence.

INT: Is this insistence always an advantage to you?

RD: The language is not vague in its activities. This becomes a very severe limitation in my poetry; it doesn't produce certain atmospheric possibilities. I can get carried away on certain sensualities—color and several others; you get *lotophagoi* passages, fairly identifiable as coming from Pound, or ideas of enchantment. But I really picture an enchantment which, if you examined it as a Freudian does when he looks at the dream that he thought was an enchantment, you would find, when it's analyzed to its particulars, isn't an enchantment at all.

INT: Do you feel that because the words are charged with multiple meanings you're coming closer to some original language lying behind English?

RD: No, no, not at all. Actually the charge is inherited from Pound's language charged to its utmost degree. The thing was laid down in Imagism in the very first rounds; poetry was language charged. And I read that "charged" as relating to every word, and you'd put in the full charge of language as far as you knew. I "*OED*" a lot. If I weren't fascinated with the language, none of this would be here. It's not *au naturel* that poets do it this way. Quite a few poets pick up "*OED*"ing and I read it as just "*OED*"ing. Particularly, of course, I'm quite divorced in feeling from poets that are inheriting some things from me: Robert Kelly and [Clayton] Eshleman and so forth, because they're projecting a personal psyche. I'm character-structured, not psyche-structured, so I find it quite abhorrent; I can't read them with any pleasure.

INT: What do you mean in "The Dance" when you write, "Lovely our circulations sweeten the meadow"?

RD: I've got very much in mind there the whole tradition of the Morris dance and its sweetening the spring. I also view poetry as participating in certain energies that are present in the language and "sweetening." In my Dante essay I address myself to the sweetness and greatness of Dante. One of my contrasting points with Spicer was that he stood for bitterness as being a reality, and I stood for sweetening. Sweet and bitter, like chiaroscuro, the mixing of dark and light, is an insistence throughout my poetry. So sweetening the meadow is one of the beginning propositions. At the point where I write "sweeten the meadow" I don't have any memories that immediately flashed on the sweetening style of Dante. And the *dolce stil nuovo* is part of my idea of what my tradition in poetry was—clear from Pound's spirit of Romance through to the courses in Kantorowicz to the whole idea of what sweetness meant to the Renaissance. So "sweetening the meadow" is loaded, although that's a very innocent poem; today if I wrote that line it would get heavy. It's not heavy in that poem.

INT: When you "sweeten" language in the Renaissance sense, aren't you bringing something to it that wasn't there before?

RD: Yeah, you bring your dance to the grass. By the way, of course, you're sweetening the idea of the meadow; I would say if I were thinking analytically of it, all dance conceives of itself as sweetening the meadow. The meadow is a field of thought, isn't it, and it's a field of poetry, so you sweeten the poetry in dancing it. Spicer so much opposes it that you find in his poetry an elimination of almost all of the sweetening activities, melody and dance, and a hostility to it, so that in his final lectures he's saying that if a line seems beautiful, cut it out. Not stop it, just cut it out, take the whole line out. Take any area of the poem that seems beautiful out, and this is the contrary to sweetening the meadow.

INT: Do you have strong views on the relation between poetry and performance? For instance, when you do poetry readings is the poetry you're writing ever affected? When you became prominent as a poet, readings were beginning to come back into force again, weren't they?

RD: By 1946 I started reading, and that's part of the reason why in the West we didn't publish. Printing was not the mode of the writing, but writing was still the mode. The performance of the poem was like the performance of a piece of music, and from the beginning I understood it that way. Beethoven exists in his notation, and he's subject to endless interpretation. But since I conceive of the poetry as notation for a performance, but not for a specific performance, certainly not for my voice, when I give a poetry reading I am not giving a poem that preexists; I am giving that particular reading of that text, and it will change all the time. Sometimes, of course, I'm reading the poem and taking it for granted, but in anything as involved as "Passages" I'm always suddenly seeing more possibilities of what it means. I'm readjusting and the notation is fairly exacting; it already contains the whole pattern. One thing I don't dream I do when I read it is give it expression or more emotion than's there. I think the emotion's in the writing, so I object to the Dylan Thomas kind of rhetoric. I am very keen on rhetoric, and consequently object to the Dylan Thomas bathetic reading of a rhetoric, which destroys the structure by putting it across. I really object to expressionism, to *putting into* it something and/or *putting in* more depth.

INT: If your text instructs and directs your performance of that poem, and yet performances can vary, does that mean that the sense gets changed?

RD: No, I'm always returning to the text and the text is the one I'm performing, not some new possibility in that sense. And I haven't listened to enough tapes to know to what degree there is a shift. I know that my way of performing is characteristic enough that somebody else can perform it *au juste*. When I finished "The Soldiers" I sent it off to [Robert]

Creeley. Now I had not myself read it aloud; all of "Passages" grew up around the fact that you have an audience, so they're auditorium pieces. So I hadn't really read it aloud at home—sitting at the table is awkward; it just would be the wrong dimension. I sent it immediately to Creeley when it was finished, and he was teaching a course at Boulder or Aspen. And so within a week of its being finished he read it aloud and they sent me a tape back—and *au juste* a Duncan reading. Creeley, however, has a greater mobility in reading—and appropriately—other people's work than almost any poet I know.

INT: What happens to some of the words that are polysemous, or ambiguous, when you render them in speech and so choose one pronunciation?

RD: My sense when I'm rendering them is that they go toward a neutral position, so they leave open their operation in other parts of the poem. And also I have certain places where the particular lines—and this is more interesting than the polysemous possibilities that are present— establish a kind of irony. And in Dante's case, since the actual world illustrates the spiritual world and also the intellectual world, these three are conceived of as being a harmonious set. In my case they may belong to different systems and one system may be in a kind of joking relation to the other. So a tone may change, and often when I read a passage, I wonder if in any way the peculiar pitch of it is conveyed. But then I hear this is a changing problem in music, as early as the shift between Brahms and Richard Strauss. Brahms's humor is notoriously rollicking—I mean if he's in a humor, he's in a humor; you can't miss it. Meanwhile, in Richard Strauss there are jokes that run through actually excruciatingly passionate passages, and they *are* jokes. There wouldn't have been a joke in Wagner at all. We do have a pitch and it's the pitch of what we're involved in. The thing that Pound so admired in Eliot was that he could contain certain jokes, which Pound really never could. In this Pound is not modern in temperament. If he could have seen a few jokes he would hardly have been enthusiastic about Mussolini; you have to take a second look at your hero to see the joke. Now, it's only if you *have* your hero; if it's not your hero, then there's no joke.

INT: Some critics have suggested that the reader can skip the difficult parts of your poems.

RD: I've asked people writing essays on my poetry to approach the question of the several natures of the reading difficulty. They should ask two questions: "What do you imagine were your reading difficulties?" and "What do you imagine would be a reader's reading difficulties?" In general, a reader's reading difficulties will exceed your own. Well, let's just take the difficulty of reference. Why does Dante come into it? Why in my conversation do I presume that we know something about *Paradise Lost*? I come in heavy over and over again on Milton because Milton was disallowed by Ezra Pound from the main track of poetry, so in general I'm making it impossible for us to read Duncan without both Ezra Pound and Milton. Now, that forces Ezra Pound into a different court, and it forces Milton into a different court, but it also forces a whole track of poetry into a different one. It was one Charles Olson would not accept; and [William Carlos] Williams attacked [T. S.] Eliot for coming back to Milton, but Eliot came back to Milton to put a memorial on top of him. That's not the way I think of my Milton: my Milton is news, not memorial. Not commemorated anywhere. I do not commemorate with my texts, although I revere, I adore, I do a series of things. But I want the reader to be involved with my primary experience. And my primary experience has been not only in Milton or Dante, but also out in the novels of Charles Williams and in Pindar, a bit of a novel, of a thriller, I think it's still read as a thriller. I'm not talking about big stuff. And in Jess's mystery canvases we find Krazy Kat, which most people read as a cartoon, but that's not the way it's being seen. So it is a conglomerate.

INT: Could you explain your use of that term?

RD: Dodds, in *The Greeks and the Irrational*, speaks of our crisis as being whether we carry a conglomerate. He sees the whole Greek civilization as having collapsed because it could not carry its conglomerate. And he says there's no guarantee that a civilization can necessarily carry its conglomerate; if it fails to, then it collapses. It knows the conglomerate is there, and it is no longer carrying it. And you get really serious rifts.

The thing that bolsters all of the Baroque, the decision that Milton made, for instance, is contained in the *Areopagitica* in its insistence that truth is there throughout, and in everything it needs all occasions. That he keeps firm—that its occasion will be found even in things you would want to censor. So you need pornography, you need every part of the range, and Milton doesn't imagine that he's encompassing the range. He's supplying something that's needed, not at the center; it needs Milton, but he is not the artist encompassing the range. Shakespeare is building a world; Milton does not. He builds a stage set like Jonson, and the line from Ben Jonson to Milton is a much more sensible line and an actual one. And Blake is not building a world; he's in the same line as Ben Jonson and Milton.

INT: It's interesting that you used the word "rifts," the same word that Denise Levertov used to describe the jumps one must make in poetry.

RD: Oh, yes; and rifts enter my poems. "The Continent," for instance, with its idea of the movement of masses going back to form a single continent.

INT: And since we're trying to avoid the rifts that you suggest ruin any society not coping with the conglomerate, are the rifts in your poems micro-earthquakes to avoid the actual earthquake?

RD: No, they incorporate rifts as information of the conglomerate, as a way of containing the conglomerate. *The Cantos* had for me the promise of a way the conglomerate would be carried. And I see myself, by the way, as still carrying that conglomerate, so that when an actual poetic genius arrives at the place, it will be there. In other words, so far there is no synthesis of this conglomerate; that's one thing we don't have at all. So the collage actually carries it more adequately; its aesthetics reveal that it can be quite vivid for us. Cubism showed us that we can carry what we thought were contradictory elements in a large composition; but a composition means it's in your mind.

INT: In developing your technique of the collage, were you influenced by what Jess Collins was doing?

RD: Well, his technique of collage has grown, along with my concepts of collage in poetry, since 1950, and in the big leap forward in his collaging period he incorporates many kinds of sources and materials and all of them have content reference, which many collages don't have in a polysemous sense. That's the same period as *Letters* and *Caesar's Gate*, when we were in Majorca. And *Caesar's Gate* begins to be complex collaging, and during the buildup years of *The Opening of the Field* and especially "Passages" we talked about what was going on in assemblage and collage. And our general lifestyle is collage. We don't have a decor in our house; we have an assemblage of objects which have one core of sentiment. A perfect example of the conglomerate—one of the efforts of Modernism, which emerged as a style—was that it thought if it disposed of nineteenth-century sentiment, sentimentality as it began to appear, if it could just rip the nineteenth century away from itself, it could then form a conglomerate of *pure* elements, functional elements. And actually critics very soon found that *A Portrait of the Artist* is a nineteenth-century work, filled with aesthetic sentiments, so it wasn't Modernist in this sense, and they began to observe that about *Ulysses*.

INT: Is this true of Pound also?

RD: Pound never accepted that he wasn't a Modernist, but his critics could see he wasn't. He was sentimental, a troubadour; he was a pure product of having read William Morris and so forth. Well, our conglomerate is not just a contemporary conglomerate. Our conglomerate is our feeling of continuity through time. And it is that which makes our predicament: a point of collapse can be shown to happen after Dante, because Dante doesn't start a Christian culture; he contains the conglomerate at a point when you couldn't believe it could be contained. After him it can't be contained again ever. He contains the conglomerate at a point when the evidence of the Albigensian Crusade was so bloody that you couldn't contain what was called Christendom. But what he did was not a typical medieval poem at all, and it's hard to place it in either the Middle Ages or the Renaissance. But in his imagination it occupied an entire time: it admitted all he knew of the pagan or pre-Christian world. And spacewise it admitted the Moslem world into its theological level; it wasn't *theologically* significant, although it may have been heretically. It was *compositionally* significant, because he made a collage (or assemblage of elements) in the Moslem world of the identity of God that was intolerable unless it was a collage to be in or to enter into the Christian theology. And yet, of course, this is a rather closed picture; the real assemblages of our time would be like *Howl,* where we've got Buddhism going along with Judaism. I find this phenomenon in many directions. Where I would differ from Ginsberg is that I see it not as that kind of amalgam, but for me in the poem it's experienced entirely as a compositional amalgam. I'm not that concerned about my spirit or soul, that's quite true.

INT: I want to take you back to something you've said about language. In *The Truth & Life of Myth* you write: "In the world of saying and telling ... there is a primary trouble, a panic that can still come upon me where the word no longer protects, transforming the threat of an overwhelming knowledge into the power of an imagined reality... but exposes me more." Does this mean that it's good that the language no longer protects and that it lets in more experience?

RD: No; it's just the very nature of it. You proceed along the line of excitement, certainly drawn into the art initially by a series of lures. Among them is one quite analogous with one's entrance into falling in love and sexuality, in which an energy appears and then an excitement which exceeds the one which you encompass in your personality, so you are transcendent—transcendent in its whole context. In general, in falling in love you feel identical with the universe, so the entire scene changes all the way to the horizon. It's the same thing being in love in the language, but all of those states are perilous. Always the quarrel with being in love is your domesticated imagined reality, which is within the bounds of the actual. Our word "suffer" struck me first in John Dewey; as a Pragmatist, when he's talking about experience, he talks about "suffering" something, "suffering" joy, "suffering" grief. We suffer, so we're in John Dewey-land; and you'd think a Pragmatist was far removed from this scene. Every bit of what we call experience is the Cross. Every bit of actual experiencing is passional, and Dewey is not a Neoplatonist, who disapproved of passions. Kathleen Raine wants to make Blake vote for the Neoplatonists; it won't work, because Blake is entirely a passional artist. And yet passional is not a pure position at all. It threatens every level of your imagined reality, and the imagination is not passional in its nature.

INT: But you're attracted by that threat?

RD: Plotinus's is a sublime imagination, as if the imagination could occupy all of creation, and I find it abhorrent and attractive. So the lure is mixed. You go into a poem, and it promises more of you than you know of, and a you more true to yourself, but it must promise that to the reader as well. There's an opening in language in which I'm going to be able to exist. But that opening is also an opening into perilous difficulties which you don't quite feel at first. My poems are all hopelessly inadequate. My early poems, of course, are in every occasion hopelessly inadequate. In the beginning you think that they ought to become adequate. Finally, in my case that's not what's at issue; it's knowing what's happening, not its adequacy to a situation. And to know what's happening in a poem is not to drive or control it, but to know where it is, and the *where it is* is the condition of it. And you almost sense it by the dread in every situation. My concept of the minimum of the poem is a place where the complete poem is happening, and in that place it apprehends and contributes to every other minimum in the poem. So the total poem remembers all its parts and doesn't have the factor of going from one place to another. As you move from line 1 to line 2, line 2 begins not to have every opportunity in the world, because everything in line 1 is there. It's a decreasing series of opportunities, so it's coming into our imagined domesticity. It's increasingly domesticated. But it's also, because it's going along the line of risk, increasingly endangered. I do not picture any domestic situation—unless it was sound asleep—as not being more and more at the pitch of this dread. Why does it increase? Otherwise after twenty-five or twenty-six years we would not be more filled with protections against that dread, but we would have to let them go and be living rather habitually. Maybe we are.

INT: You're saying that your poems need to go into a place where the word no longer protects?

RD: As the poem really gets there, the word doesn't protect at all. In the original lure you thought there might be something—the word promises. I think the poem is entirely a protective form. The realization of form that's in the poem is analogous to the use of a pentagram in magic, where you're going to call up demonic powers. You measure accurately, and you close all the things, and you have more and more complicated features of the poem to cover its situation. But I'm talking here, of course, about proposing a poetry that's going to be more open. If you open rifts and you still conceive that you're in this territory of suffering the situation of the poem, you are opening up rifts that you *have* to suffer for. They must be part of the lure of the poem. Of course, it is for me. The rifts are not merely open because I'm bored by going, or I *see*, but because I'm tremendously aware that what I see is not the only thing that's there. There's a reply from a Hasidic master: students ask, "Why don't you write, master?" And he says, "Because whenever I open my mouth to say anything, the world floods in and drowns me." And I say, "Yes, brother." Now that's the rift part of it—the world. You've got to be flooded by the world, and yet, more and more, *how* to be flooded by the world becomes the question of the artist.

On the New Poetics

(with L. S. Dembo, 1967)

This interview was conducted in 1967 by the late L. S. Dembo, longtime editor of Contemporary Literature. *There is an extensive, fascinating exchange about the Adams Cantos in Ezra Pound's* Cantos, *Cantos that some readers find unpoetic and lacking in deep meaning. Robert Duncan sees these Cantos as poems having a collage-like quality, with complex inner rhymes "like fast Stravinsky." "We're not diverted by the development of metaphor and theme. Everything is in the sound." Similarly, the catalogs and unadorned factual passages in* The Maximus Poems *function "like a magical evocation." Duncan was not entirely satisfied with the results of this interview and tried for a time to rework some of it for clarity. This is its first publication.*

—Ed.

L. S. DEMBO: Mr. Duncan, I'd like to begin with a fundamental question. Given the difficulty of your poetry and that of Charles Olson, with whom you've been closely associated, how do you view the relations of the poet and his reader? To bring up the old controversy, does the poet have to communicate something in order to reach an audience?

ROBERT DUNCAN: I imagine the answer to that depends on what you think can be done with language. Take Olson's *Maximus,* where part of the design is that this entity "Maximus" is going to be able to come into existence only in the poem—because while it resembles Charles and has access to Charles's experience, it's not Charles. Now that poem is existing in relation to the reader in the same way it exists in relation to Olson reading the poem as he writes it. As a matter of fact, he's the first person who gets to read it. Many poets don't read. For instance, take an awfully good one like Robert Frost—while he writes a poem, he does not read one. So nothing happens at that level.

LD: Exactly what do you mean by that?

RD: Well, the writer, let's say, following images and meanings which are composed along the lines of melody or along the lines of rhythms and impulses, gives the poem its own entity, but as a reader, he will ask the question that you are asking about the reader in general. Now the poet as a reader may be very interested in the poem *not* reaching him. He might be interested, for one thing, in the fact that, as I read *Maximus*, only too soon does everything compose, and I think it's very strong in Charles to want to have propositions that won't compose in that way. In something like *Maximus* or my later work the thing that made for a conversion point was Williams's *Paterson*. On any immediate level that you look at in that poem, quite an exciting formal thing is happening. I don't mean that simplistic form that Williams takes over from *Finnegan* in which a man is compared to a city stretched out like a giant and a woman is compared to a river, or Joyce's cyclic year form that he also borrows. Temperamentally, he knows these forms are large and give a kind of field to almost any kind of poem. But *Paterson* happens to be very much more interesting in its movement. Williams thought that was a form, and yet obviously by the time he came to Book Four he felt that he ought to have a fifth, because he himself must have been crushed by this 1-2-3-4 thing.

LD: And this *movement* was what you called a "conversion point" for you?

RD: Yes. My own experience as *Paterson* began to come out—and it was on that occasion that I felt the combination of *The Pisan Cantos* and *Paterson* most strongly—made me not want to go on any longer as in my earlier work but to undertake something similar. And certainly to imagine a poetry which would be an *open* thing. One knew right away in reading *The Pisan Cantos* that Pound must clearly no longer be writing a poem that was a hundred cantos long—and it was clear because *The Pisan Cantos* had such a great and absolutely moving reality that Pound certainly could no longer be thinking that he was producing heaven, purgatory, and hell in any Dantean sense. That's simply not what we were reading.

LD: You don't believe that a mythic or historical theme is being developed in *The Cantos*, then—one with a beginning, middle, and end, so to speak?

RD: Well, look at the Adams and Jefferson Cantos, which are absolutely unyielding of the historical meaning we would expect them to have—I mean of the poet's intuition of history. Now if you were setting about like Dante, they would have to yield such a meaning. The fact that they didn't means that Pound himself must have been puzzled. There he was: he knew that it must go the way it did, because he could feel it—the poem has a way of dictating itself. But if you reflect on it, the whole section becomes at least, for one thing, a metaphor of how thoroughly blocked his mind was in relation to Adams and Jefferson. He wanted to have these Cantos say something, but they became symptomatic without the poet coming to the stage where he was able to read the symptoms.

LD: You're saying, in a sense, that Pound's approach is the opposite of Dante's?

RD: Yes. For one thing Dante and Cavalcanti sat around in a group and talked about love, and when they sat down to write, they had an area of agreement about what they were going to say. But when Pound and Williams corresponded with each other, they dismissed all the major things poetry is going to say. They said, you know, we've had enough of that talk about love. As a matter of fact, they had had none of it.

And so, at the point, let's say, of introducing politics, Pound had only the intuition of a Jefferson or an Adams, although that one was quite right. They are the only two we could take that would clearly give us voices that stand for what would be a rational government. And yet the whole poem in which they're appearing is one which does not have an eighteenth-century center for its order or its "government." Pound takes up Confucius from eighteenth-century sources—which is, after all, what was interesting in the Adams and Jefferson sections. And yet, though profoundly anti-Taoist, Pound tries to make an anti-Taoist Confucius. Yet *The Cantos* themselves are an order of exactly the opposite kind. They *are* the kind of order that depends very much on something like the Taoist.

It becomes apparent in *The Pisan Cantos* that all those long cantos of Adams and Jefferson can go on because they're like chunks of a man's mind. But had Pound understood what the potential was, they would have begun to move.

LD: And you say that all this applies to your own and Olson's poetry—or, in other words, that you yourselves are trying to realize the potentiality of this kind of "form"?

RD: Right. Charles certainly had the same discontent and expressed it first. That's part of what he's doing in proposing the poem as a field. We both felt that *The Pisan Cantos* and *Paterson* make very clear the job in poetry that is exciting. And this is a matter of temperament, of wanting a kind of adventure in the poem. Also, both Charles and I share the fact that we're intellectuals; that is, we not only want our feet dancing, but our brain dancing as well. It's at that time I realized that, well, the brain is an organ we've been rather ashamed about, as if the mind existed apart from another one of those physical organs, or as if the poet ought not take mental pleasure in the poem.

Now Dante took mental pleasure because he liked holding ideas and arranging them and talking philosophy and love. D. H. Lawrence can be taken as a man of ideas that have moved things, but he had such a conflict, that he's like a "sexy puritan." He liked the voluptuousness of this little organ in here between the ears, and at the same time he disapproved of it. You shouldn't think about sex, Lawrence would say. So you get a man who's angry every time he's having the pleasure of his ideas. He can only think if his thinking is combined with anger because anger's the only thing that will override his prohibition that you shouldn't use that dirty little organ between your ears.

LD: Let me interrupt you for a moment. Didn't you say in "Yes, As a Look Springs to Its Face" that "I write my poems for unthinking things"? Wouldn't that contradict this whole poetic that you've been developing?

RD: But I was talking about the brain having pleasure, not thinking.

LD: Doesn't the brain take pleasure in thinking?

RD: I don't have the experience of thinking when I'm writing poetry. Certainly I don't feel the poem as a problem, for instance, that I'm trying to find the solution for. The experience I have in a poem is very much as if my brain were dancing, not thinking. Right now I'm trying to think what thinking is and something very different happens than when we were talking before and going along with meanings and ideas—if I can get that across....

LD: Yes, well, I think the dance metaphor is what does it here.

RD: Well, actually I've got a lot of references to the brain dancing, and so I must mean something else by those "unthinking things" you mentioned. Oh, I know: When you're dancing and you're still counting in order to waltz to a piece of music, you're thinking with your feet. And as long as you're doing that, you're not dancing. You've got to get to the place where the numbers have entered your feet.

LD: And this is what you do in your poetry?

RD: Yes, with language. When I'm writing a poem, I no longer have access to the meaning of a word. I use the *OED* not because I think I can give the word a history or because I can get to a root meaning, but because the *OED* provides me with a story—an immediate sort of material right there. If I were thinking, I'd be thinking about the definitions and meanings, and that's the last thing I want to do. My poetry is filled with talk about boundaries, and especially intriguing to me is that the universe has only the boundaries that we imagine and so we're constantly imagining other boundaries.

I think of a poem as taking place on the ground of language, which is a pure creative ground. We don't make up language ourselves, and we don't think it. The *OED* snaps me out of what a word does mean. It gives me reference all the way across to the word as it actually exists in a communal sense, and I work with words thinking of them as communal, not expressing something in me. It's like the absorption of a child building with blocks. He's not thinking; he's building architectures.

LD: Just what do you mean by "communal"?

RD: Well, any experience we have that might be our own individually can reappear only by its participating in a language which we didn't originate. When I'm talking, I may not be immediately confronted by the commonality of language, but I am when I'm really composing in a poem—especially as we do when we've driven that musical phrase of Pound's back to the place where every word is potentially active.

LD: Well, where does this idea about "imagining boundaries" fit in?

RD: You mean about the universe having only the boundaries that we imagine? One of the things the imagination does is *to draw*—and actually an area that is very important in our intelligence is making drawings. In our culture, still thinking about human values, we tend to believe we're producing pictures or being artists. But children are *exploring,* as long as they're painting in their own styles. And they're exploring what I'm talking about, boundaries and ground: then great artists come back to it. The same thing goes on in a poem. In poetry we show that the whole world of meanings we live in are imagined boundaries that are drawing and redrawing a figure—that are endlessly producing figures. It's like Gestalt.

And in this sense words have exactly their own reproduction of the total universe because they are of the same process that's going on in it. Here I'm more interested in the way in which, as human beings, we are not merely humans, but chemical facts, and in our mass can be related to things. The behavior of human beings in a mass, for instance, can tell us much about the behavior of cells in a microbe.

LD: We seem to be getting into biology now.

RD: As a matter of fact, there are some biology books that point this out. A community of bees or of human beings is like a community of cells, and all life-forms seem to have a message that can be read in this way. And yet that seems to be degrading to our human values; the struggle that the humanist has against statistics is the one of not imagining what this thriving ground of life is telling us. He keeps thinking the human being is the living thing and everything around is for him.

But I want to get back to words here, which are absolutely a process of life. It's true they disappear into air, but they bear the same stamp—and the real message they are going to bring is about something much more fundamental than personality. And their vitality is going to exist in the way they group and disgroup themselves. We can *make* them do certain things, but no matter how we make them do it—get into a sonnet form or something else—the real thing is that we can go from one man's sonnet to another and find them entirely different in texture.

LD: But how is this idea related to your theories of form?

RD: Well, a poem has its composition from intuitions that are not only like normal intuitions but have behind them the fact that we are thrilled by the patterns of our actual chemical being. They are intuitions about balance, movement, and so forth.

Now our consciousness wants to participate in things, but form exists and it is through form that consciousness must actually participate. It's certainly curious that we pose chaos or formlessness, because it so happens that all our areas of consciousness proceed by form. Seeing is form: you're somehow aware there's a lot of data, but the eye happens to make a form out of it, and consequently we see. We have intuitions that could be of chaos—and yet we really can't experience chaos, because we have no apparatus for it—because experience itself is only form.

LD: This seems like a Kantian conception. But let's get back to the poetry itself.

RD: That's my point. In language we're in an area which is just like the one our senses absolutely form. Why, then, a poem? What happens when the form is intensified and begins to operate differently from prose—when the form begins to operate very intensely for the person writing it and then for the person reading it, so that every single part is resonant in every other part? We finally arrive at what looks like art, but actually is a deepening intuition or increasing consciousness of our operation and form. We are participating fully in the world of forms. This kind of thing, of course, is too exciting to keep up, and I'm terribly dependent on having some inertia between writing poems.

We'd be out of our minds, for instance, if we really participated in the intricacy of our total body composition. Your consciousness would love to exist in a larger and larger area, but it would be mad long before it got to the place where it was aware of—participating in—its atomic structure. In imagination our consciousness begins to participate in other forms, and it also draws back. You can only go as far as you can tolerate, even though you can tolerate orders that increase far beyond your reach. So you draw boundaries around you and they go out a *little* beyond your reach. In language you just have to . . . those sounds! And we work with what look like very simple ones. How many actual vowels do we have . . . 10? 8? 9?

LD: Would you say that these ideas are similar to Olson's theory of "proprioception"?

RD: They would be similar because Olson did have a lot of influence on me, although those proprioception notes are very rocky compared with the lectures he made earlier. The main thing in the *Projective Verse* piece was picturing poetry as a field of activities related to a larger field of activities. He thought of that larger field as one of energies moving in history—in which almost any man unknowingly is participating in activity that actually stems from the beginning of human history. But what do you do when you begin to imagine history so that it comes to be present right where you are? Whitehead talks about this in *The Aims of Education*. You're not really removed from it at all, because the minute you imagine it, you're participating in very early events.

Now if you wanted to investigate what really happened, your participation only becomes more complex. You begin to get a fugal action, something as complex as Bach, with several layers going at once. And your anxiety increases because you cannot go intensely farther without an intensifying form. That's one thing a poem does: it's a particular kind of intensity.

LD: A "high-energy construct," I think Olson calls it.

RD: That's what he calls it, yes. But sometimes poets want to diffuse their excitement and so they don't want a high-energy construct, or they want a construct that will at least neutralize the energy that is painful. That is, both painful and pleasurable. And the poem does have a goal, I think, of arriving at a place where it is productive rather than self-consuming. Getting back to that earlier point, one of the problems in our discontent with *Paterson,* and in our realization that maybe *The Pisan Cantos* had no terminus, was how to participate intensely in forms without bringing them to a conclusion. For instance, the conventional poem permits an area of certain intensity by formalizing a beginning and an end. It thought of a creator who did the same with the world; that is, it saw the world as a paradigm and in the Deist period thought of it as having a happy conclusion. So it had no conflict. And the poem was supposed to arrive at such a self-supporting system.

But certainly Charles did not think of the body itself or the human species as self-supporting. If you knew evolution, you wouldn't think of man as an end result unless you had hindsight too, because it happens that all forms of life today are evidences of what life's forms in general are. Now the questions that Olson asked—the relation of the word and the poet and what he was experiencing in the line, what was the real root in relation to the language—were based on his readings in morphology.

He was interested in linguistic morphology, the life and evolution of forms in the word itself and in the word as syntax. After Stein and Joyce and Virginia Woolf, you almost had to consider the problem. Now Charles went back to physical morphology and saw that the universe puts its stamp on everything and that it's one universe. And, like me, he became very excited when the one consistent theory came up again— the idea that one continent separated into a number of continents and is in the process of congealing again into a single continent. *Maximus* begins to bring in the actual geology of that; only in a few places, like around Labrador, do we actually see the movement. And that's the way Charles wants the poem to move: from a oneness back to a one-ness, but so slowly and so far beyond its own lifetime that it cannot conceivably be composed. And yet it does keep composing into forms. That's the other part of the experience; he tries to undo the forms. In the parts that he read at Vancouver, which still haven't been printed, he becomes too thematic and I was a little disappointed. You're composing too soon, I thought. Certain things were hurrying up and being done and not done.

LD: But can't this "morphological" theory be used to excuse a great deal? The Adams Cantos of Pound that we were talking about, for example, are actually just fragments of words and phrases, with the transitions excised—from John Quincy Adams's biography of his grandfather. And many of the *Maximus* poems are simply documents or catalogs.

RD: Denise Levertov would agree with you. She can't accept this operation, which actually has attracted not only poets but painters who have gone in for collage. You wonder what the artist has done. He hasn't painted anything; he's lifted somebody else's thing and put it in the middle. But those elements in a collage are like signs or intuitions. Even if Pound himself didn't come close to understanding what those Adams poems are doing in *The Cantos,* my temptation would be to try to understand the kind of poetry in which something like that could appear. I think Pound was proceeding by *feel* at that point. Certainly his generation believed that "beautiful thoughts" and "deep feelings" were not so important as the feel of the language. So Pound takes bits of phrases as if he felt them to have a certain quality, but he doesn't allow them to follow through to their meanings or to their original quality at all. It's like assemblage sculpture, but he isn't making another figure out of it and that's why we find it baffling.

Well, these fragments don't produce emotional upheavals, so I suppose the average reader is left terrifically cold. He's faced with words that are inert. Stein, for example, is witty and eventually you can see that she isn't wholly abstract. She gives me all the pleasures of reading without the rewards. But Pound didn't intend his readers to get any pleasure—he meant to force the "feeling." That's what I still get from *The Cantos*—the pure feel of English words without any distractions.

LD: By the "feel of words" you mean just what?

RD: The way they go. Now I think Pound meant more than that. I think he felt that, say, the words of Van Buren contained within themselves *arête,* a strength that would be a kind of intaglio. We wouldn't ask, "What did the man think?" or "What's he saying?" Rather he would *feel* the stamp of the man. Pound very much believed that men had such stamps.

He depended a great deal upon it and that's why the Chinese characters were so important to him. They started operating later as symbols and meaningful elements, but most important was that they were a stamp, like the shape of a poem in general.

LD: Are you saying the poem as a whole is *a stamp*?

RD: I'm saying that a poem has an absolute distinctive shape in itself, which is part of what the poet experiences. And this seems to be the poem essentially... what most intrigues the artist. We have the *feel* of Jefferson and the *feel* of Adams, or at least the way Pound felt them, without any idea of what he felt *about* them or what they meant to him. The ideogram is the shape you make, and for Pound it was the shape of history, the list of people that you're going to look at.

LD: But what about the feel of words as words? Isn't there a rhythmic element involved?

RD: That's what I was getting to. There's a passage from Canto 65 that really shows what I mean by getting the feel of the language. We're not diverted by development of metaphor or theme. Everything is in the sound. This is at the bottom of page 124:

> Mlle Bourbon is grown very fat, Chatham so dampened the
> zeal of Sardegna
> BLUSH, oh ye records!
> congress has XX'd me
> How will they wash it? I
> dined with M. Malesherbes uncle of Luzerne
> tiers état contains 30 classes
> Dined at Passy: S'il règne un faux savoir
> which inflexibility has been called vanity Policy
> of frog court to lay stumbling block
> between England and America

Now what's going on all the way through here is fine little syncopated rhythms of place rhymes. We are almost certain, for instance, that he says *Passy* because he's just had *classes* and he follows it with *inflexibility*, on the right beat. Now there are no major ideas of Pound developing here, nor is this rhythm Adams's. Adams's sentences don't move this way; they're much more balanced, although probably not as much so as Jefferson's. And Adams wouldn't say "frog court."

LD: Well, doesn't "frog court" put a jarring note into the whole passage?

RD: No, because you've got "un faux savoir." It comes because of "faux savoir" to "frog court." It's *music* that tells us he wanted to use "frog court," which makes for a disjunction and consequently heightens that jazzy syncopation. But what I really wanted to say is that in reading this passage we aren't able to expand by metaphor, or if we do, we'll be exhausted before we get very far. But look at the sense of rhythmic structure: "congress" and "double-crossed"—and "tiers," which would be related to "30." I meant there are very little subtle plays, and it's all going by the sound.

LD: If this passage is all a matter of sound, though, what is to distinguish it from highly rhythmical gibberish?

RD: I don't think it would have to be distinguished, because here a poet is simply showing his skill in manipulation of the language. Though I'm sure Pound meant to give a tone of Adams, didn't he?

LD: Right. And he *is* saying something, isn't he?

RD: Well, "congress has double XX'd me," meaning the Congress did double-cross the President—"How will they wash it?" All right, if we immersed ourselves in the whole situation of the poem and we got the material that's been reset here and put into music, we might arrive at the reasoning back of it. Why did he pick this and how does it fit, and so forth? But these elements are remote from the poem; that is, the poem refers to them rather than being built with them.

LD: I can see your point very clearly. The question is whether this passage is really rhythmical.

RD: Well, at least there seems to me to be a very high music in "congress has double XX'd me / How will they wash it? I / dined with M. Malesherbes uncle of Luzerne / tiers état contains 30 classes / Dined at Passy."

LD: That really appeals to you?

RD: It absolutely sends me! My God, to be able to place rhymes like that! It's like listening to Satie—no, he's even simpler than this. It's very much like fast Stravinsky. And it's the kind of thing that makes poets gasp at what Pound can do in the writing of a line. Because with inner rhymes, you see, words have to be placed so they create a balance. Now this isn't always a balance that shifts forward—it's a much harder thing to do than to write end rhymes. You can't calculate it—you have to have an absolute feel for it. I'm not even tempted to figure out how the ideas operate. I have a pure sensation of the mastery of this writing from the way Pound manages that long passage—and it goes on much longer than I've read.

LD: Would this argument apply to *Maximus,* which does seem to have something in common with *The Cantos*?

RD: Charles will certainly present situations like the ones found in the Adams Cantos. "The Record," for instance, really throws people. This is on page 117 [of *Maximus*]:

> Here we have it—the goods—from this Harbour,
>
> 1626, to Weymouth (England) consigned to
>
> Richard Bushrod and Company
> & Wm Derby and Company

fr Cape An   dry fish[1]
corfish[2]
train oil[3]
quarters of oak
skins:...

And so forth. Now this is very straightforward compared to the Pound. The document is coherent all the way through—it hasn't been shuffled around. It also extends as a metaphor, even though Charles loathes the idea of a metaphor and would like to get away from it. Its prototype is that passage in *Paterson* in which they're drilling for water.

LD: You mean that table [in Book Three] of what was found at each stratum?

RD: That's it. Now we understand it immediately in the context as drilling for water in a period of absolutely dry language. We're no longer reading it as just a document. Now this is precisely what Pound does not do. Pound does not want us to reconstruct a meaning, because he has already *deconstructed* it from its original context, so we can't follow it as we did in Charles's piece and recognize right away what it is. But neither Charles's poem nor this passage in Williams is composed as music. It's in prose, anyway.

Actually, Charles's lists, "they required / 7 hundredweight biscuit bread / @15 / per hundred" and so on, may be thought of as a kind of magic operation. You almost have to read the *Maximus* passage metaphor- ically. One thing that Gloucester colony is is the colony that poetry is. In his lecture at Berkeley, Charles said at one point: the colonists wanted to come to Paradise, and they were no sooner there, when they wanted to cash in on it. "And that's what you do with language," he said. "You no sooner have got a poem started, than you want to start cashing in on it—to have it start producing things." This, of course, is part of Charles's whole historical vision of an original Golden Age, after which everything falls. Usually he gives 1500 BC, the century of the Aryan migrations and the great language changes, as the critical date.

Incidentally, that's one place where I have a fundamental difference with Olson. He goes into etymology, because he's going to the time when men were Adam and the word was Adamic. Whereas, to me, Adam is the sum total of all men who have ever lived. In *Letters* I realize that he must contain Mae West and Hitler; we can't discard any of humanity if we're going to examine what the final Adam age is. It's the same with language: the earliest root we can find is not really early; it's simply one of those parts of the total life of the word.

LD: Could you elaborate on this totality concept of man? It seems to go back to what you were saying about "communality."

RD: Well, I mean, in a sense, that we are fulfilled not only in just one chapter, but in all the other human beings that have existed and will exist, because we're fulfilled in the total human thing. But I don't think the total human thing is the universe. The universe fulfills itself in many forms besides man. On the other hand, I think a man might tell us a lot about the shape of the universe, because the universe is undoubtedly printed. The essential message is everywhere within it. That is why I think the poem can bear the real thing in language and why it gets beyond our reach in the areas that we feel. Meaning is men, but when you get into poetry and become more excited about sound, you have already gotten beyond what you think is your human area. You share that experience with animals and babies. As I was saying, that is a larger area of the poem, and the largest of all is the one that includes intuitions of form—when we are responding at a genuinely physical or chemical level. All the universe may be pressing us with such feelings of form—or sequence in time. After all, the universe shares with the poem movement through time and eternal being, and it also shares projections of space and things that are sounds.

LD: But getting back to Olson, you were saying that "The Record" was metaphorical in a way that the Adams Cantos were not....

RD: Yes—and moreover it's like a magic evocation. If you are working magic and making a potion, you would have to have such a list—what the colonists required in order to set up Paradise in the New World. Now we think, of course, that there's nothing magic about it: you had to live through a winter, so you needed "7 hundredweight biscuit bread / 7 hhds of beere or sider / 2/3 hhd beef" and so forth. But only if we go through that list do we comprehend how absolutely solid is what one needs to get through that winter. The colonists didn't know about the winter so it's pure calculation—what they took with them to perform the magic of getting through the winter. Their formula was wrong; things didn't develop into Paradise.

LD: Well, that's one way of looking at it.

RD: But, don't you see? This kind of magic runs throughout the whole poem. There's a little song of Maximus—what is it? "In a time of fullness, go with your ass bare"—and it's really instructive. It's Heraclitean magic to be sure that you keep the strife going so that you "get on with it," as Charles put it in *Projective Verse*. And it also means that when the poem seems to be good be sure to prevent it from really getting there: man thwarting himself in order to prevent himself from being realized, when realization would be too quick.

I may be reading something into this, because I had a notion like it when I was working on *Letters*. It began to occur to me that if I *saw* an idea, then so would the reader. So I'd better get on to something else.

LD: One might call it de-composition.

RD: Yes, and decomposition in the physical or biological sense too. There's an image I'm working on (so I really shouldn't talk about it) having to do with cells and meanings. In cancer, cells are invaded by viruses and the cell is either willing to die, and it then spills out viruses like a pod, or it is unwilling to die and begins to multiply itself instead of multiplying the original virus. Well, metaphorically, *meaning* is like the virus, and the cell can give back those meanings or it can keep the meanings inside and become productive of itself. Cancer cells no longer have the key to an orderly interrelationship with other cells and simply swarm all over each other.

LD: Are you saying that *The Cantos* and *Maximus* are cancerous, then?

RD: No ... well, yes, that's true. They make an enormous ... No, I really don't think this applies to them.

LD: But what about the way they proliferate themselves?

RD: They do, but so do I. I proliferate poems all over the place.

LD: That's true, but your poems don't yield their meanings that easily either.

RD: No. So they probably are cancerous, because they form great mounds. But we don't know what the cancer's doing. It's very bad when human beings get cancer, but look at it from the point of view of life or nature in general. There are cells which, after all, are individual units and as far as they're concerned the body is just their "neighborhood" or city. Just at a time we're facing overpopulation in our bodies. And in our language we're facing overpopulation. I've got to manage language like someone managing traffic coming in by the twenty tons. I want to see every layer of that traffic. One of the ways you keep cool with a word is not to remember it's got a life—to let it be just what it was in, say, the eighteenth century. But you don't keep cool if you insist that the story be ever-present. And that's what a cancer is: the cell ever-present; more than one cell in one place.

LD: That's an interesting analogy.

RD: Oh, but it's not an analogy. It's an activity going on all over the universe and in various areas of ourselves.

LD: The universe is a single, vast activity?

RD: Well, we have to admit that human activity is part of the activity of the cosmos. It is my keen feeling that life itself, from its beginning cell, is some cooperation of the radioactivity of the sun and the life of the stars and whatever chemicals were present in that first water, chemicals which we manufacture inside our bodies in order to be like the water was in that original period. We are literally—it's no myth—or else it's both myth and reality provided by biophysics—we are so literally children from those rays of the sun and the stars, that when they happen to irradiate again, we mutate and are potentially another species. And the beginning of life is something that happens in chemistry when you have those irradiations of light. That light makes it possible for them to produce the water.

LD: Well, all this is very interesting, but it does seem to me that your poetry is often concerned with more specifically human problems, even when it appears to have a cosmic dimension. For example, in "A Poem Beginning with a Line by Pindar"—that anthology-piece that everybody has read—you wrote, "There is the hero who struggles east / widdershins to free the dawn and must / woo Night's daughter, / sorcery, black passionate rage, covetous queens, / so that the fleecy sun go back from Troy, / Colchis, India . . . all the blazing armies / spent, he must struggle alone toward the pyres of Day." Now actually doesn't the poem *compose* here, in your sense of the word? There seems to be a coherent, internal conflict going on, which on at least one level would signify the experience of the poet. In "The Structure of Rime" sequence doesn't the poet struggle to master language or apprehend the Master of Rime, undergo anxieties and terrors? That is, he must "woo the Night" or descend into the depths before he can reach the "pyres of Day" or apprehend some kind of Logos. I know I may be reducing it to a kind of cliché. . . .

RD: Specifically what was on my mind, as the passage was unfolding, is the story of Jason freeing the fleece at Colchis. Medea is one of the daughters of the sun, who binds the sun so that it cannot rise, and Jason must free it, to make his trip in the other direction. He has gone into black magic because he has to go against the direction of the sun to release it at its beginning point. But I had no sooner started with this idea, than I thought of Alexander, who also went against the sun. It's a haunting thing in history, because going against the sun, he destroyed his whole civilization. Hellenism passes into its Hellenistic stage. But he also returns and dies—that's his "pyres of Day."

I always have trouble with the word "sun" and it often operates in my poetry with the word "night" because of their full puns. "Sun" itself is always "son" and they come together in Christ, but they also refer to myself as my mother's son, or father's, the son. Especially since I too was freed. I returned to my birth name (Duncan) from my adopted name (Symmes) and released from this other, third, identity. Somehow this widdershins movement, doing something in reverse order, counting back, has been very meaningful to me.

LD: Then you definitely would not want to read those lines as I have read them—metaphorically or symbolically?

RD: Oh, but I would. I'm only telling you what was on my mind when I was writing the passage. It's just that when you have so straightforward a theme, it almost makes the poem unnecessary. You could just announce it, put it up in letters.

LD: But a poem can have a theme and still be a poem, can't it? I know "Structure of Rime" doesn't "compose" quickly, but it does seem to have a certain content.

RD: When I started that sequence at Black Mountain, I announced that I was giving myself permission to have a prose poem in which things would talk to me. I would let rhyme tell me certain things about itself, instead of the other way around. At the same time, I wanted to do an open series—one that does not have a beginning or end, but simply takes place. It refers to a very real realm that exists: I *go* to it, I don't make it up.

So I ask the sentence, "Speak! For I name myself your master," and the text speaks back to me: *"Have heart . . . you that were heartless."* I have the full thrill of reading a text right while I'm writing it. *"Suffering joy or despair / you will suffer the sentence / a law of words moving / seeking their right period."* It's almost like watching a movie, or you might say simply that it's a hypnagogic experience. I'm receiving certain things and I'm initiating others. Now that's very much the "Structure of Rime"—over and over again. Even when you come to the image of Glélé in VII, that big African fetish figure driven full of nails. When I say, "These are the counsels of the Wood," then I'm listening to the wood, from which I've never heard, although I apprehend it immediately as the wood of Glélé and the wood of Christ.

LD: Well, you've certainly been most informative on this matter. I wonder whether you'd like to talk for a while about Black Mountain College. Exactly what was the philosophy of what a student should learn?

RD: Well, as you know, when Charles became rector of the College in 1954, he began to make it a center for the writing of poetry. He was aiming at something like those colleges the Celts used to have for their bards, where you would submerge a candidate in a tub of water for fourteen hours or all night long in icy water and make him emerge from it having composed and being able to recite by heart an epic poem. Education becomes a trial: you're not aiming at discovering the potentialities of the individual or how he will develop them, but you want the student to undergo the ordeal whereby he will become "the Poet"—acquire an "office."

But as for myself, going there in 1956, I taught two courses: one in beginning techniques in poetry and the other in the meaning of forms. Then in the summer I taught a course in Rimbaud's *Illuminations*, which we read in French—though the students were more confident than I was about the linguistic problem.

LD: The techniques course was essentially prosodic, I imagine.

RD: Well, we never dealt with the poem; we dealt with exercises. Beginning with vowels, moving toward a structure of tone-leading by vowels, and then going on to consonant-clusters, syllables, and stresses. I didn't know about "junctures" at the time to describe them, and certainly not enough to teach them. There's a difference between feeling something as an artist and being able to present it as a teacher. Anyway, it was a very rich time for me, as far as developing my own techniques went. One thing I discovered was that I do not have a syllabic measure beyond three or four syllables. There was one girl in my class who had an accurate measure of eleven. She could write an eleven-syllable line without having to count. Dante tells us of a Provençal poet who could go up to thirteen or fourteen. But if I get a word that's more than three syllables long, just the word itself, I have to analyze it consciously. Well, I guessed that this student was going to have trouble in stress, and she did—was almost in tears over it. Yes, I was teaching prosody, but a prosody based on linguistic elements.

LD: Was there any special ideology at the school—beyond the merely technical, that is?

RD: Well, in the '50s [Robert] Creeley and Olson were asking themselves questions that Denise Levertov never asked herself, questions they'd inherited from Williams. And that was what was the nature of the American experience? Now I'm not interested in that problem at all.

Creeley viewed himself as the New England conscience and the New England spirit. Even in so late a volume as *Words* you'll still have some intimations of it. And Charles will view himself as an American; *Maximus* represents something of the experience in Gloucester. I suppose that even in the Pindar poem and "Apprehensions" there are Western elements, although I don't try to present the Western experience at large. Certainly not in the way that, say, Robin Blaser would—he says in his brief biography that he's from Idaho and that his poetry tries to return to that area. And Charles's later *Bibliography on America for Ed Dorn* advises taking an area of the country and knowing it thoroughly. This is an inheritance of what [C. P.?] Snow and [F. O.] Matthiessen at Harvard taught him in relation to how you'd write on Melville. You'd have to know thoroughly all the economics, and so forth. (This, of course, was the '30s.) So at Black Mountain the question was, "What is the American thing?" and there was a great prohibition against the European, though the school gradually moved to a more cosmopolitan position such as Pound's.

My own feeling is that just as we should discard race, certainly we ought to discard ideas of nationality. It's Man as a totality that's the interesting thing. And Charles moved toward this conception. His Hittites are closer to him than the Americans. And so are his Mayans and Sumerians. But what was not taught at Black Mountain is just as interesting as what was. Henry James was not taught, for example. He was not the American language. Pound's essay will show you [how] little he was paying [attention] to the real nature of James.

LD: Just one more question—although it's a leading one. Among the poets writing today, whom do you most respect?

RD: Well, two poets that I consider superior to myself in technique are [Louis] Zukofsky and Olson. They are both capable of making certain kinds of decisions at points in the poem where I would not be as fine nor as discreet. Also, of course, they're ten years more experienced than I am. Since my world is so different from theirs, it's chiefly in the area of technique that we can be measured. Whereas with Denise Levertov and Robert Creeley I take pride that I am their equal. I can see them making decisions that I might not make, but I don't quite have that feeling of distance—of something going on that I couldn't be sure I could learn.

LD: How about some of the poets like Jack Spicer and Larry Eigner?

RD: Well, Eigner means a great deal to me because I've taken over some of his structuring of the line and so forth. But the people I read most are Creeley and Denise Levertov and Olson, and I read Pound's *Cantos*. This means I read them like you'd read Shakespeare or Keats or Shelley or Coleridge—not only for pleasure but because I'm still hunting. I read Zukofsky. Now Spicer is an absolutely solid poet, but somehow I can't imagine the structure of poetry depending on him. I feel that it was insane (and I think it was perfectly permissible on his part) to have converse with demonic powers, like he had. He himself discarded poetry or twisted it.

LD: What of Robin Blaser?

RD: In Blaser's case, that's a pure poetry, and it'll probably last in the area [where] pure poetry always lasts, like Mallarmé. At the present time Blaser hasn't advanced any poetic theory that will make his work available to us. You almost have to become a connoisseur of Blaser's world—like a gourmet. Certain foods are good for gourmets, but I like to eat all sorts of things. No, we don't need Blaser for a vitamin. I did need Mallarmé for a vitamin at one time, though. I can see why the New York school doesn't like me, because, while I think there are some beautiful poems in Frank O'Hara and John Ashbery, those are individual incidents and I don't find them very nourishing, either. There are times when I'm aware that my poetry, and say Charles's, have to do with the larger concerns of poetry—I mean the propositions of language and so forth. But on the other hand, a Donne was also interested in primary propositions, but people ceased to view them as such. The risk of the intellect is that it will not always recognize yesterday's primary propositions of the universe of language or anything else.

PART III

"Toward the Liberation of Human Love"

With Jess, circa 1955–57

"A Vast, Nervous, Contradictory, Worldly Life"

(with Robert Glück, 1984)

This discussion with Robert Glück, professor of English at San Francisco State University and longtime friend of the poet, appeared in The Advocate *in 1984. Glück asks about Duncan's sexual encounters and romantic relationships in the 1930s and '40s, and endeavors to define some of the poet's distinctive views on homosexuality. He comments: "He takes issue with attitudes of inferiority and also with cult superiority—with strategies of isolation as well as group affiliation, regarding them as violence against a larger sense of humanity."*

—Ed.

If Robert Duncan were a racehorse, he'd be world class. He's a poet whose work is already part of American literature. Duncan's three major books are The Opening of the Field, Bending the Bow, *and* Roots and Branches. *This spring, after a silence of fifteen years, we have* Ground Work: Before the War, *published by New Directions. Coincidentally, Black Sparrow just released a biography by Ekbert Faas called* Young Robert Duncan: portrait of the poet as homosexual in society. *It's mostly an account of Duncan's turbulent life in the '30s and '40s—"Husband, gigolo and homosexual, gold seal student, anarchist rebel, and university dropout."*

I liked the biography for its portrait of Duncan and the times, but its prose is stilted and the book doesn't live up to the complexity and zest of its subject. Still, Faas includes plenty of Duncan's own prose from diaries and letters. Duncan never throws anything out: "I burn nothing because I would leave, not a record of something realized...but...a vast nervous contradictory record of the worldly life I have come to celebrate, almost to worship. Not to seek a synthesis, but a mêlée." Two diary notations from 1941:

I sailed over ... with the wings of my coat curling behind me—I tossed my head and dropped an eyelid—when I moved it was from the hips

and the navel. I walked from the hips. I stood from the hips. I laughed
and turned my head from the hips. . . . I would coo in a deep pigeon voice
and he would say—do you want another beer—and yes I could coo.

I saw as he undressed the little legs come out of their frames. . . .
He unbuckled the last metal frame and slid along the bed to my side.
From the dark, forbidden, lower center of him, from the pit below the
belly where the tabooed legs twisted came the penis that belonged to his
magnificent body, a cock like a God's.

*Faas's biography ends when Duncan is thirty-two; we have a picture of
work, ideas, romance, politics and learning, and psychodrama in which Duncan
is Mercury, fabricator of identities. By 1951 he had created a poetic mode that
satisfied his desire to include everything; he had met, corresponded, or worked
with Henry Miller, Anaïs Nin, Tennessee Williams, Kenneth Patchen, H.D.,
Kenneth Rexroth, Ezra Pound, William Carlos Williams, and Allen Ginsberg,
to name a few. And we see the start of the Berkeley Renaissance group (Robert
Duncan, Jack Spicer, Robin Blaser, and others). Duncan's part in the Black
Mountain School, the Beats, and other postwar movements is still to come. But
in 1951 Duncan set up housekeeping with Jess, a reclusive, visionary artist who
has been Duncan's lover for thirty-three years; and, as Duncan says, a household
is not matter for a biography, "which is a story, like the* Odyssey *—a long trip.
When you arrive home you are not really charting the seas anymore, charting
how you got by this point and that point."*

Duncan presides *over San Francisco; more particularly, over the Poetics
Department at New College. He's a man of letters who dispenses generosity
(and fierceness!) like the Great. Still, his life and art continue to have an organic
relationship where truth-telling is oppositional and risky, where the urge to bear
witness—nakedness—is the province of Outlaw and Clown. Three years ago, at
a performance space in San Francisco, Duncan reenacted his 1955 play* Faust
Foutu, *in which he strips while saying:*

Now. Look at me! This is me, torso. . . . This nakedness is me not
because it is beautiful, this nakedness is beautiful not because it
can be endured, this nakedness can be endured not because it is
strong, this nakedness is strong not because it is craved and craven,
this nakedness is craved and craven not because it is shameless.

It has shame! It *is* shame! Alive with shame so that living through shame I may claim my place among movie stars.... It is *my* torso that strikes wonder so that the gods are dismayed.

Duncan was born in 1919 in Oakland, California. His mother died when he was born. He was adopted; his [adoptive] parents studied the Occult and Theosophy, beliefs that informed his childhood. When he was three, he became slightly cross-eyed and had to "rediscover his place in the world." His family moved to Bakersfield in 1927. He returned to the San Francisco Bay Area in 1936 to study at UC Berkeley, where he edited a radical journal and also found Ned [Fahs], his first lover.

Last month, over coffee and pastry in my kitchen, I taped the following:

ROBERT GLÜCK: So Ned was your coming out?

ROBERT DUNCAN: No, in high school I simply made advances toward the son of my father's two best friends and found two boyfriends. Ned was an ideal male type for me: sort of preppy, taller just as Jess is, and romantic. He was notorious on campus as a scorer. Ned was my real coming out—falling in love, yes.

When I think back, I had a very aggressive stance of sexual approach coupled with wanting to be allured. In general I'm an aggressive predator, and yet with an important person, as Ned was, I wasn't at all. And quiet as Jess is, I still force a play in which I get to be the one being sought.

The grief of getting older is: Do you have an image about the older? The lure, as it was spelled out in the '30s, definitely was youth, and I tried that lure. Meanwhile, you land a lot of men you don't want: The one thing the bait on the hook doesn't choose is the fish.

RG: What was the scene in the '30s; what were you brought out to?

RD: By that time I was in my freshman year. I heard there was a place you could dance with men, so there were arrangements like that....

RG: In Berkeley, Robert?

RD: Yeah, that was in Berkeley. And I tried it out. I knew they would have sex on the premises, so it wasn't just the pickups. I could fascinate.

167

I could turn it off and on, and at the same time it was like acting—it was a way to allure a person and then to find out later if he would or would not work out. Have times changed, Bob? I don't know.

I had from my teens a definite idea of the special meaning of being a homosexual. Because I could see it was different, and I also could see that it was not easy. Adolescents are forbidden sex anyway, but here very specially forbidden. It made it clearer there must be a terrific drive. But the erotic life would also demand everything. You haven't got time to write a poem if you're fucking. So eros reappears very strongly in imagination—that's clear quite early. I knew that people would be attracted to the poem when I had all this secret eros in it, and consequently you got 'em. When what you really wanted was readers who follow the rhythm of the poem.

From 1939 to 1945 Duncan lived off and on in Manhattan. He was influenced by Henry Miller, by Anaïs Nin, and by European Surrealists fleeing from the Nazis. He edited experimental journals, was drafted and then discharged for homosexuality, married Marjorie McKee in 1943, and had his brief, famous career as a Florida gigolo.

RD: Marjorie was the first person that I met who was a true peer and really a challenge, and who could play the role of glamour ten times around whatever I did and with a good deal of psychological depth—very adroit at living in the scandals and mysteries of what a personality could be.

I was guilty in that marriage all the time. Not at all guilty for the fact that I might have affairs with men. Guilty that a) I was in the marriage, so I'd betrayed the man who had not yet appeared; or b) that I was always secretly looking for death. I still had a strong picture that I was meant for men, so I'd lost my destiny, had been rejected by my destiny.

When we say eros it means so many things, but eros for me was never psychoanalytical; eros is the one that appears in my poetry all the time, which is the terrifying power that sex has over you, that you recognize does identify you in a way you didn't know about yourself. That's important. So you're frightened because it's another you you haven't discovered yet, and it contains all sorts of things that frighten.

. . . .

I thought a Being more than vast, His body leading
    into Paradise,   his eyes
              quickening a fire in me,   a trembling

     hieroglyph: At the root of the neck

  the clavicle, for the neck is the stem of the great artery
    upward into his head that is beautiful

         At the rise of the pectoral muscles

  the nipples, for the breasts are like sleeping fountains
    of feeling in man, waiting above the beat of his heart,
    shielding the rise and fall of his breath, to be
    awakend

         At the axis of his mid hriff

    the navel, for in the pit of his stomach the chord from
      which first he was fed has its temple

         At the root of the groin

    the pubic hair, for the torso is the stem in which the man
      flowers forth and leads to the stamen of flesh in which
      his seed rises

. . .

    For my Other is not a woman but a man

    the King upon whose bosom let me lie.

(FROM "THE TORSO, PASSAGES 18," *BENDING THE BOW*)

*This is the most ravishing poem about homosexual desire that I know. The torso
is Ned's. At the same time Duncan reveals the Form behind form; desire becomes
concrete and external, it explains reality: "I know what you desire / you do not
yet know / but through me . . . Gathering me, you gather / your Self":*

If there is a social duty which is mine it
will be to free us sexually—to erase just
as the slave negro can be erased the psychopathology of homosexuality.

(FROM 1941 DIARY NOTATION, QUOTED BY FAAS)

Forty years ago Duncan published his landmark essay "The Homosexual in Society" in a journal called Politics. *The editor suggested he leave the essay unsigned, but Duncan protested, "It is only by committing myself openly that the belief and desire of others for an open and free discussion of homosexual problems may be encouraged." The essay is reprinted in the Faas biography and also in the second edition of Jonathan Katz's* Gay American History.

It's 1944; for the first time an American writer makes homosexuality a topic in a public forum. He says, "It is precisely this will to uproot and uncover what other writers are content to let lie that has distinguished writers of integrity." Duncan seems completely fearless; characteristically, he takes more than one tack and shocks everyone. He detests society's ghettos (mental and geographical). More fiercely, he denounces the limits homosexuals impose on themselves and each other. He takes issue with attitudes of inferiority and also of cult superiority—with strategies of isolation as well as group affiliation, regarding them as violence against a larger sense of humanity.

What I think can be asserted as a starting point is that only one devotion can be held by a human being as creative life and expression, and that is a devotion to human freedom, toward the liberation of human love, human conflicts, human aspirations. To do this one must disown all the special groups (nations, religions, sexes, races) that would claim allegiance. To hold this devotion every written work, every spoken word, every action, every purpose must be examined and considered.

Having used sex for so long to punish and to achieve victory, I can make no real connection between what I mean by sex, by lust and what I mean by love.

(DIARY NOTATION, 1946)

In 1946 Duncan moved to Berkeley and harnessed the energies of numerous writers to produce magazines, lectures, theories, readings, books, and finally a literary movement: the Berkeley Renaissance. As Bruce Boone points out, the Berkeley poets were new on our horizon, a gay group, and it gave Duncan a context in which to find his poetic voice. Boone says:

I'd suppose these points: the Berkeley group stood opposed to institutional authority on grounds of bohemianism or anarchism; but authority was probably important to them on some one-to-one basis as an erotic glue to hold things together; learning's so important to them it's probably the core of what they want to do, all the misappropriations of the university notwithstanding; the key to their gay-identifiedness is in some relation to a long distant past; and all these factors would be meaningless if not seen as an ensemble or nexus working together.

(FROM "ROBERT DUNCAN AND GAY COMMUNITY"
IN *IRONWOOD*, NO. 22, DUNCAN ISSUE)

RG: Robert, a few years later you traded promiscuity for domesticity—in the spirit of self-preservation?

RD: Yeah, but a confused one: because you aren't the self you want to preserve. I aimed at a lasting condition in which I would be able to work. I think that had to do with a sense of energy. By the time I was thirty, I was canny enough as an animal to know I couldn't go on with endless energy: I've got to have a conservation of energy itself, not of identity.

In the early period I could be pretty well carried away by sex. By the middle twenties, if I hadn't fallen in love, it would have been very easy for me to be disgusted by it. Loving is a one-way distance for me, so I don't think I would pay attention to am I loved or not; on the other hand, it's rather fortunate that I am.

RG: So in 1951, when you get to Jess—

RD: Well, I was in despair by the time I came to Jess.

RG: Now gay men are making the same decision to bond in the spirit of self-preservation.

RD: But that's true of any of us—that we're faithful to what really concerns us. Writing didn't promise us something; or if it did, we're out of our minds. But we didn't sit around and make bargains with it. And that tells you something about your relations with what you love.

Is there a dialectic of the people that I fall in love with? Is there a dialectic from Ned to Marjorie? There is in a way. And from Marjorie to Jerry, and from Jerry to Jess. They're recognized in relation to each other.

When I was first out, they had no cure for syphilis and none for gonorrhea. And people died of syphilis in those days. If two people fall in love, would they really sit down and make a bargain: Well, we're going to wait and find out if this is healthy? Falling in love has never not had a challenge of that kind; in the days of the plague, people fell in love, and even saying hello to somebody was a dangerous proposition. In AIDS, liberation doesn't meet its defeat at all; it meets a test, which is a very different thing.

I never encountered a disease, except one: gonorrhea. I came in to get the report, and the doctor turned around and looked at me and said, "It's it," and I fainted. I went out like a light. It was the only time I ever slept with somebody in the social register. I went back to his mansion and rang the bell, and a butler came to the door and then a young woman shouted down the stairs, "He's sick." And I said, "I know, that's what I came to tell him."

Duncan's first collection in fifteen years appears this spring. Ground Work: Before the War *is a meditation of enormous scope—on time, affection, the apprehension of reality, eros, myth, language. The history of literature takes its part in the discourse both as history (with its patina) and as an "eternal" contemporary. Duncan is always testing parts against his larger goal: to admit the full range of experience. Sleep and waking, light and dark, rational and irrational—contraries are the emblematic starting point.*

> In dreams
> insubstantially you have come before my eyes'
> expectations, and, even in waking,
> taking over the field of sight   fleetingly
> stronger than what my eyes see,
> the thought of you thought has eyes to see
> has eyes to meet your answering eyes
> thought raises. I am speaking of a ghost

the heart is glad to have return,   of a room
I have often been lonely in, of a desertion
that remains even where I am most cherisht
and surrounded by Love's company,   of a form,
wholly fulfilling the course of my life, interrupted,
of a cold in the full warmth of the sunlight
that seeks to come in close to your heart
for warmth.

(FROM "INTERRUPTED FORMS" FROM *GROUND WORK:
BEFORE THE WAR*)

RG: This is a gorgeous poem; the sentiment here is practically Victorian.

RD: Oh yes, but I love Victorian poetry. I don't view modern as that modern; I mean, Gertrude Stein to me is more a Victorian—is just a hotter Victorian.

RG: What about the hiatus in publishing?

RD: Oh, you mean waiting the fifteen years? That was calculated; I'd seen Rexroth, where the writing becomes really grumpy and then posing, the amazing pose about being the sage-old-fart-on-the-mountain sort of thing that I loathe. I wanted something that was just as mysterious as it was in the beginning of writing.

If something's going on I want to know it. I don't think there are any sins; I think there are things you don't admit, look into, or confront, so confrontation is my response.

Poet of the Light and Dark

(with David Quarles, *The Advocate*, 1976)

This lively conversation with writer and poet David Quarles appeared in The Advocate *in 1976. Although he does not consider himself a "gay poet," Duncan speaks of his experience as a homosexual throughout his life. He says he is "a poet of emotions" and that his own personal homosexual love experience belongs "to our larger experience of love." He mentions that many young gay poets are unfamiliar with homosexual themes in Western literature, and speaks of an individual's rights rather than "gay rights," and a future in which there are "no labels, gay or straight," adding, "we must just be."*

—Ed.

Gay literature goes hand in hand with gay liberation, thinks Robert Duncan, fifty-seven-year-old San Francisco poet. The author of more than twenty-three books of poetry, Duncan started a poetry group at the Society for Individual Rights to educate the gay community about its own literature. "Young [gay] poets coming along had no measure for their expression," Duncan said. "You had a lot of sexual expression and great poverty in emotional expression and, certainly, in passional expression."

Duncan thinks that the great modern event in gay literature and in the poetic world in general was the publication of Allen Ginsberg's *Howl* in 1956. Although the proliferation of gay writing since that time may be something new, Duncan points to the long history of homosexual themes in English and Western literature. "Ancient Greek myth and classical Greek poetry created a tradition of sexual and romantic Eros for both male and female homosexuals, and classical Rome provided models of sophisticated social comment from the bias of homosexual wit," Duncan commented. His own exposure to the homosexual tradition in literature began in high school with Marlowe and Shakespeare. Of Marlowe's *Edward II*, Duncan said, "The picture was grim, but getting to know about homosexual hubris and suffering was valuable." Shakespeare, in both the sonnets and plays, "ran a gamut of homosexual idealism and youthful dejection and conflict."

Although he is homosexual and published in 1944 the first public literary discussion of the subject in the United States that includes a declaration of his sexuality, Duncan does not consider himself a "gay poet." "Since I have been in love with women in my lifetime, I admit that love as a theme as well as the presiding homosexual love. I am a poet of emotions," Duncan explained. He noted that the majority of people who have written on his work and the eight who are writing doctoral theses on his poetry are not homosexual. "They have been entirely sympathetic in their reading of my own personal homosexual love experience as belonging to our larger experience of love," Duncan said.

He does, however, recall a different time. In the late '40s, Duncan, Robin Blaser, and Jack Spicer were participating in a student organized writers' conference at the University of California at Berkeley. The conference was ordered off campus by Josephine Miles, Mark Schorer, and Thomas Parkinson of the English Department. The excuse used was that the poets' writings did not meet University standards. The real reason, Duncan recalls, was because "we were all three homosexual and were thought to be contributing to the delinquency of the young—the young being a group of new writers who were precursors of our current gay liberation writing." As for the present, Duncan is glad to enjoy the benefits of the gay liberation movement. "One thing that is very noticeable and extremely pleasant is that the young people don't have to camp, and they don't have to give the signals we used to give, which were very debilitating. Built into them, as into black minority signals and women's minority signals, was a good deal of social hostility," Duncan commented. "If you want to be a clown today, you can be a clown, but you don't *have* to be, and you are not a clown from a loser's position," he said.

Addressing himself to the question of rights, Duncan pointed out, "My view on rights is that you have to fight for them. We won't ever be through fighting for our rights, but the main thing in a fight is to define it correctly." He thinks that there are no special gay rights, but the question is one of an individual's rights. The issue should be fought on the basis of consenting adults. Recalling his own struggle with his sexuality, Duncan said, "In high school, all of my sexual contacts were mutual masturbation or petting. And so when I read *Ulysses* and Molly Bloom wants to suck a young boy's cock, I really thought she was crazy. You wouldn't do something awful like that. And I remember telling a friend of my mother's about this, and she laughed and said, 'Well, tell me that when you come home from college next semester.'"

Duncan was born in Oakland, California, and adopted by a family of Hermeticists and Theosophists who have no prejudice about homosexuality, "although they had a rather puzzling view—they thought if you were a homosexual you may have been a woman before, and so you were a woman in a man's body." He tried out that theory and discarded it—and drag, too. "The first man I fell in love with didn't go for drag. I'm not sure if I would have taken up wearing drag anyway, since I would look something like a gorilla in drag or a friendly chimpanzee," Duncan laughed.

Returning to the gay liberation movement and literature, Duncan cited the language breakthrough. "We now talk about cocksucking and buggering and not about fellatio and sodomy," he said. The way for this new freedom in language in serious literature was prepared in the '20s by [James] Joyce, [D. H.] Lawrence, and [Ezra] Pound, according to Duncan. Later, the publication of [Henry] Miller's *Tropic of Capricorn* and the battles against censorship in the '50s consolidated the gains. "What is important lies ahead," Duncan declared. "To be able to talk publicly about these acts means that we are just beginning to be able to bring them into the storehouse of meanings and values. We have yet to begin to create the psychological and mythological tradition that will be needed."

He contrasted the present situation in gay literature and life with the nineteenth century by pointing to Walt Whitman. "Although Whitman's poetry acclaimed the sexual emotions of a man's love for another man, especially in 'Calamus,' he seems to have been very uneasy about some imputation of perversion that might be made," Duncan said. When a friend of Whitman's asked if "Calamus" was an endorsement of homosexuality, Whitman denied an "undreamed and unwished possibility of morbid inference—which is disavowed by me and seems damnable."

Edward Carpenter, a Whitman disciple and rumored to have been Whitman's lover, preached a doctrine of sexual union without penetrating the body, according to Duncan. Carpenter advocated this practice for heterosexuals, too.

Turning to his own poetry and its roots, Duncan said that he is an intellectual poet with pantheistic and anarchistic leanings, tutored by William James, [A. N.] Whitehead, and Freud. "I have nothing like the following that counterculture poets have. My book sales run around ten thousand at the present time," Duncan explained. "My poetry comes right along the line of modern music. I'm music centered," Duncan said and noted that his poetry started centering on music, especially [Anton] Webern, in the '40s. "I stem from poets like Pound and Williams who had great difficulty in their reactions to homosexuality. The entire '20s were not only anti-Semitic, which was the style in the '20s and came to its grievous end, but were also, like the total society, anti-homosexual. But you don't, after all, pick up their bad habits. I was no more going to be crushed by the signs of anti-homosexuality than I was going to be converted by other poets' anti-Semitism or their attitude toward women," he said. "I am a child of one William James," Duncan continued, "and I even read my Freud as a descendant from that psychology. It's pluralism I'm aiming at, and so of course it's going to be pantheistic, and noticeably my pantheism includes Christian gods. The divine interests me because, again, it's a dimension of human life." He favors an increased delineation of homosexuality in the realm of the divine and in the myth of the Homo-Eros. "In my work I constantly address the homoerotic content of Christian theology and theosophy."

Duncan was married in his twenties to an artist and has ambivalent feelings toward women. "In poetry my attitude was seriously influenced by Robert Graves's doctrine of the White Goddess. My ideas are built on negative and positive mother figurations. Mostly negative. So a very powerful woman figure for me is the authoritative, tyrannical woman. I am very impressed—superstitiously—by women's minds, so I will tend to be angry when women don't measure up to the mind I assume they have, which means I think they know something we don't know. A figure that fascinates me is the sorceress or the wise woman.

The grandmother figure emerges as a wise woman, and probably my grandmother emerged very strongly as a wise woman."

Duncan noted that while married he experienced hostile and sadistic feelings. "That didn't make me want to go much further in heterosexual relations," he concluded. Love and hate are combined in Duncan's poetry, which he describes as "chiaroscuro, mixing the light and the dark." This term also encompasses bisexuality. "I would agree with those who feel the imagination—and Freud feels the id or the libido, too—has no such character of male or female. It has both, and it projects both. We would properly be mixtures, and we form ourselves by shaming one side and promoting the other," Duncan explained.

As for his personal life, Duncan admits to having become quite domesticated with his long-term companion, Jess Collins. "My own warp is that I'm almost fanatically monogamous. By fanatical, I mean that when I fall in love outside of my household, I behave like any monogamous householder does. I go through guilt or go through sacrifice or go through pain. This is ridiculous, absolutely ridiculous animal behavior. And yet, in the economy of an artist's life, in the society we are in, monogamy gives me the greatest energy. My energy is not sidetracked at all."

As for the future, Duncan believes that the important goal of society should be to allow everyone to love consciously whomever he or she wants. "We must pay attention to the least inclination of the body, but first with all liberal permission. There must be no labels, gay or straight; we must just be," he concluded.

Gay Sunshine Interview

(with Steve Abbott and Aaron Shurin, 1978–79, excerpts)

This conversation with the late Steve Abbott and Aaron Shurin origi-
nally appeared in Gay Sunshine, *nos. 40 and 41, and it was subse-*
quently reprinted in Gay Sunshine Interviews, Vol. 2, *edited by*
Winston Leyland (San Francisco: Gay Sunshine Press, 1982). Another
interview session on poetic form was published in Soup, *edited by Steve*
Abbott, 1980, pp. 30–57, 79. In the long Gay Sunshine *interview, only*
excerpts of which are presented here, Robert Duncan describes vividly
a violent sexual experience he had in Bakersfield as a teenager, as well
as discusses being a member of a fraternity house at the University of
California, his first love affair with Ned Fahs in his early twenties, his
long relationship with his partner Jess, and the nature of "manhood,"
which he notes can be more consciously integrated into homosexuality
today. He says he wrote the essay "The Homosexual in Society" (1944)
as his reaction to watching a young poet at a fashionable gay party and
"seeing what I feared I might be too, in his affected voice."

For easier reading, not all omitted passages are indicated by ellipses.

—Ed.

This interview took place during three daylong sessions in December 1978 and
January 1979 at Aaron Shurin's house in San Francisco. There was a definite
feeling of generosity in these discussions, a feeling that we were sharing expe-
rience, and in fact we all brought material to the interview; our own poems
offered became part of the texts to be studied and were referred to in the course
of our exploration.

Duncan's enthusiasm gives to his speech a head-over-heels impetus that
often finds him interrupting himself to further his unfolding language. We
tried to reflect this urgency in transcribing the tapes. To flesh out the picture,
there is Duncan with his white tufted hair at either side of his commanding
eagle-like face—one eye holding you down and one roving.

—SA and AS

ROBERT DUNCAN: I still feel my first lover [Ned Fahs] is an eternal person for me. I was raised in terms of reincarnation and karma belief; and falling in love was, and still is for me, experienced as an appointment. That first love relationship was absolutely painful. It must have been painful for him too, incidentally, because I could have an absolute scorn for his mind where he did not share my sense of things. [Ned] was not an artist in temperament; he was a schoolteacher and he was up against a kid who, when it came to modern art, [Ezra] Pound or [Igor] Stravinsky, was demanding, absolute, very little willing to allow sharing unless sharing included the world of painting, writing, music I had come to believe so in. He thought of himself as the rational one, and I was taken to be irrational, imaginative. The excitement was the union of opposite types.

The world of my mind and of my work was, even then, the most important. I sought a lover where sexual needs and response and daily companionship would extend fully to include the central intent of an art. That's what I had to know fully in my heart about Jess before I went further with him, to recognize how much of an accord we were in our arts and responses. I had fixed in my account of falling in love that union of opposites, not here male and female, but of contending forces united in their contention by love; working out a karma struggle. But I broke through that fixation to admit that I was in love with him where the sense was of a deep accord, not of winning or losing, but of going on with him in a common life.

In my [early or] mid-twenties I had quit writing poetry and tried to settle down into the terms of one relationship. I tried to cease my driving concern for this mind and this work I had had, because it seemed so much more important that the sexual love and the companionship be there. I was in love with him, and I did not want to come to judge how he responded to art or poetry. My absolutism remained. I guess I only put it aside by staying away from the area of concern. He was an artist but a commercial artist. We could share fully our going to galleries to see art, but whenever I got off about poetry and ideas and philosophy or structure, that look of the rational male barely countenancing the irrational flight of fancy would come over his face.

New York City, circa 1940. Photo courtesy of the Poetry Collection,
University at Buffalo.

STEVE ABBOTT: How long did you stop writing poetry?

RD: Well, it was 1943 and '44. When Pound was finally captured by the American forces, I was moved to write "Homage and Lament for Ezra Pound in Captivity, May 12, 1944." The basic forces of my poetry had been stored awaiting that time, but if I think of the revelation of my sexual nature in its development, I think of how important loss was, and lament. Early poems in the loss of my first lover are eaten through by self-pity as I remember them. Then in the earliest poems, a poem like "Persephone," written in 1939, the theme of rape, rapture, and dread. And the blood in those poems comes forward from actual initiations in blood. . . .

The next blood thing came after my father's death. I was about seventeen. My mother was having suitors, and we'd gone to a Chinese restaurant in downtown Bakersfield. They wanted to do something so I said, "Well, I'll walk home." Now it was near the end of summer so we've got that valley heat sort of thing. For some time I'd already experienced the area of fascination and played with it as a child. I'd catch a man looking at me, and I'd look into the gaze and suddenly they'd behave like I'd never made men behave before. I did it once when I was in a car and a man was in a barbershop. He got so upset he had to get up out of the barber chair. [*laughs*] I would catch a look and go deep into it. What was on my mind was I had discovered something I'd read about in Greek myth. It was really true like I thought it was true. My family believed in elementals, so satyrs were real to them and nymphs were real to them. I found out there was something satyr-like about me, something nymph-like about me. I could fascinate . . .

Now we've got me, I'm sixteen or seventeen. I picked up one of those glances and it followed me. It was a boy of about eighteen or nineteen, a fairly husky road-boy as there still were in the late Depression. And my experience there was Oh! here we've moved into an entirely different realm! I knew there were other realms so I experienced it as a new dimension. Everything's changed! I could see everything's changed! That's what this gaze means. Now I understand in a new way the heat of May. Now I can hear what the grass and the trees were saying. Now I'm in entirely the same dimension as birds and water. And in this poem of Persephone you have me back in a winter landscape where I used to cut out from my house, going to see a girl I had a crush on, and walked to her house some five or six miles, walking through the Kern River bed. And all the way I used to have fantasies about what kind of men lived in these houses and are that close to this landscape which seemed to me, when I was fourteen or fifteen or sixteen, almost *dizzyingly* sexual. And yet I had not yet admitted to any threshold that I could possibly masturbate although there was mutual masturbation going on. At school they talked about boys who went and jerked off in circles, and I couldn't exactly understand what jerking off was, but I knew it was some kind of rite. I pictured a rite that the boys who were in the know did. And yet when I went the river way, I waited for a river spirit or nature spirit. So with this exchange of glances, in a way we get right to the Persephone rape that underlies it.

The dusk was already coming and instead of stopping at our house—between our house and the park was a fairly large field, about four or five blocks, that wasn't developed. Now I knew I had this power but I never connected this eyepower with playing sex games with kids in schools or necking in cars. . . . The first time I'd encountered one of those people I was looking for in the river valley! And those people were always male! But then no wonder that I caught an absolutely lunatic glance. Probably by the time one of these glances got through to me, and I was taking them up, it was a very disturbed person, a tremendously repressed homosexual.

So we went to an area far enough from the tennis court that it was dark, though it was still quite visible. I had no dimension in which I thought we should not be in public. The tennis courts, to me, looked as if we were already in the realm I'm talking about, the realm of my near hypnagogic self, the visionary realm. And right over there was the other realm. The people playing tennis were lit up. It made it more clear that the park where we were was in that other domain. I had no calculation that we might be seen or arrested, any of this. . . .

It's moving with a terrific rapture and I see "My God! but this rapture is not only moving somewhere I ain't ever been before but it's actually *scary*." So I move myself from it in a *very* weak tone of voice, very, and I say, "I gotta go home. It's, it's kinda late and I. . . ." Well, I *had* to go home because I knew, my God, that something appalling was going to happen. Now what's interesting about this threshold is that I'm not sure exactly what would have happened, and at this time he says, "I've gotta piss," and he turns away from me. And that's still logical except I'm shaking and know, instinctively, I'll get in trouble if I start walking away.

Then he turns around and the face facing me, his face, is one of *maniacal* fury! He has brass knuckles on and says, "You dirty little cock teaser, I'm really going to give it to you." He grabs me by the—suddenly the physical force is very present—and starts hitting me on the chin first. You can still see the scars though I was on a plastic surgeon's table afterwards. And at this point I'm still in another dimension. I can see the people playing tennis. They're close and the court absolutely lighted that I can see their faces and their studied not hearing. I start *screaming* just as loud as I can. It's *inconceivable* to me! There's quite a lot of confusion because that was a magical realm as on a lighted stage, and they almost look supernatural because they're so far away but not physically far away. What does happen is a woman four blocks away phones the police 'cause she can hear the screams and has no trouble reading that there's bloody murder going on. So the police are on their way....

I meanwhile had moved into still another dimension. Everything is absolutely clear. I realize I have only to wait a few seconds more, almost as if I had an interior timer, and my coat would be so bloodied that when I—I could wiggle out of my coat, I knew that. But this is how calculated it all was. My coat would be so bloody he wouldn't be able to hold onto me. So I slipped out of my coat, grabbed it, and started running. By this time there are police cars all around but I don't connect to them or they to me. They went to the park but there was nobody there except for the tennis players, who said: "Well, we were so intent on our game here ..."

Now in the Depression years we had a Catholic schoolteacher renting a room from us. I used to talk about God with her and interesting theological things. So when I got home I went to the bathroom because, well, my first problem is I can't explain my bloody coat and bloody shirt. But when I went into the bathroom to clean up and saw the *bone* of my chin exposed and shreds of flesh around it, I mean, already I was a little sick at the idea. So I walk down the hall and tap at the door of the Catholic maiden teacher. She says, "Come in, Robert," and I open the door. At that point she turns around and faints and I faint. [*laughs*]

Luckily my mother soon arrives home and when I come to, my mother and the chief of police are bending over me. I was in the hospital waiting to be rolled into the operating room and they're saying, "You've gotta describe him, he . . ." And, I say, "I was to blame. I was the one who led him on. I was to blame. I was the one who led him on." And my mother says, "No, no. You don't understand." And the chief of police says, "He's killed two boys already. We've got to get his description." And I refused. I would not give a description.

My family whisked me away soon afterwards, but while I was in the hospital I talked, so certain levels of Bakersfield knew what had happened, not so much in my mother's circle but telephone operators and the like so that when I went to college, I met old friends there who knew what had happened. Even here I think we both, the attacker and I, belonged to what happened, hmm? But what I knew in the aftermath is that when I went back to T., my schoolboy crush, I was afraid of him. I was afraid something was going to happen that would go beyond what we had been talking about. . . .

AARON SHURIN: Now were you writing poetry at this point?

RD: No. Well, yes, I was writing some and I have some because my mother saved poetry from this period. When my high school teacher, who started me writing, was asked, "What was his poetry like?" she replied, "I only remember darkness and blood." That's what it was. But really, writing poetry starts after this episode. . . .

AS: In these early poems . . . you're first beginning to find a language.

RD: I'm drawn to Pound because of the hypnagogic sort of thing. In Pound I found those nymphs and maenads with the same charge as I felt them. I found an identification with trees which is very strong for me. Trees are not phallic for me. They're beings, and that's very different. I see roots and branches in trees. And a stream of water is a power of force, and I wanted to become water very much. I wanted to become tree and talk with trees and water with a lot of confidence. They seem to be talking back to me.

SA: You often have birds singing in your poems and songs in your poems. Is singing a part of the feminine in you that's coming out?...

RD: Yes ... Medea's song upon seeing Jason [in the play *Medea at Kolchis*] is at the point when I'm at Black Mountain. Medea is really seeing the way I saw N., seeing "the man." The feeling was so strong, by the way, that I don't have that feeling again. It's not that feeling I had when I met Jess. I was reading Lady Murasaki when I was living with N., when it was breaking up.

Genji has a mistress and cannot fulfill the relationship, so he makes a reincarnation promise to give her a life that he will consummate. With N. I very strongly felt—I was shattered really. I mean *I* was breaking up, but then intense as it was, during the last year I got engaged to marry Virginia Admiral [?]. I was hitchhiking to New York all the time from Indianapolis. I had torrid affairs, I mean I was picking up people as frequently as any little nineteen- or twenty-year-old. I wasn't figuring the arithmetic of this at all. I'd demolish the whole place if the least straying came on his part, but *I* wasn't straying. My diaries at Cal are in the aftermath of all this. Still, when I first met Marjorie, I'm so wrapped up in the fact that I have been, that N. had to rescue himself and that I've been sexually disowned....

I'm circling around your question of how come I had a sense of the social punishment that would come down. You couldn't miss it. In the '30s we had friends who at fifty were back on a scene they'd been off thirty years because they'd been in prison. You didn't miss *that* heavy ticket. Being in closets was serious business, not frivolous coppin' out in those days. And when I had no inner reserve about it, everybody was warning me over and over again about my outrageous behavior because there were not a lot of people who were gonna be visibly queer....

What I wanted was love, not lust. Lots has to be aroused, lots of romantic foreplay, before I was actually sucking a cock. I mean I've done lots of cocksucking, but I remember coming to Sanders Russell where they had just picked up a soldier, and he had one of those hard ones you couldn't get off no matter what. They were lined up in a row to suck it, and I was just disgusted. The whole thing looked like a deformity. Not on your life! [*laughs*]

SA: It looks to me like the energies were coming from different chakras. The lower chakra is simply the physical sensation, but your sexual fantasy was coming from a higher, more magical plane.

RD: We've got a struggle in which the two are uniting. Rightly it starts from the higher chakra if it's ever going to get there, because the society doesn't ever want it to be there. It doesn't want a connection between the higher chakras and the lower chakras. It wants to believe the lower chakra is not a chakra at all.

AS: Even in terms of homosexuality, they don't want connection between the imaginative and the actual. They like to keep that separation.

RD: You see me constantly going towards naturalization and the spirit of realization. You find me, over and over again, *realizing* things. One of the most important things for me in poems is realizing. . . . Olson in *Maximus* has an imaginary body, yet with his own body, he didn't exercise it. He misused it. To him it was a broken-down automobile, the opposite of what he announced throughout the poem. Meanwhile he's galloping toward advanced emphysema and announcing the breath is the thing he's coming from. He does *not* say breath is holy or he wouldn't be smoking. . . .

SA: You are quoted in the magazine *Christopher Street* as saying, "We have yet to create the psychological and mythological tradition to build the gay culture and gay arts movement that would be needed." . . . Do you want to expand on that?

RD: Oh, yes, let's go first, did we ever *have* such a culture? I've written on this [in] chapter three of *The H.D. Book* in the *TriQuarterly* review, and it is the chapter specifically on the Eros. I traced through there how inadequate it seems to me are the tracings even in the few areas where our Homo-Eros appears. . . .

"The Homosexual in Society" article of 1944 arose from my reaction to a fashionable gay party and seeing a young poet, seeing what I feared I might be too, in his affected voice. Hadn't he lost his own natured voice, having lost his manhood essentially? And if you think about the term "manly" today it's a very forceful and troublesome word; it's avoided a great deal. What are you if you're a man? So we're full into the center of what is my picture. I think we're discussing a homosexual manhood in a more solid ground than was provided in the Greek world. In the Greek world they [homosexuals] were thought of as a very special cult; Plato doesn't propose anything other than that. Higher thought: by being removed from women they were removed in their minds from triviality, and among the trivialities were daily life, how you cook. We don't any longer believe that knowing the nature of food and nutrition is demeaning to a mind; it's the center of our idea of what mind properly is. So when you're talking about manly and manhood it goes along with our new ideas of nutrition, of food good versus food bad. We've got a charged politics today, Nader would represent that, that people are putting out false food as well as false fronts. So when we list the goods, we're in the actual territory of manliness. When Plato lists the goods, he knows nothing about the goods of food and the bads of food. We don't even find that data when we move back to the Greek world; it doesn't seem to be as complete a picture as ours. And your poem (Steve's "Night on Amoeba Mountain"), for instance, addressing the green at the end and an alliance with the plant world and its natures and what is in it, this is also central to us in what the mind and the manhood is realized in. And in Plato's day, the whole classical period is so far apart from it that when it attempts to give a description of the plant world it's got very little picture of it, very little observation.

So if we go back just to the place when we're talking about the homosexual world, first I can't separate that from finding our manhood. Women's liberation and what it says today—I do not hear more than very clear evidence that they've been so deprived and closed away that they're giving expressions of acute pain that they can't locate what womanhood is. So that we're [too] very far away from finding out what manhood is. Now we come to why and how I see the homosexual is closer to that. A man in love with a man not only finds himself in the presence of the other's manhood, and so he cannot but know the agony and the separation from nature. And his formula can't be as simple—although it certainly is—we hear it on the stage, it's done over and over again—yes, the formula can be we both flunked out from manhood. . . .

A Conversation with Robert Duncan

(with Robert Peters and Paul Trachtenberg, 1976)

This interview with poets Robert Peters and Paul Trachtenberg was conducted at Duncan's request at their home in Huntington Beach, California, in May 1976. This first half of the discussion was published in the Chicago Review *in the fall of 1997, the second half appearing in the winter 1998 issue of the same magazine. Here Duncan touches on various aspects of homosexuality and the models for it in his life. He discusses, among other subjects, his childhood reading, costume, love and conviviality, his household life partner Jess, astrology, and again what it means to be derivative.*

—Ed.

INTERVIEWER: Robert, it is a pleasure to have you here with us, and we hope that we can range over many aspects of your life so far inadequately treated in other interviews and conversations.

ROBERT DUNCAN: I have felt dissatisfied with most of my interviews to date, and they have been numerous. So I have come here to you and Paul, to see if I can't do better. Until now, I've had trouble sorting out the matters that pertain to my writing, and those that appeal to the gossipy side of my life.

INT: I see the risks. But why not talk right off about homosexuality, and where models for your life have come from?

RD: Primarily, our notions of how we should approach our readers derive from psychiatrists' case histories. This is a case history of Duncan. My first impulse is to tell the story of my shock and personal alienation when I was a hustler. And the topic is salacious. A hustler's story, including mine, belongs to storyland. We as yet haven't had our homosexual Proust who relates his personal story in depth. If we had, it might be easier to avoid more superficial stories. We need to understand our gay selves better.

INT: I envy you for living an active gay life from the time you were a young man. Apparently you didn't sit around in the libraries as I did reading Krafft-Ebing to educate myself and understand that I wasn't the only male in the world suffering sexual turmoil.

RD: Oh, no. I did read Krafft-Ebing, and I've seen my own life in terms of those case histories. When I was interviewed by this guy from *The Advocate,* I tried to explain why I don't go in for drag. In the process I obliged him by talking about how I felt about buggering and about cocksucking, and how I was afraid of these experiences, and then not. If I were writing all this myself, I would be less controversial, kinky, and would explore the stages of my homosexuality. But, being interviewed, I was trying to lay a claim: "Yes, I am a homosexual. And I am not a boring homosexual." As William Carlos Williams in *Paterson* said, "I AM A POET! I AM A POET! I AM A POET!"

You realize the proud pathos Williams felt—that he was opposing a society where it was profoundly embarrassing to declare you were a *poet.* When he says it up front, recites it, he touches upon part of the courage and the importance of what for gay writers who publicly acknowledge their gayness is their contribution to "gay liberation." Eventually acceptance and tolerance wouldn't require our making such assertions, especially exclamatory ones.

Today, what's so interesting is that it's now possible, regardless of whether you're searching to understand your own homosexuality or not, to find many published treatments of the subject, ones that extend knowledge about this condition. We don't read *Crime and Punishment* because we are going in for crime and punishment. We read it to understand more of the human condition. And that's why Dostoyevsky wrote for us, not for a friendly murderer who had just broken open the head of an old lady who had loaned him money.

As for "homosexual literature" in America, even now the word "homosexual" has not yet transcended prejudice where you can write about your gay life because it *is* a human life and not a bizarre anomaly; we still invite hatred and bigotry. We can, of course, go back the other way. When we were searching Krafft-Ebing we weren't really searching for the man Krafft-Ebing; but we did learn a lot about human lives extending beyond ours. I know that I judge sexual acts outside my own areas of feeling with much less sense that they are unnatural because homosexual acts (mine) have been declared "unnatural." So I do have a glimmer that I'm not "unnatural," that this business of drawing a line around nature diminishes us, for we reject performing acts that are frowned on by society. You are expected to agree that homosexual practices are horrible; you are so aghast that you yourself wouldn't perform them. Well, there are plenty of people today who in fighting to dismiss violence from literature would argue that if you begin a novel with an old woman being murdered then you should never, that you *could* never, have any human community with the murderer, a perpetrator of an "unnatural" act. So, this is one area that opens up.

Though I used to go to the Krafft-Ebing volumes to search for myself, as I'm sure you also did, I didn't find much help. The self I sought, I knew, was not really different from the self I was in the family I grew up in. I was looking for another story, possibly, and certainly took a long time before I was comfortable living that story, a homosexual one.

INT: When did you first begin to live the story?

RD: Well, I was all along inside that narrative; but, of course, I couldn't locate it. In my earliest poetry, when I was still in college, I was very attracted to Ezra Pound's *Cantos* and to T. S. Eliot's *Waste Land.* I read them as rituals of identity, earth rituals that struck me in the early Cantos particularly. In the first place, I obviously loved fun and adventure, and adventure beyond my being able to understand it. Today it's hard to explain what it was like in the 1930s. While people were beginning to accept Eliot, there were few essays explicating *The Waste Land,* there were no essays at all exploring *The Cantos.* So *The Cantos* were more exciting to read. I've always wanted to be inside an unexplained poem, a poem that was an adventure that you couldn't sum up. I loved that.

INT: Did your childhood reading help you?

RD: Yes, much. A crucial early "adventure" was reading the story of Ulysses, a favorite hero, first in the Lang, Leaf, and Meyers edition, and before my parents were beginning to tell me those legends. And so my love for complex poems started at a fairytale level. Some of the other stories I'm talking about dealing with my sexuality also arrived as fairytales. Another major experience in my self-revelations was falling in love, something so biological it does not much derive from a pattern of fates within the human community, from magic that you don't originate yourself. The sense of giving love between two people is the gift that two people bestow on one another, hidden in a fairytale series of gifts. Sometimes these would be Christmas presents, but also they were gifts of tasks to do. In King Arthur they were gifts of quests you journeyed on.

I've always tended to read new worlds I enter, both at the level of Greek myths and at the level of fairytales with Celtic magic. None of this would I find in Dos Passos or Krafft-Ebing. When I first had strong sexual attractions and fascinations (I was fourteen or fifteen), I would emerge entirely into a world identical with those two worlds. One was the Celtic world that James Stephens presented in his novels where spring was part of it, the change of weather—this was in Bakersfield, California, where the beginning of the heat, the redundancy of going into sexual heat and the whole nearby Mojave Desert going into extreme spring temperatures were a literal heat that shimmered and danced, so that it was always identified with landscape.

Then, of course, the Greek world revealed to me what fauns and gods were. When I read The Cantos, Ulysses and fauns and nymphs were waiting for me. Now, I never felt that Pound wasn't speaking for my condition. The Greek world didn't ask, "Are you homosexual or are you heterosexual?" And, also, since I loved Pound, I saw that to him the vileness of usury was as vile as sodomy. He comes down heavier on Sodomites than on Semites. So, very early I discovered that I can love an author without forwarding everything he says. So I don't see Pound as prejudiced against me. His prejudice is accidental. Fairytales tell us this, don't they? In the revelation that's coming, everybody is locked into some nonreal form, a bearskin, or a whole series of magical shapes, beneath which there's an extraordinarily valuable person and all sorts of terrible things to countenance. We've returned to Raskolnikov. Dostoyevsky brings us right in: here's a terrible person, but he's also a person, and the whole revelation of the novel is of human value.

INT: What you say about putting on a bearskin reminds me of gays who don leather as an extra hide suggesting a world of darkness and evil, as a commentary on how we gays are seen by much of the hetero world as demons and monsters.

RD: Oh, yes, right. And it also symbolizes a world of unfeeling; for leather suggests, in Reichian terms, that the surface of the skin has been tanned, and the mystique is as much about the business of the actual tanning of the surface as it is about the hide itself. The hide, insensitive through tanning, has lost much of its vulnerability. Leather is a form of armor. It's interesting that after [Wilhelm] Reich in the 1930s—his book on *Character Analysis* along with the *Function of the Orgasm* is one of the first places there was a real shift in thinking seriously about sex in a life context—we see sex as something more than a way of exploiting other human beings. A deeper reading of sexuality, I think, than Freud had proposed, but continuous with it, reinforming the Freudian proposition. Jung called attention to the fact that people develop character armor, ways of feeling and invulnerability. He was also fascinated by sadomasochism, because he sensed that sadism was an effort to tear armor from character, that the whipping and the chains were both resisting and tearing away from being caught over and over again at a stage of coming out of an armor. And if you go back to insects and think about, say, how a sea insect like a crab develops, their entire skin becomes rigid, then they crack and break it open, writhing, bursting forth to a metamorphosis, before reentering armor. So, on a trivial level, we see "costume."

INT: How significant is it that the leather world dominates so much of gay public life?

RD: It wasn't always that way; but it was around in the 1930s. I can remember it at bars. Only a very particular and small segment of gays wore leather. One of the great jokes in San Francisco was that standing in a leather bar didn't mean you'd arrived as a "leather boy." But leather queens do put on and take off armor. In dramatic terms, they are donning, then doffing social armor. You reveal that beneath the habiliments you are a fleshly, vulnerable human being capable of loving and being loved.

INT: Are leather jackets, then, toys?

RD: Toys, yes, because children with toys play the life-story they hope to enter eventually. When I was a child I was always wanting to play household and house, along with other games like being abducted. They were fantasies . . .

INT: Did you ever play you were a mother?

RD: No, there's nothing very motherly about me, I think. [*laughter*] Fatherly feelings I have, yes, because I don't feel motherly. No, that's not true, for when my lover Jess is ill and I'm nursing him, my idea of tending him, my idea of who it is that tends you when you are ill is a mother. The fact that my mother was the most immediate person tending me when I was ill supports this. I'm very motherly then towards Jess. And when my father sat and read to me, that wasn't quite the same. All those acts of bringing food, solace, and so forth were so much mother roles, bits of mother.

INT: You had no fantasies though of being an actual birthing female? I often had one, played out with my sister. I was a mother sow, and we would put chairs in the front yard, on the grass, in a circle. This would be my sty, which I would enter wearing one of Father's heavy winter mackinaw jackets. I would lie there on my side squirting forth piglets, feeling udders along my belly, thrusting them forth for all my little pigs to suck away on. . . .

RD: Wow! That's fantastic! What gay man wouldn't want a whole set of cocks in a row running down his belly for multiple fellations?

INT: Back to leather. Is it valid to say that gays in leather are imitating archetypal human torturers?

RD: In part. The military association. But, of course, I'm not into any kind of leather scene myself, so we're talking of an area about which

I'm clueless. There is another thing, though, about our sexuality and imagined situations in which we don't actually find ourselves. They arise from fantasies that may not be quite near us. I'm sure that when you start wearing leather you find out something entirely different from what your original fantasies told you wearing leather would be like. You saw men in leather on motorcycles, Hells Angels. I do think that to enjoy the full impact of discovery and novelty, you have to be young. If at fifty-seven, I chose to start wearing leather, I would be another *me*, not just another leather queen. And these ideas threaten me.

I had a period once in Florida where I was a gigolo—there you enter a very specific world of a gigolo amongst immensely wealthy people and with women. I was a fuckout as a homosexual gigolo. I remember Charles Glenn Wall once said of me: "Once most boys get their first bicycle as a reward for doing 'it,' and you give your bicycle away in order to do it with someone you really crave [*laughter*], you'll never be able to earn any money in that field, no matter what. You've gotten too vulnerable."

You do need distancing, and the ritual of distancing that gigolos go through. There's also an alienation from yourself, a situation with costumes and postures—the way you dance, and so forth. It's most complex.

INT: You're then a kind of Prince Charming.

RD: Right. You walk into your own fantasy figure. I think we're coming around where we can see all those areas of homosexuality that have to do with costumes, and areas of fantasy as very particular uses of appearance, as appearances that threaten because they possibly alienate me from this other *me* more true to myself than I've so far discovered. I felt this powerfully when I read D. H. Lawrence. I mean, if you could read Lawrence—actually this insight for me began when I read Robert Browning's dramatic monologues. I found the promise there of some *new me* when I would be at the end of an evening of outrageous camping, as last night, for example, we got more and more campy. And that was the play; but we were at a household of people for whom it was not a "play," who did not understand one thing we were doing. We sensed that our host can only meet us by being campy, so we went over and played with his playthings, and since that was very incidental for us, that was fun.

Well, if we had an evening in a leather bar in a leather outfit, that isn't what I'm talking about. The leather bar is a real practice, and obviously there are people within that practice who are in no way self-alienated. We can't talk about a poet like Thom Gunn [who has taken part in the San Francisco leather scene] alienating himself, because he understands . . . his poetry . . . he understands. The very step [into leather] would alienate me, because I've seen myself in terms of a middle-class household in which no leather is worn. Dresses yes. Suits and ties, yes. At the same time, I suppose my affecting ties is not dissimilar from wearing leather. Both are uniforms. I'm very seldom without a tie. Even when I walk out my front door to go shopping I'm dressed as my father dressed going to the office. I didn't really start doing that until I found Jess.

INT: Why the change through Jess? Wouldn't you dress this way if you were going to a regular job?

RD: Finding Jess made a householder of me. Not only did I view poetry as a profession comparable to architecture, but I viewed love, the person you come to at the end of the fairytale when you feel you have found the person true to you or the person you haven't yet found, but whom you idealize, as transpiring in a household. I am a householder.

INT: To most poets, wearing a tie and coat would be bizarre.

RD: I know a tie is bizarre. That's *another* outfit. I don't think it's a question of leather as bizarre, though we think wearing leather is bizarre. To someone who does, putting on a coat and a tie and walking to an office is part of another world, another bizarre world.

INT: Leather-wearers may be either straight or gay.

RD: Oddly, leather has come to mean "gay." You are right to say that it actually is neither gay nor straight. I'm sure there are lots of Hells Angels bikers who would protest.

INT: What about drag? Is going in drag gay or straight?

RD: Neither. Since the majority of transvestites by clinical record are heterosexual, cross-dressing certainly isn't gay. As a matter of fact, I think homosexuals tend to go into transvestite clothing not in a transvestite way, to appear convincingly as a female, but in order to be absolutely mad "queens." Transvestites walk the street not to "look" outrageous but to look like your grandmother. Most of them are "out" all their lives and never notice they are fighting other women at rummage sales for clothes. Those "ladies" are never picked up by *men* at all [*laughter*], and they comprise most of the case histories. So, I think that we are in a delusion, a delusion of a minority, to think that costumes are something that homosexuals, and homosexuals alone, don. Housewives put on housewife costumes.

INT: Yet, Robert, when you go out to shop and are dressed in tie and shirt, nobody is going to point at you and say, "Oh, look at that man in that outrageous getup."

RD: They are likely to in San Francisco. [*laughter*]

INT: There are protocols, right?

RD: Right. If in my outfit I walk down the street in Bakersfield, California, nobody's going to notice. Bakersfield's my imaginary town, one I haven't returned to since 1936. In leather, now, they might notice, and be repulsed, unless I were scroungy enough to pass as a heterosexual Hells Angel.

INT: I'm fascinated by the household idea. The way you live, write, share your life with Jess. For Bob and I have something similar.

RD: We talked before about where I wanted to put the picture of my life. I'd inherited the conventional fairytale idea of a household, consisting of wife and husband. So I actually married, and always felt guilty in the marriage, although I married because I was in love. I felt guilt because in dreams and in poems it was the male I craved for marriage. In fact, my first poems where a woman really appears came some years after my marriage, and had to do with fairytale experience.

INT: You didn't rush into your marriage. You lived with a woman for two years.

RD: Yeah. I didn't rush into it. Or maybe I did rush into it, because we may have gotten married because it's a way for both to say, "We are not at the end," when that was what was really on our minds. In other words, the marriage was a step that itself had built into that act once we both realized that we ought not to have married.

INT: How does homosexual marriage differ?

RD: I feel homosexuality, in marriage, creates the same bind; and it happens because it must find out how it feels about marriage. I recall the first of my poems where the word "marriage" comes forward naming, "Yes, it is a marriage between Jess Collins and me," was in "Passages," about the ring and so forth; and *marriage* is referred to. It was a very sweet pang indeed that I felt, having taken a terrible risk, for I was not at all clear about *marriage*. Was marriage a church sacrament or was it a life sacrament? And had I intruded upon a sacrament? Obviously, in the poem the idea appears, and from then on I felt that with Jess I had a true marriage.

INT: How formalized was the marriage? Paperwork? Rings?

RD: We've never had a license or a contract or an agreement, and I mean we don't have such governing us. That's a great gain, because we've always known why we are together. Yet after twenty-six years we've accumulated such real estate that our money has never been in a separate account; it's always been in common; and everything is hidden in common. That itself comes to be a marriage. It's an economic agreement, isn't it? Economic agreements are contracts. So I have very mixed feelings still about "marriage," Bob. I realize I have inner contracts, deep inner contracts with Jess. For one thing, I knew him six months before I moved in with him. And moving in then was not yet a deep inner contract, although I knew I would never move away from loving him. That would be disastrous! In prior relationships I had such needs and they were under such compulsion that I had no confidence they would continue. And I'm not talking about would you live together always. I now understood that you don't move away from loving as a matter of fact. Where you have terminated a relationship the love continues. You can't wrap up and destroy the fact that you love. So, by thirty-one I did know that much.

INT: How long has your friendship with Jess lasted?

RD: We met in the summer of 1950 and I moved in in 1951. So this is the twenty-sixth year.

INT: Have there been times when you've both had to get distance from one another?

RD: No. Never. I have fallen in love with others. I don't understand the mystery of falling in love. And I have sometimes been ruthless. In the beginning, when I first fell in love, because of my commitment to Jess, I both had to consummate it and at the same time had to cut it off entirely. I had such powerful feelings almost immediately, reaffirming my love for Jess. But I also felt his pain more than I could feel much pleasure in consummating with someone else, so I simply backed off. We went off together to Europe, Jess and I. I knew that distance would help, and I have always felt that Eros would punish me no matter what I did to try to rectify matters. I still had erotic feelings I attributed to the ancient, priapic Greek gods. And more than that the sense of being punished was reaffirmed because I'm deeply Freudian, not Jungian. Freud places the burden on Eros and Thanatos. Not a lot of fancy archetypes. In recent poems I've been writing about *He* coming to attend me. This *He* consists of all the lovers I have had, and is the figure in the fairytale. Jess is of far more value to me than the figure in the tale. He is not, in fact, that figure. He's Jess.

And since one's actual love for a living person is always stronger than any in a fairytale, I could tell the fairytale to go and fuck itself. I mean, the fairytale of the ideal lover is not anything tremendous. But I was raised by my adoptive parents as a reincarnated person, as one in a fairytale. I came to feel, "Okay, fairytale, you can lay it on me over and over again and remind me that that's the order, but here and now is the only time I'm [in] and as long as the two of us are alive together, and all your heavy orders—and I know they can be heavy from the gods—I stand solid, and I'll take the full consequences. But *you* don't get to conquer in this area, fairytale, because my simple human life is stronger. I don't care if Jess were to die and it was revealed that I was totally dependent on him, and the hill came crashing down on me, and because of the many times I fell in love and did not obey that primal order of Eros, so Jess gave me the works. You can give me the works, fairytale, but not while Jess is here."

INT: There's more than a little mysticism in what you are saying.

RD: True. My magic now is stronger than any other magic. And if it is a mere magic, I don't care. Later, give me Reality. I'll take all the reality Eros or Fairytale can dish out. You can land on me again. You can throw me back. Say that I'm meant to go to hell. I wouldn't drag Jess to hell for company; but I'm not going to make a hell here and now in order to practice being in hell. This all has all along been my reaction to Good and Evil. If there's a war between them, tell me that Evil will conquer. I don't take Good because what I understand is Good is going to win. As a matter of fact, I choose Good over Evil because only if I practice it will it exist. Its existence is more important than its winning.

INT: I'd like to return to your household idea, because I assume from what you've said that much centering is required. Perhaps you'd review the idea. Say that your center is not Jess. Yet you imply that you have an energy source, a place of *quietus* you can visit to be restored and refreshed, and move into the external world of your numerous readings, lectures, public appearances. You know that Jess is there securing the "home."

INT: Haven't you been lucky to have found a beautiful man to work all this out with?

RD: We are so close, very cooperative in temperament. We had that point of decision: I was able to move in with him only by realizing that I felt as enthusiastic about his painting as I did about my own poetry, that it was a "thing," a process of art taking place, and I would not worry about whether we would be successful or not. I had in my own work, especially in the late 1940s, tried to aim at qualifying in the full profession as one would understand that state of poetry, which meant being drawn to something we call "English literature," a dual attracting force. Initially, Robert Browning's monologues, as I've said, showed me how to expand a person within a poem. My family had valued Browning as much as they valued architects, painters, and doctors. So they gave me a sense of qualifying professionally for what a poet was, a faith that beautifully contained the promise of the *poet me* who was yet to emerge. And this: my family was achievement-centered, as the professional middle class is—and I was blessed to be nurtured in such an environment.

INT: I'd like to hear more of your connection with earlier critics, as it explains the development of your poetry.

RD: One of the first things that gave me shell shock was the question I'd framed for myself: "Are you going to qualify among THE poets?" I read statements by other poets and critics about how they value originality, and then how they value the presence in poetry of immediate experience recollected and defined. Poets who admire these two qualities greatly derogate poets who derive more from literature than from life.

The poet I so much admired, Ezra Pound, disturbed contemporary critics because he derived so directly from Homer—the purest, in a sense, of all literary sources—and from other ancient poets, some of them "anonymous." In Robert Browning's day it was taken *au naturel* that you derived from other poets. In his day he was fantastically admired. Today, though, he is in great disrepute. This great poet, so seminal in the development of my own work, is now viewed as having no psychological depth, an ersatz monologuist. When I was in my early twenties I was aware, and, gee, wondered whether I had any style of my own. Did I have originality? The part of me wanting to qualify as a poet would see this lack as a real disqualification. I could see that if I were to complain of the style and originality I saw in most known, active poets, I would be disqualified by the Establishment poetry world. In 1950 to 1952, the period when I came to know Jess, I went way beyond where I'd been before, absorbing being a "poet," and became almost entirely a "consequence" of

The Pisan Cantos and of *Paterson.* I had written a long poem in the manner of Williams. I had not yet found the "hard line" I was driving towards, one that I hoped would distinguish me from other poets who were also following Williams, now an acceptable model, almost a tradition.

I sat down, and for two years wrote entirely like Gertrude Stein. I had her recordings, owned the first ones when I was seventeen, so I could hear her voice and imitate both her writing and her speaking manner. I wanted to think like Stein. I gave up completely any possible original-ity of my own. I had been drawn to Stein because what she had done had been so despised by people as a fake or a fraud. She wasn't thought of as being sufficiently derivative of the "literature" readers and critics were comfortable with. She insulted the profession of writing! So I took her indifference to public acclaim and her listening to her own voice as my identification with the god Mercury, or the mercurial element of my professional drive.

INT: I'm delighted to hear you love Stein, for we share that. When I was in high school, I discovered her novel *Ida,* bought the Virgil Thomson 78 recording of *Four Saints in Three Acts,* and listened to it on a windup Victrola—an unusual passion for a Wisconsin farm boy. Her voice and manner were infectious, and my first feeble attempts at writing, continuing well through my army days, were almost always evocative of Stein.

INT: You strike me as deeply imitative of voices that influence you.

RD: Again, we can think of the other evening with those LA friends with the big swimming pool and all, and we find ourselves in a lifestyle of camp. Or, if I go to England, where everybody uses that accent, I'd keep trying it out and would probably return home disillusioned with myself if I hadn't succeeded in a good imitation of it. So I do have an imitative drive. Aristotle saw poetry as imitation: imitating emotions, ways of behavior. So, actually, we return to our teens when we were trying to discover ourselves as homosexuals. We went and we read literature, though in the 1930s there wasn't much to find, although I did find Christopher Marlowe's *King Edward II.* The Renaissance poured forth its homosexual feelings, the very thing you as an adolescent were feeling. You didn't have to strain when you'd reached your thirties; older, you had to adapt particularly campy mannerisms if you hoped to find yourself accepted within a little caste within a society largely hostile to you and your kind.

INT: We talked about Krafft-Ebing before, when I would go to the University of Wisconsin library and hope nobody was watching to see what I was reading, as I stood in the library stacks, engrossed, and amazed.

RD: How embarrassing if someone had actually seen the page you were reading.

INT: Right. I would also frequent the art books section, grooving endlessly on Michelangelo's nude garland bearers on the Sistine Chapel ceiling.

RD: Too bad that his Adam has become a gay cliché, as has Bronzino's gorgeous young man.

INT: And don't forget Géricault's great self-portrait, John Singer Sargent's portrait of a young athlete, nor the great fleshy sailors in Paul Cadmus's paintings.

RD: When as a boy I admired Greek statues I worried that they didn't have fur on them! Where was their pubic hair? No pelf in those glorious armpits? I wondered if I would go through life hairless. Boy, was I narcissistic. I ended up growing ten times the hair I wanted—even over my back. As you saw yesterday at your friends' pool, my penis is hardly visible in its nest of fur.

INT: I also remember a beautiful Ingres—of Apollo or somebody, a young nude male wearing a cape, possessing a superbly sculpted pair of nates, talking to a sphinx. He was pretty hairless, and so sensuous.

RD: My principle of gayness is that the more body hair you have the more you admire males with scant hair, and vice versa.

INT: I've haunted gyms all my adult life, and have even taken swimming courses, just to be near and among gorgeous naked men. I never get enough.

RD: Robert, every male is going to be a "male body," right? Through athletes and swimmers, we were trying to create a central picture of the male, idealized, one that we could probably never touch, caress, suck, or feel. In a way, that's not sexuality—that's more like conviviality, living together in great physical intimacy, as the Greeks did. That's been broken in our society, and such urges or pleasures have been channeled so exclusively in the sexual direction that our sexuality becomes very extraordinary. We simply do not permit conviviality unless we're going to follow through and cash in on it sexually, making it. It's hard for us to learn that there are men we may love who are not sexual objects. That's proved very hard for me, for one thing, to learn. There are men I love and hug and kiss who are not sexual objects. How silly to assume that simply because someone wants to hug and kiss you that they want to share orgasms. Of course, it's always remarkable living with others that you fuse your loving and fucking. Such implies coercion, forms of bargaining that can go two ways. This is what I think D. H. Lawrence found so abhorrent he was almost ready to dispense with loving, and he was surrounded by people who loved him and by people he loved. But the presence of this bargain—"I'll love you if you fuck me, or I'll fuck you if you love me"—brings you to a place where you no longer recognize what you are doing; your motives are confused. You fall into what I call "psychodramas" where you want to be sure that you will have a fuck at home so you won't have a lonely evening if you're doomed to prowling and questing and finding nothing. All of that anxiety when you fear you may find yourself totally lover-less! Everyone in the whole society feels this, including the heterosexuals. We have come back to the fairytale. There are people who meet together to talk about their bisexuality. In their fairytale they require both sexes. There's more to it than simply having intercourse with both men and women—that's not bisexuality. Bisexuality must mean the fairytale stance where your Prince Charming knows his role and seeks for others who also require a mix of male/ female. So we no longer have a psychodrama based on bartering. The true bisexual tries to arrive at a secret inner appointment he has with life and with a substantive partner who will manifest both genders.

INT: Have you found Jess such a partner?

RD: I don't know, but I think so, for he has truly opened up life for me.

INT: The bartering business probably goes back to our parents, right?

RD: Jess and I both had similar parents, ones we wanted to get away from and households we wanted to leave, because in both cases they were coercive towards their children. Parents do a counterpart of: "I'll fuck you if you love me, or I'll love you if you fuck me." They say, "I'll be the parent, you be the child I need to have, and I'll love you as that child."

Jess and I both have strong feelings that when we reached adolescence our parents were loving us as the child they wished to see, not the child that we were. If they had seen the real us we would have betrayed them, for they would then not have possessed the children they needed to love. In my case, they decided I was to be an architect. I decided otherwise. Even so, if I had been an architect, they wouldn't have wanted the homosexual architect I would have become. And that element of dominating parents brings me back to my responses to Jess's paintings. No, I'm not a parent about his work. I'm not threatened by his art, any more than I am about difficulties I face writing my poetry.

I love to play without risk. So, if I'm a derivative poet, is that so bad? And I'll write, I decided, and find out what it's like. And it will be *me*. There's only one me, and I'm writing this poetry. How strange, for I know I am not truly original, as I hoped I'd be. Even if I went into leather, I'd be an imitator. For, yes, leather was (and is) threatening, and I avoided going in that direction; but, I know now, today, that if I had adopted the leather world, it would be *me* in leather.

So much on the story of my alienation. I was not alienated when I decided to write like Gertrude Stein.

INT: Do you see yourself in those explorative years as a series of shifting selves around different sectors?

RD: No, as a matter of fact I feel a tremendous oneness, an overcenteredness, and in my poetry, an overcomposition that I'm always trying to disperse. Perhaps I've been too self-conscious a writer.

When we were talking about the Jungian proposition of integration the other day, Jung had a very deep experience of schizophrenia. I have an almost psychotic integration. It's always hard for me not to find that I'm right there still. It's very different for me to move, and when I start a poem—here emerges again this overwhelming centeredness of self—a self so confident it's barely able to experience its risks. And, of course, I've been surrounded with love. How do you experience these edges when love has to be initiated all the time?

INT: Your adoptive parents must have felt extremely centered for themselves and for you.

RD: Oh, yes, well, for one thing. . . .

INT: Lots of people reject their parents. I don't want to play amateur psychologist. . . .

RD: No, I recognize those values, and my mother and father had this statement of their love, that we were in an adventure. And my mother in her second marriage was actually happier than in her first. She blossomed then. My father was an architect; my mother had no lifework. She was an architect's wife. Now it was important to me (Marjorie, whom I married, was a painter) that people I live with either have an art or are going to be artists, so eventually Jess and I got together. I saw that his painting was exactly like my writing. It's strong. It's going to be independent and form itself apart from my work. The lendings are reciprocal, for my writing will draw from his painting only to a degree, and will move on from there to its own voice. Our works will often, then, intermingle, but at the same time will be very independent. So in our marriage, unlike that of my parents—he is a professional; both of us are artists.

INT: Good Housekeeping is not then just a problem homosexual couples have; heterosexuals should also require that both partners be professionals, so that one is not seen as the "housewife," and, hence, inferior.

RD: Jess and I do our housework cooperatively, so strongly do we loathe the idea of having hired cleaners in the house underfoot. Since we both have professions, our housework is just one step ahead of playing house. We do a lot of washing. Jess washes the dishes. I'm the one who mops the floor. When I find myself brooding over why nobody mops the floor, I remember that I'm the one assigned to do it. This has nothing to do with Jess, who may, though, call me into order for my own good. And believe me, I can get out of order. Nothing in Jess's nature is really going to come over, sit down, and make bargains. I have known households that solve problems of living together by making maps, maps based on very intuitive relations—astrological maps even.

INT: Robert, I've known so many gays superficially immersed in astrology. They seem particularly prolific in Laguna Beach. One household, for example, appropriately situated up on Skyline Drive, has a dozen "family members," each in a bedroom reserved for a different sign of the zodiac! Astrology has obviously determined your life: your adoptive parents saw you as an "appointed child," one they sought out for a conjunction of birth signs they read as particularly advantageous for them, and for you. Would you agree with me, though, that a lot of the fascination that gays in particular have these days with birth signs, horoscopes, and conjoined planets is essentially superficial?

RD: No. I think they are all scenarios for life, fairytales, with at the outset a touch of magic. My parents' sense that I was "appointed" was profound, for they had worked through various astrological charts. I had to be born at dawn, on January 7, 1919. This they told me about when I was a child, long before I understood it. My sister was also adopted according to similar readings, and she was also told early. We were "found," our parents said, which distinguished us from our cousins who were born naturally and were thus "found" in a different sense. Our parents desired us in an unusual way. This of course is reproduced in my feeling that I have someone in Jess I've been "appointed" to find—though I didn't quest through astrology.

Artists more than other people, I think, are sympathetic to astrology and such things. Astrology is yet another form of the fairytale. If you walk on stage and are told to be Cleopatra, you know who you are to become, and you also know you'll be delivering great lines, but you don't

207

know whether they'll be Shakespeare's or George Bernard Shaw's. But no matter whose Cleo you are, you know there'll be a Caesar and you know there'll be a Mark Antony. Say you never know who the author is, and you don't know who's going to play Caesar and Antony—the cast hasn't yet been announced; and you might be in a movie where Olivier plays a role, or you might be in a play with ten-year-olds, and some ten-year-old will appear to play... but all we do will be in these terms set by the author and by the director of the play. Being of the zodiac, among the stars, is a form of being on stage where we are assigned predetermined parts as part of our destiny.

The way I see astrology is that in a chart constructed around your birth time you are placed among the stars. You see, we're getting back to what I started when we talked about Pound's *Cantos*. Viewing my life in relation to the feelings of the earth, astrology was very important to me. So, I wrote poems of ritual, thinking I must if I was to participate in earth days like Christmas and the onset of the spring solstice. This idea still influences me, and very recent poems are about emerging into life as living trees appear, along with grass. My earliest poems were filled with ritual sacrifices made in order to nurture your own life-sacrifice: like the grass, you appear, thrive, die, and return again to what Whitman called "earth's compost." That's a great scenario.

INT: How specifically does your zodiac relate to this?

RD: I spoke earlier about being in a drama. Our roles are so designed that my being a Capricorn will vary widely from any other Capricorn's. A cluster of American poets, ones I came to know early, were Capricorns. Kenneth Rexroth was one, born on Christ's birthday. Maybe Kenneth thinks he's Christ, but I don't think he's Christ. The 25th gets to be a very strange day. Henry Miller, Kenneth Patchen, Philip Lamantia, George Stanley, Charles Olson share the birth sign with me. I've just named a few people who are known and who were all born under that sign. George Stanley was actually born on my birthday, the same day. And, in order to put Jack Spicer in his place I once told him: "But you're not a Capricorn." Here, I can recite them—all those tremendous poets, but you see there's a legend of Capricorn poetry, isn't there?

INT: I love the idea of the shared birthday, for there are strange twists. Michael McClure and I share October 20th, with Oscar Wilde.

RD: You must know a lot about poets born then?

INT: I've made no search, so perhaps I'm not actually curious enough to feel there are energies to be drawn from such conjunctions.

INT: How does being a Capricorn affect your life with Jess?

RD: That Jess and I live together means that people apprised of such matters check out our horoscopes and say, "Well, Jess sort of redeems you, because a Capricorn is cold, acquisitive—all these negative characteristics. But his sun is in Leo. So where your sun is frozen in the ice of December and January, his sun radiates from its home sign, from the power of the lion, and comes through warming the whole, restoring your sun." I do love these legends. Yet, I don't love astrology, because my parents were always making me do things by astrology. And I felt so clamped into this awful . . . and I'd read these accounts of Capricorn and didn't want to be influenced by those.

When I first realized I was in love with Jess, I was sitting at a table with him in his apartment house. I was having an affair with the artist then living with him, and I was writing. I'd picked up [Jacques] Prévert and was translating, writing, and gradually this translation began to turn into a poem, "Song of the Borderguard." The Prévert became more and more haunted by a poem of Cavafy's, a poem of a military guard being on the borders of the Roman empire, being invaded, and losing his Roman identity. I was writing a love poem! So Henri Rousseau's famous lion appeared in the poem, and when it was through (we'd been talking all the time and I was also loosely translating). This is typical of how from a strange series of circuits my work arises. I was there sitting with two people both of whom were my intimates, arguing art, talking, as I was writing, translating Prévert, losing track of the Prévert and turning it into this poem. I recognized dimly that I was writing a poem about a man and his beloved: *believe believe believe.* And so I was confronting the issue: *Do I believe in love?*

INT: Now there is a re-placement.

RD: As I move deeper into the content of the poem why does the Cavafy appear? I'm flooded from the outside into the empire of whom I had assumed I was, a Greek or a Roman border guard. I'm then flooded with another identity, the living *me* who is in love, something I'd not yet admitted. I am a *barbarian* who is in love. I don't then know what the poem will be titled, and won't for some three or four months when at last I enjoy the full confidence of the poem. Once it was finished I *knew* I was in love with Jess, not his roommate artist with whom I was having an affair. The issue became complex, for I maintained the affair, thinking "how strange." Always before, I'd been in the torture of being in love, and maintaining an affair with things going wrong or right. It dawned on me that this person I'm sleeping with, playing at sex with, and getting love from, and loving, I'm beginning to love in another way. My love then shifts to Jess. Hitherto I had to feel I was literally *falling* in love, for ten miles down, smashing my face into concrete. And then you break the concrete. That no longer seemed to be true.

INT: I love the notion that there's serendipity when you find others you admire who have the same birthdays, as well as others you don't admire. My birthday, for example, as I said earlier, I share with Michael McClure, Oscar Wilde, and Arthur Rimbaud, all writers I much admire. On the other hand, one of my rare professional nemeses, Robert Louis Peters, a New York poet of less than modest talents, was actually born on my birthdate exactly, though he was one year younger. That his middle name was "Louis" was uncanny—for that's an unusual name, in a sense. My mother had named me after Robert Louis Stevenson. He began writing me when my first book, *Songs for a Son* [W. W. Norton, 1967], appeared, demanding that I change my name, for he disliked my verse so much he feared contamination if anyone thought he had written *Songs*. He proceeded to send flyers to all journals and critics in the country labeling me "the false Robert L. Peters." His threat to sue me for libel if I didn't stop the publication of *Songs* without changing my name came to naught. The following year we actually met in Boston at a meeting for a foundation sending American college students to bike through Europe. Curiously, we had almost nothing to say to one another. By 1970 he was dead, due to what causes I was never able to determine.

RD: You must have had no trouble shucking this albatross.

INT: None, really. An arcane blip on the screen of my long writing career. But whatever juxtaposition of planets produced us at the same time still intrigues. There's no way, of course, to find out the exact ramifications of such conjunctions.

RD: I may have heard of him, for when I saw your *Songs for a Son* I had a mixed impression, as I did when I first read the two Dickeys, James and William. And James Wright, because of overlapping with three or four other *Wrights* who were poets, was also hard to decipher. When either of the Dickeys published we'd say "tricky Dickey," because you couldn't tell whether James or William was at work. James clearly was the powerhouse of the pair, and is a shamanist poet, as the other Dickey is not. William Dickey writes New Criticism poetry, not very interesting or demanding.

INT: One complication I don't like is that several of my publications, including some scholarly ones, are cataloged in the Library of Congress as his, with his birth year rather than mine. I've tried several times to get this cleared up, including two visits to the actual DC library. But, I've never succeeded. So the mangy man has a claw or two in me still, wouldn't you say?

RD: Well, I'd account for this as astrological, which returns us to the notion of the play. He happens to have been handed your name and a similar role in life's play. You, though, Robert, are writing your own play, and are the author of your astrological sign, as I was not. For my adoptive parents were. Their authorship was so powerful, attractive, and informing that it remains parental to me. That's why I don't employ much astrology in my writing—if you author your own, as you have, you are bequeathed a special creative power. And I've not had that luxury. I have not, then, "authored" myself.

INT: I'm not sure, Robert, why scriptwriting is so important to us poets.

RD: You remarked that people are busily "taking up astrology" almost as an element of gay culture, like a parlor game perhaps. I'm fascinated, though I remain critical, for, since I was born into all this I've never had the experience of discovering it for myself. You may of course eventually find yourself converted in some terrific mystical experience; in my case, though, the nuances I should enjoy never truly come to life.

INT: Readers, though, regard you as a leading mystical poet, right?

RD: Readers err when they interpret my poetry as more mystical than it is. I admit to a high regard for great mystics, Donne, Blake, Hopkins. Certainly, I do have a language of mysticism, since I do feel that poetry opens up a geography for me, a mixture of linguistic wondrousness. When poetry changes me, I've had a mystical experience. Unless you see what I experience as "language mysticism," I don't want to be seen as a "mystic." There's a difference. People keep trying to read me out as religious.

INT: You don't fault them for this, do you?

RD: I'm a poet whose work is flooded with religion the way landscapes are flooded with grass and trees. I'm also a tree. [*laughter*] I'm constantly producing leaves and seeds, but I don't think I'm a leaf or a seed. I know for instance that I carry seeds, yet I am not a seed. I'm removed from—"seed-dom." I'm not about to sprout into a tree.

I've read St. John of the Cross, St. Francis, and the Old and New Testaments. I respect truly religious people whose doctrines reveal to us what the religious life is. I find it puzzling, and wonderful, that St. John of the Cross is a poet and a saint. That's a great mystery. But I'm a poet, and I share that with him. It's not incidental that my poetry is a record of human love. I'm a lover, that's true. [*laughter*]

INT: Can't you also say of your poetry that you are into more than intrauterine devices, or sperm, as part of a total vision? The eroticism?

RD: In addition to the eroticism, there are elements of simple human religion in my work. You'll find that sometimes a father will be my father, but not often. In my verse, the father is often Zeus-Father. In that poem where I actually present the Lord's Prayer, I pray in extremity. An extremity is when I'm not feeling endangered, but when I feel that my soul may be endangered, and I want to see it elevated, placed where it can be calm and, hence, restored to me. I place it in God's hands, and if I were to think about it, that God would be the one I find in Alfred North Whitehead. When I'm in extremity, I pray almost as though I am still a child, and pray to the wrathful and fearsome Father of the Old Testament. I see myself as a Judeo-Christian poet.

PART IV

"Surrounded by Love's Company"

**With Charles Olson and Ruth Witt-Diamant,
San Francisco State College, 1957**

On Pound and Williams

(with James Laughlin, 1983)

It is appropriate in this part devoted to "Love's Company" to give fore-most place to a tribute to Ezra Pound and William Carlos Williams, two poets Duncan highly revered. These observations were recorded in the home of Duncan's publisher James Laughlin in Norfolk, Connecti-cut, on April 22, 1983, and published in American Poetry *(vol. 6, no. 1, Fall 1988). (Laughlin's questions and promptings were not part of this transcript.) Duncan describes the overwhelming effect on him of Pound's* XXX Cantos *and the "real Visions . . . occurring within the poem itself." Speaking of Pound's desire for a scheme for his* Cantos, *Duncan notes, "It isn't the power thing that holds it together, but the deep inhabiting of the emotion."* Paterson *was exciting "because every immediate area . . . is opening up" and "at every moment that poem bursts its own outline."*

—Ed.

ROBERT DUNCAN: Let's start out on Pound as I did when I was a freshman in college with *The Cantos*. I was on the freshman staff of the college literary magazine and had already discovered that when I thought something was good there would be a whole staff full of "nos" and I would be the only "yes"; when I thought something was lousy, there would be a whole staff full of "yeses" and I'd be the only "no." Actually, this made me feel like I had an identity for the first time. I asked to return one of these manuscripts that interested me—it was a sort of precious imitation of Edith Sitwell—and I asked to meet the young woman who had written the poem. She turned out to be a marvelous bluestocking, endlessly amusing. Her name was Antoinette [Krause], and she came from St. Louis and knew Tennessee Williams. I was wide-eyed and impressed. She was reading Proust in French. She knew streams of names I didn't know. And her consort—which is the only name you would use at the time for Robert [Bartlett] Haas, who

217

eventually married her—was writing a dissertation on Gertrude Stein. This is Berkeley 1936, or at the latest early 1937.

We met for tea, and I left poems with her. As they walked me back to campus down Bancroft, Haas said, "Should he read Eliot?" She said, "Oh no, his work is much too lurid as it is. He should read Pound." I rushed off to a bookstore and opened up a volume which was called *XXX Cantos*. I'm not quite sure that at seventeen going on eighteen that I wasn't merely reading "x-x-x"; it took a vast summoning of my intellectual powers at the time to realize it meant "thirty." I opened and read, "And then went down to the ship," and it was just too much, I was overcome. I looked around the bookstore and shut the volume. I kept going back to the bookshop to read just this one line, maybe sneaking the next two, but it was just too much for me, so I ended up buying *The Fifth Decad of Cantos* first. My Pound volumes are all dated, and by the time you come to 1938 I had everything that was available.

It took me some time to go back to *Personae*, the earlier Pound, because I was so absolutely fascinated with *The Cantos*. Before I could read, my parents had read me Langley Meyers's *The Odyssey*, and here it was in a poem. Then one of the pieces that I wrote in high school (it survives because it was printed in the school paper) was a sort of prose take on [John] Masefield's poem on the ship loaded with spoils. I obviously had some kind of attachment to this setting out on a boat. It became a prime model for me.

In the years just before the war we faced the baffling collection—the Adams and Chinese Cantos. It is very hard for a Romantic poet addicted to rhetoric to make his way through dutifully and begin to hear the music. It's interesting to note, though, that for a poet who supposedly deplored rhetoric, the rhetoric of *The Cantos* is commanding. One of the things Pound did when he "modernized" or reconsidered *The Cantos* was to open with a commanding rhetoric, not talkative like the opening of the first proposition in the original first three Cantos. I knew the music was there, but it wasn't as clear as in those remarkable Adams Cantos that refused to yield to any rhetoric. The music was a fineness of finding rhyme, sensing the rhyme then breaking the lines of Adams in true rhythmic verse in which you'd catch a kind of music in the middle of the prose which was a letter.

By the way, very shortly after that I did read Eliot, who *was* too lurid, and *The Waste Land* governed a lot of my early poetry—"The Venice Poem" especially.

In any case, by the time we come to *The Pisan Cantos*, the sense was of a terrific immediacy. You clearly grasped historically that in the [detention] camp at Pisa everything had come home, and now it didn't have the distance of the earlier Cantos. One of the troubling things in those early Cantos is the distance, the distance in which Pound could almost make choices and almost be constructing a poem. Suddenly the meaning of all those constructions changed, and it was a change in the dramatic monologue. One of the things that interests me in Pound's own origin in Robert Browning's dramatic monologue is that there is always the potential in the dramatic monologue that you might be the person you were pretending to be. It's like doing your own portrait. When Rembrandt goes back and back and back to look at Rembrandt's face, he is looking at the face the way he looks at faces as such, so we don't think of it as egotism. He is always really seeing.

Certainly that's the character I get in *The Cantos*—it's not confession— Pound is suddenly one of the people present in the same way that other people are. There is tremendous contrast between *The Pisan Cantos* and the presence of the poet doing his autoportrait (not doing his autobiography) and the work of the Confessional poets, for instance, who always really proposed to us that we are hearing their local whine. In our gang we turned away from the Confessional poets with distaste about what they did largely because it was seen as a misuse or misreading of what the dramatic monologue was. They failed to imagine themselves and became the victims of their own forms. That was very different from what was happening in the later Cantos. Think about the distance in "Mauberley," where there is a persona. In *The Cantos* there is no persona, but rather dramatis personae.

Eventually, it became clear to those of us who were following the poem that there were not going to be one hundred Cantos. Fairly early R. P. Blackmur saw that the poem could only have a purgatory and heaven in a secondary sense. Pound doesn't even do a tour of hell, for example, but rather goes straight to his own circle. He is rescued by Plotinus, who freezes the whole thing over and brings Pound up out of it. These are parts I take very directly as actually far more interesting than, say, ghosts at a séance table. You feel the reality emerging on that plane, seeing Blake running in the distance. These seem to be real Visions—no visions had before the poem, but rather Visions occurring within the poem itself. Pound has no guide, which is striking. Virgil takes Dante through hell but Pound, who couldn't accept at that level what Dante was, goes immediately to the part he loathes. In *The Divine Comedy* Virgil stops Dante at one point when he is with the barrators and says, "If you stand here gloating while the devils punish these people you will stay here." In Pound's case, when that freezing moment comes he is simply rescued. So there must have been a feeling that there was a hell but that there could be no guide through it. Pound would have been as removed from Dante's world as Dante would have been removed from Virgil's. So in a way I see that in the hell Cantos, Pound does much more gloating than Dante does. Eliot's remark was that he seemed to be punishing people he disliked.

In the year Pound spent with [W. B.] Yeats I'm convinced he got brainwashed. He was enchanted by Yeats, who knew that Pound was attracted to the Neoplatonic material. In earlier poems Pound had already shown how vivid the gods were for him, and Yeats was encouraging about this. So it is a very real Plotinus who appears and freezes over a surface of hell, which Pound both believed in and didn't. And because he is simply rescued from hell, this makes him unable to go deep into a purgatory or deep into a paradise. The most eloquent passages at the end of *The Cantos* center on Pound's sense that none of us can do it [ourselves].

The lot my generation faces is that we don't have the confidence of hell. We don't have the confidence of purgatory or of heaven. I don't necessarily mean this to sound negative, that we are lacking something. We may be the first generation who writes without any guarantee. We can't even wrap ourselves in the evidence that we might have fame, which was very attractive to Pound's generation. Historically, I see us facing such a likelihood that the civilization that maintains that part of itself will just collapse. Pound's depression in part was his sense that *The Cantos* were not shaping to the great poem he dreamed they could be. And yet we were excited by that very thing. He despaired over the form, yet we saw that despair of form absolutely the given thing—in the modern experience. This wasn't a negative despair. Despair is such an essential part of experience, yet it in no way robs me of daily life. But the despair of a form which Pound was suffering is actually the form of *The Cantos*. To have the courage of coming to its consequences.

All along Pound asks isn't everything draft and fragment, so that in the end we are back to the beginning. Looking at Vortex canvases, Pound's idea of composition was that you could give it a kind of force that would force a composition of the total poem. In my generation we weren't looking for that kind of closure. It was a shock to see [Charles] Olson bringing *Maximus* to closure. Of course he left fragments which Butterick has had to assemble, but what I mean is that he had refrains appear, things that promised a closure, where originally he had proposed that *Maximus* would be open.

I'm a bookish temperament. Books are as real to me as mountains and trees and bushes, as they obviously were to Pound. Books haunt my poetry, so it was a sitting duck to find a model in Ezra's *Cantos*. "Passages" is not a long poem at all, by the way. It is a field, which is a constellation. Constellations might enlarge but they are not long; you are not going from one place to another. I see things as collages, assemblages, a step Pound didn't seem to take. His idea of Vortex or ideogram is still a figure of a power, an area charged with a very specific power draws everything into a constellation. That's part of what I think he hoped *The Cantos* would have, then despaired of it. As the poem progresses there are centers, but they didn't do what he long dreamt of after the Vortex period, that there would be [a?] commanding power that would shape it.

Part of the aftereffect of both the German/Hitlerian thing and my own family preaching "the will to power" to us when we were little made me feel whenever anyone mentioned power that I practically wanted to wind down so that you couldn't even run a tinkertoy with it. I was not interested in some center that would form, make a dynamo. Henry Adams tells us a lot when he has the virgin and the dynamo. It's a sort of proto-*Cantos* and makes you wonder if Adams and Pound were first cousins or something. Thus I wanted no rhetoric but rather a launching out, which takes us back to the ship.

I had a more difficult time with [William Carlos] Williams. The early poetry was difficult for me until I got hold of *The Wedge*, which taught me how to read it. After a time I came to see that there really was music in it, but at first I just wasn't going to hear it with my own volunteer ear.

One of the great things that happened was the restoration of the *Spring and All* poems to their original context. Until that occurred, they'd been approached as oddities—why is he paying attention to that wheelbarrow? Yet after the fact, you can look at that individual poem in context and see that it is beautifully made. One of the most outstanding delusions is that those poems are casual, that they aren't measured.

After the war those two strands came together. We had *The Pisan Cantos*, and *Paterson* was begun. Much of our energy at that time was spent in absolutely foolish debates about how the *Four Quartets* was real and *Paterson* wasn't—the kind of thing only universities would set up. I was earning my living typing theses around Cal, and the literary powers that were would challenge us nuts to a debate on *Paterson* and/or the *Four Quartets*. I got so that I wanted to throw the *Four Quartets* down the well. As a matter of fact, I couldn't even read them decently, had no humor about them left at all because of the outrages that went on about refusing to listen to *Paterson*.

Much of our time also went into imagining the poem. I pictured Williams as imagining the poem also. It was a very active thing. There were very few of us reading *Paterson*. There was a bookstore off campus which we got to order ten copies of volume one. Robin Blaser and I each dutifully bought our copies, but no one on the faculty did. So when it came to volume three, the bookstore ordered only two copies. Volume three is where Randall Jarrell jumped off the wagon, saying this was too much or too little. That's when we started having our debates.

The great adventure of *Paterson* was when Williams wrote the end, then suddenly discovered that the end in our time doesn't really mean the end. Gertrude Stein had already seen this in *Four Saints in Three Acts*, where she keeps announcing this is the end. We weren't diminished at all when after the end Paterson was still there. I think it was a great moment in the question of the open poem. We were puzzled when *Paterson* first appeared by the fact that he had taken the structure out of *Finnegans Wake*—what Williams himself had written about in *transition*—of having the river as a woman, the city as a man, all laid out in sort of a dreamland. We began to see that there would be four books, as in *Finnegan*. This was one of our main critiques about the *Four Quartets*, that it was a regressive form. "The Venice Poem" is written in movements like a sonata, and Ginsberg's *Howl* is of course written in movements. Yet resting back on a preexisting musical form was not the excitement we sensed moving in *Paterson*. The lucky thing is that for all the heavy business that William Carlos Williams borrowed from *Finnegan*, he was not writing a circular form like Joyce, one turning back into itself. At every moment that poem bursts its own outline.

It was so exciting to read because everything was numbered and looked like it was under control, but every immediate area of that poem is opening up. By the time he comes to the theme of radium itself—the pitch-blend—we have the sense that throughout some element is there, but more than that now multiple elements, and this is how we read. With Concrete poetry we see what it is, so that's not pitch-blend; it's already separated out and we see the point. But the poems which draw us to read them over and over will re-reveal themselves, like that radium passage which is so loaded.

On one level, radium is radium for Williams. The one thing that totally redeems his mind is that things are things. In Ginsberg's "Plutonian Ode" plutonium is a symbol, but nothing is that way in *Paterson*. A symbol is always a limited meaning that comes from looking at an actual thing. If you return to a thing more symbols will be there, which is the opposite of what people expect of a symbol. Pound skirts this question. Very early he wrote that image is not metaphor. That's a place where I think Pound got something very, very clear—an image is actually a point you can return to and make metaphors out of. The image itself is actually a source, and if you look again other meanings come from it. *Paterson* is a lively exploration of this. What he takes from Joyce—the Falls are language falling, for instance—which is the symbolic level, is rescued, because when he is looking at the Falls they turn out to be falls, which is much more than questions of the language going to pieces.

In some funny way I don't remember things being closed down when Book Four of *Paterson* was posed as the end. I actually feel that we made a breakthrough when we had a floating book following. And yet the first poet with this kind of thing happening wasn't Williams, but Spenser. Once he gets *The Faerie Queene* into form he has the "Mutability Cantos" that just float. Imagine. There is a period in poetry going from Spenser through Williams in which there is always going to be a mutability canto, there is always going to be "and then . . ." What you've neatly made in four movements is not the end of anything.

When we come to Williams's later work it was so immediately human to me that I had no aesthetic judgment. His line interested me. The line and rhythms I built on all the time. My own long lines relate to his tercet, his triadic line. In the correspondence in *Origin* he told us we didn't have measure, and I wondered why he put it that way. Everything has measure. What we lack is observation of the measure of what we have done. In a way what he meant was that we didn't have a consciousness of the measure of the things we were doing. He himself certainly has consciousness of it in the late work. You can't dream that this wasn't a demonstration of feeling the presence of measures. Yet no one had given him a language in which to talk about it. When he writes to describe the measures he does a pretty good job of it, but he keeps it diffuse and confused so that other possibilities are there. He loves to be in a muddle when he's talking about what he's trying to get at; he doesn't want a summary statement. In my own work I still build on the implications of this, and find that I don't exhaust it.

In that fifth issue of *Origin*, where my work appears (which is retrograde, because I'd stayed with the work I'd written four years earlier), he has that astounding poem with the bridge and the dead dog. A tremendous breakthrough. Nowhere did he have Pound's structure of opinions that Pound had already framed by the time of *Kulchur*. In part he got caught in that because he felt he ought to have a solid structure. Where Pound wanted systems and schemes, for Williams things would come and go. Pound's facism sat there as a scheme, not just a political picture of power but a scheme that would give structure. After "The Venice Poem" Pound wrote to me that I should have had a plan, and already I saw that I'd *over*planned that poem. It was like a bridge, but what truck was going to go driving over the poem? In each movement there's to be a work of art and so forth, as if I was reading *Ulysses*. Now that you've done that would you ever want to see a plan again? And here comes Ezra's inevitable, "You should have had a plan." You didn't just write back, "One thing you don't have, buddy, in *The Cantos* is a plan, thank God."

I'm thinking of the button-maker clinging onto this one raft in the sea. One aspect of Ezra is that way. Not only is it fragments and wreckage from something in his mind, but he's got to be sure he's got this one log—his plan. It's a real contrast because Williams had the most simplistic of plans—an architect would have said fine, you've got four sections, you're not going to get in any trouble, Joyce has already shown how to do this. But then when he's got into it he pays no attention to the plan at all, constantly remodeling the architect's house, where he does everything the people who live in the house suggest. Finally, you can't even find where the plan was; you just see ghosts of what was. Ezra is just the opposite, constantly telling himself the plan is there, yet beginning to lament that there couldn't have been a plan anyway.

Williams had aspects that you'd think were collage—the introduction of letters—and immediately I responded to that. I don't think I ever responded to the thing Williams was haunted by in that very dramatic section of *Paterson* where the language goes to pieces; that seemed again like something borrowed from speculation on *Finnegan*. He was imitating in that section of the poem what he thought was all around him. I don't think in my own work I was attracted to things as symptoms. That's where I'm close to Ezra: I just roar if I don't like it. Collage in my poems, the things that are brought in for assemblage, are included because of the feel of them, the musical contrast. That's typical of *The Cantos*. As you go along you see that he feels he needs a section that moves slowly, and knows right away what to build in there. Once you are in *The Pisan Cantos*, it is already somewhat easier to see what they add up to, compared to each canto in the *XXX Cantos*. There everyone was wondering what the thing about [Sigismundo] Malatesta was. In my imagination some of his despair about *The Cantos* was finally that we don't find out what and how Malatesta works, yet there he is.

I think I would have more a tendency myself now to respond to Pound's idea that you stand by your word with "yes, and look at it." In *The Cantos* it isn't the power thing that holds it together, but the deep inhabiting of the emotion. The heroic pathos is that he is the only poet I can think of in this century who actually plays the hero. In the '30s, because anthropologists were talking about "culture heroes," everybody said that Pound and Eliot were culture heroes. I don't think Eliot was ever a culture hero or wanted to be. But Pound turns out to have been a culture hero in a culture he saw doomed. He becomes the eloquent text of the doom and despair of the hero who undertakes the hubris of a culture that he knows too well is going to pieces. He undertakes the futile battle that in itself is wrong.

The World of Jaime de Angulo

(with Bob Callahan, 1979, excerpts)

This excerpt from Bob Callahan's discussion with Robert Duncan about the Indian shaman Jaime de Angulo appeared in The Netzahualcóyotl News *(vol. 1, no. 1) in 1979, and it touches on contemporary physics, C. G. Jung, linguistics, Ezra Pound, and being a "systematizer." Duncan says he's more like Jaime, whose figure was a parabola, and who declared "there's no center, there's no center in the universe."*

—Ed.

At the conclusion of a year of rebroadcasting Jaime de Angulo's Indian Tales *on radio station KPFA here in Berkeley, poet Robert Duncan kindly came over to the studio one afternoon to talk with co-host Susan Ohori and me about his feelings for the world of Jaime de Angulo. Mr. Duncan was a particularly welcome guest not only for his own unique intelligence, which he happily shared with us, but also because he had lived in the de Angulo household as the family typist during those years immediately preceding Jaime de Angulo's death.*

Upon hearing that particular program, I was moved to make a transcript of our talk, and such a reconstruction is presented here. The following interview, however, should in no way be taken as representing a formal statement by Mr. Duncan. "I dislike intensely the publication of talk," he has elsewhere written, "which I would distinguish on the one hand from a prepared lecture, and on the other from writing. I'm a writer, and as a writer, neither in poetry nor in prose do I proceed without care and design." What follows then is meant to be understood as an informal, free, open, rambling kitchen-table kind of conversation, as is offered to our friends and readers in just such a spirit and manner.

—Bob Callahan

BOB CALLAHAN: Robert, you were de Angulo's typist back in 1949?

ROBERT DUNCAN: Yes, I came to know Jaime de Angulo through Ezra Pound's correspondence urging me to get in touch with Jaime, though I had already met Nancy de Angulo, and she was an immensely attractive and impressive person. In the summer of 1949 I rented a room from the de Angulos, and stayed there through 1950 during the period when Jaime was dying of cancer. At the end of that period Jaime had become almost inert. And yet, although the doctors had surrounded him with painkillers of every kind, he would refuse to take these pills. You see, he dreaded going to sleep. This may have had something to do with his shamanic experiences and so forth, but he really had a great dread of sleeping. Not only of losing time, but of any loss of consciousness whatsoever. So he wouldn't take the painkillers and he would just lie there, and it had come to the place in the disease where the pain would just be a ripple going across his skin; there wasn't enough energy left in him to even have a spasm. And then when the pain had passed he would get out one or two more sentences of material that had become rather disjointed by then, as I remember. I would spend time with him, but I can't really remember what I was jotting down. I think he had just lost track of the material.

It wasn't until Jaime was in terminal illness that he addressed himself to the realization that his lifework was not yet accomplished. It hadn't really been typed up. There were stories written in longhand on various sheets of paper, stories to be typed. And I was the typist for most of those, and for all the manuscripts that appeared during that period. The very first typing job I had was Jaime's textbook on language.

BC: You mention Pound. Had you heard of de Angulo prior to your correspondence?

RD: Yes. There were rumors about Jaime that I had heard before I ever came to know him. I think that I must have heard of him first in the late '30s when I was in Berkeley. That the very young man that D. H. Lawrence had fallen in love with in Taos, and the reason Frieda had dragged Lawrence off to Mexico to get away from Taos, was Jaime de Angulo. Jaime's memory of D. H. Lawrence during that period was that Lawrence was an utterly repulsive man. Jaime hated him, but he was never very clear why. Apparently when Lawrence's relations with people became uneasy and troubled he began to sweat a particular kind of sweat which seemed to him to be a 100 percent reaction to the people of the

Jaime de Angulo. Photo by Gui Mayo.

British nobility. Both Bertrand Russell and the Sitwells also thought of Lawrence as repulsive and dirty. So maybe that's de Angulo's aristocratic background coming through. Lawrence's writing is clear on that, and so is Mabel Dodge's biography, although no one actually comes out and names Jaime.

So I had heard about this man who lived on the Sur, and who lived like an Indian shaman. And in the '30s they still talked about how extraordinarily beautiful Jaime was. He was certainly a very beautiful old man. In one of the ironies of the time, in a treatment for cancer, Jaime took female hormones. And I remember coming into what is now your kitchen–dining room, and Jaime was washing himself stripped to the waist, and he had female breasts, of course, because he had been taking female hormones for some time. It came as a great shock at that point; I mean, he had become a hermaphrodite in that sense. Another aspect of Jaime was that he was also a transvestite, and he liked to put on Nancy's clothes and go to San Francisco and seduce young girls, who never discovered he was a man because his sexual activities were not of a kind that would display that little secret to them.

But I think the transvestite role was certainly keyed to Jaime's constant fascination with what was a shaman. I have a very pronounced pelt on my back and neck, and Jaime told me that I would qualify in the Sur community as a were-bear, and he was fascinated because in my poetry bears had already appeared. Since I spent my childhood at Yosemite, why of course bears appear, along with snakes, but Jaime's very immediate fantasy was, and very seriously, yes, [that] exactly.

In Jaime's generation's writings on the American Indian they had noticed immediately the homosexual shaman, and Jaime's transvestite was a male lesbian, which means that you cross sex lines. I think that the crossing of sex lines meant to the Indian that you could also cross between the living and the dead. One of my observations of the shamanism of Gary Snyder is to raise this question—he seems to be a very straight character compared with the shamans we read about. Jaime's shamans have not only crossed sex lines but crossed every line entirely. They rob, they break the law, don't they? This is like that movement in the Jewish world in the eighteenth century in which you simply break all the commandments, turn them upside down. You are still related to the tribal commandments, but you break them all. And that means you have a kind of magical relationship with them, because you have transgressed, you've gone across. And of course the central idea in shamanism is going across.

Jaime, when he was dying, wanted more and more to tell about what he thought was the reality that was going to be there when he died. And he said he understood what it was the Indians were talking about. The model could be found in contemporary physics. Jaime would draw a parabola that went out into endless space, and say this is it: "I pass into this, and go back into the universe." So he had an Orphic conception of the universe. In its prayer of death Orphism says: "I return myself to the universe, out of which I came." And Jaime remained intensely interested in contemporary physics, and would read it over and over again. And yet he was always angry when a physicist like an Einstein or a Bohr or a Max Planck would try to put his model together with the Judeo-Christian concept in which the universe assumes a personality. Because for Jaime he was already a great personality, and that was quite enough personality to have around. Here he comes in line with [Charles] Olson; like Olson, not being a physicist, Jaime searched the mythology of what is our physical universe. He died before we have our picture, our contemporary picture of merging realities at the particle level. But it was there, the great questions were there, and they excited him, because then he could enter the ground of great questions. To die, for Jaime, was a very great thing.

BC: Robert, what was the connection, or disconnection, with Jung? Jaime seemed to move in and out, and around that world.

RD: Well, Jaime's first wife was Cary Baynes, who became a convert of Jung's, and was also a Jungian translator. So Jaime heartily hated Jung. But also Jaime and Nancy, like the rest of the Kroeber group, and those people who actually worked with that generation of Indians, had a good deal of scorn for Jung's usurping the Indian mind as being one he could talk about, and taking over a mythology as being in conformity with what all of us can now see happens to be a mythology of the German upper class. Yet, as a matter of fact, one damn well better study that mythology, because the powers that be all move out of Jungland, and they're as big and happy and hearty, for both good and evil, as ever we are liable to see. Yet we live in a world now where that contemporary ego out of Jungland has identified itself with the self, not to be part of the universe, or to be a child of the universe, but to be the universe itself! And that is quite astounding.

BC: Could I nudge you a little more on the language question? Jim Herndon, for example, once told me that Jack Spicer was among the first to claim Jaime as a language master, and a teacher. . . .

RD: Well, it's interesting hearing about Spicer in that context, because during the period when I was living at the de Angulos's, Spicer was in one of his feuds with me, and one of the terms of that feud, or one of the expressions, was Spicer's dismissing Jaime entirely from consideration. As I remember, when I was typing Jaime's book on language, and had showed it with some excitement to Spicer, who was then getting his formal academic training in linguistics, Spicer was quite scornful of the amateur character which Jaime very deliberately kept in his text. You see, Jaime was the guy who writes those letters to various linguistic magazines while sitting on the top of Big Sur with a theory about how you can get euphonics by using the number on a broken typewriter, or any other such eccentric idea. He would have a million of them, and put them all out there. And, as against this, in the realm of linguistics Spicer was absolutely, shatteringly, dogmatic, a closed piece of information, except when he is in a poem like *Language;* in the poetry he would be another person. But the minute somebody would supposedly hit on that field, Spicer would then turn on a series of classroom-like right or wrong answers, which came off like he was giving a test. So you were never able to get from Spicer the student of linguistics what you knew Spicer the poet actually knew. He was absolutely a dual person in that regard.

Jaime, on the other hand, would be very pitched against anything that would be settled. He always wanted to be unsettling. A part of his character was . . . I think it was a little like Rousseau, the painter Rousseau, who said to Picasso: "I'm the only modern, because I went to the Louvre and everything looked like you, but nothing looked like me."

Jaime avidly read all the linguists. He loved Sapir and Whorf, and put me onto them right away. They're the only ones to read, he'd say. Plus his own book on language. Both Jaime and Nancy had known Sapir, and had come to love him as a person.

Now wait—there was one time when I remember Spicer coming into this line, when the poet Spicer was talking to me about linguistics. It was during the period when I was writing about how much we got from poetry by beginning to consider the sounds instead of thinking about rhyme, and of alliteration, and all those other terms that we can throw out of doors now, thinking instead about the actual sounds of words as the linguists had then begun to describe them. And Trager and Smith had so extended the notations for junctures and for sounds, and for contours in recording speech, so that I felt very beholden to Trager and Smith. And Spicer was the one who had given me Trager and Smith to see how far they had gone once he realized I was really interested. Yet then, in an article when I referred to Trager in the context of Sapir and Whorf, Spicer said: "How can you put a schoolteacher like Trager next to real poets, real geniuses? Sapir and Whorf are all alone . . . and Jaime . . . Jaime's another one that is all alone." So, yes, at least the poet Spicer recognized the insights of de Angulo.

And of course Jaime always delighted in the impact that his deal-ing with Indian materials had had upon that field. But he would do so without having anything of the aspect that Spicer would present, one of a dual personality, one of them wanting to be an authority, the other one a poet. I think there's a contradiction between an authority and a scholar. And the university today is destroying scholars faster than they destroy poets—as a matter of fact, they're being nice to us poets now. They feed us, and pay us nice fees. But scholars are really out of court, because what the university wants are authorities, people who will produce new authorities to pass on an authoritarian line, and keep the thing solid.

. . .

One thing that strikes me about the whole generation of anthropolo-gists, and it comes out in the book *Ishi*. We tend to think of them as having this abstract subject called anthropology, an interest in primitive people or something, but in fact that is nonsense. They were fascinated by people! These so-called informants are people, and often, as in the case of the de Angulos, very close friends. Nancy would talk about how preposterous it was when they went up to Alturas, or into the Modoc territory, or the Miwok areas, living and talking with the Indian peoples there; but equally how preposterous the other way around when they would invite their Indian friends to Berkeley. We always think of Ishi, and how out of place he was living in modern Berkeley; and yet every-body is out of place, living in somebody else's house now, if we are really sensitive to it. You don't have to go to another tribe to be out of place. If you stay longer than three days anywhere you're out of place, and you don't even know how to line up for the bathroom.

. . .

I'd like to return to the question about Jung. I said that Jaime really hated Jung. This also means he didn't read later Jung at all, and he never reflected very much on what Jung came to say. He'd tell only certain very scornful stories about this German guy listening to these Indians. But he had another very personal reason in doing this. I think before I say a little more about Jung, one should bear in mind that Jaime's picture of what happens when you die is very different from Jung's need to have a center with a circumference. This of course is a great figure in the Christian Judaic ego relation to the universe, i.e., "I am the center wherever I am."

Now Charles Olson always kept that. His death figure was "I am the center." I said: "I've come to see you die," and he said: "I'm not dying now." As if his "I" was the Center. His "I" had become identical with the It, the Center of the Circle. But also Charles was devoutly Jungian; Jung had given him his whole replacement for the Catholic. So he had retained that Catholic figure of God as the Center of the Circumference.

Jaime, on the other hand, was profoundly not Catholic at all. His figure was a parabola going out to no center. He proudly showed me: there's no center, there's no center in the universe, he said. Get it out of your head. Look at contemporary physics. There's no center. But here contemporary physics was just illustrating his own profound feeling. What's most important to realize, however, is to realize we don't have just two profound feelings about/within the universe. We're talking about many profound feelings in the universe.

I'm more a Jaime-kind. It does not interest me that I might be the center of a circumference. I play with both of these views, and tend to be mercurial with coexisting possible universes. But the one that thrilled Jung, and steadied him, was the one he thought he had found in Indian designs. The importance of that symmetry is what drew Jung to the Indians. But the trouble with the redundancy of Jungians looking for Jungian designs is they don't look at *all* the designs. And are we going to believe that the designs they select will stand for the whole universe?

No. I think if you look around you will find various accounts. This is why the figure of Coyote Old Man is so fascinating, because him don't have no center. Him bad boy.

BC: I remember Carl Sauer often giving me one of those incredible synoptic overviews of American prehistory, and then when I'd try to get a handle on it he'd caution me: "Now remember, I'm only talking about New Jersey. I didn't say anything about New York." So that's also a tradition out of good ethnology—good German ethnology by the way—Sauer on this continent, [Leo] Frobenius on Europe and Africa. By the way, do you know Jaime's sense of Frobenius? It came up in his letters with Pound.

RD: I'm not sure. I don't remember Jaime talking about Frobenius. His reading matter was mainly physics in the period I knew him. But as for his exchanging letters with Pound, though, his first note to Pound was: "You're sitting there in that loony bin, and I'm sitting here in this hospital, and now we are both terminal cases." And this terrifically excited Pound's immediate sense of humor. That's one great thing that's often missed about Pound. My first correspondence with Pound had to be—here you are a totalitarian, and I'm an anarchist; and here you are with my parents' anti-Semitism, which I threw out the window with miles of other junk; and still you happen to be an absolute master for me in poetry, so poetry must be something completely different from something we assume it actually is? I mean, I had to find out. Did he really have an *idée fixe* there? Because, although I am fascinated and always will be with the idea of order, I believe that what he called order was disorder, and I still do. And order that comes from the state, any order that comes from a law placed on someone is disorder, not order. It's ordering somebody, and that's very different, very different indeed.

And so I advanced to Mr. Pound Vanzetti's picture of Volunteerism. It's the opposite of what Marx proposed. Marx said from each according to his ability. Vanzetti said from each according to his wish. And that's a lot different than ability. Ability really comes alive when it's volunteered. And when we volunteer something we discover abilities we never dreamed we had. The volition is what is removed in that other hard-line thing, what I call the "little red hen" message, i.e., "If you don't plant this week you don't get this bread." Vanzetti completely rewrote that message. And Jaime was very much of that feeling; he'd gone directly back to earth, because he didn't want to consult man about what he's going to get back. It was his volition that gardened, and it was his wish that the earth would constantly return.

Now in correspondence with Pound I simply threw that directly open. No, Pound didn't have that kind of *idée fixe*. You know if he'd actually been paranoid I would never have heard back from him. I'd have had his curse, and so forth. But I am certainly not going to be able to write to a man I revere and keep back what I think of his anti-Semitism, and not because it's anti-Semitism, not because we can't say all sorts of things about Jews, or Indians, or Celts—I mean we are all abominable—I think we Europeans in particular were eating children only three hundred years ago—certainly at the beginning of the Christian era we were notorious for setting a great big wicker basket image of Bridget full of children alive, and burning them up. I mean isn't that a fine tribe to come from? There are no tribes that are not sickening beyond belief!

. . .

BC: How, or where, do you locate Sauer, say, with someone like Jaime? I remember in particular that Carl would love to play with Chardin a lot, like you love to play with Jung. With fondness and real respect.

RD: Well, there is a big difference between Sauer and Jaime, and one that ought to be pointed out. It's the one I touched on before. I talked about the Jaime who, when he came up against Nancy, who was a scholar, he always wanted to be irresponsible in turn. Well, Sauer was also always responsible for what he knew. No, he was not building a system, either, but he was answering to "Is this the case?" And Jaime would be quite contrary; he would be patently irresponsible to anything he would come across. Jaime would want to be contrary; not contradictory but contrary. He would want to present contrary, troubling ideas. And here he was much like Pound . . . Jaime was never really clear about where he placed gods, and towards the end it became insignificant to him. For me gods are beings of our communal dream, and we have large human possibilities, and this wouldn't get too far from the Jungian thing except that Jung posits them as given contents of the psyche. When I say beings of our community, I think of them as created beings, creative ideas. That's very different from ones that are stuck in your psyche, and that you conform to or don't. And they are not archetypes. Creation of things is the thing that Jung disallows. Jaime was very much creation of things; after all, he had created an Indian world for himself, a nontraditional Spanish-Indian world of his own imagination. The authenticity of the world didn't interest Jaime. But more than that, when he was excited by authenticity he would attack it straight on. He was always the anarchist. Whereas Sauer has to be authentic. When Sauer is tracing his movement of people, he is responsible to an actual map—which is extremely valuable, but in an entirely different way.

Olson was attracted both to the Sauer, the authentic; and, as he explains in his *Mayan Letters,* Olson also loved the kooks. He loves the crazy ideas about outer space, or the people who would claim that Homer was a woman with four heads.

Sauer was not a systematizer; yes, there he would be like Jaime. But Sauer was not pitted against, or polarized against, the thing he's responsible to. And yet the imagination does flow in much the same way—the prose is just beautiful. . . . We are not picturing authentic as repetition but as authentic in the real sense that the material might be present through thousands of years, and through the storyteller, constantly revivified. That's where the real authenticity comes in.

BC: Okay. We've cut the full circle, and appropriately the tape is running out as well. I'd like to thank Robert Duncan for coming over here today, and also for all the support he has given to our press on the de Angulo project in particular over the past half-dozen years. Thanks again, Robert.

RD: Well, thank you. I've enjoyed it.

Charles Olson and
Black Mountain College
(with Ann Charters, 1969)

This vivid evocation of Black Mountain College in its last phase in 1956 touches on both the appealing and challenging aspects of the school, including the living conditions and intellectual atmosphere. Duncan brings alive the community in which he wrote poems and plays and where he taught for the first time. A portion of this conversation appeared in Ann Charters's introduction to Charles Olson's The Special View of History *(Oyez, 1970). Charters wrote the first biography of Jack Kerouac in 1973 and a number of seminal studies of Charles Olson and the Beat poets. She eliminated in the text her questions to Duncan.*

—Ed.

ROBERT DUNCAN: Early in 1956, Ruth Witt-Diamant wrote me from the Poetry Center in San Francisco that she'd gotten a grant, and would I come back and be assistant director of the Poetry Center, a three-year appointment. When [Charles] Olson heard that, [Robert] Creeley had left Black Mountain so Charles didn't have anybody to teach in the Spring semester, and he wrote me would I come early and teach the Spring and Summer semesters of 1956. So that was actually how I came to go at all to Black Mountain. On our way to Europe in March 1955, Jess and I had gone to Black Mountain to see Charles, driving from California, and we saw him just one evening. It was that time he read the 2.4.6.8.10. of *O'Ryan,* which he had just written.

I had first met Charles some years before. In the summer of 1947, I hitchhiked back to the East Coast and saw Ezra Pound for three days, and I came back to Berkeley in the fall, '47. *Medieval Scenes* had been written, and Muriel Rukeyser had read it and talked to Charles about it, and Charles read the poem and wanted to come meet me. But I didn't have any idea he was interested in poetry. We met in Berkeley and talked the first afternoon about ecology. He was doing work in history himself and was wound up about poetry. I hadn't read *Call Me Ishmael*. He was doing work on the expansion of the West and had thought of doing a book on the Donner Party. So the Charles of *Origin* was a discovery. I got much more the range than I'd ever seen before, and the full force of a near contemporary of mine who had the same [mind?] [D. H.] Lawrence had. Or the early Pound. Pound up until 1915 was a creative critic, as creative in his essays as Lawrence is, and a generative critic in the sense of the crisis that bears on the times. This was the whole impact of Charles's early essays.

Creeley was in Majorca in 1955, and that's where Jess and I went then. We went to Majorca because Creeley was bringing out a book of mine. We didn't yet know what it was going to be, but he said he wanted to publish a book of mine in his series, and it gave us a place to go. We stayed in Bañalbufar beginning in April '55, and were there until November, when we went to Paris and London, and then back to Majorca. [Cid] Corman and [Paul] Blackburn were in Paris, and I met them there. Blackburn was a poet then as interesting to me as Creeley and [Denise] Levertov and Olson. Of course Olson was a different dimension, because his sweep of imagination and time was very appealing to me. My range in my poetry was not short of his, could [not?] be satisfied. Creeley and Olson were imagining what writing was going to be—and that's a correspondence; they wrote every day, over a thousand letters. Even when Olson had not yet met Creeley, he sometimes wrote three or four times a day. Creeley sent his first stories and some poems to Olson, and Olson would write back in great length. Olson was also conceiving his own poetics and his own drive—it was the greatest poetry correspondence course ever—about what was going on in poetry and should. Out of this comes the concept that first you find in issues of *Origin* and then you find shaping the *Black Mountain Review,* a concept of what could happen in poetry. The strange thing is that Charles had fixed in his mind that I would be an element of this New Poetry.

I read *Projective Verse* when it first appeared, and I really had no comprehension of it. What is mysterious to me, I took it as saying that you should just read poetry aloud, and saw no more in it than that. I didn't feel it was hard to read or couldn't be read, it just hadn't dawned on me.

It dawned on me slow, and I was also working along lines in the same direction, so I won't say that it hit me on the head, but I then found it opening up ways for me. Olson didn't have the same effect on Creeley. They were building up the idea of writing together. Creeley and Blackburn in 1955 talked about poetry too, but in Majorca they discovered they didn't speak the same language. It's the imagination that links Olson and Creeley and myself and Levertov and [Larry] Eigner. In Cid Corman I see no more than a post-Williams sort of poet, and there are many of these kind. They're literalists. The imagination is very much involved with us. It's the imagination, the revelation of something as dream, as magic. Whereas the literalists will plug along as if the most solid thing was solid. Magic, I think—and I would read it the same anytime I find it in Charles. . . . You still have the art of the poem holding what it is that's going to happen, and the magic directed to the inner orders of the poem and not the way I've felt about [Robert] Kelly (and other post-Olson and post-Duncan poets): diddling. Making out the magic experience as the poem.

My first impression of Black Mountain College was that it was very run-down. It was winter, between semesters. We stayed in the big so-called Gropius building, which by that time was a derelict piece of Modernism—nothing looks more run-down than an art moderne building ten years later. Nothing was gracious about it. Everything was meant to be shipshape, and if it isn't it's a very wrecked old leftover of the ship. By spring, 1955, Black Mountain had lost its lands. It was no longer the Black Mountain one had heard about in the late '30s, where there was a coordination between the land and its farms and the College. By 1956, when I actually stayed there, the large dormitory building was not too bad to live in, but the school then was very noticeably derelict. One had only to walk about to find deserted laboratories with broken glasses and splendid kiln equipment which had just gone to ruin. I think we were paid something like $75 a month, embarrassing to recall. You also got your room, so you were paying only for your board and so you made no money. You were living on $75 a month. That was a partial salary, because when they sold the land the check probably amounted to something like another $75 a month. Although we had about fifteen students, most were there—like [John] Wieners—on scholarships. They

With Jess at Black Mountain College, 1956

saved up money to be able to eat while they were there. It was a closed community; nobody took jobs in town. They'd drive into town once or twice a week to go shopping.

The building that had the big dining room had been sold, so that whole part of the campus was gone. It was being renovated while I was there, and a boys' camp opened the next year, after I'd gone. The theater for my productions was in the basement of the dormitory building. Classes were in the dormitory building, and I was living there too. I had a suite of rooms where I could cook. Charles was in a little faculty house, and the Husses had a house, and the students were in various

241

little houses. I don't remember any students in the dormitory building. I was the only person living there, I think. During the Spring semester, Tom Field had an apartment the floor below mine. The building was on pilasters, giving the effect of a big shelf floating in the air. This left quite a big space beneath. It was enclosed, and we improvised sets. My plays are filled with described sets, so there wasn't much of it. When I was there, the earlier swinging days of the College—when Charles sang Tristan and M. C. Richards, who was then rector of the College, sang Isolde—were well remembered. Charles didn't act at all in the plays I was writing. He came and watched.

One negative impression was that by 1956, Charles was coming to the terminus of the College, and there was no force there that was in any way going to carry the College on ahead. Charles's own idea of education was so entirely centered on the poem and writing, that it was in some fields absolutely incognizant of the role of the arts. It's my impression that he thought of music only as an accompaniment and that painting was a form of therapy. But of course back of this was the fact that the great opportunity to form a school of writing at Black Mountain, and for Black Mountain to be what it was in its last phase, which was the home ground of Charles Olson's imagination in education, came when he opted to remain at a time when John Cage, M. C. Richards, and a body of the faculty went north to form what they thought was a campus away from New York. One can see that they also had lost the idea of education, because Stony Point, where they went, never was a college. Originally it had been proposed that they would form a Black Mountain near New York. In the last of 1956, one of the ideas that Wes Huss and Olson had frequently about going on with Black Mountain was to desert the campus and have a college on wheels, which would be like a gypsy college really. I came back to San Francisco at the end of the Summer semester. I had written two plays at Black Mountain, and I was in the middle of the second play of the *Medea* trilogy, so the cast of that play—but that was practically the entire student body—came along with me. I was the only one who really knew where he was going, so everybody went there. That was my own impression. As a matter of fact some went there before I did. Tom Field left at the end of the Spring semester and came to San Francisco. San Francisco in '56 and '57—when John Wieners was here—had practically the entire student body. [Ebbe] Borregaard was the last to turn up. He appeared at Black Mountain at what should have been the beginning of the Fall semester of 1956, only to find everybody setting out for San Francisco, and he came along with them.

When I first went to Black Mountain in the spring, 1956, and had conferences with Charles, he asked that I not go to anything of his, and he wouldn't go to any of my classes. In a way I could understand this. He wanted me to be completely free, and he would have been impatient, I'm sure, much of the time with the way I would deal with things. At the same time he wanted to be free himself—free, that is, from somebody who'd have ideas and come on with the same strength. So I was able in my own classes to do just what I imagined I would want to do.

I had two courses. One I designed to be in techniques; no manuscripts and no poems were read at all during the semester. We met every morning in a seminar room with a table. People would sit around and I'd plug in the coffee and we'd have coffee all morning long. It might have met as early as eight o'clock. I'd run around to get students and have to wake them up because they weren't used to having a morning class. On the other hand, at Black Mountain they didn't care if you went to a class or not. There were no grades, and if you were there you were there. We dealt first with vowel sounds and took quite a long time with that. Then consonant clusters, and then we did syllables. These were exercises, not instructions or information I had to give them. Perhaps thinking of the work [Josef] Albers had done earlier at Black Mountain, my idea was to work with the materials of poetry, when a technique applies, and everything else would be their own account. Outside of that, they could show me poems, but it would be in the same way they were looking at poems themselves. There was no sense in which I was more skillful than they were. These were just their field of materials, and you only have your own field. Actually I had spent two years or so in the early '50s imitating Gertrude Stein in order to come to a field of materials, aside from any worry about whether it would be my own or not.

By the time I came to Black Mountain I was more interested not in imitating something but just dealing with the sounds and the syllables and the stresses themselves. We didn't get any further than stresses, but I had ideas about other things we could come to. The other course I taught was in the meanings of form. Along those lines I have one essay on the meaning of conventional form. I hope one day to write more on the meanings of form. In the design of those first lectures at Black Mountain—they were talks, really—I ran it like a seminar. We had three meetings a week, and they were in the evening. The first two meetings the students took the theme and presented it—we talked about it the second time—and the third time I would present what was on my mind. I had one on genesis, and there was one on law. The one on law, for instance, Joe Dunn had the assignment of giving the first meeting on it, and out of it came my "The Law I Love Is Major Mover" poem. I went to the library and found Joe Dunn reading in encyclopedias and everything else on the law industriously, and when we came to the Monday evening he gave an absolutely garbled account of what he thought law was. He thought law was "the law," like cops. When he got through I remember I said, "Well, Joe, don't you ever feel like you're under a law?" He looked at me very startled, an ex-Catholic asked if he's under a law, and I asked, "But if you start a sentence with 'if,' aren't you already under a law?" I'm not sure I could get it across, but things got across in many, many ways. This was not a concept of a class in which you teach, although I would lecture once a week in that evening course, and I certainly had lots to say. I talked for several hours, and it'd be a lucky student who'd get a word in edgewise. But they were seminars. The basic possibility of this kind of education would be the context in which you could hear each other talking, a confrontation that those ideas existed.

I was working then on the plays and on the beginning of *The Opening of the Field*. I was in a little gold mine. There was plenty of time at the College. These aren't things that you have to prepare for. You're talking from the fund of whatever you know. And Charles wrote poems, too, of great distinction in that period. Those three songs, "Variations Done for Gerald Van De Wiele," belong to that spring or summer.

When I was thinking of the negative things, I was thinking about my own sense of the potentialities of the teaching situation. The difficulty in so-called higher education is that it should be only a conversation. You don't need to acquire new materials at that point. You need only to explore the use of them, and then you're all on equal footing. You know, what are you going to do with *Ulysses*, not have you read it.

In the faculty there were Wes Huss and his wife; Wes taught drama. And Charles and Betty. And [Stefan] Wolpe—he taught music—and Hilda Wolpe. [Joe] Fiore taught painting. No science teachers, history teachers, and all of that. The diversified faculty had disappeared. It was an arts college. Huss's drama group was going strong. It was a core at the College. I could get a cast of six—more than six, since some would double in a performance (we did two performances)—and there were just barely more people in the audience than there would be in the play. Out of it came the idea of having a play with everybody in the play, and no audience at all. It's another possibility. We didn't do that but it's a lingering idea from Black Mountain days. Many times now when I go to universities the more earnest members of the English Department will ask, "Is Black Mountain still going?" or "Could there again really be such a thing?" This Black Mountain which Charles had really sort of inherited was an opportunity just as long as its own faculty was interested in running it.

When I was there, it seems people could feel most at home taking theater. Huss's idea was all working out from people. Oddly enough, he's closely related to some of Charles's ideas—not oddly enough, since they'd gone through the winter at Black Mountain and some years together. But Charles's fascination with stance, for instance, was I'm sure related to Huss's actual use and exploration of the stance you can take as an actor: I mean, you can stand one way or another, by posture, and how totally different the whole situation will be dramatically when you are merely and entirely standing. For Charles this stance was not merely metaphor, because the College was small enough so that even if you didn't attend somebody else's classes you were very aware of what went on. Ideas went through the whole school. They are related. I imagine stance originated with the theater and came back into *Projective Verse*. But also Huss would take ideas and translate them into the theater.

Charles had formed a concentrated little group of writers at Black Mountain. He just wasn't interested in the general student unless they were writers. The period before me had been very rich. Of the students when I was there, only John Wieners is known, although Tom Field's writing is very interesting. Eloise Mixon also wrote some fine poems, but I'm afraid they were very much along the lines that Robert Duncan was interested in, technique, and that's not the same thing as going to be a poet. [Edward] Dorn and [Michael] Rumaker and [Joel] Oppenheimer had all been there earlier in the grand period. And Wieners had also been there at that time, and Fielding Dawson; and Jonathan Williams is an earlier student. The ones who are actual Black Mountain writers are from the early '50s.

Creeley had been at Black Mountain earlier, part of '53 or '54. Duncan, Creeley, and Olson are known as the "Black Mountain Poets" because our work became known through the *Black Mountain Review* (and Don Allen's anthology). I suppose we might be designated as sharing ideas that come out of Olson's *Projective Verse*, but I'm not even certain of that. I'm still fascinated by composition by field, and I think Charles is, but it would be a hard case to make it that Creeley believes in composition by field, and some people identified with Black Mountain don't even enter that realm of ideas, like Denise Levertov, who thinks of form as organic. Actually, we came to know each other's work in the period of *Origin,* beginning around 1950. The first issue of *Origin* featured Charles Olson. Charles and Creeley had corresponded and wanted a magazine. They felt something new was happening in writing, or was about to happen. Their own writing was just beginning, happening. Corman had a radio program in Boston, and Creeley wrote to Olson—I've seen that letter—saying he'd heard this man Cid Corman and maybe this was the opportunity to have a magazine. And since they had an idea, of course that idea dominated *Origin* to quite an extent, but if you read *Origin* you'll find that every once in awhile Corman put his own oar in and then it wasn't like that at all. And eventually Corman dropped all of us. But Corman certainly does not belong to what we could call Black Mountain. So Black Mountain means something different from just being post–Dr. Williams and Pound. I think the vital key, and one which would work for

Olson, and work for me, and work for Creeley, and work for Levertov, is that there's a combination of D. H. Lawrence and Williams.

At that time Charles was interested in alchemy and magic. Certainly I got a lot of drift from Charles in that period just talking with him. The alchemy things are clear in earlier poems. He also brought in Pythagorean ideas of number that would appear in his lectures. Recently I've become more interested in number; I don't know how you could say "more," but it seems to me number might be the heart of the poem, rather than the terms in which number appear, which might be sensory things. This is an essentially magic view of the poem. Not magic in the sense of doing something that you mean to do in the end, but in the sense of causing things to happen. An evolutionist doesn't aim at a magic spell which is going to produce an ice-cream cone, but aims at magic being set at work. It's a very different thing, and Charles, I think, saw alchemy that way, although we argued enough about the gold. In my own work, because certainly these terms were very suggestive to me, the gold in alchemy—the rendering of good—seems to me intelligible only if it is not a teleological end, but is part of what one celebrates in what is created all the time. It seems to me the potentiality for the creation of good cannot be greater than the potentiality for the creation of evil, because the thing that increases is potentialities. Most of what is called civilization is to lower the potentialities so that you don't incur anything but very mean evils, and consequently you don't incur anything but very mean good. Here I think I would be very much in concord with Charles's view.

But basically there's another issue that interests me. Charles is Roman Catholic in origin and I'm not. My parents are that funny kind of theosophizing which is very upsetting to a Roman Catholic. Charles tends to dogmatize, and I tend to spin endless whatevers. And Creeley views himself as Protestant, doesn't he? Charles's access to alchemy, to Renaissance thought, to Pythagoreanism, always goes along lines of dogma: correcting the dogma of the Church or being super-Pope, and he's an incarnationist, and I have quite a battle with the incarnationists. I'm convinced that Aristotle is right, that the soul is the shape of a life, but when I get through I've got spirit left over to go . . . But what I've got in mind here is that a great deal of the force of Charles and use of the school was—he saw education as spiritual attack. On the first level we can take it as to attack a subject. There was a kind of spiritual attack, it seems to me, on students frequently. He wanted things to happen in them. I don't mean he wanted things to happen in his classes. He wanted things to happen in them spiritually. There's a very important difference between me and Charles. I guess this is what I meant when I started that picture of a Christian. Ginsberg shares it. Charles wanted to produce a new and redeemed man. This is actually Charles's alchemy. I sometimes can get angry at the idea; certainly I would never want to be a new and redeemed man. The big thing for me is what is.

But I thought the College should have had more and more variety in its teachers. I tried to persuade Charles to get Jack Spicer there, but he wouldn't hear of it. He really didn't know much about Jack after all, but I thought if Jack Spicer had also hit Black Mountain! He did meet him in San Francisco when I cooked up the Magic Workshop and there they all were, under the spell of Jack. Jack was a Calvinist. There was no Calvinist at Black Mountain. If Creeley is a Puritan, intellectually the school isn't equipped with all the paraphernalia of Calvinism. Students do not respond to dogma by obeying the dogma, taking it upon themselves— I think maybe to some extent Dorn did, but he moves it around—but outside of Dorn, Creeley never took Charles's dogma.

Charles as a teacher did not produce little Charleses. The little Charleses you see have nothing to do with Black Mountain. Charles—and Jack Spicer too—were immensely excited with the potentiality of a person being a writer, and both of them wanted something to happen in the person. Now they didn't want that abstractly, and they could spot out of five different kinds of people, one who could really be creative (but sometimes creative only means disturbed) and they'd go to work on it. They could really produce a psychodrama in two seconds. They're experts indeed. Spicer's force was as strong as Charles's impact must have been on that group of Black Mountain students from Jonathan Williams on. Spicer acted on Joanne Kyger, Ebbe Borregaard, George Stanley, Harold Dull—they are four who have really lasted from the Magic Workshop.

In 1956 the exciting poem for everybody at Black Mountain was Edward Marshall's "Leave the Word Alone." Ginsberg has said that Marshall's poem had given him the key to *Howl*. People had copied Marshall's poem, and Charles was very excited about it. Ginsberg sent *Howl* to me at Black Mountain during the Spring semester. I took it to Charles, and I remember Charles said, "He isn't doing anything with syntax." I looked at it and realized he isn't, although I'd just been wild by the ideas. Look at *Howl* and Marshall's poem. Both of them are about mothers who are insane, and I think that's what unleashed *Howl* for Ginsberg, out of Marshall's poem. It's not a simple thing to remember, but in that Black Mountain concept of "projective verse," that concept of the poem, not doing anything with syntax means not doing anything with content, not making, not seeing what is happening. A poem that's all effects and not operation. Marshall's poem is one that delves into person in a very different way than *Howl*. *Howl* is orational and Charles's sense of the poem is not orational. Spicer's response to *Howl*—I was in Boston in between semesters and saw Spicer—was, he's stolen our subject matter, meaning homosexuality. Actually *Howl* was the poem those of us who were writing felt challenged by. You could not write like it, turn out another *Howl,* but I tried to write a page after first reading it. That energy, one really wanted to see if one couldn't do that.

Black Mountain was the first time I had taught in my life. I have no degrees from anywhere, and the first time I was ever tempted to teach, and the first time I ever taught, was Black Mountain. But I was full of ideas in the '50s, and of course I was trying to convey the ideas of the New Poetry which was hard for me to read. My essay on *Maximus* was because I just couldn't make heads or tails out of it. That appeared in the *Black Mountain Review* in '55, but I'd written it in '54. I'd written it in my notebooks just to make myself deal with that poem. I had a great sense that it was a magnificent poem, but I had no way of getting at what it was that was magnificent. I can lose my temper at people who assume that it's meaningless, that anything's meaningless. I don't believe anything is meaningless, so I'm angry if people dismiss it, or assume it's meaningless. But this poem had a tough meaning, and I think that part of its meaning may be actual unobtainable things, truly obscure things;

that's okay, though I still work away with it, because so many things have moved in time and become not obscure at all.

The positive impressions of Black Mountain College are certainly the strongest. Number one is: there was no reason, and everyone understood that, to do anything with the idea [of what?] your classes or your workshops or your lectures were going to do. They were really the business you were about at the time. I know of no other context in which the intellect was proper unto itself. I think this was very much Charles's concern. I've given one picture of 1956, that the school was winding down, with lots of people feeling that, but in back of that was that Charles had a positive intuition in this, and that was that even this that looked like the ideal school was not the proper place for the intellect to develop a freedom to develop ideas, converse, and teach.

The limitation for Charles was the administration of the school. Even if it had been operating at its optimum, he would have kept fiendishly busy keeping it going. Charles of course had a year or two in which he was just winding up the business of that school. That must have been extremely disruptive to his whole creative life. The positive value was that where we operated at all, and Charles's classes were mostly at his optimum hours, which happen to be between one and four in the morning, the students would meet him, and Charles would give out with what was there. There was no administration there demanding that you do something that wasn't in your rhythm, in time. My rhythm is morning. I told students okay, you want to meet [then?]. Nothing suggested they were going to be bugged if they didn't show up. I'd wake them up if they asked me to wake them up, but at the same time gave them the leash: if they didn't, okay. Charles's class met at 1 a.m. or 11 in the evening, whenever he was going strong. I've always thought that universities don't know anything about using time. I kept the grind of everyday technical workshops because I thought that's what you do, like piano lessons, finger exercises. This was my first teaching and I tended to teach as I had known, been taught. Faculties and students are not now blowing up universities for very good reasons, and the main thing about Black Mountain was that it was still thought of as a school. Charles went back to Gloucester; people clustered about him to come learn. I learn more from poems and bits like that. I know Charles wanted very much then to be supported as a creator who teaches, part of what he does. That was on his mind, the perambulating university.

At the teaching level there were disagreements. Students weren't agreeing but taking up ideas. Charles's ideas were Charles, and their experience of Charles, or their experience of me, was the paramount thing, not their agreement. They liked the experiences, but that doesn't mean they carried the ideas over. Certainly characteristic is that students didn't develop along imitative ideas; this was very important at Black Mountain. Other kinds of teachers would have wanted to instill ideas of poetry, and we presumed that poetry was not going to be like us. This interests me very much. I think of our poetry as dated; it would have a center someplace around, come to a fullness of its own being there for all of us by '56 or '57, certainly by the time I was beginning *The Opening of the Field*. I don't think there's been any development since, any conversion of my poetry into a new area. *Paterson* and *The Pisan Cantos* had most to do with my poetry in the early '50s. It's that that was everybody's, so it's the late '40s when it's taking place. That's actually a long time for a movement to take place, and the people who are in it will continue all their lifetimes to be in it. It doesn't change style, which has a locus someplace in the early '20s. Then you've got enough that all your lifetime you're exploring that. There've been quite decisive movements and schools since us, and some of them have very strong feelings of their identity. Don Allen's anthology [*The New American Poetry*, 1960], which is informed by the leaders, those poets forming the schools at that time, is in retrospect *the* picture of the schools at the moment. Strikingly, there've been no anthologies since which have that sense. Most of them don't like schools or movements, although "Concrete poetry anthologies" are pictures of the Concrete movement.

Students at Black Mountain at that time would have, let's say, a library of ten books. They'd have *The Cantos, Paterson,* Charles's work, and mine. Also they'd have Lawrence. Charles and Creeley liked *The Plumed Serpent,* which outside of its first chapters I've thought a dud of a fantasy. But students would know Lawrence's later poems. There'd be no Henry James, no Joyce. It was thought pretty wicked to read *Finnegans*

Wake. Charles felt stronger even than Pound perhaps about the betrayal of *Finnegan.* These books may have been in the library, I'm not sure. The first entertainment I gave at Black Mountain then—because I knew how Charles felt about *Finnegan*—was to read it, and everybody turned up but Charles. No Virginia Woolf; she'd be thought of as genteel. There'd be Jung. That came from Charles, but it was temperamentally across the board. That meant no Freud.

In 1957, the Poetry Center raked up about $200 for Charles to come to San Francisco. We had a group of about twenty people, and he gave five lectures. He was presenting [Alfred North] Whitehead's *Process and Reality,* and this was a case in which I'd never read Whitehead, and right there in the middle of *Opening of the Field,* this was a real blast for me. I take it that Charles was reading *Process and Reality* at the same time. That was how he functioned. I have a feeling that in the spring of 1956, Olson had already been through—but recently enough so that he was filled with it—the picture he had been building of morphology. Eventually he came out with *Proprioception.* There's an interesting gestalt that went along with it, Jungian. We can assume he was ransacking *A Picture of the Psyche* [?], because he was trying to build in that period a picture of the psyche. I was ransacking in very much the same way, so I was over much of the same ground. Charles was very thoroughly, very solidly into morphology, and I have only really been in that to the extent that I had a definite sense Charles had been in it more directly. So in the later part of '56 and '57, just the period he's also involved in closing out the school, he was occupied with *Process and Reality.* After all, it is projective verse; it enlarges the idea of field. He probably got the term "field," my own guess is, out of Gestalt, where the term is an explanation for the arts, for what you are doing in a poem or music. The term "field" was intelligible to me by the time I returned to *Projective Verse.* Through the period '52 and '53, I was reading with a new understanding Gestalt theories of composition.

When Charles talked in San Francisco, it was the Whitehead view of history as past and future, and the fact that we're at the point of genesis and that the end of things is back of us. I'd come across related ideas earlier, but this really conjoined with a lot of ideas on my mind. That

**With Charles Olson at Olson's lecture on Whitehead,
San Francisco Museum of Art, 1957**

you're always working at the point of genesis I'd still be with. The most meaningful concept of form is the one of something taking place within a field. If you have a larger sense of the field in which it belongs you begin to see it as form finally. Well, in the context of these Whitehead lectures, Spicer brought Tarot cards, the cards Pamela Colman Smith had designed, Art Nouveau designs directed by [A. E.] Waite. Charles turned with an absolute fury and smashed Spicer right there with a crushing remark, with also everything of his weight and size back of it. A rotten deck, and so forth. Well, of course this rotten deck was merely my own too, my theosophy of that period. But I know Charles and I talked about the Tarot in '48, and Charles was wound up with the Marseilles deck, and the authenticity with the first. That's another thing I don't share with him, that primal is as true and no more true than today and any other minute. And for Charles, in Whitehead's sense, it would work, for we're at the primal now. For Charles it wasn't even decadent, for that would have had a meaning. We just were not to deal with this thing at all.

In correspondence and in moments of personal insight in his essays and poetry, Charles sees mythologically. This is also the feeling I get from the new *Maximus* poems. The "Okeanos"—long orphic piece—is a real piece created mythologically. Charles very much wanted to be mythological. He's the least disposed to all the allegorical or psychological possibilities. He's coming straight at it.

The Spectrum Interviews, 1982

Part I: "Out from Under 'Olson's Push'" (excerpts)

These excerpts are from a two-part interview with student Carol Balzano that took place at the State University of New York at Buffalo in 1982 and was published in two issues of the student newspaper The Spectrum. *The first part touches on Duncan's relation to Charles Olson as a contemporary who had "a kind of seniority, a kind of superiority." In Part II, Duncan discusses the "backlash" to himself and Olson, along with his view of Language poets, poets in universities, and stream of consciousness, which differs from his work, which happens in a nondirectional, nondialectical field.*

—Ed.

"I took the art of poetry to be essentially a magic of excited, exalted or witch-like (exciting) speech, in which the poet had access to a world of sight and feeling, a reality, deeper, stranger, and larger than the world of men's conventional concerns, and I took the craft to be a manipulation of effects in language towards that excitation."

(THE YEARS AS CATCHES, FIRST POEMS (1939–1946)
BY ROBERT DUNCAN)

An American poet of great distinction hailing from the original Black Mountain College, Robert Duncan was in town last week to give a lecture ("The Continuity of Christian Myth in Poetry"), sermon, and a poetry reading. The readings included poems from his soon-to-be-published volume of poetry, which is the culmination of a fifteen-year retreat Duncan took from the publishing world. A man of privacy, Duncan also granted an interview with the Prodigal Sun. *This is the first of a two-part interview.*

—Carol Balzano

CAROL BALZANO: I know that [Charles] Olson visited [Ezra] Pound at St. Elizabeths during the early '50s.

255

ROBERT DUNCAN: Yeah, that was previous to 1950? Again, I'm not sure in there. But that was part of what we [Olson and I] talked about. But I had also had sessions with Pound before Olson met Pound . . . in the summer of 1947. So it would have been later that I met Charles. Dates are hard to fix, aren't they? I have to spot where they would be. Dorothy Pound invited me back, and I stayed with Dorothy Pound and went to St. Elizabeths. I had none of the disaffections and quarrels with Pound that Olson had. It doesn't mean that I agreed with him, but I mean that I didn't have quarrels with him. My relation with Pound would be truly filial. The main thing I was worried about since . . . Not only was I not racist, but I was anti-racist. This means that not only don't I approve of anti-Semitism, but I don't approve of Semitism. I don't approve of people who put their race out front. Race is interesting, like personality, but I do not believe in race. So it's atrocious that Jews think they're a chosen people. Or even a people.

. . .

And the other one was that I was an anarchist and not a fascist at all. And that I believed that order was in the individual, which Pound believed. But the place where I not only didn't believe what Pound believed was quite the contrary. I still feel the order that is put upon us by government is not order. The same orders that are put on you by a teacher if you're a student—that's disorder, not order. So the only thing I believed was: order is the one that comes from the individual outward toward the community. The individual's disorder is when the individual doesn't adhere to the community it belongs to. So the most essential thing in Pound for me was the theme of order. And that one was subverted by his dreams of having an order imposed. A plan on a poem.

. . .

But I also experienced this contemporary [Olson] having a kind of seniority, a kind of superiority to. He could do things in the poem that I can't do today. And the time, of course the person's ear, the delight and response to delight that they take in hearing the music of the poem, is very individual, so there is no competition. But in the case of both Zukofsky and Olson, I'm still learning today things about how a poem's built.

So I experience them as teachers. In Zukofsky, I don't dream of him as a contemporary. Olson, it's because he begins writing so late, in a sense, that he, ten years older than I am, would be my contemporary. Olson, before he starts breaking out, breaking through in that essay *Projective Verse,* there'd been years dreaming of what writing would be. Of thinking, thinking, thinking, thinking about, and also, in his case wondering: could he ever possibly be a writer? And then overnight, there he is. So other people were having an age of Auden. I had an age of Olson. Felt a little off the hook once Charles was dead, because then I thought now I can go back to writing my own thing that's not part of history. While Charles was alive from 1951 on to his death, I did my duty as I saw it, and vivified by my sense of what was going on in, in Olson's push. Sherman Paul called it Olson's Push; in London I said we made it "putsch"—

. . .

Olson discovered, what really lined Olson up as his true contemporary to himself was [Robert] Creeley. And they were so different in temperament, and the impact of their poetry was very telling. Creeley has never had the disposition of a leader, but there's much to be learned about Creeley's verse. I had a hard time with his poetry at first because I'm rhetorical and he wasn't. I had to uncover his rhetoric in order to get to his verse. I had never read anything, not since Lawrence or Mary Butts had I read anybody writing a story that was in the order of *The Gold Diggers.* So it was rich; it wasn't only Charles Olson. Then this small group of writers, what we all shared was that we were followers of William Carlos Williams, who read him in the light of D. H. Lawrence. Charles and I could have been called post-Poundians, but it isn't very fruitful in relation to Creeley or Denise Levertov, who was another one.

CB: Did it ever disturb you, as you put it, that you were under "Olson's push"?

RD: Oh, that was so voluntary, as a matter of fact I was never quite to be trusted to be under his push. . . . Oh, it never disturbed me at all. I had no trouble about that. If I see something really good, I'm in there dutifully and give my heart. Not at all. In my own world I was taking it over; well, you could say it took me over. That's like, does it ever disturb you if you're in love with so-and-so? No. It doesn't disturb me—Olson is very dogmatic, as you know reading Olson. I never paid attention to the negatives of the dogma. I mean, it was the whole feeling of vitality and the subject. My poetry never reflected, it's got some of the what you might call American history in it. Never sat down but I did map work. My subject was history. I wasn't in American studies, I was in medieval and Renaissance studies in history. So Creeley I know would feel at times, should he have history in his poems, which he didn't. His poems are Creeley. . . . Olson was always coming on as if he was gonna change you. I don't know anybody who has changed into Olson. And the ones who are foolish enough to try and write like that are just lost, because he had an absolutely, extremely individual temperament. Creeley's seems to me the verse that can be a learning ground for other people. But my poetry and Charles's are very unfortunate learning grounds. But Williams's poetry is a great learning ground that's back of this whole thing. Williams opens up your own way of going about it for you, and doesn't load on that you oughta be doing *Paterson* or something. Whereas Charles, if you read all the way through, it was clear that Olson obviously wanted a million little helpers that would carry on his projects. Especially at Buffalo. At Black Mountain he was more concerned with the individualization of the students and their terms. But I think by the time he came to Buffalo and was afraid of dying, that he wanted to have some people who would go and carry on his work. I realized there that I was entirely different.

CB: Then do you disagree when you see young poets, modern poets of today writing in projective verse?

RD: No. I wonder what it's going to turn into. Listen, [William] Empson wrote seven kinds of ambiguity, although he was trying to point out that you shouldn't have, and I was trying to find if I could even do eight kinds of ambiguities. I mean, I was always trying something on. I've seen striking poets start out with Robert Creeley poems, and then they change very rapidly into their own thing. But Creeley's poetry, immediately, I mean, when the line breaks, the crisis between two lines is very telling in the relationship to the period of those poets who are now in their early thirties or coming into forty. There are areas where *Maximus* is like *Paterson* of William Carlos Williams. But it's not like Pound. And the aspects of which it's like *Paterson* only call more to one's mind how much it is not like *Paterson* at all, how much it's absolutely amazing. And you know another poem that was going on when we come to the mid-'50s, and most people were asking me, What do you think of *Howl*? Well, I didn't relate to *Howl* at all and here nobody in those days—their minds were not tuned at all to this other tremendous poem that had started in the early '50s, too. The *Maximus* really was so—I loved it. All the rest of my life I will answer to what's going on in *Maximus*. But I sure hated the years I thought I was invited 'cause they were interested in my work. Then what they wanted to know was, What do you think of *Howl*?

The Spectrum Interviews, 1982
Part II: "Revolt against 'Backlash'" (excerpts)

Recapping last week's interview, poet Robert Duncan (hailing from the original Black Mountain College, where he taught and worked with contemporaries Charles Olson and Robert Creeley) spoke of his artists-bond and associations with Charles Olson, Ezra Pound, and Robert Creeley. "And I read Projective Verse *... but I didn't really understand it. I thought I agreed with it, which is even more disastrous than when you don't understand something." "I wasn't committed to write like Charles Olson; I was always writing." "So the most essential thing in Pound for me was the order. And that one was subverted by his dreams of having an order imposed." "I don't know anybody who has changed into Olson. And the ones who are foolish enough to write like that are just lost...." To quote Gertrude Stein, a remark which Duncan agrees with and exemplifies in his writing process: "The composition is the thing seen by everyone living in the living they are doing." This is the conclusion of a two-part interview.*

—Carol Balzano

CAROL BALZANO: Well, this brings us up to today's modern poetry. What do you feel to be a depreciating element of today's modern poetry?

ROBERT DUNCAN: Depreciating? Gee, that's a stacked question! I could name a million descriptions of depreciation. One of the most interesting and coherent movements—a movement that takes the name of a magazine. The name of the magazine *Language*—one of Spicer's late books was called *Language*. And the movement, at least in San Francisco, is the Language poets. And I find them reductionists.

They're after effects that come from [Louis] Zukofsky, reduction in which there's a kind of—I usually quip, you start out with logical positivism and you end up with illogical negativism. All sorts of things that are ruled out in language: it can't refer and so forth. So language is turned over to a kind of logic. I'm never illogical, but I'm never logical, for in my head logic is zero—zilch. I'm a poet, not a logician. Yeah, I'm interested in the operation of the words, so I'll go pour over logic in order to find that words also behave that way.

The Language group has set logical rules on their language. And I see them not merely as being reasonable or rational, but as rationalizing. They set their premises, and then they rationalize what language should do, so now there is a depreciation, because they begin to rule out subjects. That is, they rule out that language really can't express love, really can't express emotions, and can't have subjects. Well, I think you see the absurdity. What they really say is it shouldn't, because it obviously can. ... I've never had any trouble being sentimental. I love it. And yet all the people who feel you shouldn't be, say you can't be. Now can't isn't the same as shouldn't. And they can't hear it. So I—yes, the most interesting group in San Francisco at the present time is the Language poets.

. . .

So this very area where we pose is there a depreciation, has increased a lot. And it is growing on rumors, on what words can do in art. It stems from how much linguists, and semiotics, especially (a field having nothing to do with writing), were beginning to tell us more than we were noticing about the act of writing. At times I think there are ways in the art in which you begin to be, you can dangerously come close to becoming sophisticated. And then you have a puritanical backwash. And the Language group that we face at the present time, almost all of them are a form of puritanical backwash. Their rules are clean lines, shouldn't have—shouldn't go overboard, you shouldn't be ... So proprieties show up. No, it isn't very proper to be passionate ... and Olson would say, sailing into the wind with an overloaded ... He really loved extravagance. What is it that he said ... you've got to overdo it? ... I'm trying to think of what ... oh, exaggerate, exaggerate. Well, that really means to pile it up.

CB: Getting back to a phrase you used just a minute ago, "puritanical backwash"...

RD: Yeah, right, backwash. What do we call it in politics, it's very much like ... We're in a puritanical phase of government. You could spend millions on munitions, but you better not spend anything on pleasure, please. And so forth. And at the same time you get wealth, instead of getting riches. I mean some people are rolling in money but are nothing rich at all. They don't want any art for it; they don't want any no-show. Yeah, let's get back to your question, because I really stopped you with puritanical backwash. But it's called a backlash. A backlash. Backlash comes into it, but backwash I was thinking of more because . . . I see the Language poets as going on from where we were going on in reaction to that. So I think there is a dialectic and they're part of it and you have to undo what looked good about us, if anything did. Foolish to talk about it, because to most of the apparent literary world, nothing about us looked good. But in their terms it did, and they undid it. So this very group that's critical of us, they don't bother criticizing [W. S.] Merwin or something; they're criticizing us right out front. 'Cause that's what they read.

Let's say, 'cause you asked me first what I think my own reaction to it [is], I think they're moving away from, they're moving away from sexual content first, or they isolate it so the thing is purely sexual. So they're moving away partly from our apocalyptic politics. All this new group announces is a new kind of communism, and communism is a puritanical, political movement, and profoundly offended by the liberalism in which you have an expansive . . . And anarchism is a liberal, has liberal aspects. So they move away from passion; it's just language. They absolutely rule out that a poem would be, could be intimate with feelings about a war. They deliberately rule out myth. One sign of the beginning of that war was [Frank] O'Hara's ruling. And yet O'Hara himself is exactly the same, of wide temperament . . . and [a] passionate poet.

CB: Do you think universities breed a lot of conventionalized, restrictive poets?

RD: I don't think you need to do something in order to breed one kind of poet or another. But universities are an environment that poets who are conventional can take over very rapidly. And they tend to entrench themselves in universities. The interesting thing about poets entrenched in universities, in English departments and so forth, is that they insist on the poem being an expression of individual feeling and sensibility and a cultivation of it. And they're very opposed to the intellectual, or an intellectual adventure. So they flare up. I mean they experience . . . What I mean by [an] intellectual poem is [a] poem . . . poems that rule out the convention. The convention of our time . . . is the one that's presumed. Let's take the really top poet who's in the area of really conventional poetry, which would be Robert Lowell. It's presumed that the poem is an expression of Robert Lowell's sensibility and his insights and so forth in the society he lives in. There is no apocalyptic. Ruled out absolutely is the prophetic, the apocalyptic things that were particulars, and almost all of the Romantics, the things that the Romantics were fascinated with. Ruled out is mystery.

CB: I have a quote here from you—can you expand upon it? "The poem is not a stream of consciousness but an area come into it."

RD: Geez! I can't even understand it! Wow! Where is that from?

CB: I believe it's from *Bending the Bow.*

RD: Is it from the preface?

CB: Yes.

RD: Oh well, probably I can understand. Well, we'll take it apart. I certainly mean it's not a stream of consciousness. Something begins in a poem, you work with it, so that's not the same as my stream of consciousness. I'm trying to figure out what am I saying. No, I have to listen to find out what I'm saying. 'Cause I thought previous to what I'm gonna say, so I have to start with that one. However, my poems are really forming a field of possible meaning. So I don't experience them in a stream of consciousness. I was fascinated mostly by the stream of consciousness in the novel . . . but if we think of stream of consciousness as Joyce proposes in *Ulysses*, it turns out not to be stream of consciousness, because he's got a design throughout, and so it seems to be a stream of consciousness out front. Dorothy Richardson wrote a stream of consciousness novel, and that stands very forward for me of what stream of consciousness should be, the form of what the arts are referring to. And the idea of field is not a stream. A stream goes in one direction. We're getting there. A stream, and the idea of consciousness, is that it flows like a river, and has a current, and that means it's directional. It also then does have a beginning and an end. That's all the concept. A road going from one place to another, a stream, going from one place to another, so the poem goes from San Francisco to New York. We decide if it didn't get there, we can decide it lost itself, a whole series of things. All based on the fact we presume the writing goes from one place to another. But if I were a naturalist, and we went into the middle of a field, we would miss the whole thing if we were going from one end of the field—we would miss the whole thing, if we were going anywhere. As I think, know, the naturalist discovers that if he looks at a square inch he discovers he's got a larger work than he can do, and he's got to convey everything in the square inch. So that what he does first doesn't relate to what he does record as a direction at all. It's simply an ability of getting into it, in order to accumulate the data of what's in the field. And so in the poem I'm concerned with what's happening. And there is a course in the poem, for me a current. Directional current remains at level one. But I'm not—I don't have problems with how does it begin, how does it close, because the true form of the thing exists in re-reading it, and re-reading it, and re-reading it. It consists in all the things existing together.

And there's the form, not that you go from one [thing] to another. And not ruling it out, but the one I'm centered on, and that one, of course, I first found in Pound's idea of an ideogram. It's a group of things, of weaving together. Now you can't talk about a stream and an ideogram— no flow. The negative side of that is that I'll agree with the critics and observe that my poetry is static. There's no dialectic, if you're fascinated by the field. And the field is tensions, but there is no dialectic. And remember, I was a student of history. It's a problem in history, because a field appears, and if you describe it only as a field, then you have the problem that you cannot account for the dialectic that's happening in it. That it is a stream, that it is changing. It's like physics, having a difficulty with—how come the movement is directional, where in the actual framework of physics, biology, mathematics, and so forth it doesn't make sense that it would go only in one direction. There is no such thing as direction in a field. And we're still in field theory—and still puzzled by how come we go from being babes to being old—and consequently have a "look[s]-like-there's-a-path-with-an-arrow-down-that-way" sign. And that between these two ideas, there's no paradox at all. They're just the things I'm presented with. There's enough excitement that the imagination can play, play, play. . . and poems are alive, no matter where I carry them. It wouldn't be alive if I thought it was just an ideogram. I think you see what I mean. Because I can't put them together, then the imagination has to create something to have them coexist. Not a philosophy, 'cause I'm not a philosopher. The philosophy that comes closest to me is [A. N.] Whitehead, in [his] process of reality. Probably it's a symptom of my age—I'm sixty-three. If we just go to the age of Creeley, or to a brilliant younger poet like Michael Palmer, they'd be drawing on [Ludwig] Wittgenstein and not on Whitehead. So we can date us cats by what we draw on. Can't quite do it with Zukofsky; he was Wittgensteining very early indeed, and he was older than Olson.

CB: Turn the clock back a little, so to close it off here. I got this quote from the preface of *Caesar's Gate:* "I do not intend to issue [another] collection of my work since *Bending the Bow* until 1983, at which [time] fifteen years will have passed."

RD: That was not a vow. Somebody said I took a vow not to. Well, that's turned out to be true, although the text of the next book has been finished for two or three years. I haven't written a preface; I'm now faced with getting the manuscript to New Directions this spring, so it will come out next year. What I wanted to do with taking all of fifteen years was to give myself a scope so I wouldn't be overcomposing the volume. I tend to overcompose because I'm thematic. I'm enamored with composition. I must be some kind of composition junkie. Theme junkie. I compose leitmotifs and themes. It would certainly be gracious if I could break it a bit. But everything that comes up I recognize, so it immediately gets sewn in. I'm like some spider who makes an elaborate web, and even gets a few flies into the web, and keeps wondering, How come I'm less and less free to freelance design? Ride in the wind.

CB: Can you part with the name of your manuscript?

RD: Well, it's *Ground Work.* But in my view at the present time it should have a name. . . . It's *Ground Work, Volume 1.* The second volume, which I'm well along into, should come out in my seventieth year, which will be 1989. We're six years away from it. But certainly not in the text today, have I found the title. So it's very, it's still up in the air. It hasn't occurred to me, hasn't come to me. *Ground Work* was the working title. And that meant working in the ground, working underground, the ground our feet come forward from.

On Kenneth Rexroth
(with Linda Hamalian, 1982)

This 1982 interview with writer and biographer Linda Hamalian appeared in Conjunctions *vol. 4 in 1983. It offers a vivid, loving portrait of person and poet Kenneth Rexroth, who was both a teacher and like a brother to Robert Duncan. Duncan speaks of their similar anarchist views and their shared "feeling of a sacred universe." He describes his rich conversations with Rexroth, touching on Rexroth's relation to other poets and his wide reading and vast knowledge, and his "almost magical and sympathetic coordinations when it came to nature." Hamalian is the author of the invaluable* A Life of Kenneth Rexroth *(New York: W. W. Norton, 1991).*

—Ed.

In late spring of last year, during the intermission of the Kulchur Foundation reading given by Robert Duncan and Edward Dorn, I asked Robert Duncan if he would be willing to discuss with me his relationship with Kenneth Rexroth, with an eye towards gleaning background information for a biography I am researching. We met the next day and he talked for several hours, reminiscing about Kenneth Rexroth and both their roles in the San Francisco Renaissance.

—Linda Hamalian

LINDA HAMALIAN: When did you first meet Kenneth Rexroth?

ROBERT DUNCAN: Before I met him I had read a couple of his letters that were printed in *Partisan Review* and *New Republic* in 1939 and 1940. I became intrigued with someone obviously older and more knowledgeable than I was who had taken the same stand on the whole Stalinist-Trotskyite thing on the Left. I had already decided that I was kind of an anarchist—I'm described as a bourgeois anarchist today—and was always looking for leads about the anarchist sensibility. I was reading Emerson and Thoreau and anarchist pamphlets and learning more about anarchism in New York. This was before the anarchist group the Libertarian Circle was formed, before the war. And Kenneth was also a Laurentian. He had sent some things to *Phoenix,* a magazine that printed my first poems. I bought the press, and asked Kenneth if I could have his poems which were still sitting around. We never did print them. But I made plans to see him when I returned to the West Coast.

The first or second day after I came back to Berkeley in 1942, I went to San Francisco, where Kenneth met me in a car. He and Maria were smuggling Japanese through a kind of underground, and like the Patchens, he was in a state of paranoia. He didn't want anyone to know where he was. He imagined that any moment a Stalinist would come up the stairs—not that they *weren't* shooting people. When we finally got to his home, he made one of those marvelous dinners of his. As you know, he was as great a cook as there ever could be.

I think he was thirty-eight when I met him. I was twenty-three. I certainly knew him for fifteen years before he became corpulent and swollen and sick, a model of high blood pressure and impulsive temper. Yet he projected the temperate in his poetry. But the picture he would give himself as a sage would be just there in the kitchen, and in a few other places, like the mountains. When he came back after camping in the mountains he would be very much restored.

LH: Do you remember what that first meeting was like? Was it a serious evening?

RD: Oh, no, no. Marshall Olbrich was there, so it was an evening of long talk and dinner. I can't remember but I might have stayed all night and gone home the next day; it was that open sort of thing. He was the only true poet we had. Josephine Miles was an Academic poet. Today there could be lots of poets who might be considered part of the romance of the Bohemian idea. Not for me. I think we were fortunate that we had a poet who was really fascinated by what the arts meant, and how his own poetry fit into a continuing line. I always wondered to what extent Kenneth owed quite a bit to [Robinson] Jeffers, despite his rage against Jeffers. Technically the fineness of Kenneth's passages on the California landscape are very close to Jeffers', as William Everson has said. Another thing that was difficult for Kenneth was how much he came out of the Ezra Pound picture of Chinese culture combined with the Cubist, European sensibility. It was easy for Kenneth to blow up at Pound's fascism and obscure how much his work came out of *The Cantos*, just like he blew up at Jeffers's nihilism and inhumanity or whatever and obscured that influence.

The person who is straight-line Rexroth is Gary Snyder. He had the same bookshelf. Both thought that Arthur Waley was a prime Chinese translator. Philip Whalen is more of a mixed thing, but Snyder is straight-line Rexroth.

LH: Do you think Rexroth was a father figure for many writers, or is that a media description?

RD: He was a big brother for me. For Everson, he was the person who discovered Everson. Kenneth did not fit very well with the image of a father figure. He was a teacher, and that was something very immediate for many people. When I first met him, he seemed to be just what I believed a person should be—a marvelous cook and a beautiful personal painter, not that he was in the paint market. But the paintings that he had around and the poetry were really positive as a continuous thing. The poetry was also trying to get that Cubist feeling that he got into his early painting, and the paintings would change as the poetry changed. The great force in Kenneth's life was one that he didn't realize, but he was always moving towards; that is, he knew the essential thing was moving down from Yeats. Here is where, oddly enough, I would come into his line. He had a brilliant feeling for the reality that was very, very close to [W. B.] Yeats. He was a deep Yeats reader, and in his imagination he wanted us to carry that through.

LH: Is there anything in Rexroth's poetry itself that you have assimilated into your own work, anything that you can point to?

RD: I don't think so. It seems to me that the strongest places in his poetry would be the grandeur of the landscape in the West, something outside my poetry. Some passages of *Heavenly City, Earthly City* sound like Wallace Stevens had gotten into the landscape. Perhaps the influence is there in the Pindar poem or "Apprehensions," where

With Robert Creeley, Majorca, 1955

ancestors come in, where there is a sweep of landscape. But I'm third-generation Californian and Kenneth was first. So it is hard to say that these things come from Kenneth's poetry, because there is my family legend too in places. I shared with Kenneth a temperament that could be called mysticism, a feeling of a sacred universe. Maybe for me there is more magic than for Kenneth, but he would have understood that. Kenneth did not understand me at all during the period of "The Venice Poem" when I became concerned with form. For Kenneth a poem was a vehicle for your own knowledge, and I went away from that. Yet he would know what that meant. Kenneth had made a choice. He hadn't been successful in his Modernist poems because he was trying to make inventions. I realized, long before we had [Jacques] Derrida, that every period has meaning. That's why I felt so close immediately to the appearance of Charles Olson and Robert Creeley and Denise Levertov in the magazine *Origin,* and a correspondence could start back and forth in the early '50s. Something was afoot that I felt related to in a different way.

It's too bad. Some of us wanted very much to get across to Donald Allen that you couldn't do an anthology of a whole generation as if it were just new. He himself resisted what emerged, which was how much that newness was not new. But Kenneth and [Louis] Zukofsky and [Kenneth] Patchen were the bridge in a kind of dialectic that moves through American letters. There were the poets who were adults by the time the Depression hit, and they had to meet the impossibility of being poets. I was only seventeen in 1936, and I knew I was going to be a poet, that it was possible. I wasn't already in my twenties, bogged down with earning a living. And the WPA, whatever else it was, was a crushing battle. Kenneth suffered because he stood up against the whole Stalinist thing that controlled the WPA. He had a lot of hate talk directed at him, and that's why he was so fearful. The same thing goes with Patchen.

LH: It is difficult to figure out precisely what he was doing during the '30s. He did participate in writers' conferences. As a delegate from San Francisco, he was elected to the presidium of the first national conference of the John Reed Club. And his poems from that era are overtly political. But it is difficult to uncover the other kinds of activities in which he was involved.

RD: Yes. I always thought these things may have been fantasies, but one doesn't have to know what he did do. One has to know what he thought, how he pictured himself, what his impact was. Then we come up right against what was prohibited in the '30s.

LH: You were very disturbed by Kenneth's remarks about Marianne Moore?

RD: Oh yes. Definitely I was. If Marianne Moore came to the door, he'd slam it in her face. It was a much more serious issue than how does one receive a poet who comes to visit. At that time I had the highest regard for Marianne Moore. In recent years I have thought about this. At that point it was going to be apparent very soon that Marianne Moore would be self-trivializing. Her acrobatics and muscle-flexing were showing up in the current book. I never paid attention to a poet's politics, but her politics were hardly out in the fore. I think Kenneth just threw everything into his nasty projection of her.

LH: You and Kenneth also had differences about the way the Poetry Center was being run. He was annoyed that people were charged admission, and that some poets received higher fees than the others.

RD: That is not the case. What probably bothered Kenneth was that I didn't schedule Kenneth one year when I scheduled all these people who never came to the West Coast—Marianne Moore, Charles Olson, Robert Lowell. Today, whoever had done that to me would be in the dungeon. Somehow when the time came we just stopped seeing one another. And then I felt guilty. I saw I was paying him back and wondering to what degree and why. One of the things I owe a generation (and myself) is writing an essay on Kenneth.

I don't think I was won over by Kenneth's picture of the civilized man of the world, which is Professor [Thomas] Parkinson's picture of Rexroth. But I loved the fact that Kenneth was an avid reader, which I am and a half-dozen poets are. But most of them aren't. And then I am convinced that he had an ideatic memory, that he could look at a page he had never looked at and *see* it. He read maps that way. There was an incident at the Tylers's [Hamilton and Mary] where while we were walking in the pasture, Kenneth leaned over and picked up a bug and said, "Ah! so-and-so and so-and-so." Well, Ham was an entomologist and was just flabbergasted. It was so rare that you could pick out one of these things. There was much about Kenneth's almost magical and sympathetic coordinations when it came to nature. He could also hit the Achilles' heel of people he barely knew. That could have also been the sign of his own vulnerability.

LH: Was it his love of literature and his breadth of knowledge that meant the most to you?

RD: No, it was his affection. For instance, he was very open right away about his knowing that I was homosexual, which didn't bother him at all. He was such an affectionate person. He would hug you, and he was absolutely direct.

LH: Did he help you get published?

RD: He always tried to get James Laughlin to print me, as well as to print Everson. But Laughlin is actually independent. Kenneth was most important to him, because he felt that Kenneth opened up so much of what made it lively all over again for him to print. But Kenneth was wild about *Faust Foutu,* and Laughlin wrote to me in Majorca to send the manuscript to India, and so forth, and it got nowhere. There was the New Directions reprinting of *Roots and Branches,* which Kenneth was responsible for. But by the time I was working on *The Opening of the Field,* Kenneth and I weren't seeing each other. But he would have had a difficult time approaching that book. And in general when he was being generous with me in an essay, it wouldn't require that he had read anything from *Letters* on.

LH: Are you familiar with the long poem that he wrote when he was very young, "The Homestead Called Damascus"?

RD: Yes. He read parts of it. He had a huge manuscript sitting around when I first met him, when he had that first volume in print. He didn't talk much about it.

LH: He was determined to get it published, no matter how much after the fact it was.

RD: No matter where or when.

LH: I think it contains the kernels for all the themes that developed later on. It's extraordinary that he could write a poem like this when he was so young.

RD: Also, he was close to the place before he started covering.

LH: What do you mean?

RD: When he begins to see what's contained, not only does he cover parts of it in order to have it develop somewhere else with force, but if these things would tell us anything, he wants them to be out and available.

LH: Were you and Kenneth having soirees at the same time?

RD: Kenneth was really having them in '42. But at Berkeley, when I came down from the farm, I started something a little different. Every week [at Throckmorton Manor] somebody presented a different writer. Kenneth presented William Carlos Williams, and I think he presented [D. H.] Lawrence and Yeats, too. Leo Litwin presented H.D. I presented [Edith] Sitwell and Pound. Also, there'd be readings from *Finnegans Wake* and *The Cantos*. It was my version of what a course on a generation of the masters should be. This was an open contradiction to the approach of the University program.

LH: Were you as hostile to the Agrarians as Kenneth?

RD: I don't really know anything about them. I was too young to be at war with the Agrarians. Kenneth had that war with the New Critics. My generation is still reading some [R. P.] Blackmur, but New Criticism is no longer an issue. In Kenneth's time it was more important.

LH: Did you often go to Kenneth's evenings?

RD: Yeah. It would have been in 1945 or '46.

LH: Do you think the description of Kenneth as the architect of the San Francisco Renaissance is accurate?

RD: Yes and no. He dreamed about a San Francisco Renaissance, and he dreamed it up first with only Philip Lamantia and myself. And certainly Professor Parkinson at Berkeley might have been in on it. And Bill Everson was there. But Kenneth was totally unprepared for Allen Ginsberg, who walked in and made San Francisco famous for something that Kenneth had not imagined. But he did imagine it with new people; the poets his own age were never part of his picture of the Renaissance. The term "Renaissance" originated with Robin Blaser and myself in Berkeley. We called it the Berkeley Renaissance. We were students of [Ernst] Kantorowicz. That did cause a split with Kenneth, who was still trying to persuade me that it was pretty wicked to be associated with him. When *Black Mountain Review* came out, Kenneth was named one of the contributing editors, as part of the plan or feeling that Kenneth belonged with the younger group of poets. But when one of the issues contained an attack on Theodore Roethke, Kenneth blew up and withdrew as contributing editor. I think that Kenneth could already see that there were other sources shaping an entire new thing that he was not prepared to be part of. All the new ideas about poetic form, like the theory of field-composition, reminded him of the New Critics. It created much more of a break for Kenneth than anything that I was doing or Philip Lamantia was doing.

LH: Do you think that he did not have a real understanding of what you meant by organic form and correspondences?

RD: He knew what that was, but he really thought that a poem was a vehicle. With Yeats, the poem was a vehicle of Yeats's thought; it was not a thing that got defined. Kenneth was not hostile, but he felt he was being deserted.

LH: What do you think is his strongest voice, his voice as a poet or his voice as a critic?

RD: I think the two would have to go together. Also Kenneth had a strong historical imagination, and could get very excited, for example, about [Arnold] Toynbee. He liked to see history in terms of cycles, and he had a strong identification with certain periods, the Hellenistic in particular, which I also have. This is what I have in common with Gary Snyder and Kenneth Rexroth, this business of relating to history in terms of spiritual epochs that we relate to and other ones that we are antagonistic to. It's all very post-Spenglerian.

LH: Yet you are all very much concerned with the immediacy of the moment.

RD: Yes, and the Laurentian thing that we carried out. It is curious that Zukofsky came over as a leading figure for us too, because of the Laurentian thing that you find in some of the passages. By the time you had Zukofsky and Olson, Olson found Zukofsky intolerable and couldn't read a line of him if he tried. And of course, it also went the other way around. But more and more in his poetry, Rexroth posed as a tempered person, and that neutralized the poetry, it seems to me. It neutralized the imagination. Until the mid-'50s he did not have to pose. He was a tempered person, a person who when laying out a meal, could lay it out beautifully, when raising his children would go into the profession of it, would go into the whole thing with great feeling.

LH: Wouldn't you say there is a religious, spiritual side to Kenneth?

RD: Yes, there is his sacred universe. Kenneth thought deeply about the inner relation. He professed to be an Anglo-Catholic who also thought that Buddhism was the deeper reality, which is of course quite possible, because Buddhism doesn't exclude having Christian beliefs. Remember that *The Signature of All Things* refers to Jacob Boehme, who became central to my work. And I can't dream that Kenneth was not giving a pointer in that title to those of us who were following him. What is so fascinating is that our period wanted a poet to be a model person, and

Kenneth wanted to be a model person. Thank God he was a real food critic and not a model, because a model is a terrible person to have a meal from. I still love his paintings. He had an immediate feeling of the mysterious; he saw the connection between Cubism and mysticism. And now we find out that [Piet] Mondrian is bedded deep in a kind of mysticism and a sense of mystery of painting itself.

LH: Did you like Kenneth's readings to jazz?

RD: I think Kenneth did that because it reminded him of a time he loved, the picture of what Chicago was like in the '20s and '30s and the hoboes and WPA. That's why he loved to prowl around Fillmore and North Beach. I think they reminded him of something in Chicago that was very vivid to him. He used to frequent jazz places. He read his poems as scat and they worked. He didn't write jazz songs. He just read his stuff to jazz. I really wondered what in the hell that was, compared to really writing for jazz.

LH: It was quite different from what Kenneth Patchen was doing.

RD: When Patchen arrived, it was a little hard for Kenneth to share the town with other members of his own generation. Kenneth was quite excited about the arrival of the Patchens, like he was about Dylan Thomas. But he had a hard time coexisting. He also talked a lot about how well he got along with [W. H.] Auden, something I didn't know. Kenneth liked the self-civilizing Auden, but us kids were all for the savage Kenneth!

LH: What do you think of his translations from the Chinese and the Japanese?

RD: They read beautifully, but I have no confidence about how I feel one way or another about Chinese poetry. I can't believe Pound's *Cathay* and then all the continuation of *Cathay* that Waley did—and Kenneth really loved Waley. What I think is moving is that Kenneth, like Pound, learned to read Chinese, that he really learned Japanese. I've never gone back to look at the [Pierre] Reverdy, now that I read French. As a matter of fact, Kenneth always said I was reading Reverdy, but I never read Reverdy. I talked Kenneth out of several things. I never read Reverdy at all. Now that I have more leads, I am reading French all around while I am studying Baudelaire. Pointers, pointers. Perhaps Rexroth is a father figure, if a father figure is someone who tells you whom to like and you never want to read him.

LH: What did Kenneth think about T. S. Eliot?

RD: I don't remember his ever being more than just sort of gossipy about Eliot. He was much more wrapped up with the Sitwells as Communist agents. He would have more fantasies in that direction. In Parker Tyler's anthology, there is some indication that Pound objected to Rexroth. So Rexroth's objection to Pound was not just that Pound was a fascist, but that Pound had not appreciated him. Rexroth was curiously loyal to *Blues*, because they carried him and didn't pay attention to what Pound told them one way or another. They were interested in Rexroth. I don't know that my reactions to the Beats would have been so different from Kenneth's. That he moved out of town I found highly significant. Had he stayed, difficult as it would have been, there is no question that everything would have had to be accountable to him, and that would have been central. On the other hand, the very things from the Japanese that he chose to translate suggest that he wanted to be out of the conflict, out of the turbulence.

LH: Is his work autobiographical, in your opinion?

RD: Yes. Some of his poems are great travelogue poems. The two European poems seem to me truly the best things he did. Now you can see that these poems are not going to be the great thing in a period like the one we're in. They are not that charged with apocalypse. But if they were contrasted with the current diary poems by people who have nothing in their heads—take a page out of those poems and place it *en face* a page by the New York school going to Europe—you'd see a terrific difference. That's how he was close to Auden, trying to get a picture of what Europe was. Kenneth did go on those hikes in the Sierras, and I'm sure he wrote those poems straight off.

LH: Did you read more of his shorter poems or his longer poems?

RD: Both some short ones, and passages from long ones, especially "The Phoenix and the Tortoise," but not in recent years. We were fascinated by his progression in the long poems. We can also talk about serious poems and how much *language* motivated the whole group. My language is serious all the way through. It has no decoration. Though there may be some fancy things in the composition, the language is not truly fancy, because rule number one is that every word is meaningful throughout the poem. And that was absolutely the ground that Kenneth walked on. It's the ground that Gary Snyder walks on. It's the one Everson means to walk on. By the way, some of the latest poems of Everson are terrific.

LH: When you say in "Towards an Open Universe" that when you write a poem it is as if you are giving birth, do you see that as something Rexroth might agree with?

RD: Yes, sure. For one thing, in later years, I came much closer to what he might have felt and agreed with at the time when he might have ceased to read me. But Kenneth had a conspiracy view of history. My conspiracy thing turned into deep dream poems, like "In Whose Name," with a certain amount of Satanic suggestion. But Kenneth could go on about how the Freemasons were running the world. It was his counterpart of Pound's the Jews run the world.

LH: Does Rexroth belong to the tradition of Modernism?

RD: It's always awkward. When he was first writing, getting printed in *Blues,* when he was trying to develop a jazz style and getting his own take on logical positivism, he might have been moving in that direction. But he really doesn't develop that way. He goes in the direction of the simplest language. Writing your own feelings in the language you get right away. But one thing that could be appalling about Kenneth was when he wanted to show you that he was well read. There were times when I saw Kenneth after he left San Francisco. I accepted, as a matter of fact, an invitation to Northwestern University because I thought what a treasure it would be if somehow Kenneth and I could have time together at one of those poetry conferences. So we had a social evening. I had just stumbled into my hotel room at about 1 a.m., and Kenneth phoned to see if he could come and talk. Well, it was just heavenly, and we talked until 4 a.m. in this whole glowing atmosphere. He was just like he was in '42. There was no way I could think, "Is this later or is it earlier?" It wasn't like we had something to clear up at all. It was just sheer bliss sharing this man's stories of Japan, wild sexual stories swiftly followed by perceptions about Japanese gardens. I didn't care if he was really sitting in Dizzy Gillespie's lap when he first hit the horn or if Djuna Barnes really did drag him into the sack. I don't call this madness. I call this part of fantasizing. It's part of what flows into the poetry. And yet that kind of fantasizing is not all we have when we read that he is in the mountains, because those mountains are so beautifully and naturally present. The mountains, I think, were his retreat until his last years. It's part of his picture of what a person ought to do. He wasn't an alcoholic, so he didn't go away to dry out. I know he had a deep thing that he kept all the time that had a cosmic frame and a deeper ground. And Kenneth was never a closed personality. He was a prickly one and could be very sensitive to whether you were for or agin' him. Kenneth was a direct person, much more so than Kenneth Patchen or Anaïs Nin or H.D. And he had strong recognition from people of his own age.

"The Closeness of Mind"
(with Gerald Nicosia, 1978)

This interview with writer and Jack Kerouac biographer Gerald Nicosia
appeared in Beat Angels *in 1982. In this conversation Robert Duncan*
describes his first meeting with Jack Kerouac in 1956, Kerouac's pas-
sivity and sexual ambivalence, some of the relations of the Beat writers
and what their work has in common, and the watershed of Howl. *He*
admires the immediacy of "October in the Railroad Earth" and praises
Mexico City Blues, *in which "everything seems clear, everything seems*
music-centered."

—Ed.

Robert Duncan—what came across when I interviewed him was the suit-and-tie
European polish, suavity, and charm, but most especially the warmth of the man.
One of our most distinguished and cultivated elder poets—the most universally
respected, from Ivy League academia to the bars of North Beach, which is as great
a span as you'll currently find in any nation on earth—he had the unassuming
openness to ask me, since he saw I was alone for the evening, to have dinner
with him at a nearby Mexican restaurant. His taste in food proved excellent too.

The following interview was conducted at the Naropa Institute, Boulder,
Colorado, in July 1978.

—Gerald Nicosia

GERALD NICOSIA: How did you meet Jack Kerouac?

ROBERT DUNCAN: When Jess and I came back to San Francisco in
1956, the first week or so Michael McClure took me by the Potrero
Hill housing project where Kerouac was living with [Allen] Ginsberg.
[Robert] Creeley was quite close to Kerouac, and so Kerouac was looking
forward to meeting me because I'm very close to Creeley. It was a non
sequitur meeting. Kerouac was soused, so his eyes were slightly out of
focus, and they tried to look deep into mine, and since I'm cross-eyed,
he couldn't decide which eye to look deep into. I found the meeting

humorous enough, a) because there was a little mercurial character about it, you can't really look deep into my eyes, so the "window of the soul" thing doesn't quite work; and b) the other thing was that he had that sort of blurry look that the drunk has, and I'm not amused by drunken effusions. So we were two sides of Creeley—I think Creeley would be the interesting one to balance off in the picture of the two. Creeley was a person much more various—he could have an intense and close relationship to both me and Kerouac. Following that, I don't think that I had any actual meetings with Kerouac, although I met him at parties or in public.

When we came to try to read Kerouac, what I liked was "Railroad Earth." I like that very much in the same way that I like [William] Saroyan. But we started unfortunately with *The Subterraneans,* and the name-dropping and the New Yorkese talk turned me off, so I was never a great Kerouac reader either. Within a couple of pages of *The Subterraneans,* people are jabbering about Kafka and Kierkegaard, and it's all in that empty cocktail chatter. If it had been sheerly for amusement, but when it's also supposed—as I do get that aspect of Kerouac—to have something of the atmosphere of Dostoyevsky, I would take my Dostoyevsky straight. But I like "Railroad Earth" very much; it was quite real, the going into restaurants and cafés, and eating in the early morning, and so forth.

GN: Is that what you mean by a Saroyan influence?

RD: No, not influence, but it had some of the same qualities that Saroyan had for us in the '30s.

GN: Saroyan was one of the writers that he [Kerouac] admired very dearly.

RD: Well, he certainly got the right message off of that. Saroyan was a writer that I liked until you come to *My Name Is Aram.* Oddly enough, he named his son after the first really lousy book he ever wrote. Saroyan had times of comeback, but I don't tend to follow Saroyan. I was a great admirer of Henry Miller, but I don't think I read any Henry Miller after *The Colossus of Maroussi.*

GN: What exactly about "Railroad Earth" do you see as like Saroyan?

RD: Just its immediacy, its simplicity. It was quite the contrary of the prose that Kerouac's most famous for, which is his spontaneous streaming prose of association. This was a prose of everyday life.

GN: But also very fast.

RD: Yes, and it also had a very real *voice* in it—the voice seems to me as quite important when we read prose.

GN: The incredible rhythms strike me, where he catches the clackety-clack of the railroad train.... Creeley said that you were very impressed with a scene from *Visions of Cody,* because you hadn't imagined that anybody could sustain a piece of that length with the only plot occurrence being the reflection of a neon light in a mirror.

RD: That I think I read in manuscript at an earlier point—I never read it when it came out in print—and I was always asking, "What work was that?" I told Creeley about it when I went to Majorca. I always had the impression that Rexroth lent that manuscript to me even before Allen was on the scene. Would Allen have mailed that manuscript out?

GN: Allen had several of the manuscripts over a period of years, so it's quite possible.

RD: Well, I know he was a one-man committee for [William S.] Burroughs and Kerouac. They were the geniuses as far as he was concerned. And as a matter of fact, the Allen that we think of had not even appeared on the scene—no one had written *Howl* yet.

GN: There's a scene in *Desolation Angels* at the apartment of someone who has a piano. Might that have been your place?

RD: We had no piano. Jess came home once and found Peter [Orlovsky] and Gregory [Corso] and Allen on the doorstep—but I don't think Kerouac was along. Jess went into the apartment, and they streamed along behind him—which he experienced as an invasion—busily asking where I was, when I would be home. Since that is not the kind of household we have, not a Grand Central Station, Jess read them out as people who go streaming into other people's houses and worlds. They were a gang. The difference between a community of poets and the time when you have an adolescence . . . you have this little brotherhood where everybody shares everything and goes in and out . . . I didn't even like that in high school, I didn't join clubs or go around on teams . . . though Jack's first contact wasn't that, Jack's first contact was to attempt an eye-to-eye contact, and to want to meet a soul that was close to Creeley. I back away if people are to announce they're going to be very close to me. At one point, where a marvelous German potter, Marguerite Wildenhain, gave a formal lunch, and announced to me that now we would use *du*, I couldn't explain to her that when you start "thee" and "thou"-ing in American, they back away. In that way I think perhaps even Allen too had the European folk closeness, and doesn't understand our WASP, Thoreauian backing-away into the pond.

GN: In *Desolation Angels* Jack describes your relationship with him—he said you were two very different types of people, but that you each understood each other and that you didn't have to talk, that you each had a great appreciation for the other.

RD: That's quite possible.

GN: What was your impression of him generally?

RD: He was quite good-looking then, because he hadn't gone to pieces yet with drinking. He had a fairly ambivalent sexual disposition—probably some bisexuality in his life—so that was part of my backing-away too. And the negative one really for me is someone meeting life in that alcoholic glow—but that alcoholic glow is analogous to being in a state of ambivalence, so I'm sure I read the true thing. That is, he wanted immediately to have close male . . . something more than friendship. And I always like people to be sexually there—"yes" and "no" sexually there—whereas of course we do have a picture, one that I understand more and more, of how much and painfully Allen existed within that ambivalence.

GN: Kerouac's sexuality is one of the most difficult points for a biographer. In his books he made himself out to be very strongly macho, and now the problem is complicated because many of Jack's friends and relatives don't want to admit the possibility that he had any bisexual experience at all.

RD: In the last part of his life he tried to have the approval of the family around him. We can certainly say that he wasn't at ease about this ambivalence. I don't trust this kind of ambivalence, certainly not by the time the person has to ride it along with alcohol. Creeley when he has alcohol has this ambivalence. He has a kind of foyer in which he's responding sexually to the males around him, and then he flares up . . . usually the form of contact it takes is fighting.

GN: In a letter to Gary Snyder, Jack mentioned that he was afraid of Creeley because of Creeley's penchant for fighting.

RD: I had an absolute sense of Jack being gentle. I had no sense of any violence in Jack at all. But because he was attracted, I sized him up in that sense, so I had the whole message and had it rather quickly. But then I was also—even while I was having the message—amused because he really wanted to look soul-to-soul. It's really poignant in this correspondence now between Allen and Neal [Cassady] [titled As Ever] that probably what Kerouac and Neal both wanted was this soul immediacy. Neal feels confused and lost in sexuality, because he's willing to go into the sexual, but what he needs is the closeness of the male love. We've got homosexuality, which is sexuality, and that's what I meant by the ambivalence. We've got homoeroticism—that's when you have a love object—and that clearly is not operative in this soul thing. And then you've got this intense need for this idealist love that is usually the one of friends when they're very, very close indeed. So there are really three entirely different things about male closeness, but in a society where we don't touch each other and so forth, it's hard to clear them up. By the time you're touching somebody, they're groping you.

GN: I've heard that Jack would often put down homosexuality, which some people have felt may have been a reaction against his own feelings.

RD: He might have been declaring it. And remember that if he wanted to come close to a man and it was a question of homosexuality—if the most important thing was coming close to find a friend—he would eventually put away the homosexuality, just as women object to being sexual objects. Jack was what would be read out as a sexual object in that period, and it isn't great fun to be sheerly an object. But he certainly didn't seem to be of a strong disposition, he seemed to be an extremely passive person. He was waiting for me to name him, and even when he gives the account, he feels I did name him—the account you give, in which he sees me as seeing him.

GN: Jack seems to have had a great deal of anguish about his sexuality, whether it was straight sex or gay sex.

RD: He could have had a lot of anguish if he were fairly passive, because there's a lot of pressure about a male being passive.

GN: From my research I found that Jack probably had a strong erotic attraction towards men as well as women. To me, his sexuality is very important.

RD: I think it is, and I'm sure it's why the traveling, why the road. We're talking about the problem of bisexuality. Our society can almost arrange its head for exclusive heterosexuality or exclusive homosexuality, because they can figure out a monogamous solution for it and that would be respectable. What they blow up about is the promiscuity styles of the new sexuality. Bisexuality is much more difficult, since they've forbidden harems and *ménages*. Although I was married in a period, I've always been just homosexual—I've never had a bisexual problem. When I was married, I was still sure that there would be a man somewhere—it wasn't "and also a man." True bisexuals have to solve certain things, and the society doesn't provide any real romance models that aren't unhappy. It isn't just Catholicism; it's the total society.

GN: Let me ask about the literary scene. Was there a feeling among the San Francisco poets at that time, was it like an invasion of these people from the East?

RD: Rexroth was really a very strong sponsor—very excited about his own recognition of the Beats before they were well known—and had a lot to do with connecting [Lawrence] Ferlinghetti with the Beats. But two things threw Rexroth, and they both happened while Jess and I were in Majorca, so I would get them via letters and not by being on the scene. One is that Marthe Rexroth and Creeley fell in love, and Marthe left Rexroth and went to live with Creeley. Rexroth then wildly blames the Beat gang for it. But the other part of it is that Allen wrote *Howl.* Rexroth was our one poet in San Francisco, and the rest of us who would be thought of today as San Francisco poets were satellites of Rexroth—we learned from him, the reading list, everything; he was our local master. When Allen wrote *Howl,* that's really the watershed. Pay no attention to the whole country; it was a watershed in San Francisco itself, so those of us who were pre-*Howl* belong to an earlier period. And yet it's a very confused watershed, because Philip Whalen to a good degree, but Gary Snyder almost 100 percent, are Rexrothian poets. Gary's bookshelf was Rexroth, Waley, Pound, and Jeffers, and Whalen's was very much the same, but Whalen would add [Gertrude] Stein, and Whalen's development was actually different. Rexroth was never quite certain about his relationship with Gary. Gary is now become a rival, because many people know more about Gary Snyder and less about Rexroth, at least as Rexroth hears it, and this is a man who's displaced. He was most tremendously displaced by *Howl.* So he had two different things confounded in his mind and actually moved out of San Francisco and turned it over to the rabble, which would be not only Allen and so forth, but us.

Philip Lamantia and I are the only ones born in the area. Rexroth himself came into the area [from Chicago], [Michael] McClure came from Wichita, [Kenneth] Patchen had come from New York—that Allen came from New York was not so important. There was an East-West thing in the Spicer circles, but that was of a different order. I've never thought of that in connection with the Beats. If you take, what do the Beats all have in common?—the whole idea is the writing coming from the heart. Where it fails of the Dostoyevsky state is that Dostoyevsky is as much conceptualizing all the time as he is coming from the heart—so he has the psychology, whereas I don't see any psychology in Burroughs or in Kerouac or in Allen.

GN: According to Creeley, Jack was upset that initially Rexroth had praised him, and then a few months later he made an about-face.

RD: Rexroth's a very outgoing, loving person, when his paranoia isn't turned on, and I'm sure the thing Jack wanted was to have a family in place of his family. That one I understand, because I have my own family in place of my family. Kerouac very much needed to find a place, and we must note that he never found it. When I think about Jess and myself living together for twenty-seven years—we're both WASPs, so we have jokes about what it was like in a WASP household, but if we were Catholic and Protestant living together, the Catholic would have moments of humor the WASP would never hear, and vice versa. So Allen is not going to ultimately understand Kerouac. Kerouac was looking for a fellow rescuer from the Catholic world, and obviously that didn't appear, and he ends up with his mother and his wife as the best way.

GN: Jack was extremely hurt by what he felt was Rexroth's rejection of him.

RD: Kerouac was writing a prose that Rexroth was absolutely keen on, saw right away what that prose was that other prose wasn't. Since Rexroth was not a writer of prose, prose did not threaten to take anything of his position, but Kerouac just inherited Rexroth's anger. The poetry was stolen from him and the wife was stolen from him.

GN: Rexroth wrote some cruel reviews of *The Subterraneans* and other of Kerouac's books.

RD: By that time you have him turning on the whole thing, but he still could have done it at the review state. In reviews, Rexroth has a persona in which he's the man of the world and of longer periods of civilizations and a kind of mentor of literatures. It's a foolishness that'll show up . . . for instance, he talks about my stemming from [Pierre] Reverdy, a poet I've carefully never read, though I've read almost all the rest of French poetry, largely because Rexroth popped up with Reverdy right away—a favorite poet of his. So he made funny judgments . . . with the requirements of civilization he wouldn't answer to himself in his personal behavior.

GN: Had you read any of Jack's poetry at the time?

RD: Oh yes! *Mexico City Blues* is a book of Jack's I solidly like, and I still think that's very underestimated. McClure was very excited about that book, so he made me more aware of looking at it . . . very much like the freedom, here I was thinking more of Gertrude Stein than of Saroyan, but it seems to me a true poetry. Some prose writers, like [Theodore] Dreiser, you wonder why he even tried to write poetry because he was mistaken about the poem. *Mexico City Blues* is very alive all the way through. Kerouac does not have any pretension to an area of poetry other than the one quite natural to him. They really are a poetry counterpart of blues, of doing sets, and that I could understand right away—though Creeley would be closer to it, and Mike probably. My music is all classical, and about the only jazz I know is good-time jazz, the kind you dance to. But one catches on right away that *Mexico City Blues* is like the voice of a local saxophone. I have no trouble with that; it seems to me one of the very best, whereas Allen I have great trouble with. The very great poems like *Howl* and *Kaddish* are very mixed as far as I'm concerned, between poetry and rant, and there's no way to take them apart. It would be a problem like Hawthorne's taking out the birthmark—that's where they made their breakthrough. But in *Mexico City Blues* everything seems clear, everything seems music-centered.

GN: I think it's a much more structured book than has been realized, a thoughtful dialectic between Buddhism and Christianity.

RD: Actually McClure made some of his break away from my poetry via Kerouac. He had been in a workshop of mine; Mike's first book, *Passages*, looks like a Duncan poem. Then he went through a heavy Whalen period, to ween [wean?] himself away from the things that I would come on very heavy with. Another thing that opened his eyes was *Mexico City Blues*. He brought that to me and said, "You've got to pay attention to it," so I actually have that on my shelves—the poetry on my shelves, really, is the poetry I read.

GN: In *Desolation Angels* Jack writes that he and Allen were upset because a *Life* magazine photographer was taking pictures of the San Francisco poets, and you and Michael McClure had had your pictures taken separately from him and Allen and [Gregory] Corso.

RD: If they did take a photograph, it was never used. The only photographs that ever occurred were the ones done in that set for *Evergreen Review,* and that sort of launched us because our faces were united with what we wrote. At City Lights, *Life* magazine interviewed me, and the guy was very antagonistic to the Beats. I went to lunch with a *Time-Life* man, who told me a story of a murder in Central Park, and who seemed to think the Beats were going to corrupt the whole world. I just sat there and listened as he was saying, "You know your friends do this and this and this," and wondered was that what *Life* was going to come out with when they printed the story. Their dossiers must be something to read—the FBI dossiers you can get ahold of—but *Time-Life*'s own little files are obviously another matter, because this was a real little weasel sitting there at lunch.

GN: Did the Beats seem very different to you from the earlier San Francisco literary scene?

RD: When the Sartre-existentialist thing came after the war, the North Beach filled with young and blackstockings with a doleful look who huddled around the bars being existentialists, so the change from *existens* to Beats was very noticeable. And actually very disturbing was the business about drugs. Two students of mine, who had been at Black Mountain and on the San Francisco scene, in really no time at all ... John Wieners became a permanent mental cripple on heroin and speed, and Joe Dunn was doing the first "white rabbits"—you could smell him ten yards off, and it took him no time at all to be completely wiped out. He's made a kind of return, but Wieners has never made a real return from that. The reason I didn't take drugs is because my body metabolism and chemistry is what I write on, and anything that drugs have been described as doing, I seem to do *au naturel*. But I would wonder, did Kerouac get into much more than marijuana? The only drug I was impressed with Kerouac using was alcohol, and anything else must be very incidental.

GN: He tried heroin a few times, and Lamantia introduced him to peyote.

RD: Lamantia is using drugs ritually, and cultishly, a little like McClure. Wieners and Dunn went to it like it was baby food, like they never had enough bottle . . . they'd just wipe themselves out—like Dylan Thomas drank in order to be in a coma.

GN: People have described Jack's drinking to me as if it were a kind of wall to keep other people out. Did you feel that when you met him?

RD: We sat on the porch looking out, and talking in general, like we're sitting and talking, so it was a meeting, and I wasn't exactly writing him off. There was a perfect invitation to meet again, but I didn't seek him out. Creeley and I are very, very close, and my feeling with Kerouac was, if he could have been close to me, then he would have been closer to Creeley—there would have been a triumvirate of a kind. But whatever he sensed there, I was in no position really to play a third in it. The Creeley we were referring to was also alone like Jack was, and I wasn't.

It's interesting because there was a three with Allen and Neal and Kerouac, and the different arrangements of trying to have somebody in between in which one would be the role that unites the two. We're not talking about an erotic closeness, we're talking about the closeness of mind. Neal writing to Allen . . . Neal feels that Allen's teaching him and constantly helping along, not his writing-to-be—writing would mean nothing—but his mind and spirit is the thing, that's what he feels Allen is guiding, and he owes Allen so much for this. And remember, Allen is the one who's doing the recognizing. Sometimes it isn't that other people don't recognize the writer, like Kerouac, but they themselves have a hard time recognizing what they're doing, so the recognizer gets to be very close.

A Conversation about Poetry and Painting
(with Kevin Power, 1976)

This fascinating, probing exchange with writer Kevin Power appeared in Line *nos. 7/8 in 1976 and in* Revista Canaria de Estudios Ingleses *(Tenerife, Spain) in April 1982. Here the reader will find as extensive a consideration of painting as anywhere in the poet's writings. He vividly describes observing Jackson Pollock at work one night, painting and painting "until the radiance was present." He evokes other painters, including Edward Corbett, Milton Reznick, Mark Rothko, Clyfford Still, the Pre-Raphaelites, the Pop artists, and most profoundly the art of his partner Jess. He points out that in both Jess's work and his own, "discontinuous elements" become of "major importance" and that language starts talking to him just as paint talks to Jess. This interview, as in its longer form here, has been reprinted in Kevin Power's* Where You're At: Poetics & Visual Art *(Berkeley: Poltroon Press, 2011).*

    —Ed.

At Robert Duncan's home in San Francisco

KEVIN POWER: You mentioned in the [Don] Allen anthology the importance of the new painting in San Francisco, of [Brock] Brockway, [Lyn] Brown, [Jess] Collins, [Harry] Jacobus, [Lilly] Fenichel, and of their teachers: Still, Hassel Smith, Corbett, and [Elmer] Bischoff. You point out that they displayed new organizations allowing for discontinuities of space and for more vitality than you had. Would you expand on this?

ROBERT DUNCAN: Well, 1950 was the tail end of Abstract Expressionism, and students were in a stage of transition, and one of the transitions was from French to German painting. It took that long for the eyes to get accustomed, since one of the misfortunes of German Expressionism was that all things German went out along with Mr. Hitler, although the Expressionists were hardly on Hitler's side of the scene. So that, after the war, when America had been dominated by French art, we were already, by the late '30s, looking at what the French Modernists said we shouldn't be looking at. We were looking at [Pierre] Bonnard and [Édouard] Vuillard, at the ones Picasso fought against, because *Verve* was reproducing them. The French tide had already begun to turn and a kind of French art we'd been thinking of as continuous was remodeled. In high school or during our first years at college Picasso was the Ezra Pound. You had them both tattooed on your mind. But things were opening up and the [Edvard] Munch show in San Francisco in 1951 was one of the first. Initially we'd always seen these things through reproductions, although the fact I'd been to New York meant that I'd seen a great deal there.

Then, also, in the years 1949–50, Still, Corbett, Hassel Smith, and Bischoff (an abstract painter at that time) were all going more towards a non-objective image than stressing the action of the painting on the canvas. They referred to themselves as non-objectivists. Well, I was looking for these discontinuities, and, in fact, in the Colnaghi shows of those years we'd pick out some of the Europeans who appeared to be moving in this direction. We'd look at an early [Wassily] Kandinsky for the dispersion of areas and the same thing in a Vuillard or a Bonnard. The first person I heard address himself to this idea was Hans Hofmann in 1940 at a congress of abstract and Surrealist painters. He said that the new painting would be Bonnard plus [Joan] Miro. Miro did, indeed, produce a dispersed and busy canvas, with lots of objects in them. I'm not talking about the grand Miro of the Spanish things but Miro of those little shapes. I like the whole feeling of a mosaic going to pieces, and that's what I wanted to happen in poetry. I knew it would have to be ingested, and that it would have to happen in a different way. So looking back at that proposition in the Allen anthology, it's a proposition I've written a lot about in a book of mine called *Writing, Writing*, where I try to spell out a writing that would be like painting. The important thing to understand is that the picture we had of a possible painting or possible poetry is not the painting we saw but the painting we could imagine from what we saw. Jess's collages develop along with my poetry. One thing in the poem was to see *The Cantos* bringing in more and more elements—in other words, the very thing that so depressed Pound. Pound was attracted to [Max] Ernst's collages, but they're homogenized; they tell a story at one remove. But that's not what Pound himself did even when he set to work on *The Waste Land;* he produces another kind of collage effect that incorporates elements that would have been assumed foreign within the poem.

KP: You wanted that lack of coherence?

RD: Actually, yes, very much so, but that was after "The Venice Poem." It's overcomposed; it's thematic. I'm still weaving too many themes, so that my score for lack of coherence is not very high. My readers don't get too many brownie points when they think I lack coherence, although I propose the possibility. I'm attracted to it although I find it difficult or impossible to achieve. In fact I think there's no language situation that isn't coherent, since language is already such a highly formal occasion. [Jack] Spicer's proposition about a real lemon in the middle of the poem is itself a word called a "real lemon" in the middle of the poem, and consequently is homogenized. The same thing applies to painting in that anything that happened in the canvas was already an image. As a matter of fact a brushstroke in which we can read the man's arm movement is already an image in movement. We're reading a trace of movement. Incidentally, one of the reasons behind that interest in gesture at that time was that the painters were beginning to look at cave drawings and how they were made.

KP: I wondered if your interest in following the tone-leading of the vowels was itself one method of dispersion?

RD: Well, you can disturb poetry since poetry's not language. Sure, you can disturb poetry by dragging it back towards the song or music, because poetry is a later compartmentalization. It used to be almost identical but by the nineteenth century they're calling them "song lyrics"; before that nobody had worried about a song in a poem. [Michael] McClure's "beast" language is one way of using sound to disturb poetry. I think I've an early poem where a sound, "brhhh," is introduced.

KP: I think there's also one in *Caesar's Gate.*

RD: There might be, but I suspect it's punning. Those were illustrational poems. The collages that go with the printed poems were done as illustrations. And then Jess had more collages done than that, so I illustrated them with the poems that appear in script. So it's a sort of composite book. The collages were all done from sixteen issues of *Life* magazine; that's all we could get our hands on in Spain. Jess actually cut it down to where he'd used up every image of the sixteen issues.

KP: In *Names of People* you make a lot of references to people who were at the California School of Fine Arts [now the San Francisco Art Institute], to people like Brockway and Corbett. Did you also know the older figures there, such as [Jean] Varda and the McChesneys?

RD: Well, you know, most of the poems were written in 1951, although the book itself didn't come out until 1968. In other words, at the time the Art Institute was very active. I certainly knew Varda and was very fond of him, probably because I'm older myself. I knew people in the old bohemia like Madeline Gleason, James Brown [?], and Varda. However, when Hassel Smith and Corbett were at the school, the old guard—and Varda is one of them—were really fighting against this whole thing. Varda had a lot of swing with the trustees, and there was a great deal of bitterness. Varda had great scorn for the new painting. But, of course, I always thought that Varda was a tinkertoy artist, and bohemia is certainly inclined to produce tinkertoy artists and poets. Varda's things are cute and that was exactly the range of his own mind. I knew Varda mostly through the associations of [Henry] Miller and [Anaïs] Nin.

Actually, a good deal of my turning against Nin and [Kenneth] Patchen as writers—and I'd actually been lost in admiration for them as only an eighteen-year-old could be—was my beginning to realize that, as artists, they weren't responsible for their art, that their art was a sort of plaything for their personalities. On the other hand, you couldn't find a more splendid group for that *not* being true of than Still or Corbett. When we come to the final score, Still is the most considerably impressive painter of that whole period. Jackson Pollock is a great event and absolutely thrilling in those paintings that project that strange kind of light. I mean, in those huge canvases. But his expressionist painting and much of his other work shows, I think, that he wasn't that bright. One nice thing in an artist is that you don't have to be intelligent, but it helps a lot if you're actually going to continue to work. Still has an extraordinary mind. I'm not saying, does he talk good? No, he talks as silly as the rest of us when he talks.

KP: And the supposed mythic quality of Still's work, did that attract you?

RD: I never really got around to that. Remember that my last rounds of thinking about art had been along the lines of Hofmann's students and of Hofmann himself, whom I knew. And that's a very different proposition about painting. So the big shock for me was the Still retrospective at the Metart [Gallery] in 1950. That was a tremendous year for me. I met Jess; Brockway, I'd known before. My mother had already given me money to go back to school where she thought I was going to get a degree. I was going to go to Europe; in fact, the trip had already been paid for. Then I saw this Still show and that changed my mind. Well, I knew one thing about postwar Europe that was rather sad and that was that there wasn't any art. When you saw it, you saw hand-me-downs of what had begun to happen in the States. And then the New York I knew—I was in New York in the war years—was clustered with Surrealists and with the last of the European painters who were refugees, and they had a lot to do with the fact that Americans suddenly realized that we could do something. By the time the Surrealists themselves went back to Europe they found the market so set in Paris and themselves so isolated from the younger painters that it just destroyed them. Painting had become an *objet de luxe*, an investment.

KP: What is it that so impressed you about the Still show?

RD: One of the effects of the Still show was that I couldn't in my way be happy about it. I like the canvas to be disconcerting, to be challenging, and Still was certainly that. Through it all I realized when I got home that I'd seen something absolutely stupendous. Stupendous is the right word, because it knocks you. In other words, it didn't appeal to any aesthetic that you could possibly advance. You could find one, and seeing the Stills at the Albright-Knox proves that. But he wasn't established and by the time he'd given those canvases to the Albright it was still only a small circle that would allow that he was what he is, and that I think is still not very large as a concept of opinion. Anyway, by the time I saw the Still show, ugly and beautiful no longer interested me; I knew art wasn't about that. Yet it was still disturbing to see such a great show; everything got translated to where even now I didn't understand what it was that I thought was ugly.

KP: Was it the jaggedness and ruggedness of the tear that you weren't prepared for?

RD: No, it was because Still also had in his early painting, and it was still lingering, something of the thing I hadn't liked about Jackson Pollock: that is, the patient on the couch, confessional, or dirty-insides painting. Oh, there's another painter whose work I love: [Milton] Resnick. His work was either absolutely radiantly joyous or intensely dark and gloomy. But it's Jackson Pollock's work of the psychoanalytical period that we first saw. When the Surrealists arrived, they made a combination with abstract painters, but the abstract painters there are followers of [Georges] Braque, along with American '20s type of abstraction. Yet certain people emerged, and they were really painting psychological symbols. One of them was Pollock and his totem-like things.

KP: [Adolph] Gottlieb and [Mark] Rothko were also working in a similar vein.

RD: Yes, and people like [William] Baziotes didn't really know whether they were Surrealists or not.

KP: The so-called biomorphics.

RD: Right. They didn't know if they were Surrealists, and they weren't. They were psychologists. They misunderstood Surrealism, like [Jean] Arp, reading it as psychology. They didn't get the fact that they were outside that reality, that you're above it. The biomorphic artist attempts to make all forms like body forms.

KP: Was it an attempt to give Surrealism an American context?

RD: Well, I don't think they worried about that right away. I do know that they didn't talk about an American context. Almost all of them were into psychoanalysis. I was married to Marjorie McKee, one of Hofmann's students, and she was being analyzed. Virginia Admiral—and you'll see a canvas of hers upstairs—was also being analyzed. They really read their canvases' interior space, whereas Hofmann didn't. Hofmann's idea of abstraction was still the classical one in which you're looking at a room or you're looking at something and you abstract. So he was a post-Cubist all his life. When he's painting what you'd think were Expressionist things, they're still in a big studio, painting the space and light and area of the studio. Elements of interior feeling come in but they're abstracted. The Americans were almost like blind people; they didn't think in terms of the abstract. They started painting an inside feeling, and one thing that you can see right away is that Miro is not painting an inside feeling. He's got an iconography, and there were some very odd propositions about an iconography that would all be lucid because of an inside feeling. In the same way *art brut* was very appealing too. I think Americans have very strong inside feelings. But to get back to Still: he was a mixture of inside feelings and grand propositions of form. I think you know what those are, those huge canvases that are clearly not an inside feeling. Though even in 1951 they were there, a mixture of these two was already present.

KP: Was Still's idea of the unqualifiable act important to you?

RD: I never really came in contact with his ideas. Jess says that as a teacher Still wasn't noted for his ideas but entirely for his attention to things. I've read some of his writings. Still also got into a controversy with the Communists. Many of these people were fellow travelers and they found themselves being savagely attacked. They'd come out of the WPA and found themselves painting the way Communists said you should never paint. I don't know that Still was a fellow traveler, but Corbett, certainly, was. So, they all felt very guilty. Still was the one who was attacked and he launched back. He was very bright and had all sorts of things to say. Somebody like Michael McClure paid attention to every aspect of Still and his work, and was picking up poetically and translating what they would propose about their art into poetic terms. To me it's a picture that proposes. For ideas I go to a poet, and only sometimes do I pick up from a painter. Ideawise I'm way back in the teeth with people who would be my grandfather, like Matisse for example. For my contemporary ideas I make them up myself, so I'm not going to be running round to someone next door.

KP: Looking at those Still pictures again, were they a place that contradictions could cohere?

RD: They might well have been, but actually they offered a contradiction of an aesthetic which immediately made it appetizing. There was a lot of talk in criticism, at that time, about the challenge. [Arnold] Toynbee had raised a picture of history in which challenge meant everything. So a crisis became more important than everything else. That rang very true to where we were in the poem. I also find it very interesting that while Toynbee was raising this picture of history, Dirac was raising a similar picture for physics. He said our ideas must all be wrong, because we can't ask any questions of them. If we've got a framework where we can't raise questions, then we don't have a language. He means not questions about something out there, but questions about self. In other words, we're incapable of doubting, because our language will not give us an apparatus to doubt with. We're in a bind, a crisis again. And Dirac is exhilarated and ecstatic when he makes this proposition, one that [Erwin] Schrödinger takes up again.

Lots of these things rang together in my mind. At that point of "The Venice Poem," 1949–50, I launched off into trying to do a duty piece. I'd been in correspondence with Pound. I wanted to take *The Cantos* as far as I could. I don't have any propositions about something being possibly larger than the thematic coherence of *The Cantos*, so the thing I suddenly realized I was like was the *assemblage*. It doesn't in fact raise the questions that I thought were maybe there at first. Assemblage is not incoherent; it doesn't worry about coherence or incoherence. But my initial blow was to ask myself if this could possibly break up some formation I had; could it break up the habit I had of constantly forming things. These assemblages of Jess from the early '60s just bring things together, and that, of course, is not the same thing as do they break something up. But much more than that I began to understand also that it had something to do with a picture of the universe, while Pound's picture of the universe was never really very modern, so that he was just misinformed. When you move something from there to there you haven't, in fact, broken anything up. So we've got one where everything in that universe, including particles, are events. And no matter what happens to that universe, events simply don't have the frame that used to be there that could be broken up. That was an important realization for me. The field in a Bonnard or a Vuillard, going beyond Impressionism, is not felt to be just a matter of looking at light. I was intrigued because it was broken up and I get that kind of texture.

KP: Do you mean the play of the various color areas?

RD: Yes, it was intensified and worked in every area. My poems are worked in every area, rime-wise and everything else. They consist of minute details which accumulate in a huge faith as to what is going to happen on the whole canvas.

KP: With reference to the Assemblage Movement, I notice that you've dedicated a "Structure of Rime" to [Wallace] Berman and another to [George] Herms. What was it that you admired in their work?

RD: Well, that comes later and is a result of certain new elements that appeared. Jess thought of himself essentially as rescuing objects. In other words, you take something from a context like *Life* magazine, which is a really despicable context, and you rescue it. You're not only rescuing its photographs, but you're rescuing *Life* magazine from itself. Sometimes you're doing what Burroughs was doing: you're showing *Life* magazine what *Life* magazine looks like.

KP: Whereas Herms was, in a sense, concerned with restoring the mystery?

RD: Well, Herms used to go to junkyards, so he was rescuing what's thrown away. He wasn't recycling, by the way; he was rescuing. [Marcel] Duchamp had something to do with that with his *objet trouvé*. Duchamp never thought he was rescuing that actual object; he thought he was finding a form. Duchamp's great at finding forms outside the frame that's given to art. But it's cutting both ways, you see, since besides making proposition "A," the Dada proposition, that he's going to do something to art that would be intolerable to it, he's also meanwhile added an art object to it. We were amused when the Surrealists gave their first show in Paris after the war; Man Ray's *Object to Be Destroyed* was shown. It had been in the Museum of Modern Art for years in some sanctified corner. Bring it out and what happens? Some literal French student destroys it. Man Ray was at the opening and he wrings his hands and says, "You're destroying a work of art." It's called an *Object to Be Destroyed*! This is almost the pitch of where it was at in that period. We were sort of isolated. I was isolated in 1950 when I wrote "The Venice Poem." I'd completely lost my earlier audience; even Spicer turned against it. My account in general was that its composition was musical. I don't mean in any advanced sense; it's a symphonic form. It couldn't have been more nineteenth century. Its decisions were all musical. They were done because this next to that does so-and-so, not because there's some theme. There were themes, of course, but they're designed themes. So the poem got entirely out of the range of what a poem is supposed to be, which is personal feeling beautifully expressed or something like that. I felt that if I wanted dynamics I could go all the way to a kettledrum. I also made full use of mixed rhythms. That's what I love about Stravinsky. It's what's been called "pastiche," but I was hearing it also as a mixture of elements. This wouldn't be like Still; he doesn't mix his elements.

KP: But the notion of a mixture of elements is clearly very close to assemblage.

RD: Yes, certainly, or like Jess's stuff. That canvas painted in 1952–53 shows the elements of drip and blob used in a canvas that's beginning to be expressionistic, but actually you can see right away that the expressionist elements are beginning to find a new space. So it relates to things like Berman and so forth. It's that kind of edge of Surrealism which is not Surrealism. But the spatial part of that is what Jess would be particularly responsive to. He is, of course, responsive to [Roberto]

Matta, where the opening up—not of a perspective to organize the space, but of the spectral character of the space—is felt. It's the spectral space that interested him.

KP: He would also have been very interested in the patina of the objects, the associated world that they held?

RD: Yes, he was always concerned with that. The primary requirement was an image that emerges and you see the paint all the time. In fact that's exactly what's going on now in his work, only it's a much more sophisticated development. Then also the fact that the painting acknowledges that the image is a skin. Images happen at the skin level of the painting. (This always intrigued Jess and we would talk about it a lot.) You see this one here doesn't just happen on its skin, and consequently there are elements that are active. There are no lines in it. What you see as lines are juxtapositions of areas and those areas are built up in layers and layers and layers. So you've got color activity that's not on the skin of the canvas, understructures that you didn't at first take into your seeing. We used to have on loan a really striking canvas from a catalog that showed that. It's the one that was done from a Burne-Jones [Jess's Translation #7?]. It has huge lumps of paint, so they're really in a struggle between the recognition of the fact that the paint and the medium were the depth and the image that you're reading on the surface of it. This would be very much like a poem recognizing that you're not saying something with the word but that the word is itself saying. And my use of the *OED* is like that; I've always thought in terms of layers of words.

KP: In "Passages" the free words that you set out there have those layers of meanings beneath them?

RD: Yes, when they're separated into phrases that's to separate them from any syntax tie, and ultimately in theory they operate throughout the entire book they're in. I conceive of the syntax of a sentence tying the words in so that we do not get to be reminded that they also go everywhere else, and consequently mean sometimes something very different from what we take them first to mean.

KP: Could I take you back to that "Structure of Rime" dedicated to Berman? You said there that they were "artists of the survival and they were willfully losing their last coins among the waves and the shadows of their work." What did you mean by that?

RD: Well, that's because I think our survival is so questionable that only art proposes it, and that's always preposterous. In other words, we no longer have any survival that we could believe in, and so we only imagine our survival. It becomes an act of faith, comparable with religion. As a matter of fact, to say that our culture will survive seems to me as risky as announcing that the Virgin Mary is pure white and so forth. I view myself as living in a world in which I don't exist. Consequently, almost every proposition is imaginary. So that the question of the artist's survival has got to be a very strange proposition. We are no longer tenable as a species is something I'd already begun to imagine when I was at high school.

KP: Is there a hint of desperation in that attitude?

RD: No, not of desperation. Jess was an atomic physicist before he went to painting, and when he was at Hanford working in the Project he had a dream in which the entire civilization was destroyed in this year, 1975. So, in a funny way he believed it, but at the same time it becomes unbelievable. But the paintings are proposed as only existing in themselves and possibly not having any future. Yet what happens is that he takes longer and longer to finish a painting. The investment time on a canvas he finished last year was a year and a half, just on a single canvas. This canvas here and that one over there are two panels of four that an Italian movie producer wanted done for a room. That one's a Chinese demonstration of a Pythagorean theorem. Well, he's finished these two so far this year, and got a fair way along with the third. So it feels almost as if he's a speed painter. We've known each other for twenty-five years, and our talk all the time was of this imagination and what it was going to be. The one who's not an artist would talk about what is art. I mean, what is this imaginary art that calls upon me to be concerned about art, since, otherwise, we'd just look at it. Even a critic should really sit down and say, "Gee, I would just be looking at it unless..." Most don't do that. They keep thinking they're talking about what is art, but they would hardly be talking if that was the question, because art's sitting right there. No, the real question is how come this thing called upon them to be answering some question about what art was. And that question we can begin to see must be some proposition that's never been there before, since, otherwise, we wouldn't have to be working with it.

KP: You said at the beginning of *The H.D. Book* that the great art of our time is the collage, to bring all things into complexity of meaning. That seems to me one of the essential parallels between your work and Jess's, i.e., the way you've both applied the collage technique. Do you accept that?

RD: Yes, new complexities and also to range widely. For example [in this canvas by Jess], you've got a Chinese demonstration of a Pythagorean theorem. However, the Chinese demonstration of that theorem surely precedes the Pythagorean theorem by some five hundred years, and more than that the Chinese way of looking at it is entirely different. It's an unfolding box and, if you remember, the Greek one demonstrates by their forms moving out from the triangle, whereas the Chinese sees it as an infolding of triangles. Yet exactly the same thing is being observed. This panel is going into a room of a wealthy Roman, who's building a house the way the Romans always did in Pompeii and so forth. We take it that these are architectural units, because he said exactly what size these panels were to be, but nothing about what they're to be. You can see a similar complexity of meaning in this panel where Jess is researching the Quetzalcoatl legend, and yet the cross is Western. Range and complexity of meaning are real propositions of this household. We'll spend three hours of a morning re-researching along some myth line for, say, the big Narcissus canvas. I'll read all the stuff that's in French and a lot of the English. Jess can crawl his way through the German. I've gone through Greek passages with a dictionary. All of them to uncork the lore that goes into a painting of his, and lore is details. Joyce is right about it. It's the artist who gets his complete focus and indwelling sense. The word "indwelling" is the important one here. It's the "indwelling" that immediately was recognized in Still. I don't worry about what myth is there—I mean, cats are the same as myth. A lot of people think you shouldn't have myth; they think you should be out of doors playing baseball or climbing mountains or [taking] some real part. Well, it's all real to me; it's just where you indwell, what calls you and what gets you completely into the thing you're working on. In our case it happens to be intricacy, something that promises intricacy in layers that may demand working over long periods of time. When I was in London two or three years ago, Jess wrote me about a canvas he was working on. He said he guessed he'd have to stay with the thing longer and longer before he could ever realize it. I wrote back [that I was glad]. It's the essence of what I've been trying to find in my life. I need a framework in which everything would exist. I'm interested very much now in design elements. Jess's collages are, of course, very different from some of the collages we love. They're different from Herms in that they get more and more intricate. Herms and Berman have a nature cult magic that's got lots and lots of lore in back of it, but it's not multiphasic. Herms was very attracted to the Sabian astrological moon-cycles, their ritual and cult. Berman, in much the same way, has an interest in Kabbalistic letters, itself a kind of magic. Riddling is much more where *we* are.

KP: You also say that Jess's work moved towards being a ground for what you call Romance, for the life of the spirit that involves fairies and Christs, saints and the present. Does collage become, here, a technique for fusing the imagination with the present?

RD: Well, Jess reads more in the fairytale realm than I do, but it's something that cuts both ways. Both Jess and I built up for ourselves the sense of Romance—it's common territory. Part of the key to that sense of Romance is that our own relationship wasn't conceived of as real but as story living in a way. For Americans "real" means the psychodrama. And I'd really been starved for someone who would recognize that the truest thing about life was the Romance of it. It's Romantic in almost all its aspects. This includes such things as Vietnam, as far as I'm concerned, since in any Romance you'd want to find out how evil things were going on. Vietnam says, clearly enough, that that's the way it really is. More and more people are beginning to see the way it really is.

KP: In assemblage the realness of the imagination is proved both "against" and "with" the realness of the objects used.

RD: Right, you recognize they came from a junkyard while you're looking at them. As a matter of fact, you get more out of these collages by Jess when you've seen *Life* magazine all through certain years, and you recognize the issue of *Life* that the picture came from. You see, then, what's been done to it and with it. It could be called trivially related because it's transformed. Its presence is enhanced by recognition. The naughtiest he ever did was cut up a Corbett drawing and use it. He said that was exactly what he needed.

KP: What was his interest in comics?

RD: *Tricky Cad* is a diversion of Jess's almost all on his own. One thing that happened with *Tricky Cad* is that, when Wieners wanted to publish it in *Measure* in 1955, Jess wrote to Chester Gould to get permission. He received a very unpleasant letter in reply, totally outraged by the idea. Jess said that he guessed Gould had seen that the evil and lunacy of his world had been exposed. Of course, this was part of what Jess was doing. Some months, in '56 or '57, Jess did some more case histories, and about that time [Stan] Brakhage arrived with a ton of material. Brakhage had collected *Dick Tracy*, but Jess never did anything with them. He doesn't read comics at all; it just happened that in a spell he picked them up and started working with them.

KP: You also mention Dick Tracy in "Structure of Rime XXVII." Were Jess's series of canvases called *Salvages* concerned with this idea of "rescuing"?

RD: I don't remember now whether *Salvages* were rescuing nonpoems, or simply proposing they were the rescuings of something. It was like a floating idea of salvaging things. And Jess's *Salvages* were canvases which had been left in the studio when he started on something else. They were, later, picked up again and radically used. I mean by that, instead of assuming that you were going to finish them, you used them as material for entirely new paintings.

KP: In the *Book of Resemblances* there's a small group of poems where you're specifically concerned with the patina of things, with their past life.

RD: Oh yes, but this was, of course, very early on. It still interests me, although I haven't returned to it. What particularly struck me there was that what you took to be *débris* on a table turns out to have its own order. As you straighten it out, you'd find that you'd actually been in it all the time in putting the things there. You can't make an assumption that when you put this in the so-called disorder you're engaged in some kind of haphazard process. Everything is dropped or otherwise into it or onto it, and if you took a time span it would look exactly as though you were composing an object. So, what we call a litter is, in an entirely different sense, a work. Only we haven't been consciously engaged in it; we don't congratulate ourselves and we haven't had the experience of the struggle of our putting something here. And remember that the poem was advancing along the lines where we wanted to be paying attention to what was happening as we did it and not to be deliberately placing something in the poem that would solve some problem of composing it. In the poem we're moving away from, and certainly in the canvas Jess was moving away from, the point at which we're concerned with the composition of the canvas. We talked all the time, with great scorn, about the propositions that were in Art School, in English courses, about how a thing was composed. It seemed to us that it was composed no matter what, and the main thing was how did you break up this tendency of constantly trying to move a thing to be conclusive.

"Passages" and "Structures of Rime," by the way, are not long poems; they simply have no boundaries. The first poet to realize that he had no boundaries was [W. C.] Williams in *Paterson,* the most bounded of poems in all of its propositions. When Williams dutifully arrives at "the end" and leaps from the Falls, he finds that it wasn't the end of the poem. Williams's intuitions were the major things we had to draw on—he went on and on. It isn't endless, like Brancusi's proposition about the form of an imaginary endless tower, but in terms of the poem it was central to us. Pound, of course, died in great distress, because he felt that he'd botched *The Cantos,* that *The Cantos* didn't have a closure. [Williams] wrote the

"Coda." I put codas on things in much the same way. My way of arriving at open form is finally the key I took from Williams, although Olson's language about projective verse and so forth had been there for a long time. It's the gestalt proposition about what's happening; you look at a canvas and it's lifted right off "The Place of Value in the World of Facts" lectures which went on at Harvard in the years when Charles was there, the late '30s.

KP: So open form itself can be seen as a kind of collage?

RD: Open form is really a field, and in field-composition you're not going from point A to point B. The reader could actually move through it in any way. If you think about a field, where you're going to enter it, or where you're going to leave it, or if you're going to leave it, or what you're going to do with it, are all your own business. The previous idea of form as laid down by Aristotle is, "I, the artist, build a path across this field called life, and the path goes from A to B." What this defeated was that you failed to notice what was going on. All you've got are two important points, A and B, and a limited amount of experience. In the early '50s, to get this across to students I'd say, you can go to New York from San Francisco direct, or with a sense of adventure you could introduce a few "digressions," as they used to call them in the eighteenth century; you could go via Charleston or the Grand Canyon, but none of this would be the same as wandering across and finding a continent.

KP: It's the discontinuous elements that again assume major importance?

RD: Right. None of this was programmatic; all the ideas were present and wandering in my mind. They're still like that. All present propositions about open form are just so confused. Recently, in Cody's [Bookstore] they started listing long poems; both [M. L.] Rosenthal and John [Ashbery?] gave their lists, but all without any background of what do you mean by "closure" or what do you mean by "opening." Charles had some feelings about opening and closure, on the other hand, that can be located. One of his first poems ends with the statement that he didn't like a closed parenthesis because, when you close a parenthesis, it's the end of the man: Charles Olson born 1910, died X. Closure. And that's exactly what was on his mind about closure. My point is that you're not there at the point of birth, unless you've recently gone right through and had your engrams and know right back to conception. I come in a blur, so I couldn't find a parenthesis preceding me and when I'm going out I hardly have that one located, so that's open as far as I'm concerned.

KP: Open form comes close then to the Abstract Expressionist idea that you finish when it stops, i.e., there's a point where the process itself takes over.

RD: Right. I actually got to see Jackson Pollock painting one of those great canvases. It must have been in the '50s. Marjorie [McKee] parked me at Lionel Abel's house, and he went and talked to Jackson Pollock all night, telling Pollock what I was doing while Pollock didn't pay any attention. What struck me again and again was that Jackson Pollock was in the middle of the painting, literally in the middle—not in front of it or in back of it, in the middle of it—and that's the way I feel in a poem too.

KP: Something you say in "Pages from a Notebook" seems like a parallel to Pollock's idea of being "in" the action of the painting. You say that "you seek in one way or another to live in the swarm of human speech." Similarly, you accept "the accidents and imperfections of speech" because as you say "they awake intimations of human being," and this attitude also seems to parallel the Abstract Expressionist's acceptance of accident as a factor in the creation of the canvas. Are such analogies fair?

RD: They're tricky, but all these ideas were certainly in the air. But I really would place that sense of living in the swarm of human speech, in the middle, with Pollock. McClure *really* felt he was doing what Jackson Pollock was doing. I'm not quite sure what he felt that was, because he would have his own picture of it. There was, of course, Jackson Pollock, the *Wolf* [painting]. By the way, there are some splendid Surrealist canvases of Pollock when he breaks through from the psychoanalytic inside Expressionism and when he's still got some of these first image things that were really amazing. Anyway, I don't hear in McClure what I hear in me, but obviously we're two different poets.

310

KP: McClure said that he was particularly attracted to the idea of a spiritual autobiography in Pollock.

RD: Well, you know that's also an area in which Jess and I were immediately influential, and this holds for McClure and for people whose art we never really got close to, like [Stan] Brakhage, since along with the Romance things we had a definite sense about spirit art. It's part of the reason why I tend to dismiss the psychological—Americans are immersed in the psychological. There can be a war between the spirit and the psyche, but there shouldn't be at all; in fact they really should be together. Americans are decently shy of spirit, and that's okay. We're rightly embarrassed with the claim to spirituality, and yet the world is absolutely a spiritual existence. And one of the great assurances that it has happened in America are those great canvases of Jackson Pollock where you see the interior light. It's not perhaps the first time, since there is some spirituality in nineteenth-century light, but the painters were often thinking of it as outside light whereas for Pollock it's inside light. Where inside there had been muck and shit, suddenly there's an interior light. It's not Jungian, it's not painted with a mandala or something, it's not Buddhist—it's a real interior light. In fact you see it in the canvases because he works in it. He's again in the middle of the light. He painted in the middle of the light. He painted at night, all night long in the middle of a light that couldn't possibly be anywhere else. Oh, of course, he's got all those nonlight lights, the blues, etc., but the paintings aren't defeated because they went to the museums. Jess is defeated because he insists on painting by daylight. But Jackson Pollock's not defeated, because he painted by the very light in which the paintings were going to be shown. I believe he painted in those big canvases until the radiance was present. So period, it's a spiritual presence, and that's what I mean by indwelling, the presence. And what I mean by saying he isn't intelligent is that he's destroyed by the very place where he is like Dylan Thomas was. He'd returned to this ecstatic painting in the light until the presence was there but nowhere could he entertain the intellectual frameworks that belong to such a light in painting.

KP: Is that close to what you're saying in the *Black Mountain Review,* where you see form as "a spirit in itself," as constantly manifesting itself or aspects of itself?

RD: Right. Well, the Dewey–Elie Faure world that I was eating in high school is the source of that. It's not an original idea, but it's part of what shows how thoroughly conventional to my earliest sources of a direction my mind would be all the time. The proposition of the litter on the table says that no matter what we do, we are always in it, and maybe our art trains us to have some sense of how much we're in it. Wouldn't you say that the mad drivings and so forth that were going on were also present in that light of Jackson Pollock? In one of those same huge canvases called *Lavender Light* or something, Chicago also has a great canvas of this period; well, in those canvases you know that, while you're looking at them and seeing the inner light, they're also built up of all that mad, drunken impulse. So we substantially go back to a life that could be called unconscious, although its devotion to the light is absolute in the painting. We all know that Pollock was like a stumble-box. [Milton] Reznick on the other hand is almost propositional, as for example in the later ones where he's trying to paint a canvas in which nothing happens in any particular area. I've a little tiny canvas that he gave me some years ago. I try to keep to a rule to have no canvases that we don't buy. To start saying yes to a canvas is death on wheels—you've got to want them, to know why. But anyway, we did want this one. What Reznick was turning to was still not abstract—gee, I wish constructivists didn't mean Max Bill, but constructing something. What he was constructing was an event that he felt. Certainly he is a transcendentalist. He was constructing huge canvases that would be pointless except that nothing was to emerge at any level to the eye as possibly being focal points. They were all equal throughout the whole canvas. And you began to realize what it was: his entire tension was almost like [he] got out of his head so that nothing violent would happen on the entire canvas. It wouldn't even shiver. It was really strange, although again this light was present.

KP: You also see this inner light in Rothko.

RD: Well, Rothko's penetrating depth of color is something like this.

KP: But there was that move into the blacks and grays at the end of his life, in canvases which, in retrospect, seem autobiographical in their sense of retreat inwards.

RD: But I think these were also social feelings.

KP: I somehow felt he moved from the passionate assertion of the earlier canvases to a meditative space that also became a suicidal area of darkness. It's perhaps a result of the Paris retrospective, where the chronological presentations of his work did mean this move from the reds and yellows to the grays and blacks.

RD: He may have been addressing death, but he couldn't have done so any more strongly than he did when he worked in violet. Violet is much more the color of death. [Ed] Corbett had the worst and slowest form of suicide by alcohol, and at the time of his death he goes into the depths of white and black. In Pollock, color becomes an element of drawing, whereas color before had been purely a means of getting the experience with the light. In other words, I think there were dialectics at the point where he ran into the tree; he was making a proposition that would have thrown him forward.

KP: The reappearance of the figure . . .

RD: Right, he's also going back to classical French art like Picasso or something.

KP: It was an astonishing experience to see those last works of Picasso at Avignon, where he filled the walls of the Palais des Papes with what amounted to a reliving of his whole artistic life, as if he wanted to feel them for the last time and put them together. Your own *Dante Études* seem also to amount to a resume of your poetics.

RD: The Dante piece was the last thing I've finished. The *Seventeenth Century Suite* was written before that, although parts of the Dante in fact preceded it. They overlap. I work in interrupted forms. I've got several poems going, including one by no means finished called "Towards the

Sonnet." In it I've done versions of Shakespeare sonnets and so forth. So it's a form I'm working in different directions. And of course Jess was copying. In a way he'd initiated this business of copying from black-and-white pictures—it could be a photograph, or a drawing, or a transcription of a photograph, etc. Rule number one is that nowhere, except in his imagination, does it have color. Rule number two is that it makes propositions of line which he transforms into mass, into area. He's faithfully transcribing—so faithfully, for instance, that a Burne-Jones scholar who was at Barbara Joseph's, who has the copy in her collection, exclaimed when he was looking at the painting, which is a copy of a page of a Burne-Jones letter, "That's Burne-Jones!" Of course he was undone, since nothing of Burne-Jones could ever be that painting, but he recognized the handwriting.

KP: The Pre-Raphaelites always seem to have held a fascination for Jess, since in the *Book of Resemblances* they're clearly central to the designs and shapes that are taken up.

RD: Yes, right. The Pre-Raphaelites in terms of English literature are bohemians, not academics. So that the academics really have a very hard time with them. They can't forget them lolling around, smoking opium, generally misbehaving, and so forth.

KP: And of course your interest in the Hermetic tradition is again underlined here.

RD: Well, my parents were Hermeticists of course. What I'm doing there is in a way addressing and trying to make intelligible to myself all the things that were fascinating to me about it when I was a child. It was fascinating to be in a household with Hermeticism; it was also a pain in the arse, like religion can be, because, for instance, I still can't tolerate using astrological lore. Why? Because it was law one: I was adopted by astrology; if I wanted to do something it was done by astrology. Lore and Romance I did learn from the household and also my father's attachment to Pre-Raphaelite ideas. There's a lot of junk in the Pre-Raphaelites, but the fascination is finding out what's real. When you go to them today you're rescuing from the scrap heap. The trouble with Matisse is that there's no scrap heap onto which Matisse has gone, so you've only got Grand Art. As a matter of fact you can almost rescue Renaissance art today, because it's really on the scrap heap. Picasso is more questionable; some parts are on the scrap heap.

KP: One way the Pre-Raphaelite influence has filtered through has been in book illustration.

RD: Yes, and the fact that the illustrational had been forbidden in painting interests me. Both Jess and myself are attracted to bringing into High Art what had been forbidden to it by the eighteenth century. There was a division between painting and illustration, a war between color and line that Blake carries on about. There was a general feeling that painting should not illustrate, and that's where the Pre-Raphaelites get read out because their painting was illustrating. Now we've never been as idiotic as to pick up a war with the Impressionists but, if you know Pissarro's letters to his son Lucien, you'll see that Lucien was an illustrator in the last great generation of illustrators. We still look at illustration all the time, clear through to the Art Nouveau period. Again it's to bring the forbidden in; in this case it's not only on the scrap heap, it has been disowned. Our homosexuality also meant rescuing the irregular. It's exactly analogous to admitting that you're fascinated by Hermeticism. Also you read the funnies and build a world of such, and you build the world as a world of spirit. I really hate something like camp, or even style. I finally realized that I haven't got any aesthetic. What I've actually got is a collection of sentiments. Even that Brancusi over there is a sentiment; mind you, Brancusi would faint at the idea, but it's so pure a sentiment that I can take a copy of it.

KP: What did you think of Jess's inclusion in the Pop show in London?

RD: Oh, that was an accident. I wasn't against it. Pop Art fascinated us, but it became disappointing. I think that was due to its lack of spiritual imagination, because, paintingwise, artists such as [James] Rosenquist and [Roy] Lichtenstein had amazing ability. It was intriguing painting, but it seemed to lack visual imagination and what that all implies. So spiritually they ended up merely adding agenda to the sadomasochistic scene. What's so attractive, for instance, in Lichtenstein is his magnificently elegant line. In other words, there are scenes as incidental to the actual spirit of the painting as the seltzer bottles in [Fernand] Léger, and Léger is sort of poppa to Lichtenstein. I don't mind the seltzer bottles in Léger, but I really can't get a boot in the face as part of my icon. They were making icons for our church, icons in which they express their anger that the icons are so trivial. I've just received this book of Kenneth Anger; his life as an artist is crumbling and going to pieces, because of his real spiritual disarray. Choosing Satan goes nowhere. As Jess said at one point, America has so despised spirit that people will hug the little imp to their hearts just because it's a spirit. [Martin] Luther is from an ink bottle. The world of spirit is everything—Rilke really starts talking about it. The Americans, and the Europeans as well, have gone in for this no-spirit stuff, and then they just get a hunger for a spiritual thrill.

KP: I saw Anger presenting his films at Berkeley, and it was sad to see him reduced to an imitation of a showbiz personality. Could I ask you now about Jess's paste-ups, itself a method to permit an inclusive open field?

RD: Jess pins up his paste-ups until they are all done so that he can still move them around, and then the pasting is very complicated. He sometimes has to paste in the most complicated layers and figures. Only in the very early ones does he paste-up right off. This one, for example, by the time it's ready to paste consists of hundreds and hundreds of things. He mixes materials and periods.

KP: I was looking at some early ones in *O!*

RD: Yes, that's almost the beginning, [like] Jess's first collages I saw when I first met him. We had lunch at Brockway's and then went over to see a show of Jess's. I bought a little painting, which is in the other room. He had some collages there, one of which was a large figure made up of male nudes—very simplistic but built up of all these figures.

KP: The composition techniques of "Passages" also seem analogous to the paste-ups?

RD: Yes, that's true, but by that time Jess has gone a lot further. What's parallel to these earlier ones are the poems written in *Letters.* They were written during the years that I was first living with Jess, and also, of course, some of the things in the book *Writing, Writing* are very parallel. By the time I'm writing "Passages"—and I was already wondering why something wasn't happening in the poetry field like that—anyway, by that time "Structures of Rime" had already begun with no closures and with no boundaries, and a field which extends beyond itself so it itself is not a field adequate to the composition where both can move from prose to verse, but one where the verse line would be the dominant mode. Prose is that block of paragraph that moves and feels differently, and verse is written in lines and can be articulated.

KP: Yet there are those prose poems in *Caesar's Gate.*

RD: Sure, and there are prose poems as early as the book *Letters.* The prose poems in *Caesar's Gate* were done in 1955–56 just before *Letters* was published.

KP: These paste-ups also seem evocative of dream states. I wonder if they have anything to do with what you meant by "night language" ("Pages from a Notebook," *Black Mountain Review*). Were [George] MacDonald and Helen Adam in there?

RD: I'd read MacDonald when I was little; I think Jess had only read one of them. We read them together when we were first living together—we read aloud. There are fifty to sixty MacDonald novels. And Helen Adam was certainly right in there. We didn't meet her until 1954; that must have been right in the thick of the MacDonald period. Night language has a little bit of Freud in it. It's not so much the language of dream but something a little like what people mean by background noise. I don't really think it was the language of Lilith. It's more overhearing things, and if you're going to sleep it's not the language in the dream but the way you listen to voices or sounds of animals and so forth.

KP: So it's again the concept of the poet as the articulator of what you've called the "shell of murmuring"?

RD: Right. For one thing I think poetry may rise—well, I haven't got an exact location for it but I have the notion that poets had as their practice, when they used to be a profession, to hear what birds are saying. We know all this from legend. I think quite literally they had to go and hear what the surf was saying, what children were murmuring in the garden. In Eliot it's children murmuring in the garden outside that's very strong. For me, it's my own memories of surf or something. So night language means to me the sounds I would listen to. And in the tradition of my family, since they had séances, there was a strong love of reading things out loud and of hearing what so-and-so's saying. I used to puzzle as a child, because it wouldn't always be words or sometimes you thought you heard words.

KP: So now as you're composing when you say the words there's a series of voices present?

RD: Yes, language speaks to me when I write and not the other way round. Well, once in a while I can be found ranting at the language. But the point that makes me want to get to the poem is that the language starts talking to me. And the paint talks to Jess; he's adamant about that. That explains a lot of this business about translating: since the picture's there, he doesn't interfere with the picture. It's the picture and the paint that start talking to him. He has to be in the painting quite a time before it happens. He's working on one now where he had to go through a long slaving job before the conversation started.

KP: This is an inner language which belongs to the work he's looking at?

RD: Right, it belongs to the work, not to the language per se. It's the same for me with the poem. The quality it has of being the poem it is, is that it, the poem, starts talking. The way that I know that I'm in a "Structure of Rime" or "Passages" is just that you know, like with a person, it's absolutely definite. I've no doubt that it's "Passages" talking and so on. I used to put numbers on them but then I started to wonder how come I put numbers, since it isn't really a progression. It's a progression up until about 36, the last numbered one, but after that I don't worry if it has a number or something.

KP: Does that explain why "Structure of Rime" can become "Passages," because you're hearing both voices as it were?

RD: Sure, the part of any form can be in any other form; that's very definite. My reaction to reading *Leaves of Grass,* which Whitman kept re-forming by moving parts around, parts of one poem to another poem, was that I thought he knew much more about poetry than many twentieth-century poets do. It seemed to me shown again with the exceptional knowledge he had of nature-form. Of course, that would in fact be a principle of collage. And that reminds me of something that happened to Jess. One of his things came back broken from a show. He collected all the insurance from it, which amounted to the price of the object. He then built another object with it.

KP: Sounds like something from Duchamp! Your interest in Whitehead also seems related to this concept of a work made up of interchangeable parts. You quote Whitehead's idea of the personal identity of man as "a matrix for all the transitions of life," one that "is changed and variously figured by the things that enter it." This seems to me to be the thrust behind the notion of "open field" and suggests that open field is perhaps one of the conditions truest to that of man himself.

RD: Yes, that's true. Another thing that is valuable to me from Whitehead and still is—I'm talking of course of *Process and Reality*—is that he treats us not as entities but as events. One of the puzzles of my family and their Hermeticism is that they propose you're an entity—I'm an entity, a cat's an entity; I still feel that in the '50s we were concerned with identity, just the thing that Stein was saying. It was Charles who got me turned on to *Process and Reality.* He came preaching it in 1956, and I started reading it, seeing immediately that my book was his book and so forth, although there couldn't be two more different readings. Whitehead made a tremendous impression, because he seemed to me to make everything intelligible; because we were watching what was happening in the poem, or happening in what we were doing, we were ourselves events of the universe. It explained how come our attentions are what they are, how come we're more real out there, etc. And it is my experience that I'm more real out here, bouncing off you, and consequently in a radar I'm here but what would I do otherwise. With *Opening of the Field* you can tell where Whitehead comes in; he comes in right away and from there on he's going to be there. Of course I'd already proposed "the field," and it was a complex sort of joke along with Charles's proposition of the field. And also in a Joycean manner I was proceeding to orchestrate it, using every possible extension of lore or field and of various structures, and even to build the book like a Roman field with the dead going to be in a certain place and so forth. And then we were also living at Stinson [Beach, California], so there were open fields for me to go walking in. In fact everything that I could do around that word ["field"]. Then when Charles came with the Whitehead it just opened that up until it was not simply a joke, it was "nature."

KP: You also saw the field as a metaphor for eternity, "open to the tracking of any possibility," I think you said.

RD: It's certainly a metaphor for eternity. We talk about *the* field, but the interesting thing about field as it's proposed is that usually a field will be changing, a series of fields exists. In other words, if we take any event it has a series of fields. Our entire field of eternity is one of those fields, not *the* field of the fields. And also because Dante with his civilization of civilizations is so very heavy on my mind, the idea of the field of fields is always there. Whitehead has something that blasts this almost along some Hindu line in one of the footnotes to *Process and Reality* where he's talking about the ethical concept of God, and he says that God doesn't seek goodness, he seeks higher intensities. It's an explosion, like in the ambar. Then the footnote says . . . this of course refers to our present atomic universe. Well, only in the grand Schopenhauer return to the Hindu, in which you've got the universe of universes, can you have a present atomic universe. Actually, I have an unsettled feeling about the universe and that's okay. That's why you don't finish your work. I'm not going to write *The Divine Comedy* and say, "Hi, buddy, there's the universe." Whitehead didn't have an unsettled feeling and so wrote *Process and Reality*. I'm happily unsettled, so art must have moved someplace else. Though you know, to go back to our friend Matisse, he seems to have been joyously unsettled. There's a lovely passage that shows him in great command, his description of what he was doing at Vence when the nuns wanted him to do the Chapel . . . and so it's a book and it's also a room; I think it's a perfect idea. And now we're back to what most appeals to me about the proposition of field—i.e., that it is an eventful series of architectures; it has no closure.

KP: Does it permit a momentary realization?

RD: Yes, sometimes. But the interesting thing is not that the realization could be momentary but that it's immediate, it's right there where you are working. Then what makes that analogy with eternity relevant is that right there where you are working, you are working in the presence of the poem, and it is in turn absolutely true to, and productive within yourself of, the realization of what the poetry it belongs to is. When I'm working on a poem in the concept of an *oeuvre,* like [Jean] Cocteau, or classically [Gustave] Flaubert, or [James] Joyce, that is not the world of a field. Joyce, for example, when he's working on *Finnegans Wake* understands it as a sequel to *Ulysses* and understands it in the design of the five works. Yet when I'm working on the *Dante Études* they entirely change the apprehension of what the poetry they belong to is, but not because they add to everything that was there before. As a matter of fact my experience of re-reading or reworking *Caesar's Gate* for the third time entirely reinformed what it was. Yet I'm working with something from 1949 supposedly. So my idea of sequences is not like the serial poem as [Jack] Spicer proposes it, or as [Robin] Blaser proposes it. My argument against is that our experience at any point is changing. Not just our judgment. Simply, if I'm to look at you, I'm immediately aware of you in a field which happens to be the one present. All right, let's say we're going to deal with something in which we would fit you, and in which you'd be related to an experience I'd had before, but immediately we would move to another field, not before or after, because it still has only *here* for me. The other thing I begin to have like an antimacassar, quoting it over and over again, is that the saints only have one place to meet and that's here where we're speaking.

What interests me is, what is it that arouses us to this immediacy. And immediacy means there's no medium going towards something else outside to where we are. Yet the poetry's present; the poem is not just a thing in itself. It again is written in the presence of a poetry. It again potentially reinforms all other acts of poetry, and they don't have to be redundant at all, because reinformed we look at them and there they are doing something else.

KP: Is that the actual continuous mystery of the sounding, that the resounding can never be the same?

RD: Oh yes, and the resonance, because sounding is not just the sound you're making but the resonance in relation to all the other sounds present, and the sense of this sound now being present in the aura of the sound where we are. All other sounds have changed for us, because they become resonant with it. And consequently there are new propositions of chord and discord and other huge senses of concordance. Fascinating to me is the scholar's pursuit of the concordance, where the work is supposedly through and then you make a concordance of all the elements. Well, a concordance is a strange thing to read as such, not tracing it back to the poem.

KP: I saw one of Taylor's works that threw up the fact that he had this pattern of off-rhymes. . . .

RD: Mine's based on vowel leadings and internal rimes.

KP: You're now teaching a course on vowels. How do you set about that?

RD: It was a terrible failure. I had a great time, and the students got to hear that there was a vowel around. It was my first venture in teaching poetry, but I think I'll beat my tracks back to the history of ideas.

KP: What was it that you did then?

RD: The phone company had a marvelous chart of phones that I used to give them a scale. My concept about vowels and consonants being elementary for the poem could be approached, I thought, by letting them see the scale they're working with. Ideas are scales. If they're anything else then the kid thinks he's writing about something. When you're asking a question I'll take one of those ideas and build around it, but that's not what schoolteachers are usually doing. They want, for example, to make certain statements about love in a poem but they're so anxious and they don't realize that there are eight hundred million statements about love to be made that if you made a huge structure they could all be there.

KP: So the inherent music if heeded will carry a diversity of meanings?

RD: The artist's responsibility is to have studied, known, and be able to hear resonances. Take a poem by Poe—its resonances are specific to poems by Shakespeare or Dante, etc. You can make comparisons and so forth, but what actually happens is that Poe seems different. Now that's already a resonance, that's already rime. To be different or to be like something are already for me too close associations. You see there are no boundaries between poetry and painting, or poetry and music, so a question about Brueghel will bring up a question about how that looks in Brahms.

KP: How do you set about listening to, or working with, the vowels?

RD: You've got to hear them while they're there and since English disguises its vowels and we traditionally try to think we've got fewer than we have, it's my idea then that time should be spent hearing and tuning up so that you're immediately perceptive of what's present and what's not present. At Black Mountain I taught it as analogous to [Josef] Albers's business of color.

KP: In one of the *Passages*, you use the vowel chart, if I remember rightly. What do you think of [Gary] Snyder's idea that breath is literally inspiration, the taking in of the world, and that expiration is man making contact with the world?

RD: Well, breath is the physical way in which the vowel comes into existence. I also got hold of the book he mentioned the other night when he was reading *Turtle Island*—*The Garland of Letters* by [John] Woodroffe— and it was quite splendid. But in his own poem about the vowels you wouldn't have thought one was present. Gary now appears to despise this level of the poem, yet his early work is this very power. I felt that we were listening to ideas; nothing was an event that needed a poem. Gary's conscious mind has never been in tune to the poem; he's always thought that the poem was an agency of communication. But that's where his head is. It's the same with Rexroth, though of course both of them can write very beautiful passages, but they're not formalists, whereas I am. Gary, since he's a Buddhist, thinks that experience is *maya* and that he's supposed to vote for something else. But even that doesn't really explain it. I feel that Gary thinks his real life means building a house or cooking or something and that words are not real life—they're referring to it. I don't know where they take place then if that's the case!

KP: But in his earlier poems he does show how the actual physical rhythms become the rhythms of the poem.

RD: Right, but I think he's lost that; he's become proficient, habitual.

KP: You quote *De Vulgari Eloquentia* in the *Day Book* where you say man has been endowed with threefold life, namely, vegetable, animal, and rational, and that what's most important to him are the fire of love and the direction of the will. This seems to offer the guidelines to your own *Dante Études*?

RD: Well, they could have been the guidelines. Yet what I found so fresh when I was working on the *Dante Études* was both my sense of household and my pleasure of the way I like to live in the city. These seem to come forward again and again, and imaginary possibilities of city living were moving in that poem quite frequently as figures. So Dante's own spirit would, of course, be a guideline all the time, but essentially I'm interested there with how much it has to do with the movement about streets, squares, areas in the city. There are some sections in the middle where I'm taking from Dante talking about stanza form and that translates in my mind to images of neighborhoods and so forth. I don't drive, so I'm always walking around, and there are a lot of city places I recognize.

KP: It's looking towards your idea of a city-state again?

RD: Yes, that was on my mind. I thought Dante and Plato are not such difficult propositions if we realize that men imagine ways of living and we don't see them as laid-down plans.

KP: The fire image is also a constant preoccupation with you?

RD: Oh, I'm not the only one in the world who's got fire under them. Charles [Olson], as a matter of fact, charges me in "Against Wisdom as Such" with not having fire; he says I'm the light. Over and over he keeps trying to make me the light. Yet there are two elements of fire, and in that little homage to Charles in "Structure of Rime" there's that image of the Indian heating the head of the drum on the fire. . . .

KP: You make use both of the fire of inspiration where the idea is to be fired and of the fire of consumption, i.e., as both a constructive and destructive agent.

RD: Yes. Fired means firing of clay. One of my earliest poems, "The Years as Catches," is filled with images that have been tested, like metal is tested. I see ordeal not as proving yourself but as being "fired." One of the senses I had of Vietnam was that as they were being bombed they were being enormously fired. So that all the people who survived are a million times more powerful than those who died in the bombings. But I also understand of course the sense of being shattered. Students in the square of Mexico City were not "fired"; they were overwhelmed. But the point is that you test it, and this means of course that there's metal that fails to hold. So I don't view a test as proving what you are but as refining or strengthening, and this could go too far and break you but you're willing to go through whatever it is.

KP: Fire's also an important image in Pound, Olson, and H.D. That reminds me of something I wanted to ask you about H.D. You mention you first became aware of the War Trilogy [*Trilogy*] in the painters' studios in San Francisco when you were working on *Medieval Scenes*. What kind of impact did H.D. make on the painters? And I also wanted to ask you if *Medieval Scenes* was influenced by the painters.

RD: I'm wondering if I ever said that. In 1942 when I was here I was very much against the Second World War; there was just a lonely group of us who were mostly anarchists. Anyway, when I was here I looked up [Kenneth] Rexroth, and one of the things he said was that there was a terrific war poem about the horrors of the war by Edith Sitwell in a magazine called *Life and Artists Today*. So I went to the library to find that poem and in the same issue was part of the War Trilogy. So I followed it through and kept up with the magazine while I was back in New York in '43 and '44. So that's how I came to know the War Trilogy. Now I was around painters all of this time, but I'm not sure that I related the two things in any way. The poem really starts catching up with me about '47 when I'm working on "The Venice Poem." Oh, but wait a minute, it was important to the second version of *Medieval Scenes* that I did, the one that got printed, in which I developed it thematically with the word "more" and "mere" and analogously to the way in which words are chained and sewn in the War Trilogy. It's also true that, even before I met Jess, I was always around painters. I was even married to one.

RD: The Germans, you know, pushed around into upper Russia, and then they pushed down into Scythia. They come back into Germany about the third century AD, pushed by the Scythians and the Mongolians. In other words, the Barbarians are north of the Roman border, and they've got their own queen figure. In 1950 I had as my seminar topic Germanic and Celtic Art, and there was this picture of the Gundestrup Kettle, a kettle large enough for them to mimic their cooking of a sacrificial victim in it. There's one picture where they're lowering a little man into the kettle and it has huge goddess figures all around it, the tribe's goddess. It is she who governs their wanderings. That gets identical to the Shekinah in the Jewish wanderings. When the Jewish people lost the kingdom it was the Shekinahs who went with them, and the hearth begins then to be the campfire that you build anywhere. Olson has many propositions of the same thing in the *Maximus*. That's what his man on the sea is; he's in the center wherever he is and this center's always moving around. So my idea of nation would be pretty much how do we survive in our way of living, not how do "we" survive, but how does the way of living survive. All those things that seem "romantic" have lasted even though they weren't present in the dominant culture, and they've survived because we're susceptible. One thing we know is that if we've been susceptible, then some other individual somewhere must have been susceptible. More than that, we've got good evidence that human beings are amazingly susceptible to Romance. Otherwise, the puzzle in poetry would not be that it was individually expressive but rather how come that it keeps traditional patterns. All the way through history the meanest centuries keep alive heroic attitudes.

KP: In other words, the psyche keeps its own ideal state inside it, as I think you said in *The H.D. Book*?

RD: Yes, as a matter of fact the psyche makes a judgment about the actual state and can be adamant about it. Every psyche will name the state, and respect or disrespect what's going on, and some when they find it unjust are fighters. But the disaster that happens within a tyranny is that those who cannot locate the injustice in a state lose heart. People wonder about the collapse of Rome, but Rome was always a disgusting state and it lost heart in no time at all. The psyche makes demands; it reserves its judgments. The demands of Love Romance, as far as we know, are created in the periods of the troubadours. They were re-cultivated out of whatever in the ancient world, but they were transformed and they became a demand for every falling in love or passionate relationship. Passionate poetry, by its very nature, its very rhythms, is how you think and how you feel when you're excited. That's what a cadence starting in something is!

KP: Love is thus the giving of form to the poem?

RD: Yes, in falling in love everything's changed, so that's very much like a poem. It's like the way in which when you're writing a poem the writer disappears or the reader disappears and the poem seems to take the place of reader or writer. So that you're completely in it, very much like any love relationship. We can't draw away from it, and when we're in it, it will judge all reality around it. Freud wanted the reality principle to judge our actions so that we shouldn't come to grief; well, compared to that, any poet wants to come to grief. Love for me is an intense part of my life, so obviously it gets into the poetry and is frequently thought of as analogous. Yeats, for example, adds hate to it so that as far as he's concerned love and hate become the driving forces.

KP: It's a dominant part of "The Venice Poem."

RD: Well, "The Venice Poem" was conceived of as a rite of passage through a period of intense jealousy or sick love. It tries to exorcise it. It's not a very loving poem, to put it mildly, but that's why love becomes its topic, because that's the sickness in it.

KP: It's also the power that formulates the propositions in it?

RD: Right. They're attempts over and over again to find a curative base so that love will not be sickened. There's a long one, for instance, in the Coda, where the prayer to Shakespeare is a prayer to equilibrium in which love can be felt again.

KP: In "The Venice Poem" you're also exploiting the Poundian notion of everything being contemporaneous.

RD: Oh yes, that's always fascinated me, even before I heard it. It's the power of the imagination again, the fact that when you're reading about the Middle Ages you'd be in it, and it would take a lot of shaking and reminding to break the spell, so that you had to go out and water the lawn! It's as simple as that.

KP: Why was that poem always so central to you?

RD: It was the decision I made in that poem to follow the poem through. I often think of it as the last magic poem I wrote, apotropaic magic. I let the poem initiate me. And there also seemed to me to be powers that one could call upon, like calling upon the power of Venus, calling upon Jealousy itself to cure itself. It's also homeopathic, isn't it! My feeling was that if I precipitated the full content of this jealousy—to that extent it's Freudian—I would also in that precipitation be changed and have a kind of cure. And at the end of the poem, of course, you're reborn. When I think about the poem, my conventional relationship with the world is affirmative, and so when terrible things happen I don't experience them as punishments but as experiences. I want to find out what they're like so I affirm them deeper and deeper. So the poem had to be that long for the experience to take place. I mean, was it nine months or not, for a pregnancy to be born! It's not a poem of self-discovery, it's a poem of self-experience. That's very different. The poem to compare with that one is another poem of jealousy, the "African Elegy," where there's "I, I, I" going on. It has very strong accusations and releases figures of discovery about my own cruelties that, had this poem not been there, I wouldn't have arrived at admissions into the content of the poem. In "The Venice Poem" they reappear, because of those voices going back and forth about the poet and the fact he's self-centered and so forth. But they are breakthroughs for me.

KP: You put out parts of yourself in the poem which you simply let stand?

RD: Yes. What shocked people about the poem was the exposition of an unresolved and nonintegrated series. For example, in the Rexrothian position, the poet presented himself as a model of classical form, and there are classical ways of being jealous such as in Catullus, who dismissed the world as tawdry, but what I was doing was opposed to this.

KP: I understood three of the propositions in the poem, but I wonder if you'd explain the last. You begin with the poem as a mirror for the whole world; in the second proposition you have a part of the whole world reflected in the mirror; in the third it reflects a realistic image of what's happening. And finally in the fourth proposition you present the mirror as imitation, as poem. But you then say it "stops, changes" and what I'd like to know is what you meant by that.

RD: The germinal idea in the poem had come from Jane Harrison, where she was talking about, I think it's in *Themis*, the origin of dithyramb. As a matter of fact, the whole book has this proposition of what was going on in the dithyramb, and she divides it up into *dromenon* and *mythos*. She says that *dromenon* is the series of things that is happening, and the *mythos* is the story that's told of the things that happen. But what sent me was the tearing up and shattering of the Zeus child, and then the recomposing of the Zeus child, all in order to give birth to a new entity, a new person, and that I thought the poem was doing. She said that what they did in the dithyramb was imitate birth, and that the theme of imitation is *dromenon,* and this was exactly what I felt I was imitating. In other words, you go through jealousy imitating something; you do not know where it's going but a new consciousness will be precipitated.

KP: It is once again the process of the poem resolving itself, and that's analogous to the Abstract Expressionist idea.

RD: Yes, it's being in the middle of the poem; it's the Pollock thing we were talking about earlier. If you think about it, the person in "The Venice Poem" is entirely in the middle. The poem precipitated its own advance. It was being read to everybody while it was going on, so it was a brutal process. It's made up of a series of incidents that would have passed except that the poem wouldn't let them pass. So it was psychodramatic for a whole group of people.

KP: In *Writing, Writing* you talk about automatic processes, and you have a poem on one of Jess's canvases where the poem parallels the way a canvas comes into being.

RD: Yes, a canvas coming into itself.

KP: You say, "The red is ready before the part of it plays."

RD: We were reading Stein an awful lot in that period. The *Four Saints in Three Acts* was issued on a long-playing record, around 1949, and we played it down to the knuckle practically.

KP: Were you interested in automatic techniques in any way?

RD: No. Stein insisted hers weren't automatic. My hand wasn't automatic. Automatic means that you are not aware of the words that you are writing when you are writing them, whereas what I was interested in was to what extent could I break associational lines and produce a certain sense. And I found that had to be by paying attention to the immediate word and by making a leap wherever I could see that it was going.

KP: Such as, for example, when instead of letting the words settle into their syntactical order you make one word react against the word that precedes it. Yet still an overall image emerges?

RD: Yes. I didn't share the non-objective fear of imagery. I mean, in Jess's canvases you might begin to see a face or something appear but, gee, Corbett would turn green if you could see a face or cloud in his work. I was not in any sense aiming at not having anything happen in the poem or in defeating the message; I'm just talking about the area in which this would occur.

KP: I know from what you said earlier that you hadn't read the Still texts, but I wondered how far you'd go in agreeing with this quotation of his. Still writes: "I held it imperative to evolve an instrument of thought which would aid in cutting through all cultural opiates past and present so that a direct, immediate, and truly free vision could be achieved, an idea be revealed with clarity." I thought this interest in revealing vision would have been common ground.

RD: Except that I go in for the opiates. As a matter of fact this is the area of my work, the opiate part, the fact I like getting entranced in a poem, which people who admire my work don't like. Still owes something to Whitman here, who, if you remember, was going to do away with enchantment and entrancement of the poem. It would also certainly be in line with Creeley's intentions and Olson's.

KP: But the idea of pushing through towards vision comes close to you?

RD: Oh yes. If you think about what happens in the vision of a Still, of what happens in a canvas of that grandeur, they're keeping alive a mode of being; for instance they produce grandeur that's not expensive. Its truth is absolutely striking. I mean, there were, around this same time, many painters who had a whole series of motives and rhetorics, the Pop artists come to mind, and who were painting canvases that made fun of the fact there was an art market. This is so trivial, or to put it another way, who made huge trivial canvases? This is something that's just not in that statement of Still's at all. And so I think that he certainly would represent a force that interested me, and that is, how do you keep alive value in a society that has none of that? Well, you keep it alive in painting, that's one way! Still readdresses the problem of how to survive over and over again.

KP: You mention Pop Art, and you've a series of poems about ordinary objects, the bath, matches, etc., where you describe them in an extremely rich language. Were these a kind of counter to Pop banality?

RD: I don't really know if I was concerned with Pop in that period. I was really addressing the household we lived in. We've also got drawings of all those various articles. Oh, wait a minute, you're thinking of the bath in "Domestic Scenes" where the things themselves are very ordinary and the language very rich. These are really about relationships to people.

KP: They're too early for Pop, of course, but there is a kind of recontextualizing?

RD: It's like this bar of soap is my magic thing. Well, one thing to come out of *Medieval Scenes* was that Jack [Spicer] and myself finally discovered where the swans were. We started a game of trying to discover them because we saw that some of them were around us. Much of it is in the Freudian principle that things that come into dreams are actually things that were in one's daily life and are reproposed. The swans were on the decal of the bathroom wallpaper, and we collected practically the whole group from what was around. So the populated poem in "Domestic Scenes" was to bring them forward and then find out that they were older things. I sometimes feel that my poetry's deficient in its relation to what Williams would call the object, the old red wheelbarrow, since so much of it is about poetry, stems so much from poetry, books, and art. And so the practice of addressing my mind to them—I now feel it's overdue, although I've not sat down to do it. But, certainly in the period of *Writing, Writing* it was very much a part of what I was doing.

KP: Did Williams's use of collage techniques in *Spring and All* make any impression on you?

RD: The period when I was writing these poems I would have had only a very poor sense of what Williams was doing in *Spring and All*. I just had the full superstition from the age of seventeen or so when I first started reading poetry that Williams's was a major poetry, but I really had no clue as to how that came about. It came from my following up of Pound and Joyce. So those kinds of things were just puzzles; I could feel them but I couldn't get at what was going on at all. Yet I must have had it fairly early since there's a letter of mine to [Bill] Everson in 1940 when I was twenty-one, in which I write to him saying that I had a sense that what he and I need is the secrets of Dr. Williams. So I must have had some kind of awareness, and I expect you can guess how only a handful of people in the country even knew that Dr. Williams even existed.

KP: And later how did his use of collage affect you?

RD: Well, in *Paterson* definitely. *Paterson* lies back of *Medieval Scenes.* It had started coming out during the war and was immediately effective. It takes a long time for it to soak in, but I think "The Venice Poem"'s shifts and movements all the way through draw on *Paterson.* Of course, as I've said, H.D.'s War Trilogy was as important, because the gods had come back in and that reunited my feeling with what had been fascinating to me in my parents' cults. I didn't belong to any cult, but I had a way now for the gods to come in without being decorative, as they'd appear in Keats.

KP: And the shifts you use in the Venice and Pindar poems, are these parallels to the kinds of effects collage produces?

RD: Sort of. The Pindar poem, like "The Venice Poem," is comprised of four sections. Its Coda builds to an anxiety, whereas the Coda in "The Venice Poem" builds to an exhilaration. Yet they've got the same parallel structures.

KP: Dance is also a central image of these poems.

RD: It's a theme in my poetry. It's part of my teens and twenties, and I also spent a fair part of my thirties dancing.

KP: There's a picture of you in Nin's *Diaries* dancing to a Varèse recording.

RD: Yes, that was around Christmas 1939, New York.

KP: Do you see the poem, like dance, to be this moment of coming together of breath, body, and movement?

RD: It's a transcendence of self-consciousness.

KP: It's that moment, to use the H.D. image you quote, that all the butterflies are hatched from the words?

RD: Monsieur Valéry, not my favorite poet, has a book on *La Danse* where he says it stupendously. When Pound talks about love of poetics I think he calls it "the dance of the intellect among words"; in that sense, consciousness transcends its attention to what it looks like itself. The Pindar poem describes feet in the poem dancing, and "you passed the count" means that you're in it. When I'm in a poem I don't count the lines. Zukofsky said to me of one of the *A*'s that it was "eights." So I said, what do you mean—eight words, eight syllables? He said, I don't know; if I haven't got a feel for words and syllables by this time I shouldn't even be in the business. He's counting eight words.

KP: It's again the idea of being in it, being inside.

RD: Well, you can find enough announcements about being inside the thing instead of being outside and stepping away and looking at it. That early proposition of mine from the 1952 "Notes" has continuously been misinterpreted, the one where I said all my visions are revisions. I don't revise. It seems perfectly clear to me that if I'm going to go back, then I'm in it again, and I see it again or I don't see it. I've got no stance that I can imagine from which you could correct it. If you're in it again, you can be back in worse trouble than you ever were, and I've never really been able to understand what in the world a person was doing revising. I remember Everson showing me a manuscript where he had some word and he crossed it out and he had about five words above it. Finally he writes in the word he had in the beginning. So I said, well, how do you choose among the others? There's no principle involved at all. There's tinkering or something to make it sound better. Yeats is a corrector or refiner, and I've rewritten passages of poems, but they've always needed complete revisions of the poems, not just of individual words.

KP: You're close here to the Stein idea that composition is the thing seen by everyone in the living they're doing.

RD: She's riding a good horse and there's none better.

KP: And it's a principle shared by many San Francisco Abstract Expressionists. In one of the *Letters*, "The breaking up of cold clouds," you make a direct reference to Hassel Smith when you write, "it releases freshets, which I've seen advancing before my speech in the paintings of Hassel Smith. These remind me of the appearance of crowds at the margin of solitude and that there might be a crowd of one who writes," and then you add something that seems particularly relevant to the painters: "thus our invention is to disturb anew the spiritual arrangements."

RD: Yes, I think this is the force of Still. These are powerful propositions of feeling. It's almost like Anacreon's laying it on Egypt. He really proposes a kind of space and a time of painting. It's a one-man revolution.

KP: Those great gaps and rips that you talk of in *Writing, Writing* (Appendix II)—do they owe something to Still?

RD: Probably, but I'm seeing that all the time.

KP: You also say, "these violent recreations betray the secret history of our time"—so again as with the Expressionists, this is a pushing up of the emotional facts.

RD: Right. This would be the "nation" again, Charles's idea of "another kind of nation." I mean, the poem doesn't provide one, of course, but it does sow seeds and seeds the ground with possibilities.

KP: The sowing that takes place on the various levels of the Pindar poem seems analogous to the Abstract Expressionist dispersal technique?

RD: Oh certainly. Charles was one of the reasons I went back to the city and so forth. I was also fascinated by H.D.'s Moravians. She came from a Moravian brotherhood. What they had was that, since Christendom was bankrupt with the Protestants and Catholics at each other's throats, Christianity could only continue, if you didn't form another Church, as a secret group of people inside the Church. And the writer and the reader or the painter and the people who truly look at the canvas are not connected in any way other than volitions, and that's the point that's so important for me. When you find a book of poetry you want to read, it's entirely your volition, it's been written in such a volition, and this is the dissemination of something. It's quite the contrary of creed that everybody takes together.

KP: What were Olson's feelings about painting?

RD: Oh, Charles thought painting was a form of therapy for people who weren't very bright. There are painting propositions, of course, in *Projective Verse*, or at least we can assume there are. And the *Lectures on Aesthetics* [?] were specifically upon looking at paintings in terms of field as in *Projective Verse*. The Gestalt ones were about looking at a canvas, and they get into trouble with music about what was happening in time. What they thought made it easy for them as Gestalts was that they saw the canvas as a boundary and something happens inside a boundary, and this gave them a whole metaphor for the way they were sure aesthetic experience moved. But for the poem, or a piece of music, its boundary is in time and you can't show it on a page of a book. Charles loved diagrams, and he may have had his troubles with painting because as far as he was concerned if you're making a mark on a piece of paper it was a diagram. I can tell you one incident that leads me to think he felt painting was therapeutic: when I was leaving Black Mountain he said to me, "I can understand why you think there should be music here because you write plays and you want some sort of music for that, but why do we have to have a painter?" This was at the time when [Stefan] Wolpe was leaving and when many of the GIs were studying with [Joe] Fiore and had come because of the previous painting reputation—[Willem] de Kooning, [Robert] Rauschenberg, the post-Albers period. As for these crossovers we're talking about, Robin Blaser is one of the few poets I know who was responsive to music and painting, and Jonathan Williams, of course, was keenly interested in both arts.

KP: Creeley would be another, and I think Olson wrote an introduction to [Philip] Guston's first exhibition.

RD: Could be he knew Guston.

KP: Who was Blaser interested in?

RD: He was mostly with the local painters both here and in Vancouver.

KP: And Spicer seems to have been interested in painting, although that didn't seem to provide any of the common ground between either of you?

RD: Initially in '47, '48, Kabbalism, the poem as possibly being a form of magic. I was still not settled on poetry as an art, as hours of work. We got magic that was directive and manipulative of situations. And Spicer was always manipulating situations and also, of course, evoking. I still evoke. In "Structure of Rime," the Master of Rime is an evoked presence like a person in a dream. Mike Davidson has just sent me a chapter of an article he's written on *Opening of the Field,* and one of his criticisms is directed against the appearance of the people in "Structure of Rime." By making them entirely fictive, like they were made-up people, they didn't come out right. The appearance of the Master of Rime was, in a primitive sort of way, like somebody coming to you in a dream and telling you something. With the Carpenter [in "A Letter," *Roots and Branches*], for example, I tell him, I know you're not and this is not a poem; I know you're not just something out of my psyche. Davidson doesn't like this framework. He talks of me proposing figures such as the Master of Rime, but I would term it calling them in or calling them up, or as simply recalling them. To stay within the boundaries of a strictly contemporary and sophisticated psychology would be that you recall them, but they were people. Whereas in his sense he saw them as improvised. I mean, I thought the Emperor of Ice-Cream might be an improvised character. I find [Wallace] Stevens shockingly frivolous, because I don't imagine such an entity, but the Master of Rime I really tried with him.

KP: In *The Opening of the Field* are the propositions of that particular poem, the propositions of the whole book. There are five of them, the first being "SKILL the precision the hand knows necessary to operate"

("Propositions"); then there's the "sending out into the field of the poem where the unexpected must come."

RD: That sending out is exactly related to what I was saying about the Master of Rime. There is a field beyond the poem that the poem belongs to.

KP: Then there's "the keeping" that allows you to bring your "life complete."

RD: Well, everything that has come into the poem has come into your "keeping"; that's why you tell the truth about it. Let's face it, for the person listening to the poem there's no way of guaranteeing that what comes into the poem is actually the truth; that's not why you're practicing truth within a poem. But when something comes into your keeping that's quite different. And also you keep to it. The other great question is how come you keep to this practice of a poem as art and as entire attention. Some poets don't. The idea of keeping keepers is also there; it's always got that double edge. I would use keeper in its full spiritual office, then give it a Freudian twist—the sense of being retentive, of not letting things go, of keeping things to yourself. Remember, "Propositions" is one of the few poems written about Jess and me; I'm not usually writing about him, so there's a little black humor in the situation of the spider and his fly. You come in enraptured into the web.

KP: The keeping as a possessive force.

RD: Right. It seems to me that it's always a question that we keep the things we love and we expect them to be kept, so that love is also a keeper. I have a lot of things about keeping vows and keeping orders in different things through several poems. Keeping also gives range; even within a single poem such as "The Venice Poem," everything all the way from dark rhetoric is permitted to come in.

KP: Another question I wanted to ask you was about the cover Jess did for *O'Ryan*.

RD: The drawing! Well, when White Rabbit wanted to do a book by

Charles, Charles sent a manuscript numbered 2.4.6.8.10., and Jess did a cover for it, which was *O'Ryan*. Jess did the big figure of Orion in the sky, a white line on a black background. When Charles saw the cover, he sent back 1.3.5.7.9., and so the cover had to be done again. I just don't understand it, but Charles said he hadn't thought of Orion. *O'Ryan's* a funny poem; it seems to be talking about Creeley some of the time. Charles was always odd about punning. I saw to it that California [The Bancroft Library] bought a letter of his to [Larry] Eigner warning him against my punning. Yet by the mid-'60s Charles is himself talking about punning, although his first instinct was to rule it out.

KP: But his use of the word "origins" suggests that he's punning?

RD: Yes, but those were the traces he wanted to cover at that point. He wanted to say, I never pun, honest John, so he wouldn't be seen as using them. But, of course, *Paterson* is a place where the pun would come in marvelously; it's very operative there. Pound doesn't like punning and practically has no puns.

KP: Was Eigner, in fact, moving towards punning?

RD: No, he was in correspondence with me, and it was one of the evidences that Charles was worried about people getting corrupted by Duncan. It was absurd; I mean, Eigner was Eigner. Spicer punned a great deal; it was central to him. One of the differences between Blaser's poetry and Spicer's is that although Blaser follows the Spicer line he really isn't a punner.

KP: When you're illustrating with Jess, how do you set about that in, say, the *Book of Resemblances*?

RD: Where Jess was drawing and illustrating, those were illustrated after the fact of the text.

KP: And the same with Helen Adam's *Ballads:* he's simply working off the images in the text?

RD: Right. The only place there was collaboration between us was *Caesar's Gate*. When Creeley and [Robert] Indiana worked together,

Indiana had, of course, done numbers before and Creeley suggested numbers. I think it worked both ways, Creeley was going back and forth to New York. They both began on the book at the same time, and it was being worked out by constant interchange.

KP: The *Book of Resemblances* contains a very broad range of Jess's drawing styles.

RD: Yes, they went over some years; the drawings for the "Borderguard" go back some ten years before the writing of the book.

KP: Your own drawings for the Black Sparrow book?

RD: This was a disaster, because the originals were not taken care of, and in order to economize in making that thing they took the notebook apart—it had drawings on both sides of the page—and picked out sixty-five drawings from all of them.

KP: I'd like you to comment on what seems to me to be a key quotation with regard to your work and Jess's work. You write, "Jess finally, like me, would emerge in an art diverse and having as its key, the collage of diversities and derivation, whatever its authenticity, returning to and drawing itself from the field of arts, not as a thing in itself to incorporate specifically painting values, but as a medium for the life of the spirit."

RD: Well, socially this city has a lot of aspects in which a life of the spirit can go on; but the figure of home, or how you make an area in which you can live, depends on making something in which you can become spiritually true. I mean, truth is not just the actual. The problem is how do you live inside an environment that is not simply spiritually vacant, as they said in the '20s, but polluted. I mean, try a room or two in one of the suburbs and let it dawn upon you what you're sitting in; the architect has really seen to it that there's no sign of grace in that space. People live in little areas; I think the reason they wear costume is to be divided away from the walls and the floor they walk on. And again, where art got derailed was when the shopkeepers started to run the whole show and it became a commodity. And now we make a living out of it, because it's gotten to be a values commodity and not just painting.

KP: I'd also like you to comment on the extension of [Ernst] Cassirer's idea that you make in *The Truth and Life of Myth* where you say that both language and myth have an origin in spiritual ecstasy and that consequently the word has power to lead us to an imagined truth.

RD: Well, ecstasy I'm [a] little worried by since it means standing outside of where it is. I can take the idea of transcendence if it means that we transcend our self-interest or purpose, purpose meaning what I'm going to gain or lose psychologically. Had "The Venice Poem" only been a rite in order to be reborn myself it would not have been a poem. When I say it was a magic poem, I mean it was both a rite and a poem. I felt the poem would deliver me, so I had a purpose, but the poem in its dimensions gets outside of that, because the poem is more thrilling than whether I was going to get rescued or not. I think it's [William] James who talks about fittingness, because it works in science and mathematics just like it works in art; it's where they're together. The most surprising thing, in the true sense of aesthetics, is that we recognize to some degree that something fits the situation. Happiness actually means it's happening in the right place, and so that what governs the writing in a poem is our recognition that it fits.

What it fits doesn't occur yet, but the fact that it's got fittingness tells us what the next thing is going to be. We don't have to select. The other picture is that you select—how did the poet select this thing? No, you follow the feeling of fittingness and don't worry if you haven't got that feeling. And that feeling of fittingness I would say is identical with truth, true to the elements of the thing. And more and more, as for instance in "Passages," I keep whatever happens. Have you seen that [NET] film where I'm writing? Well, I knew there that I had to keep it. I have to discover both what it's true to, this abominable little line of alliterative m's, and what it's doing coming in a passage which is charged with political opinion, which is the least likely place for anything to be true to anything. The atrocity of the alliterations is more shocking to me than my swinging out with my loosely conceived outburst at what goes on in the political world. I think that my controversy with Denise [Levertov] about the poem and the [Vietnam] War and so forth was that it seemed to me that the only actual model a poet provides for behavior is how entirely attentive to the poem he is and not self-interested. You see, in a dream you can't be self-interested; you don't get to choose. You can be attentive or you can lose it, but you don't get to start not being true. When you tell the dream, you can start fudging it, and then you lose the whole thing. Truth to me is still not given. We could earnestly follow the truth and discover a year later the truth about it, and a year later the truth, etc., because in the beginning the sense of fittingness is the apprehension of all the things that might belong to it. That tells us what the fit is. But as we see more things it can belong to, the whole sense of fitting can change.

KP: The authenticity is simply the being present.

RD: Right and that's the essence of my criticism of Blaser's translations. Spicer also argued that there were spirits outside the universe and that they were invading language. He came straight up against my feeling that the powers of the language were the actual words' existences extending in time of human uses, as we know they do. One of the lines is associational, the potentiality of the word is quite actual; if we imagine ourselves endlessly researching, we unwind in any word this huge lore of the word. And that seemed to me to be the source of the meaningfulness of the poem, not something that I knew, but that I recognize when I'm working.

PART V

In an Order of Orders

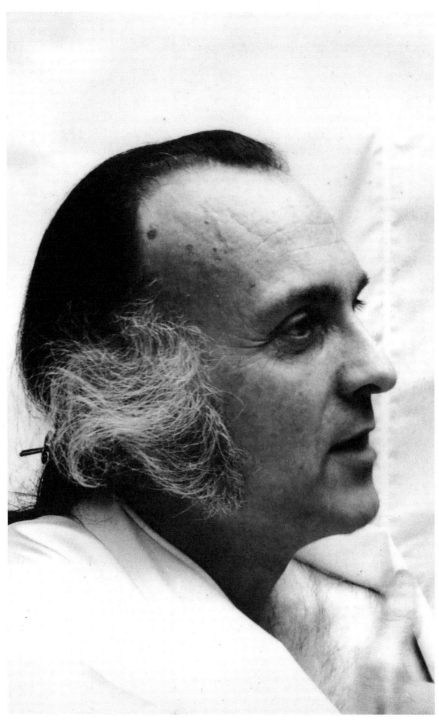

Robert Duncan. Photo by Matthew Foley. Courtesy of the Poetry
Collection, University at Buffalo.

boundary 2 Interview

(with Ekbert Faas, 1980)

Ekbert Faas first interviewed Duncan for his book Towards a New American Poetics: Essays and Interviews *(Black Sparrow Press, 1978). This second discussion was published in* boundary 2 *(vol. 8, no. 2, Winter 1980). It provides a description of Duncan's view of Modernism as a continuation of Romanticism; his reading of Whitman, Pound, Williams, and Stein; and of the composition of his earlier* Medieval Scenes, *"The Venice Poem," and* The H.D. Book, *which illustrates "living on art... [which] very few of us do."*

—Ed.

1.

EKBERT FAAS: In our interview for *Towards a New American Poetics* you told me that you read Modernism as Romanticism and that your ties to Pound, Stein, Surrealism, and so forth seem to you entirely consequent to their unbroken continuity from the Romantic period.

ROBERT DUNCAN: Right.

EF: In a similar way you suggest that Whitman's sense of the "ensemble" is larger than Pound's, Williams's, or even [Charles] Olson's.

RD: Well, for one thing Whitman had a confidence about his material whereas Pound and Williams, for most of the time, had a terrific lack of confidence. *The Cantos,* of course, was our lead to the new poem. I mean, I am not saying that *Leaves of Grass* was my lead to the new poem. *The Cantos* was an immense lead to the new poem. *Leaves of Grass* is homogenized milk by comparison to *The Cantos.* And my critique of *The Opening of the Field* and of *Roots and Branches* and *Bending the Bow* is that they are too homogenized. So how do I break that up so that it can be a larger area? So I would say: Gee, we are way down to the confines of an "I" in the *Leaves of Grass,* and yet we are in that whole ensemble. Pound recognizes collage when it occurs, as when he is doing [François] Villon.

But his mind could never cope with the notion of a conglomerate. When in [*Guide to*] *Kulchur* he comes near to the notion, he thinks he is out of order. Williams and Pound both thought that Whitman had a very poor mastery of the poem. But I think that our modern adventure is to have maybe no guarantee and maybe no mastery. Cybernetics has shown us what we can mastermind. But at the same time, it shows us that what we can mastermind is very trivial.

EF: As early as 1947 you hitchhiked from Berkeley to Washington, DC, in order to visit Pound at the St. Elizabeths Hospital.

RD: Yes. And in our conversations I noticed that Pound had no sense at all that a statement could be duplicit. I asked Pound about it because I knew about his violent reaction against *Finnegans Wake.* I said: What do you do when statements have the character of a pun in which they go both ways? He would not allow that a single event or a single statement could be duplicit. Now my figure is not even duplicit. It is complicit. I don't see it as two. Duplicit merely means we are in a Gnostic sort of world with black and white and good and bad, and both are present and operative. But in creation every element is cooperative. I read Dante that way, and Dante really does have Shakespeare's sense of the cooperation of all the elements.

EF: D. H. Lawrence seems to have had Whitman's kind of freedom you were talking about throughout. Pound had it in the early period of *Personae*, I think.

RD: When you go through the various editions of the *Leaves of Grass*, you find that Whitman advances to the point where he comprehends that any element in his poem is particular. That is, it may be assembled at any place. So he takes a thing from one poem and in the next edition, it appears in another poem. Now, theoretically, that is also true of *The Cantos.* But it is not true in Pound's mind. When Pound comes to the conclusion of *The Cantos,* he is in a profound depression. In *Kulchur* he already says that *The Cantos* are in a state of disorder which he associates with Bartok, who I always thought had too much order, too simple a sense of order. And Pound identifies order with Boccherini. And strangely enough, with Linnaeus. So Pound, I think, is profoundly anti-Darwinian. It is very strange. Pound wants *The Cantos* to be consequent; he wants them to have a heaven and earth and hell. But he doesn't even think that way. And Pound organizes his whole poem from a rigid ego position, whereas Whitman swings the whole thing on the "I." And swinging it on the "I," he gets closer to a sense of the ensemble. So what I see as the beginning of the modern mind in Whitman is the ensemble, the sense of ensemble. And Whitman's reading of Darwin is just fascinating. The same is true of his reading of Hegel. He realized right away that both were pertinent to his *Leaves of Grass*. Pound suffered because there was no guarantee to the poem. Apart from the "I," there was no guarantee. But I think that the great adventure of the modern mind is that this modern mind no longer has any guarantees.

EF: Unlike Olson, you have never openly attacked Pound for his anti-Semitism.

RD: Remember, there is a whole group of Jewish writers, [George] Oppen, [Charles] Reznikoff, [Carl] Rakosi, and [Louis] Zukofsky, who did understand what Pound was doing. And early in exile Pound asked: Are there any intelligent Jews so we can get things moving here? The Jew was increasingly significant, and in their work it was posed in an Objectivist sense, bringing forward first-generation and second-generation Jewish New York experience into the main floor of the poem, into our American experience. So that those of us reading them became in good part Jews. Now it's into that scene that Pound's anti-Semitism came. Williams, for example, can be outraged by it straight on, but for us and my generation, we were reading Reznikoff, Zukofsky, and Oppen, and we were becoming part Jews. So there was no other way to experience Pound's anti-Semitism than as an interior conflict. We couldn't just dismiss it. It was like something in a dream. I read the anti-Semitism of the European world as being their pagan sickness, and their conversion to a Judeo-Christian religion. And I think we always keep man's dreams. Now Ginsberg being a Jew acknowledges to be postPoundian. Pound is his master as he is mine, and when Ginsberg visits Pound, Pound has absolute confidence. He no longer remains in his silence which he keeps where he is not going to be understood anyway. To Ginsberg he pours his heart forth and speaks of his "damned anti-Semitism." But even that I read in the poetic sense. Not that it wasn't there. It was there. But it's really more than the actual fact. Pound was too much a real poet.

EF: One gets the impression that the impulse towards open creativity which to Pound and even [D. H.] Lawrence was something they thought of as a dangerous risk-taking, to you tends to assume the nature of something that is simply taken for granted.

RD: For one thing, it's our experience of the universe really which makes open form seem appropriate. If we only take the local fact of our life, we don't really have much of a memory of being born. We come out of a darkness, and we cannot account for the first years of our life. And one thing we really don't get to catch up with is how we die. But if we have even a rudimentary imagination and if we then write a poem, it has more meanings, more lives than we ourselves in any way posited by way of actual experience. Even if we posit a closed form, its readings aren't closed, and never have been. And when we have an open form we let the poem ride the vitality that language always has, and we ourselves adventure into that.

EF: Nevertheless, I guess you would subscribe to Pound's dictum that poetry is language charged to the utmost degree.

RD: My sense of the total poem is that it is a community where every word is a worker. And none of them get to be idle. The one place where I get intolerant is when I find that there are words which are just decorative. That they don't add anything or are in any way operative. I find [Gertrude] Stein fascinating that way, because you feel that words like "on" and "to" are just as operative as any other. And colors are really colors. So the charging with meaning is when you admit that a thing is a term in your poem. Essentially, this is any word in a poem. But you also recognize that charging it with meaning to the utmost degree means that you have to have constant researching and reinvestigation and reinformation of the terms that are your essential terms. So I have read and re-read a million different versions of the myth of Christ, Apollo, or Orpheus. The simple Orpheus story in the beginning is pretty thrilling. But if it enters the poem, I begin to charge it with its meaning. Now that's different. Its coming into the poem means that it is mine. I have an appointment with it. So it's not a business of redigesting. You have to come to know more about it. That's one of my critiques of *The Cantos*. That Pound didn't investigate history any further.

EF: You once stated that poetry was not a revelation of personality but of language.

RD: Exactly. Freud, for instance, was valuable to me not because he led me to a Freudian analyst but because he led to one of the areas, only one of the areas, in which you saw the operation of language going through and through. And more important than *The Interpretation of Dreams* was *The Psychopathology of Everyday Life,* in which everything in your daily life was read as a poem. I mean, with that kind of attention. Now I wouldn't want to read my daily life as a poem. But when a poem is going on I'll read it through and through like a poem. I would like to read it like Shakespeare reads anything: very, very clearly. Like the word "come" and "die" in there is not mist. And at the same time it's serious and not just a joke. His jokes are not just jokes, so that means that you are not in for free when you're laughing. Everything has its resonance. It's not a feeling of homogenization. It's the absolute opposite: total freedom in the interaction. And the interaction means that we finally are aware that the meaning of each term of the poem has been charged by the total composition.

EF: Poets today often try to enlist the creative participation of their audience. You yourself once announced that your reading was to be taken as a ritualistic performance.

RD: Well, at the present time I disengage it by chattering in between poems. But I have read straight from the ritualistic strength even in recent years. All you have to do is not talk in between poems. You don't even have to announce it. Even without that the audience gets shaken out of the applause. Applause I think comes from trying to bring it to the performance level and, of course, the audience very much wants to get back to where they came from. So I usually say: Now I have given you the poem and now you give me the clap. [*both laughing*] Also there is a kind of ritualistic applause. *Howl* brings a whole audience to its feet howling and roaring back, and it's entirely ritual.

EF: You get that in the Apollo Theater in Harlem.

RD: No, but I don't want that kind of event. I'm quite the opposite of [John] Cage: the poem is not communal in that sense. It's over there between us. Not from you and me. And yet my delivery, people respond to it as priestly. I would say it's a mixed occasion, and once I am within the poem I don't view it as at all personal. I still have a strong picture of the poet as a kind of Orpheus, and I do not think of the poem as a personal communication. By the way, even talking like that I almost don't feel like a person who is trying to find something. I find myself trying to focus on some imaginary place, running back a track to find what's going on in this life.

EF: But you still would have a sense of somehow wanting to affect your listeners or readers.

RD: Well, no reader is ever persuaded by a poem. But a reader's world, even at the moral level, can be transformed by the poem. I don't have any argument one way or another about certain things going on in Lawrence. I only know that I'm constantly reading and re-reading him, and there are not that many poets that I read and re-read. Every time I read "The Ship of Death," it's not that it morally instructs me. In the first place it presents to me very strongly Lawrence's lifestyle. Now that's not my lifestyle. Certain parts of it are; other parts of it aren't. But what's essential in it is that "The Ship of Death" is absolutely going on in me like a poem of my own would be. And I'm struck by lots of poets whose own poems are not going on in them that way. I'd want to know how many of your own poems are going on in you as admitted and constantly there, reconsulted and informing the entire concept of the poetic level. Lawrence enters just as my own work does here.

EF: One thing every reader of your poetry has to contend with is your love of enigma for its own sake.

RD: It is interesting that the term of not being understood was a territory I found fascinating from very early on. For one thing, all occultists, like my adoptive parents, are attracted by especially those things which they can't understand. They want un-understandable things. So as a child, any un-understandable thing you did was fascinating to your parents. I mean oracular voice fascinates me and enigma fascinates me. And my parents thought of those as omens. If you couldn't translate the omen it had a good deal of power in their imagination. And that attitude, oddly enough, I would share for whatever reasons. Zukofsky has lots of facets like that. We cannot tell what he is saying. And we finally understand that he is standing there in the aura of our not being able to tell what he is saying. I mean, the reader not being able to tell what he is saying. And this is one of the major experiences we are going through. Olson, by contrast, would batter his head against the wall if it doesn't yield meaning. He wants to break a code, so to speak. So he attacks over and over again areas that won't yield, that won't be translatable. Because he wants them translated. But then, he loses interest when they are translatable. And he keeps hitting, hitting, hitting: I am sure this means something, I am going to hit it again. With an amazing fury. But, paradoxically, you gradually see that if Olson had a great obsession in his life, it wasn't really that he was going to crack Linear B or Mayan. It was the fact that language in its most important area was so totally encoded that we can't possibly break it without giving our whole lives to it. And that is where the poetry comes from.

EF: But your fascination with enigma, I guess, would have nothing to do with a belief in *maya*.

RD: On the contrary. With the grand Buddhist assumption that everything is an illusion, I turn off completely. My mind doesn't operate that way. It operates with absolute life instincts in which certain things are true to me. As a matter of fact, if we posit *maya*, I must be spinning *maya*. If there is any place in it, I'd join the spinners.

EF: Also, your ultimate sense of reality seems to be one of process rather than *Dasein* or *être là*.

RD: My parents believed in the reincarnation of civilizations, and the reincarnation of universes. And in this we were Brahmin or Hindu rather than Buddhist. Later when I came to [Alfred North] Whitehead, there again was a series of universes or in other words one universe in process. As a consequence, form also is present in every event in the same way as the universe is present in every event. It is not *Dasein*, but it is an "event" in Whitehead's sense. And to me the question of being disappears completely if you are concerned with events. So one might say: Gee, it's a little like Buddhism. Because things are significant only in the sense of *where* we are. That is to say only the particular is significant, and the particular remains the same throughout. And that shows up quite clearly in my poetry. For instance, people have criticized my *Medea* because there is no catharsis in it. Again in *Faust Foutu*, the event so dominates that there is no regeneration.

2.

EF: You have repeatedly stated that you didn't know what you were doing before you wrote *Medieval Scenes* in the spring of 1947.

RD: I would simply be in the poem and simply would have to go through it. I didn't even know what I had when I finally had the poem. Whereas in *Medieval Scenes*, I knew exactly what I was to do. I sat each evening and did one. And that was strange, because I hadn't yet started any medieval studies. Just as I went to Florida after writing "King Haydn of Miami Beach." I never went to Miami Beach though, mind you. So, I didn't start medieval and Renaissance studies until after I completed *Medieval Scenes*. In fact, a year after *Medieval Scenes*. So, the poems were the lead that told me that I should go into medieval studies. Of course, I knew people like Jack Spicer at that point who were already in medieval studies. And I heard a lot about it. Spicer, when I first met him, wanted to know what I knew about Albigensians. And he was excited that I knew something about what Gnosticism was. In fact, he was himself deepening his own Calvinism. Of course, in those days we didn't have any of the books that now exist on Gnosticism. So one had to find it out of medieval Manichaeism, which gives you a lot of hints. But I had already spotted it in Yvor Winters's criticism of Emerson. That's why the Emerson quote begins *Medieval Scenes*. It's in his crusade against heresy in poetry that you see Winters as a true poet who is always charged with a good deal of fear and consequently giving these dramatic definitions of poetry. You could see that the poets I had come to ally myself with were the very poets he didn't want to allow to happen. So he would give you a negative reading list.

EF: Like the Church Fathers.

RD: Right. You would get a good reading list from what he attacked. So Gnosticism was the kind of thing that aroused attack from the very sort of mind that would attack you.

EF: So *Medieval Scenes* was written one poem each evening.

RD: Yes, one piece each evening. As a matter of fact, Spicer and everybody would attend, and it got scarier as it went on.

EF: How scarier?

RD: It got scarier because I had to take whatever it was, and that had to be its section. The whole sequence goes towards a frenzy at the end, but I meant it from the artist's point of view. That was a point at which I had to make do almost. I mean, I had to do a poem while they were watching. I mean, make a poem as fast as I could write it. So, this was the prototype of Jack Spicer's dictated poetry.

EF: While he was looking over your shoulder?

RD: Yes, and very excited that a poem could happen in that way.

EF: Was "Domestic Scenes" planned as a kind of companion piece to *Medieval Scenes*?

RD: Right. "Domestic Scenes" parallels *Medieval Scenes*, but they were done as a kind of humorous piece. They were written at a time when I had become centered on Jack Spicer and were actually done for him.

EF: They almost read like a parody of Williams at times.

RD: Well, remember that Williams had attacked my *Heavenly City, Earthly City*, asking me never to make such statements as "The earth has tides of desolation and bliss." But they also have a lot of other things in them. There is a lot of Laura Riding in them, and they also have a lot of [W. B.] Yeats in them. Because we were reading Yeats very heavily at the time. The whole poem, however, is a parody of itself.

EF: You have remarked that "The Venice Poem" first showed you how to write a poem. Yet "The Venice Poem" doesn't seem in any way to provide a pattern for your subsequent writing.

RD: No, I didn't mean it in that way. But it sort of showed me how to do it when it was called for. No, I didn't mean it in that sense. Because, as a matter of fact, it didn't prepare me for how to do another poem at all. But I knew what I had to do. Whatever happened in *Medieval Scenes* was quite a surprise to me, whereas with "The Venice Poem" it was quite different. For one thing I knew that I was doing a symphonic form. That's why you have that Stravinsky thing at the beginning, the evocation of the Allegro.

EF: Had you read his *Poetics of Music* at that time?

RD: Yes, that had just come out, and that's built into the text. That's one of my guidelines. And I also knew, although I was already right in the midst of it, that the whole thing was going to be some kind of psychic mystery or rebirth for me. Although I wouldn't know what it was. It would free me. Of course, it didn't free me into any great thing. The baby wasn't having a great time. The baby, in fact, had a very bad time for about a year or so. But at least I was not again in that psychodrama. Although the bitterness of the poems that followed, like *Caesar's Gate* or the *Book of Resemblances*, shows some of the aftermath of desolation. Of course, the Korean War was also appearing in that. And the impact of the Korean War for me was exactly like the Vietnam War was for people more recently.

EF: I like "The Venice Poem" very much. The only thing I would criticize is that it is almost too perfect as a structure. It almost seems like some kind of exercise.

RD: And then imagine Pound saying I should have had a plan. That's the one thing it didn't need at all.

EF: The symbolism, for instance, seems so deliberate.

RD: Of course, it is something different from symbolism.

EF: Or the "binding matter" perhaps.

RD: Yes. I was binding myself so that in each section I was to be governed by the powers which presided over it, like the Rousseau [painting] or whatever. And it would be a very specific series of images almost as if you were setting up a tribal house. These were ancestral figures that were being invoked to take me through every section of the poem. As, for instance, William Shakespeare is invoked at the close of the Coda. There are two questions that are quite puzzling to me as to what happens in my poetry. One is, how come Christ came into it and remains there. That, in a way, of course, would seem self-evident. But then the second one is how come Shakespeare is so dominant. Because I am not on the stage or anything. And time after time, he seems to appear. In the "African Elegy," for instance, Othello and Desdemona appear. And in "The Venice Poem," that's the one time that Shakespeare himself is *evoked* to carry me through with a candle, as it were.

EF: You have referred to your life in 1948 as a period of trial and error while you also felt unable to return to an earlier impulse.

RD: Well, one thing that was lost, I think, totally, was whatever I had tried to do in *Heavenly City, Earthly City*. Preposterous as it may sound, I was actually trying to unite myself with what I admired in *Paterson* in that poem. Of course, Williams has a city in there, and I don't. My city is a metaphysical city in my mind, and then it gets rescued by being a [Wallace] Stevens fiction at the close. Nothing could be more like Stevens than the whole passage about the sun and so forth. All of that was an enormous release for me to write. But Williams nevertheless was a necessary discipline for any personal self-indulgences on my part. Pound, of course, was not much of a discipline for what is sometimes called my aesthetic. For the Pound that I dearly loved shared my admiration for richness and glow and light. But at the period we are talking about I had the instinctive feeling that what I really needed was Gertrude Stein. And Stein had already been a discipline to Williams. In *Paterson* and in Williams's writing at that time he refers back to Gertrude Stein the way Pound had referred to Ford Madox Ford. It was important for Williams to remember that the word was there. Especially in Williams's major phase.

EF: But you are so unlike Stein in your whole spiritual drive.

RD: Yes, right. But I am not talking about a guru. A discipline ain't supposed to be a spiritual force that you recognize, but rather, a force that's foreign enough while you can still recognize it as a power. If you recognize that power too easily, then it might just be a power of your own persuasion. I had no major persuasion about wanting to have Steinian common sense. I mean, I love reading Stein. It is restful. It is also without the kind of tensions that would exaggerate my own.

EF: You wrote almost a whole volume of Stein imitations.

RD: Yes, I started writing Stein imitations, and then she comes forward very strongly in "An Essay at War" which precedes "Of the Art." Originally, I thought I'd never collect either of those two poems in a volume, and I was going to have an in-between pamphlet called *Two Botched Poems*. But I realized later that "An Essay at War," which seemed too Williamsey to me at the time, was really my own poem. So I put it into *Book of Resemblances*.

EF: So the whole thing amounted to a kind of dialectic development.

RD: Moreover, it was planned at that point. And while Pound was saying that "The Venice Poem" should have had a plan, I thought it had too much. So the other reason why I wanted to go to Stein was to see if I could single out syntax as the local plan of anything.

EF: I got the impression that you used Stein as a kind of discipline against what you had done in "The Venice Poem" and in *Heavenly City, Earthly City*.

356

RD: Right. As a kind of balance. Discipline is perhaps a poor word. It was to open the range. I even did a Steinian version of *Heavenly City, Earthly City,* but it only was to be about ten lines long. It was the kind of Zukofsky thing you do. In 1952 for Christmas, Jess gave me what had been his huge chemistry notebook while working for the atomic project. And I started writing right away. The tiny little Stein book that Diane di Prima put out came out of the first two pages of that notebook. Every day I would just make up things. That notebook went on into *Faust Foutu,* and other things were entering in there. In other words, I was really in a way designing a non sequitur field of influences which would balance off the intensity of the Pound, Williams, Eliot, Stevens directive I had taken. Because you are no longer making up fictions when you follow Stein.

EF: *Letters for Origin* show that Olson was rather suspicious of you initially.

RD: Of course, the first time I sent work to *Origin,* I didn't at all send them what I was currently doing. It was material that I hadn't been able to get into print, that is to say, work from 1949, what's now in *A Book of Resemblances.* So I didn't really send them stuff to show them where I was. And observably the first place where I could really see new things happening in the poem was in Denise Levertov's "The Shifting." From there on I began practicing moving the lines around. And in a way, simply for amusement. Today if you took the three books from *The Opening of the Field* to *Roots and Branches* and *Bending the Bow* (outside of "Passages") you would find that the majority of my stanzaic practice and line practice and everything else hasn't moved outside of [George] Herbert. And it constantly goes back to that base. But I do use, concurrently now and even in *A Seventeenth Century Suite,* the multiple margins of [Larry] Eigner and other modern techniques. So, it is continuous for me now. Whereas for Olson, it wasn't to be continuous. It was to be a break. There is that first essay on the meaning of form in which I say that I am very opposed to conventional verse in a very hysterical manner. So I keep thinking that I really ought to redo that. It's just too bizarre.

EF: You mean, lashing out against Elizabeth Drew?

RD: Well, she was only a nonentity, and you always choose that kind of nonentity to lash out against. No, what I mean is that I stopped that essay by saying, as it were, that I am never going to be caught doing one of these conventional poems again. I mean, I don't have any boy scout honors when I write a poem.

EF: What was the occasion for Olson's essay "Against Wisdom as Such"?

RD: Originally, that was a letter to me. The essay, written in 1953, was an outcome of that letter, which was written in response to *The Artist's View*, in which I proposed my major terms of childhood, etc. And what got Charles was not so much the "wisdom" as the fact that I was talking about things which simply hadn't existed before the Victorians thought them up. I mean straight Victorian household magic. And that kind of thing was just anathema to Charles, of course. And then I gave that long list, that maze of authors which had influenced me. And I don't think that that list includes Olson. That simply wasn't on my mind yet. But it did include Jack Spicer. And Olson, of course, never was at all responsive to Jack Spicer's writing.

EF: [Robert] Creeley once told me about that embarrassing incident when he first met you in Majorca. You were all sitting around some sort of fireplace when suddenly, talking about somebody else, he blurted out, "that cross-eyed son of a bitch." Creeley remembers how Jess turned white, but how you quickly turned the whole thing into a joke.

RD: I don't remember that. But it's quite plausible, because Creeley himself would have been worrying about his eye. So we probably both were on the edge about what were we going to say about an eye. [*both laughing*] Did you ever talk to Creeley about the letter sent to Olson where he says something like "Why do you bring this lavender or something into the group?"

EF: I didn't bring it up directly, and Creeley didn't mention the letter. But he admitted that given his East Coast puritanical upbringing he had great difficulty accepting anything that wasn't straightforward. But that that was really his own prejudice and a rather absurd one, because he had had homosexual friends before. So he didn't comment on the letter directly, but I guess that is what he had in mind.

RD: The letter was really responding to the kind of overripe writing I do. Because the kind of writing I was doing then and have been doing at all times had passages in it that could be called purple passages in the sense of what was used in the Pre-Raphaelite period. But when Creeley read "The Venice Poem" he realized that it was also straight and that these weren't just purple passages. And the most authentic thing in Bob wouldn't have liked mere purple passages. But it was straightforward purple passages frequently that I was trying out with Anaïs Nin. Because she wrote lots of them. I was trying to find out how you get this kind of pet-me sensuality. I mean, it is somewhat related to John Crowe Ransom's protest about my advertising myself in my poetry, after he had read my "The Homosexual in Society." Because, in fact, I have always done a grand job advertising what my poetry is all the way along the line. And certainly some homosexual advertising is also going on. Homosexuality has always been built into the advertisement. I mean, I could have extricated it from the contents, putting it in small letters like: smoke eight packs of this a day and it will make you want to travel. [*laughing*] But if that was the message, then I put that in very large letters indeed to let them guess what it was that they were smoking.

EF: Creeley also told me of the complete and empathetic understanding you had of his rhythms when you first read his short stories back in 1954.

RD: Yes, storywise I had it. But remember, I told you that I had great difficulty with Creeley's poetry. Luckily, I found the rhythms for myself before I met Bob. And then I found my own findings verified. I think we have a basic resistance to a poem unless its rhythm is totally recognizable, like "Chuck, Chuck-Chuck." That is to say, unless it has a basic recognizable rhythm. So we are in a position of sitting at the piano and playing a piece by Bartok, and trying to find out, what is this telling me in terms of the rhythm. And you are looking for something that resembles, as in science, the elegant solution. The kind of thing that would contain all the factors that you have begun to observe and tune it until it's productive of even more. And then you know you are on the way and then you arrive at something. But, when I picked up Bob, I couldn't find any factors. It just looked as if I had little empty poems—like most critics think. Then, when I picked up the stories, I knew immediately that nobody could write stories like this and be that cross-handed.

Similarly, when I first tried to read Williams I had a very hard time. But all of the established avant-garde of America—mind you, there were only about ten people—told me that this was key stuff I was looking at. So I had to puzzle over it, which I was very willing to do. But then when I heard Williams on a record, I thought: Isn't that terrific!

EF: So, initially, both Creeley and Olson seem to have had their misgivings about you.

RD: Because I had already written the kind of poetry which wasn't like the poetry they had in mind. So, while recognizing me as a peer, both Creeley and Olson found me doubtful. And in literary terms, I was indeed. I had been writing for over ten years, and I had been mixed up with things that they wouldn't want to be mixed up with at all. So their confidence in me seems extraordinary to me now. It must have been the counterpart to my recognizing in *them* a kind of locus which I felt I belonged to finally. I mean, a situation in which my writing can be defined and feeling that what they were about would clear up everything. Which is what they did. I mean, it was really their adventure, between Olson and Creeley, and it took place in their correspondence. That's where the major part of the intelligence is, and that intelligence was entirely feeding the intelligence of my own work. I mean, it is not that my own work was limited to that drive. But my sense of myself as not being a historical poet now that Charles is dead shows how specific that drive was. So that drive was very, very significant to me. I mean, I had been trying to focus my work along the lines of Pound. But that didn't give scope. And I guess, even the proposition of a field gave scope, because that's what a field is. Everything fits together in a field you have confidence in. Or in a series of fields folded.

EF: When did you first conceive the idea for *The H.D. Book*?

RD: In fact, Norman Pearson handed me the idea in [the] form of a commission for a book to be handed to H.D. on her birthday. That was in 1962, I guess. I am not quite certain of the date. But the date that you find on the *Daybook* gives you the exact year.

EF: Was that little present ever published?

RD: No, it wasn't to be published. It was simply to be given to her. Funnily enough, it was my first reading at Yale. He was driving me to dinner and he said to me: Susan and I have decided to give you $1,000 to do a little book on H.D. And I said: If I do a book, it certainly wouldn't be a little book. Because at a very definitive point H.D. was crucial to me, which she was not to Olson or Creeley. As a matter of fact, her War Trilogy showed me the viability of treating religion as an extension of the imagination. Although even in her Hellenic work, of course, she had always been Hellenistically inclined. Then during the war she had met with a young guru and started reverting to things like doing séances. Also she had undergone Freudian analysis. And Freudian analysis, too, is, of course, a psychic mystery cult.

EF: But then Freudian psychoanalysis seems to me to be so rationalistic.

RD: So are the mystery cults.

EF: Did H.D. see the various sections of *The H.D. Book*?

RD: Yes, she had the chapters as they would be written until she had her stroke and developed amnesia. In fact, I have a letter from Norman Pearson in which he tells me that he had been reading the most recent section to her aloud, not really knowing whether she was registering what she heard. He just couldn't tell, because she had serious interference with speech after her stroke, and she just couldn't talk back. So she may well have been listening, but he just simply didn't know. All that was very shortly before her death.

Of course, her death was a great disturbance in the writing of *The H.D. Book*. The death of H.D. and the death of William Carlos Williams both occurred during a period while I was writing about them. Then Marianne Moore and my own mother died, which left only Pound, so *The H.D. Book* was slowly becoming a Book of the Dead. I don't know if that stopped me, but I know about one thing that did. I didn't want to drive the whole book through at one stage. So I did conceive that it would be a book of returns, although I have only returned with a few sketches over recent years.

EF: When did your personal contact with H.D. begin?

RD: Well, I sent her "The Venice Poem," and had a letter back, although that didn't start a correspondence.

EF: Was her reaction positive?

RD: Yes, she was the only one who was positive. But my real contact with H.D. started through Norman Pearson at a point when I was sending out the manuscript of *The Opening of the Field.*

EF: Around 1959?

RD: Yes. And then, it was arranged that when she came over I would be there early, and I would have sessions with her while she was in the country. It was at that time that Norman suggested that I should write the book. Of course, he didn't mean that I should write a great big tome as I was going to do. In a funny way, I am thinking of my *H.D. Book* as some kind of *The Education of Henry Adams,* except that I am not coming from the Adams family. But it is about an education. I knew that I had to tell, in some way, what the poem meant to me and how it was that I read the poem. And more than that how it was that I lived by the poem in places where other people were thinking I was living by a religion or something else. I could find no poet giving such an account, although poets sometimes seem to be thinking about it. When people read my announcement on the blurb of my first book [*Heavenly City, Earthly City,* 1947] where I list everybody from John of the Cross to Jack Spicer, their only response was, like he has got a big reading list. When actually I am not erudite. But I draw on every source where I find something that speaks for my case. And that's what that book tells about. It tells of coming alive through poetry and being guilty of the one thing that our time very much worries about, which is living on art. In fact, very few of us do, and there are lots of others who tell us we should stop it. While we haven't even *started* to do it. It is only the rare few at any time, anyway, who are doing it.

EF: *The H.D. Book* has remained a fragment so far. Do you have a plan for it?

RD: Yes, I have. All the chapters of part I, for instance, have to do with women in my life. And part I is written all the way through up to chapter 6 on Participation. Chapter 7 is on my mother and there is a very brief sketch of what it will be—only a couple of paragraphs long. And the chapters 8, 9, 10 following upon the chapter on my mother will be all about Lady Bluestocking. I mean, literary ladies. For instance, Robert Haas's mistress, Antoinette Krause, the couple who introduced me to Gertrude Stein and Edith Sitwell. And those chapters would also include Anaïs. Because in a sense they are all the false H.D.s. And one of the chapters will be on my wealthy cousin Mercedes. Because I want to show what female glamour was like in 1927, when I was eight. Mercedes with her red hair and her green eyes, everything else in emerald and jade, and draped in green materials that have totally disappeared today. This entire magic of a female creation of her own universe. Her sitting room, her bedroom, and her bathroom were so entirely a realm apart and so much her own realm that it was an awesome thing to see. And that could only take place in the '20s. In the '30s, they lost all that possibility. They couldn't even behave in this way any longer. And I really don't know in which order all this will appear. But there are ten chapters to part I, and that means four chapters which I have not yet written. Then, of course, one chapter is going to be on my marriage.

EF: And part II?

RD: In part II where I talk about Lawrence and Williams and also about women writers, there are several chapters in which I portray the war between men and women and the confusions which arise from those conflicts. All that is very fascinating to me. So, the reason why I felt I needed to address all those pictures of women was to create a kind of background for the second part. My very strong feeling which has not changed at all is that all those women, Virginia Woolf, and H.D., and others who are even more doubted, like Gertrude Stein and Edith Sitwell, are of the same order as Stevens and Williams and Pound and Joyce. You remember that I was shaky at times with [T. S.] Eliot because he never went into a major phase. And because his work doesn't show the kind of creative intelligence that some of the others show. One woman I forgot is Dorothy Richardson, who is not at all established in the literary mind. And that is absolutely unbelievable. She is one of the few peers of a Joyce or Proust. But I know that I am anomalous in this demand and in this reading. So I ask myself: Shouldn't I better account for what is my relation to women? Since I have an entirely different picture of them than the one men give. And there is one thing that is always and quite frequently laid upon me. Kay Boyle has it, for instance, and I repeat it in a scene in *Faust Foutu:* Well, he isn't the regular man anyway, so his relation with women is to be discounted. So I thought that I had better tell what my relation to women is.

EF: The second part is called *A Daybook.*

RD: Yes, because it takes H.D.'s War Trilogy for its basis and it follows ten days of day-by-day living with that book. So it is really a *demonstration* of how you live with a poem as an exercise involving your dreams and all things happening during the day and so forth. In other words, you take H.D.'s War Trilogy as the text to which everything refers, whether it's dreamt or lived or meditated. As a mantra, but in a larger sense of a kind of governance of your entire life.

EF: And the third part?

RD: And in the third part, I want to do a kind of mimesis or *explication de texte* on *Helen* [*in Egypt*] or one of those last books. So it is a literary performance piece in the genre of what thesis prose is and never is, because it is not written for the kind of reasons that you write a creative piece.

EF: Thesis prose?

RD: Right. Taking that as a form. Like you take the novel as a form. There is one chapter in the first part, the chapter on H.D.'s novel *Palimpsest*, the one published in *TriQuarterly*. That anticipates the form of the third part. But the third part is going to contain a lot of other things. It's the third part really that tells me what has to be in the four remaining chapters of the first. Those are the very last I am going to write. Because it fits together. In my mind it's like writing a novel. So it does have sets of parallels. But if I pre-knew the parallels, I would go home and never write anything.

EF: So, it goes back to your personal relationships with these women.

RD: Yes, in a way. From the most extreme case at the end where like anybody in a thesis I am not there. Where I am talking supposedly in a totally objective way.

EF: Why did you make the announcement that you wouldn't want to publish another book of poems before 1983?

RD: Yes, exactly fifteen years from *Bending the Bow*. I simply didn't want to be working on another book again. You see, when I finished *Letters* I was very excited that I had composed a book. And after that, I felt that the poems I was going to be working on would belong to a book, and they did right from the beginning. That is, once I had centered on the poem "Often I Am Permitted to Return to a Meadow" as being the beginning. Of course, there were poems in between that I didn't take up. But I right away recognized the notion of field, which I took from Olson's notion of composition by field. But that also gave me a pun in the way Thomas Mann or James Joyce would use it. It gave me another field, which was that of Machpelah.

EF: I didn't catch that.

RD: When Abraham sees the field of Machpelah he by vision sees into the earth and recognizes that this is where Adam and Eve are buried. So he buys that piece of land with some deception, and it proves to be what he suspected it to be. Then the *Zohar* describes the counterpart of Blake's fourfold vision, and the counterpart of Dante's proposition of the polysemous, which at that time were both very much on my mind. And the *Zohar* discusses that this is a field folded. So there is the question, of course: Why it is called folded in the earth? It is because time and space are interfolded like layers, and it is in the folds that you have realms of being. Now all of these terms were not only promising of the book, but after I had finished *Letters* they were thoroughly ripe and ready to go. *The Opening of the Field* then is composed throughout. And *Roots and Branches* lifts the composition; that is, it doesn't illustrate a single concept through the whole thing in an organized way, but it still, of course, was driven by compositional habits and shapes. And then, by the time I wrote *Bending the Bow,* I thought: all of this is overcomposed. So I took a guess saying that the only way that I will be able to write poetry again, not haunted by a book, would be by making a fifteen-year break. And fifteen years was a nice, large double seven with another one thrown in sort of thing. But I really didn't come up with that decision until three years after *Bending the Bow.* At that point, James Laughlin wrote to me saying: Are you ready for a new book? As a matter of fact, Creeley just had a new one and Denise [Levertov] was coming up with a new one. And he said: Oh, we would like to go ahead this spring with your new book. And it was at that point that I wrote to him saying: Well, J., it will be twelve years from now.

EF: Some people think of you as the future Academic poet who is going to be read mainly by students.

RD: Luckily, I am at the present moment. That is where most of my income comes from. They use my books in courses. At least a thousand copies of *The Opening of the Field* and *Bending the Bow* are sold every year. And they also use *The Truth and Life of Myth.* And these books were doing very well because there wasn't going to be a new one coming out too soon. [*both laughing*]

I think we write for college seminars because that's where the money is. Poets wrote for the stage when the money was there, or, like Donne, they wrote sermons because the money was there. For almost a hundred years poets were Protestant ministers. Because that's exactly where the intellectual money was. And they weren't mistaken. Only one generation before Herbert, all the poets were in the theater and when the theater collapsed, they were all out on their ass. So today it is the university, and in that way we write very good seminars.

EF: But then, think of your lifelong feud with the university.

RD: But do you think Shakespeare didn't criticize the plays or the stage? As a matter of fact, it barely survived him. And my critique of the university goes both ways. Yes, I wonder how long are they going to last. I mean, the Church had a slight collapse by loading itself with all those earnest Protestant ministers.

EF: So it's more like writing for the university in order to explode it.

RD: Well, scholars have problems long before poets do. Hannah Arendt and several others have observed that the intellectual life couldn't survive in the university. That also was the interesting thing about the distraction of the Renaissance university wits in the city of London. They were distracted because everyone could see that the intellectual power of a university wit like Marlowe went into the theater. So they wrote these scurrilous pamphlets back and forth trying to give vent to their dissatisfaction and trying to unload brains that were overcrowded. It's a physiological fact that brains can be overcrowded. I mean, I've got a thoroughly distracted mind myself. If I started going down one little road, eight hundred other roads would appear. And by the time I have tried to make a quick sketch of the labyrinth, I have launched myself into unknown territory. I mean, you need a poem to get yourself in and out of it.

"Nematodes! Nematodes!"
(with Michael McClure, 1985)

Biology and physics are "imaginations of the world," Robert Duncan states in this dialogue with poet Michael McClure, which was first published in Conjunctions *vol. 7 in 1985. At the time, both Duncan and McClure were teaching in the Poetics Program at New College of California in San Francisco. They explore in part the relation of poetry to living organisms, which both have a self-originating force and yet are connected with the whole universe, and also the depth and meaning of postwar American painting. This interview was reprinted under the title "Talking with Robert Duncan" in McClure's* Lighting the Corners: On Art, Nature, and the Visionary: Essays and Interviews *(University of New Mexico Press, 1994).*

—Ed.

MICHAEL MCCLURE: Robert, those familiar with your writing know your scholarship and your studies in history, Kabbalah, and alchemy as well as Gnostic and mystical traditions, and they are aware of your involvement with linguistics and language. I see a powerful effect of concern with biology and the biological frontier in your poetry. It seems to me that your interweaving of "Structures of Rime" with "Passages" throughout your books is a biological as well as a poetic/linguistic process. "Passages" and "Structures of Rime" are streams, and they meet and circle around or move through blocks of poems like the *Dante Études* and the "Metaphysical Suite" and the long poems. And the long poems in sections appear to be something like physiological organs. The new *Ground Work* appears to be a unified work comparable to *The Cantos*, but your expression is much less "structural" than Pound's work. Your poetry seems to be organismic. It's complete with living streams, like blood flows, and it surges and explores, and it does not fear to be unsymmetrical in nature. It unifies itself with its living quality or sensations. And in fact the symmetry is present.

ROBERT DUNCAN: Of course it's going to resemble a blood flow, since right at the forefront of my own consciousness all the time are my own orders and disorders of blood pressure and especially during the period of writing *Ground Work* my debt was that I had been for a long time in hypertension. And there are many signs of a poem having its origin in and riding the crest of a hypertension seizure. I'm sure "Up Rising" was just before my high blood pressure was diagnosed in 1964, and it seems to me a symptom. But my thought is I'm never deliberately biological in my reference in a poem unless my thought of the structure of the poem as I'm working on it is very closely worked with vowels and consonants, and again it will go back to the biological because I feel measure as body weights and shifts in the lines. Now that's different from your sense of the waves. Perhaps I didn't really have to feel the waves at all; the waves are going to be there, no matter what, because of the rush of my blood. And now having gone through the kidney failure I'm more conscious of the presence, the ruling presence, of the blood pressure. But I don't know that that's turned up in a poem. The asymmetry of a poem for me does have something to do with [Erwin] Schrödinger's marvelous picture from *What Is Life?* which influenced me, more than biological pictures of it, Mike, I think. That is, that life is present as long as it hasn't settled into a symmetry, so that life produces itself by constantly throwing itself out of symmetry, postponing the moment of its arriving at composition.

MM: In the introduction to *Bending the Bow* you wrote: "So, the artist of abundancies delites in puns, interlocking and separating figures, plays of things missing or things appearing 'out of order' that remind us that all orders have their justification finally in an order of orders only our faith as we work addresses." There's a fellow named Sydney Brenner, who was originally an associate of Francis Crick, and he has made an intensive couple of decades' long investigation of the development of the nematode. It's about a millimeter long, and it has exactly 959 cells. It's the ideal laboratory animal for certain reasons: its tiny size, quickness of reproduction, and because its number of cells is the square root of the number of cells of a drosophila (fruit fly), which is the square root, more or less, of the number of cells of a human being. So that one can make many projections. In the process of doing an anatomy of this 959-celled creature, Brenner has determined that these organisms are not assembled by a linear or tidy process and that the assemblage of this animal cellwise is not even sequential. In fact, he determines that the development appears illogical unless one would, in my words, acknowledge there's a Dionysian or Orphic principle of organization that is involved in the development of this creature from its first cell to its last cell. The processes of organization are utterly baroque. Lineages of cells may lead to a cell that then differentiates into four or five other types of cells. An organ may be the result of cells blending together from apparently unrelated lineages of cells. So now we find out that there is no program unfolding the organism from the genetic codes outwards. There is something complex that is going on, it's punning, it is creating and removing, some structures of cells are made and then disappear.

RD: Within a structure there are programs, but a program is not a whole. Programs intrigue me, but not a program that would govern the whole poem. The kind of poem that has a point just disappoints me. I think the poem with a point is one in which the poet is convinced the universe has a point. Of course, some of it's so shallow they aren't even thinking that. But in a universe created by a God with an end that's named and everything has meaning and significance toward that end that is known, then you get stories and poems which point toward an end and have closure. I am absolutely a creational materialist, because I do not understand the universe as anything but a creation, and also think there is only one.

MM: I think Brenner sees that the development of this organism, and, by extension, the development of all organisms, is metamorphic, playful, and expanding. I think, as in your *Ground Work,* one has this sensation that everything is going on at once. It is not sequential.

RD: Yes, that is out of Philo: God does all things simultaneously. And Heraclitus would be nearest to the universe as I feel it until we come to [A. N.] Whitehead. They made fun of Heraclitus and accused him of blasphemy when he said the universe created itself. The opposite of that is the Aristotelian idea that there must be a creator outside the universe: that I don't understand at all.

MM: I'd like to come to that in just a minute, because I want to ask you something in regard to what you say about Aristotle. But in this frontier of biology, which is no longer what we had forced on us as kids, the life process is seen as a cascade of complex interactions and there is a grammar of assembly but not a program. That's the relationship I see to your work.

RD: That's exactly it. That's what a self-creating and selforiginating force is. But then you have to realize that the immediate force such as myself or such as an amoeba is, in itself, only an immediate instance. So although it is self-creating, the important part of that self is the fact that the whole universe is proceeding in the same way, so the interactions are far beyond anything individual. In other words, we hear them as poets, or overhear them as poets; we don't control them or initiate them at all. In writing a poem I think of my job as recognizing right away what's happening in the poem, so that I am not redundant and continuing to keep everything alive in the poem. That determines the length of it: I can't exceed the length of my own recognition of the presence of its very first impulse. Its opening words are not first in that sense. They're conceived of as being simultaneous, that's true.

MM: Several times in conversation you've quoted Aristotle's *De Anima*, saying "the soul is the body's life." I wonder what picture that makes for you.

RD: It makes a shape. Life has a shape, so you are living a shape and that's the feeling of identity and nonidentity. You can't inhabit the whole shape. I'm not a Reichian. But if you suppose a Reichian life-picture and you could remember the first engram, as they call it, that's really the fantasy of not just inhabiting the shape of this life but being able to remember it. Poetry is the area of what you can remember. Language itself does not cover this area. The organism, in time, is a lifetime and it extends. If you could run forward and backward in time, by the time you are at the baby you would have forgotten what the old man looks like, and you'd run to the other end, and by the time you got to the old man ...You'd have to remember, you'd have to *re*-member.

MM: Do you think the 959th cell can't remember the first cell?

RD: They do remember, in the sense of resonance. That the organism is alive means to me—life itself means a resonant continuity. And that resonant continuity is never balanced.

MM: Brenner has the idea that the original cell, or the original cells, form a—there are two systems going on (this I don't think necessarily relates to poetry alone)—that there are two systems going on. The one system is creating a sort of rough worm being, and the other system is refining that rough worm being into a sharper worm. But a naturalist friend of mine has a much clearer, or different, thought. He thinks that the original cell of this nematode projects out an image that then becomes worm and then feeds itself back to the original cells, which then sharpen themselves, so there is a back and forth process going on.

RD: I see, a process of feedback. And the feeling of Soul would be a feedback going all the way through time. Taking that the present is the only area in which we're conscious, then memory, like prophecy, becomes an area of self-creation. You don't really go back to the beginning, but you read every present happening. And how you read what really happens is creationally colored, because you have to re-create and pre-create— you re-create the past and pre-create the future. And a form like a poem has a past and a future. Now in the poems that bore me you don't have to re-create the past or pre-create the future, because they're actually moving from one place to another and the point at the end of the poem is more real than all the things in the beginning.

MM: The poems we like the most are the ones where everything is going on at once.

RD: Yes, but also I still arrange my poems chronologically, for instance. So sequence is extremely important to me, or the sequence of lines is important. Although, in theory I thought the lines can go anywhere, and though I rather admire that in a poem, that is not my body feel or my life feel. So I recognize why I don't do that in a poem. There are two systems present in all my poetry. The fact that everything is simultaneous is present; but the fact that the order is the form and that any other order would be another form. You see what I mean, the simultaneity doesn't give you a form at all.

MM: Possibly one of the reasons Books 11 and 12 of *Paradise Lost,* in our recent discussion group, were difficult for some of us to take is that they become so historical in the sense of being fixed on telling a story.

RD: Milton has an outline, also. He is doing what he ought to be doing at the end of the poem. Yes, that was a thorough bore in that regard. The poem is not. While there's brilliance in its passages, and there would be an example of our feeling that that brilliance came from Milton's own deeper poetic temperament, the idea of what to do with the poem, his address in the poem is very anti-poetic and he had to carry it out. You don't feel this at all in Homer. *Paradise Lost* is not a true narrative.

MM: I want to go back to an older discussion we've had and haven't been back to in a good many years, and I wonder what you think about this now. [Edward] Sapir says that language precedes thought, and it occurs to me that the energy of language, which is a very physical sensation, precedes both thought and speech. It also appears that it is a more complex process than Sapir presented. I'd imagine that Whitehead and [Charles] Olson and [Robert] Creeley, as he acknowledges in *Pieces,* work like Einstein (who said he worked with his body sensations).

RD: This is what I call "feel-thinking." If the thinking has its origin in feeling then it is not brain thinking, and our computers are beginning to show us how poor brain thinking is, how limited. Because when we get a machine to imitate the movements of our bodies they're all the same, they're all limited by the brain's picture. There may be certain other intuitions present in the machine. Yes, the machine also imitates things that we know from our own kinetic movements.

MM: How do you fit in with [William Carlos] Williams, looking for that dance step that he carried out in his body-mind sensations?

RD: Well, those body-mind sensations ... in poetry begin with Carlyle, who said that poetry is musical thinking and musical speech, so it lies at the level of what is music. Computer music shows us what music ain't.

MM: It certainly does.

RD: I think in the first place that that isn't what I'm talking about. What music ain't ain't body. We know very well that the body itself can be inhabited in different ways. The body itself can be felt in a whole series of different ways. The body is a brain regiment. Every impulse of the brain, as the newest organ of the body, comes as an order or command. As I think of it in evolution, the brain is the organ that eats up all the calories. And the brain is new, so it is much less experienced than the hands, and much less experienced than the rest of the body. And the rest of the body tends to be fairly unconscious, and I really wonder that if we got down to a nematode whether the rest of the body *is* unconscious. Our consciousness, to us, is our brain. It usurps consciousness from all other parts of the body. Its only concept of body consciousness is for it to return and direct everything, which happens in meditation and so forth. You know, through Yoga forcing your intestines to do so. Let's say I experience the failure of my kidney as a condition, as a given physical condition in the universe: it's what you are actually living in. And if you start talking about it as an illness or a sickness, you're not paying any attention to the actual environment, because the environment is now the one you are in. You're co-inhabiting your own.

MM: Let me insert in here in regard to the last few things you said. In speaking of the consciousness of the nematode, apparently Brenner and Crick as they worked with this creature became so respectful that they began to question their right of sacrificing countless of these tiny...

RD: Nematodes! Nematodes!

MM: Their respect for them grew, and I think that's a respect for consciousness that is taking place.

RD: Well, Darwin called that the vanity of the human image, which makes us worship organization in the universe. Darwin doubted it; he said it was simply the Narcissus effect, that wherever you see something that seems like your own organism, that answers to your own pride in organism. Of course, what Darwin was thinking was he didn't think there was an organism in evolution itself. It was more inscrutable. And the inscrutable part of it is also what I aim at in a poem. I trust in the poem as something that "comes into my mind" that is going to be the poem. Then I start working with it, because it is all material. It isn't an idea that I "have," and I don't really think in a poem. I have no impression that I think in a poem. I don't think that's what goes on. That's why if I'm teaching I teach poetics, not writing of poems or even what is in a poem. Poetics is the part you do think. But all of that is brain thinking. I'm not devaluating brain thinking; it's quite necessary for a complex organism. If you just think of our bodies, without a brain, nothing is clearing through. But I'm interested in the eyes; the total news coming in from everywhere, they convert it very quickly into "think news." Going back to biology and physics, what interests me is that both these sciences are imaginations of the world. They are not really thinking of the world. When they turn to think of the world that is usually in order to support their imagination. The astounding things, breakthroughs for us, are not their thinking out and plotting it but the combination of their intuitions and absolutely free imaginations. So science, for instance, doesn't become antiquated, because in our rational process we've shown that it doesn't meet the data we have got. In the poem, too, you have to *admit* into it things that are present, although they seem to make impossible the form that you felt. But that's the faith you have to have. That's the governing faith in science. It can be falsely expressed. Einstein will say that "God doesn't cheat at dice," or whatever, doesn't play games. Well, that is actually Einstein's own nervousness. The imagination does indeed play games, the playfulness of the imagination is expected in poetry, and we are meanwhile terrifically repressed about that playfulness when it takes place in physics.

You and I are not really nervously trying to check out what kind of universe we're in. The controversies are not that interesting. We are fascinated by what we'd call the play of the mind. And "mind" is not at all identical to brain. It is mind that has a life through time. The body after all—each cell of the body—dies. Am I right that no cell really lasts the lifetime of the organism? Organism, as a matter of fact, is given in the first place, as language is. I still take it that the life is created, but the body is really given. And that is just what happens with language. We're surrounded by language, we take what of it we can use. There are so many analogies, Mike. You can make analogies that we digest it, that we throw some of it away, that we shit lots of it out, that other parts of it enter into systems of nutrition. I am most fascinated now—because it's what I'm involved with—in just these elements and their balances. It is not nutrition, they're not nutrition. Jess says they have to do with electrical exchanges and all the mineral elements that I have to balance or unbalance.

You'd have to be sure you're going to use only one kind of logic, and logic is—logic ought to mean what words do and don't do. And what words can't do they don't do anyway. I mean, if you understand the difference between "oughtn't to do"... I mean, lots of logic has what words ought to do or oughtn't to do: that is of no interest at all, besides what words can do and can't do. That we can think about that, that we can frame propositions about what words actually can't do.

MM: Here are some words you said, that I gave a lot of thought to, and it is a framed proposition in my mind. You said, at a discussion group, that Shakespeare has equality of souls. And then you also added that Spenser does, and you pointed out that Whitman also has it. It's this equality of souls that's part of hugeness, the huge sensation of childhood, as I see it.

RD: Oh, yes, this is also what Crick is finding with his nematodes, is equality. There is no hierarchy of life. There are kinds of life. Now, when the helix and the proposition of DNA appeared, it seemed to me a real, a true revelation, that was present in Darwin but didn't have a principle, so that people could misinterpret Darwin. Because life is a series of variations, not a series of hierarchical achievements. The original proposition about complexity is that a human being must be much more complex than an amoeba, and that just doesn't work out at all. So we find out that we're really asking each time what is going on in this organism. The non-Darwinian picture of evolution was that evolution was a constant improvement of species and individuals of species. Well, that's exactly what Darwin hit, because he showed no matter what you would call an improvement of the species it has no way of knowing whether it's fit to survive, because the slightest change in temperature or anything else would make an entirely different condition for survival. So it is the ratios we respond to, and that's the change of temperature in which some species survive, and some don't.

MM: It seems that in childhood, though, that we're not applying ratio to the faces and the arms of other human beings, but each one is allowed to be a star in whatever their own particular universe is. They may be minor characters in the cast of our drama, but we recognize that they're important characters in other dramas.

RD: Well, the other thing in childhood is that there seems to be a child-hood style that is universal whether it's a child in Africa, or an Eskimo, or a child in New York. When you think about children's drawings and so forth in contrast to the adult arts in widely different civilizations, or the stylistic periods, children's drawings seem to belong throughout to one undifferentiated language. In Africa if a child has promise as an artist he's suddenly forced to desert his childhood style, and he's initiated into the highly sophisticated and differentiated tribal art of the adults. When this realization hit Europe it was a while before they even realized what they just suddenly saw, because their own stylistic sophistication had begun to approach that point where tribal art was no longer alien. Cubism took Africa as part of its language. Adult sophistication in art is had at the cost of an extreme repression of all sorts of things you can do. Tribal art is extremely repressed.

MM: Probably almost as repressed as—

RD: Whereas, for instance, the Renaissance, which doesn't have repression, also doesn't have style. Style fascinates us. Now, in metamorph-osis—I do think going through periods of repression, like going into a dark mood, like into a melancholia, which can also go along with style—

it is, when you go back to your metamorphosis figure, this strikes me over and over again, that we plunge ourselves into "cocoons" in which something is at work. The two things at work: the creative in us has to go inert in order for the unfolding genetic design to enter another phase. You see, the second phase isn't an improvement on the first phase at all. But it really is at a level of species and rehearsal of species that the individual hardly knows the use of. But the transformation of the worm to the butterfly is one of the most fascinating things of childhood. Because it is some sort of analogy: adolescence is some sort of horrible cocoon.

MM: I was just looking at that same metamorphosis, speaking of painting, in an adult. I love [Mark] Rothko's early, what I would call "energy-spirit-surrealistic" oils. But there is a period of about five years, I think it was roughly from 1940 to 1945, where he is seeking, he is actually undergoing a metamorphosis, where he is endeavoring, without knowing, certainly, but knowing in another way, endeavoring to move himself from that spirit-surrealism of those sprawling seashore surreal canvases to his color-fields. Those five years are like the five years of incubation.

RD: Yes, and that incubation was all through New York, much of it coming out of [Hans] Hofmann's teaching of color-field.

MM: It's very exciting to see what change a man can make in five years and when the change is made it is rather sudden, breaking the shell of the cocoon, getting a leg out, climbing out of the cocoon, and drying his wings in the sun while he pumps air into the veins of the wing. It's a complex process, but it is relatively swift when it happens. That for me was a very exciting event to discover in the catalog of Rothko's works, as in the Guggenheim retrospective.

RD: When you started talking about the child's view, I want to point out we re-create in our mind Nietzsche's statement that we're striving to become a child; if it were put back into our picture of metamorphosis, the butterfly itself will be laying eggs, and worms will now proceed with a voracious appetite—and so in a sense the butterfly can be said to be striving to become a worm.

MM: In [Jackson] Pollock's paintings in 1951 when he was dripping paint but faces and figures began to appear in the painting, he goes back to a kind of simplicity that could suggest that he was looking for childhood art again.

RD: I think Pollock is the creation of our art market. For instance, [Joan] Miro does not look like child art the way [Henri] Matisse does when Matisse is drawing, because Miro is calculating and being childish, which Pollock isn't. [Paul] Klee is. These are styles in art. Matisse is drawing from the way the hand sees. Remember that the hand is a good part of our seeing, and in order to have the technique of representation what you do is to repress entirely how much you actually are feeling. The hand obeys. I would be more than aware of this, being cross-eyed so that all my sense of distance is my own sense of movement through space or my sense of touch.

MM: I agree with what you are saying. What I was guessing about Pollock is that what he was doing was a very complex, very developed kind of drip painting. And there is one period in 1951 when actually beatific, huge simple faces and figures began to appear in the drip paintings. I don't think it was in his control. It doesn't resemble child art the way Miro does, but there is something childish and fresh and dancing and exuberant that's come back into the work in a new way. And it is after that that he has his crisis with painting and retreats from painting. I think it scared him.

RD: But also he drank as heavily as he did, like Dylan Thomas, in order not to encounter what was going on in his work. And this can be the terror. People clinging to their personality as if that were an identity. Actually, most people don't want to encounter the feel of soul and that they are a lifetime, because the terms in which they present the personality wouldn't have been present throughout that lifetime, and they suddenly feel it's made up, this personality is made up. Then it can't be real. This search for the realness. Or somebody's "Do you really love me?" That is already one who has mistaken the whole nature of love and of life.

With Michael McClure in Duncan's home at 3267 Twentieth Street, San Francisco, 1985. Photo by Joanna McClure. Courtesy of the Poetry Collection, University at Buffalo.

MM: And, you know, in other terms if you acknowledge that you are a star in this galaxy you find you don't want to be a star where we are blowing up Asians with napalm, or electing Reagan to the presidency.

RD: And yet if we weren't in that universe—let's pick any other ones—there could be a broody elephant thinking, "I must be to blame because lions eat dear little gazelles." And you say, "But you'd never be able to eat a gazelle." "But no, how can I be happy, how can I be eatin' leaves in a world in which poor little gazelles get eaten?"

MM: Shall we take a rest?

∞

RD: When you go back to the picture of Pollock, his astounding and great paintings, the big canvases, where he was inside the canvas and moving about: in all the painting of that period there are two kinds of things that are present, and they aren't necessarily the same. One of them is action painting. Well, Rothko isn't action painting. Color-fields are really indwellings. What happened in the big Pollock canvases is that they were action paintings—he really enacted the very act of painting, and at the same time, since he was inside it, they were also indwellings, because when we see them they do not just convey what one says of [Franz] Kline, that it is the will making shapes. They seem like huge networks of light and presence. So one thing in poetry and painting and music that most interests me is when it becomes a presence. This goes back to our picture of the biological. In the biological there is no bio-illogical. I'd go all the way back to Schrödinger, where he shows that, in fact, the biological is not an illogic within a logical universe that is mathematic throughout, because he says he knows of nothing in the material world that is not biological, that doesn't have life, that doesn't move between being born and dying. We can see that the sun is dying; we can see it of the earth. Once we understand that the earth has a lifetime, that it wasn't just made by somebody, it is *indeed* self-creating. It's like here in California, where people build silly real estate on the sides of mudhills. Don't they look around? Where do they think these hills with their soft contours come from? Our landscape is constantly self-creating itself by collapsing on itself. And that is what is beautiful to us, on top of that. But how idiotic, then, to start building a house on the sand. But let's get back to this picture. Jess talks about indwelling in the work you are in. It even erases any sense of being inspired. Inspiration is another thing that happens. Something comes in. Yet when things come into the poem I don't think of them as inspirations, but as material. Remember that in my poetry there is a tenure of constantly reestablishing myself, but that is different from repeating what I've just done. Repeating must be something that's present in the biological, for where else would it be? I think the place where I would agree entirely with your approach is I don't see anything, any other place for painting and poetry to belong other than that they're flowerings of a biological kind out of a species, and the species does not create painting as a whole; only certain individuals create these flowerings.

MM: That leads into something else I wanted to bring up. The Romantic movement in English poetry is very strong for many of us. What I see in Shelley is not just the discovery of nature just at a moment when the Industrial Revolution was beginning to eat it up, but also I see in him the internalization of the organism into poetry. That is, Shelley's poetry absorbs and breaks the forms that precede it, and it ripples like a muscular being, and it surges forward, and it invents its own rules, as in "The Triumph of Life." What a strange poem, and what a beautiful poem. It changes constantly and fluidly, and daringly. So that it has the qualities of sensation, movement, fluidity, organism. A long poem by Shelley seems almost like a living being to me. I realize, of course, this is also true of Chaucer, Aristophanes—

RD: Any poem that you're going to respond to. In part it mirrors your living being, and since it mirrors your living being it seems intensely to be a living being to you. If we have no hierarchy of souls, then as a matter of fact—let us take a really "jerk" poetry, like L-a-n-g-u-a-g-e poetry is to my mind—it also is organism. And the reason I can't read it is because it doesn't answer to me, to my on-going lifeway.

MM: I wonder if Structuralism is organism. I see L-a-n-g-u-a-g-e poetry as Structuralist.

RD: Oh, no. What is your idea of Structuralism?

MM: Structuralism is where you have a schema—

RD: Oh, no, no: that is Conventionalism, because Structuralism means that you approach things and ask questions of the structure. Structuralists include the psychologist [Jean] Piaget, who is concerned with the organization as consciousness; that doesn't mean you have a schema. Let's use the term the right way. Because Structuralism is extremely important for me in freeing my poetry of any sense of being literary.

MM: So you want to call what I was calling Structuralism in literature Conventionalism? Where you have a set of rules that you follow?

RD: Yes, and it's a form of game, because you agree. It's like playing bridge; you agree what you're doing, and you make the cards go that way.

MM: I don't see much possibility for organism, or for the qualities of organism, in a Conventionalistic approach to a work of art.

RD: And yet it's got to be organistic, because organism doesn't get not to exist. In other words, it's organisms that produce those conventional forms. Now, Mike, let's look back at the species. It's got an underlying map and method. And it's only when we look at thousands of individuals do we begin to realize that there are metamorphoses going on.

MM: But the very thing that Brenner finds out when he works with these nematodes is that there is no blueprint for the organism in the genetic code.

RD: Yes, but then where do you think blueprints come from? They come from organisms. This is exactly my objection to the idea something can be illogical. Everything is biological. And the reason we find that we respond to certain works and not to others is because there is not just one life-form, there are multitudes of life-forms. I find it very healthy that there are just lots of different kinds of poetry. Most of the time, having heard something once I don't want to hear it twice. Yet it is so mysterious what you can be drawn to that can seem different to you. But I think of all of these as being drawn again with a life sense, of what belongs to your life and what doesn't belong to your life. When *Howl* was written and suddenly everyone rightly recognized that that was the age of *Howl*—like [T. S.] Eliot was the age of *The Waste Land* from 1920 clear through to the end of the '30s—established poets at large responded to it so that [Richard] Wilbur, who is a very solid, talented, conventional poet, and his admirers, behaved as if *Howl* were some sort of offense to whatever Wilbur wrote. But admirers of Wilbur were never going to be reading *Howl*; and the admirers of *Howl*—who had never before admired *any* poetry—were certainly never going to be reading Wilbur. And we've got much more variety than that at present. That's the healthiest sign of human beings, not the unhealthiest sign.

MM: For me that's the same thing as saying "All souls are equal" in Shakespeare, all souls are equal in childhood.

RD: But that does not mean that all souls are familial, or familiar. And that's what we're seeing in poetry as it's more and more vivid, it's more lively. I certainly was not saying that *Kaddish* and *Howl* were not lively, although Allen has, as a matter of fact, significantly deserted poetry for Buddhism and thinks that that's the primary reality. And he's written fewer and fewer poems. He writes long rants, and so forth.

MM: What poets are you reading right now, speaking of plurality of poets?

RD: You mean right now? Troubadours.

MM: I mean in the last three years. Classical poets and new poets.

RD: We could take that up next time, because my mind is not—

MM: You've been reading [Edmond] Jabès, and Homer.

RD: Yes. And in the French—I heard him at Cambridge—it was Jean Daive, and I carried his *Décimale blanche* with me, practically memorizing it. [Charles] Baudelaire, of course. I spent two years on Baudelaire.

MM: Are you reading the *Journals*?

RD: I'm reading the *Fleurs du Mal,* but I have read them, of course. Oh, yes. But I'm talking about the poetry. Of course, in the Poetics Program at New College of California Robert Kenny was doing his thesis on Baudelaire, and preliminary to that he translated everything in *Les Fleurs du Mal.* He had a tutorial with me, and we compared translations. The question always with a translation is not does it represent the original poem, but what is happening in the translation. Again, if we think about two lives: there's a disproportion when a Richard Howard translates Baudelaire. We recognize right away that they don't even resemble each other. What I want is a differentiation upon principles, a sense of structural signs as there is a sense of significant structure underlying biological definitions.

My first reaction to Don Allen's anthology was that he should have an arrangement . . . and I did not want to be in the sort of circus where the polar bear is brought in right after the monkey is brought in right after the—and that's the way all anthologies were. Actually it would be the polar bear then the polecat, because they'd be alphabetical.

MM: Did Don consult you about the arrangement? I understand some of it was Creeley's suggestions.

RD: I was relaying ideas through Creeley, relaying them through Robin Blaser, and I was refusing to be in the anthology unless it had an organization, on historical principles. And of course in the second anthology Don no longer arranged it. But the feeling of identity was a little intense in that period. If you remember, not only was I objecting to being in the wrong categories, but I saw absolutely no meaning at all to being in something called San Francisco.

MM: This is a little bit of a change in subject, but one of the things that strikes me is how much things feel like the '50s now. I feel that there's a polarization going on; I feel there's a great sense of clarity under the political oppression that's going on. And I feel a strong sense of creativity and personal identity. I feel this in the '80s as much as I felt it in the '50s.

RD: Now we've had three crops of students in the Poetics Program, and they're all interrelated, and they're all of absolutely great potentialities. We're also in the situation of having no magazines we can contribute to.

MM: And that's exactly the way it was in the '50s.

RD: Exactly the way it was then. You had the *Hudson* and the *Kenyon* and so forth. And now *The Southern Review* is doing an issue on me and, after badgering me for a year and a half, will be printing a chapter of *The H.D. Book*. Well, this is just unheard of. In the first place, *The Southern Review* is extinct. But we have emerging, however, magazines, like David Levi Strauss's *ACTS*, right here where they were emerging before.

MM: Yes, I find that now I go to see people like I did in the '50s. My interest in painting is strengthened; my interest in serious music is strengthened.

RD: Some of that is because our past writing now feels to us very much achieved, so we have the same problem we had in the beginning. We aren't really carrying out something; we're not still carrying something through. The fifteen-year break that I wanted between *Bending the Bow* and *Ground Work* (and the title *Ground Work* itself) I wanted to be back where I was when I was writing *Letters* and making things up.

MM: Somebody asked me what you meant by *Before the War.* I said I think *Before the War,* as Robert's using it, has three meanings.

RD: Yes, oh listen, I've made up a million. And at the present time I wonder what does *In the Dark* mean, the following volume. The volume doesn't answer "before the war," although every one of those suckers is living as if they're before the war. If there is a universal sense in the world today, no matter who, everybody thinks there is going to be a third world war, everybody dreads the third world war, everybody promises there won't be a third world war. And that's the only thing they're living before. Like, before the mirror. I think that's one of the strongest meanings of *Before the War.* Before the sphinx, I'm standing before the sphinx, I'm standing before the war. And my idea of a war is that you don't object to a sphinx, or to a volcano, but that you're "before" it.

"Realms of Being"
(with Rodger Kamenetz, 1985)

This interview with Professor Rodger Kamenetz, which appeared in
The Southern Review *(vol. 21, no. 1, Winter 1985), focuses on the
thirteenth-century Jewish sacred text the* Zohar, *or* Book of Splendor.
Duncan mentions how he became acquainted with the Zohar *and what
it means to him. He delves into the nature of the imagination and the
primacy of "the law" and his adherence to it. "Finally, imagination is
my ground, and I hold to it," he declares.*

    —Ed.

*In 1974, Robert Duncan's publisher, James Laughlin, asked him if he had a new
collection of poems to offer. It had been, after all, five [seven?] years since the
appearance of* Bending the Bow. *Duncan's reply must have been somewhat
startling. He said he would have a new collection ready for publication in exactly
ten years. True to his word,* Ground Work: Before the War *has appeared, and
Duncan has already projected a second volume,* Ground Work: In the Dark,
to appear in 1989, in time for his seventieth birthday.

    *At a time when many poets seem all too eager to publish, this sort of delib-
eration is unusual. It does not bespeak so much a modesty or reticence, but
rather an extraordinary commitment to a life in poetry, what Duncan calls
"devotion to the poem." This devotion has already led him to a poetic achieve-
ment unique in contemporary writing. With immense scope and erudition,
Robert Duncan—especially in his open series the "Structures of Rime" and
"Passages"—has written lyrical poetry on an epic scale.*

    *Though clearly he belongs to American avant-garde circles, particularly
through his association with Charles Olson and the Black Mountain Movement,
Duncan has termed himself at times a "derivative" poet, even a "traditional" one.
Partly this is because he considers the entire field of poetry as simultaneous and
has drawn as freely on the poetry of the past—particularly Herbert, Dante, and
the Sufi master Rumi—as on more contemporary sources such as Pound, H.D.,
and Olson. What is also fascinating is his use of theological and theosophical*

materials, among them the Jewish mystical tradition known as the Kabbalah. Not since Milton has a poet put to use such a broad range of religious lore.

When I contacted Robert Duncan to read in Louisiana State University's 1984 Gathering of Poets program, I suggested an interview to explore the place of the Jewish tradition in his thought and work. In agreeing, he described this as an "on-going study."

I had first met him in 1973 when we were both participants in a San Francisco Bay Area poetry workshop. Although Duncan had proposed himself as just another member, his presence could not help but be a focus for the rest of us. There weren't more than a few sessions, in any case, but they were revelatory. He opened the poem before us—no matter where it was—to many further levels of possibility. He showed us how our failures could lead us to a greater awareness of what the poem was doing. He insisted, very much, on the poem as part of a life process, which came, to me at least, as a relief.

The Zohar provided the poet with a mythology, but as Duncan notes, there are many choices of mythology available to the Western mind. The particular significance of Kabbalah was its focus on language as a source of creation. Thrown back on the Torah as unique revelation, the Jewish Kabbalists made myth of the very materials of language. Behind the literal meaning of the law, the Kabbalists believed the Torah contained all the mysteries of the universe, was indeed one long living name of God. But such mysteries were revealed only through inspired meditation on the letters themselves, and through systems of encoding and decoding that we would identify with the poetic process.

It was both a personal and intellectual connection that brought Duncan and me together in Baton Rouge to discuss the place of the Jewish tradition in his work. What added to the excitement was the imminent publication of Ground Work: Before the War. However, during Duncan's visit, another element intruded which no one anticipated. He became seriously ill—was in fact, in medical terms, "in heart failure." Naturally, this overrode any concerns about an interview, although Duncan completed his obligations with a great deal of aplomb in the most distressing of circumstances and gave a very moving reading.

Back home in San Francisco, Duncan's medical problems were diagnosed and problems traced to the kidney. As a result, he seemed to be in much better shape when I went to San Francisco, a few months later, to complete the interview. We had two sessions for an hour and a half each at his home. I also visited a class *on Milton at the New College, where Duncan and poet David Meltzer teach in the Poetics Program.*

In the course of our talks, several references came up in a shorthand kind of way that might need clarification. The work by Gershom Scholem that Duncan refers to is Major Trends in Jewish Mysticism. *It is Scholem of course as translator and scholar who opened up the field of Jewish mysticism in such a fertile way for so many poets and writers. In terms of the Kabbalah, the doctrine of "letters" (*autiot *in Hebrew) is already present in earlier works such as the third-century* Sefer Yetzirah *(or book of foundations), one of the fundamental texts of Jewish mysticism. The mystical Torah, written in letters of black fire on white fire, is the Creation. The letters of the Torah are conceived of as having creative powers of their own. Robert Duncan in the '40s and '50s was already realizing the implications of Kabbalistic letterism for writing. Its first impact is in* Letters *(Jargon Books, 1958)—the title, as he explains, comes from the* Zohar—*and thereafter Jewish mystical themes are a "part of the weave."*

Despite the charge of obscurantism leveled by certain critics against the body of Duncan's work, what strikes me is its remarkable consistency and intelligence. Though Duncan's mind is, like the Zohar, *"crowded with splendors" ("Circulations of the Song,"* Ground Work: Before the War*), he has emphasized careful composition throughout. Technique in Duncan leads to transcendent postulates. As he notes beautifully at one point in the interview, "realms of being seem necessary to pose in order to give things their just place." His subtle and constant use of "ryme"—Duncan extends the meaning from assonance to "realms of being"—has created a tightly woven structure in which the poet, as in Philo's dictum, "does all things simultaneously."*

. . .

—Rodger Kamenetz

I. Initiations into the *Zohar*

RODGER KAMENETZ: You came to the *Zohar* first, or at least you heard of it, through your parents' teachings?

ROBERT DUNCAN: Yes. And I thought of it as something they knew about because of their initiations so I never dreamed it would be sitting on a shelf somewhere.

RK: You said there was an initiation to get to read the Kabbalah?

RD: Remember I knew nothing about the initiation except I knew there were initiations at different levels. In the complex that arises in the '80s and '90s and very rapidly after the death of [Helena] Blavatsky, Theosophy projects different cult groups. The group my grandmother was in was quite similar to the Hermetic Brotherhood [W. B.] Yeats was an elder in.

RK: What was the name of the group?

RD: The Isis Temple. But so was Yeats's.

RK: How large was the group?

RD: My cousin thinks maybe at the most it may have been about twenty people.

RK: So it's fairly small?

RD: Oh, all these groups were. I mean in history when you turn around and find out, what were the Gnostics? They weren't hundreds of people running around. The Valentinians may have been twenty people or fifteen people. [The Valentinians were a Gnostic cult led by Valentinus, in Rome circa 140 AD.]

RK: Was it centered around a dominant personality?

RD: There was a teacher, Mrs. Reynolds, and then a man that I knew in my childhood as Uncle Fred became Master of the cult, but it became smaller and smaller. You only need two people reading, practically, to continue a cult. I know nothing about it in its later days. And since it's syncretic—in this my poetry is like my parents' religion—it has no orthodoxy at all, and consequently the Leaves of Grass was read as a bible, along with the Bible.

RK: So the interesting thing about Leaves of Grass is that it first came to you as a religious book.

RD: Yes, as an absolute truth that was not just poetic, right. But then it first came via the cosmic interpretation of Maurice Bucke. And these cults are all cosmic cults. One of the troubles about Judaism is, it's not cosmic; it has no cosmos. Whereas the Hermetic trouble is that it does have a cosmos, and therefore undergoes reorganizations. But the Kabbalah is the area in which a cosmos appears, a series of cosmoses. When we turn around and read Genesis and ask if there is a cosmos, we are mostly dismayed unless we get into the letters and reimagine a series *[of creations]*. It's so anthropocentric and in such contempt of the universe and of creation—then of course it is almost Gnostic. The created world *[in Genesis]* is a piece of scenery.

RK: You never got to the Kabbalah and the *Zohar* specifically within the context of your parents' religious practices?

RD: No. And in general my parents tended towards the ignorance of fundamentalism when they were in the material that was in their mysteries, the literalism that appears in people who are in their religion. Things were literal for them, so they didn't have the range the imagination has, and so they weren't about to study Jane Harrison or something, really rich sources about what was going on in the mysteries, because their own mysteries to them were real.

I came to the *Zohar* because I discovered it belonged to both an anarchist and poetic tradition. I knew already it belonged to a poetic tradition, but I was confused about whether you had to know Hebrew to get into it. I think that rose in a discussion with [Kenneth] Rexroth when I was aware of how much the *Zohar* was in back of Milton and Spenser. And Rexroth said: "It's all there, you can read it yourself, on the shelf over there in five volumes. You don't have to wonder where it is, or join something in order to read it."

RK: You're not a joiner.

RD: I'm not a joiner. We discussed before the difference between imagination and belief. I'm not a believer; that's much more important, neither believer nor disbeliever.

Some things appeal to the imagination, and some things do not. What attracted me to the *Zohar* was not that I was going to find something I believed in, but something that so far looked like it would not disappoint

391

the imagination. I find absolutely repulsive the features of the literalism and sectarianism it's very hard to read any Gnosticism without . . . because Gnostic cults were so beleaguered and persecuted that only the toughest elements remain, and they were all elements of belief. After all, they remain because people were martyred in testimony to their belief. And yet some of the systems are fascinating; Valentinianism is fascinating.

RK: Harold Bloom seems interested in the *Zohar* as a "belated" text, one that comes after but pretends to come before. The *Zohar* is written in the thirteenth century but pretends to be contemporary with early Talmud. That's not at all your interest?

RD: No. As a matter of fact, this is one place where, whether it's that or the Ice Age, I'm not like Olson, who thinks that the earliest has an authenticity because it's first, that origin has authenticity. I don't see any sense in that at all, and I don't see any sense that there's a progress. Then again, that would be my concept of what is, which is not a constant improvement, of course, nor is it the loss of innocence, or the loss of a real thing. So that's what I meant, that I don't read the *Zohar* in order to get to the real thing that my parents should have believed, at all. Simply that it was a book of wonders, and so it is. As a matter of fact, while I think of it, doesn't it mean splendor?

RK: Yes, the *Book of Splendor.*

RD: Well, does splendor qualify by being more true or less true? It either is or is not splendid.

RK: Scholem attributes the great popularity of the Kabbalah in the fifteenth and sixteenth centuries, especially the Lurianic Kabbalah, to a reaction within Judaism to the expulsion from Spain.

RD: First of all, they're safe as long as Spain is Moslem, and once it becomes Christian then they're in trouble. So are the Moslems in trouble. It's a pan-Arabic world that produces the background the *Zohar* relates to. The angelology in the *Zohar,* for instance, is developing along with the angelology in the Moslem world, as we discover that many of Dante's angels come from the Moslem world, not the Christian. It's a universalizing period. It's harder for the Jews to universalize, but *Zohar* is universalizing. Dante is amazingly universalizing. He's an imagination of a larger order. The best the *Zohar* can do at one point when they're quarreling about the nature of hell and the fact that hell would not be very much of a punishment—because pain becomes redundant—and one rabbi says: Well, if any Jew breaks even a letter of the law, he'll burn forever in ovens and always be entering them. Because they're very literal and see right away if you're in the oven that problem number one is you'd be burned up. No, God would not permit that; it must be continuous torture of apprehension and, at the same time, can't be redundant.

And then they say: Well, what about the *goyim*? *["Goyim" are the Gentiles.]* Oh, but they're wet dream children. They evaporate. They're not real. So you find for all the universalizing, still the Jewish community can't believe in the human reality of other human beings. And then you have the wonderful story that Adam went and shacked up with Lilith after Cain killed Abel, left Eve, and for a thousand years begot wet dream children who are all the other people of the world. Well, this is so far from Dante, who says God needs every being and event throughout time. Milton will reiterate this. He will reiterate that there is no hierarchy of civilizations, because that's a picture that everything is needed in the universe, which is quite different from there being certain significances, and the other things are not significant.

II. *Zohar* and the Imagination

RD: There are two things which would make Scholem's book on Jewish mysticism particularly of interest to me in the first place. One was, I knew my parents were Christian Kabbalists and that they worked with the Hebrew alphabet, but since that was part of their mysteries I was never permitted to. Second, I'd already begun to get into letters and serious puns through *Finnegan* and to think more about them. *Letters* [1958] is influenced toward a creative veil or world-cloth which would be identical with the *maya,* in which it's woven all the way through. The warp and woof are connected, and the figures emerge and disappear. All of that was there and working with the idea of letters—the letters of fire on a ground of darkness, isn't that it?

393

RK: The Torah is conceived as black fire written on white fire.

RD: All of those ideas have a good deal of cross-resonance, and in the most intensified place where people lived entirely in the book—and it's the book I was writing—the two would be James Joyce and those mystical Jews who live in the Torah. As a matter of fact, the Torah would not be The Book for me; The Book is a nonexistent book, like . . .

RK: Like Mallarmé's?

RD: No, like it is in *Finnegan*. Not Mallarmé. Mallarmé has a much more elusive idea of The Book. But The Book is there . . . years before I came to the idea of the *livre* of Mallarmé. It really rests in a sense in Dante— and not in the *Zohar* or someplace else that I've ever found it—and that is, as I've said, that God needs every being and every thing and every event throughout time and space. Needs it, so there are no true events and false events and so forth. And that's pretty much the texture in which I compose.

Already by the time I'm reading Scholem I was not at all in search of religion, but in search of the nature of the imagination. It seemed to me that in mystical traditions of Judaism, religion was passing into imagination, including the imaginary. But the imaginary is not significant in relation to the imagination, because imagination is the final ground of reality. That's what I mean by the imagination. And this is, of course, an abomination as far as the religion goes, because there aren't any boundaries to what's in that final ground. If you can imagine it, then your job is where is it, not that it is or is not, or quarrel does it exist or not?

Through the mysticism in Scholem, I was also very fascinated, right away, with the giant figure of Adam, because that was worked into *Letters* and is challenged in *Letters*. In *The Opening of the Field* there is a set of Adams including Adam Kadmon. [*Adam Kadmon, or Primordial man, is identified with God in his aspect as Creator. That is, as Scholem puts it, "the God who can be apprehended by man is himself the First Man."*] There was an Adam before there was an Adam and so forth—all of that was contained by that time. Even the name *Letters* comes from the *Zohar*, which I was reading in that period. I only read the first couple of volumes of the Soncino *Zohar*, so I didn't get too deeply steeped. I insist I didn't go beyond Joseph in Egypt. I think Michael Davidson found me out beyond Joseph in Egypt.

RK: The Jewish thread in *Letters* connects with the search in "Structures of Rime" for an "absolute scale of resemblances and disresemblances." In Kabbalah the letters are activating, creative. If God says "OR" (which is "light" in Hebrew), the word actually makes light. The words are conceived as being the same as the thing created, and of course for a poet that's a wonderful notion.

RD: But that's exactly what happens in a poem, unless the poem is referential. The *fiat lux* excludes the possibility of referentiality.

RK: How so?

RD: Because in creating something, you don't refer to it. You can't refer to it. And what you then create doesn't resemble something else. Finally, imagination is my ground, and I hold to it. That is, I'm not a philosopher at all, but I'm still confronted with philosophical impossibilities with everything that goes into my weave. And I'm not a theologian at all, although the constructs that are in theology fascinate me; but there is not just one construct. All theologies I've come across exist on the idiocy of not seeing that their very first premises are not first premises but coexist with a lot of others leading to other pictures, to other constructs. *Roots and Branches* has a lot of uncovering of both of my parents, but also parents at a cosmic level, an intense feeling for "the father," whom I do not believe at all to be identical with the Creator of the Universe. [*Duncan is probably referring to such poems as "A Sequence of Poems for H.D.'s Birthday" and "A Letter."*] Creation to me is a mystery of the Universe—I'm a Heraclitean in that the universe creates itself, and human beings have these ideas; they have them like plants have flowers. We don't have tulips, but we have ideas and religions which are our distinctive way of blossoming, sorting out, mating—the same as the flowers. Then that makes sense to me. The other way around [*i.e., in which God the Father creates the universe*] does not make sense at all, because the whole thing then becomes an absolute hell of not just two, but all sorts of liars killing each other in twenty different directions. It can be summed up like Joyce did when asked about Ireland, "Well, it's one bloody fool hittin' another bloody fool over the bloody head over bloody nothin'," which could give you the whole history of Ireland; it could give you the whole history of any country. So the one that's purely poetry is: the imagination is the ground, and it's only in poetry that the imagination is the ground.

RK: I'm interested, because what I find proposed in your poetry is an idea that these relationships in language that are discovered, or uncovered, by the poet in a sense preexist and are real.

RD: Yes, you're right. The poet doesn't "fiat lux." But he doesn't refer to something either; he discovers, uncovers. When we started in the early '50s the slang in the street talked about, "Do you dig it?" And Olson very quickly had caught on that: yes indeed, that's what you do do when you write, you dig. In the archaeologist's sense, the *OED* had opened up the layers of language, and the *OED* is another one of the complicating factors at every step of the writing, because that gives me the layers of every single English word through its layers of time, and then we turn to assorted dictionaries of other languages with special fascination for roots. It's going to look very odd, because it's a temporary thing in poetry how much we go by a belief in the magic of the root. The root is the one we're picturing in the fiat lux. That there is a root [which] binds us again very much to the Kabbalah. We're not content with text on the page; we've got to find a way to surround it with a million different numbers until you arrive at its possible root. *[Duncan refers here to the Kabbalistic practice of "gematria." Since, in Hebrew, numbers are written with the alphabet, a page of Hebrew letters is also a page of numbers. This led to a Kabbalistic numerology-as-hermeneutics.]* And to work from a sense of the root. In that sense, it's radical.

RK: So it's the *OED* and also *Finnegans Wake*. . . .

RD: Well, they came together. After all, Joyce's *Finnegans Wake* is drawing directly on the *OED* all the time. He draws on the counterpart; the fact that the Germans, the French, and the Dutch were all making *OED* dictionaries too from the nineteenth century on gave him the resource of writing in a kind of European . . . He was aiming at a trans-human language, because he brings in every possible kind of language.

RK: Mallarmé wrote a little book, *Les Mots Anglais,* in which he tried to elucidate letter values; so for instance a "b," he'd point out we had "breast" and it's a sucking sound: b-b-b-b.

RD: I haven't read *Les Mots Anglais,* but I got a lot of that out of Freudianism. Earlier, in the '40s, when I was reading Melanie Klein and [Geza] Roheim and Freud, and Ernest Jones's early essays, all of those led, especially Ernest Jones's essay on the M-R complex. It's mother-murder-murmur. Those were really eye-openers. Remember, when we reach things like this *[i.e., significant sounds in a poem],* we don't get taught them but we recognize them.

RK: They're already there.

RD: Right, this kind of thing *[sound values]* strikes ideas already forming, joins them and reinforces it in our mind.

RK: In psychoanalysis, we have the level of individual experience, where everything, including mis-takes, are significant. In the Jewish attitude towards history—while you have different significances—the attitude you took over is that everything in history would become significant. . . .

RD: Ominous, that's right. And also prophetic in Blake's sense, it tells you what's happening now. If it told you what's going to happen, then it's all a bunch of balderdash, because none of it worked out.

RK: In relation to your own book, to your own life-book, your life-creation, do you ever have that sense of ominous, you have to finish in this way. . . .

RD: No. And some very important things were never there at all. Like I didn't see kidneys coming in my work, yet they entirely changed my life. No, I don't think the poem is the same as . . .

RK: . . . the life?

RD: They're not redundant, poetry and life. Consequently, you can give one over to the other entirely. You can ruin the poetry by the way you live or you can ruin the way you live by the poetry. If they were redundant, if they were the same thing, that isn't what would happen.

RK: So you can make mistakes in your life that would hurt your poetry?

RD: No, I don't mean mistakes, simply that the life, for lots of people, is much more important than the poetry, and poetry never becomes a ground of reality at all. Reality is taken on the day-to-day, physical reality we're usually calling our life. The poetry's my life too; it wouldn't exist without it, but its relation to it is radical as a flower is radical, because that's the flower's own essence and signature, but it's not radical like the plant can grow without any flowers, and even promulgate from the root when there are no flowers. There are plants that can go for long periods without ever blooming. It would be an analogy. But analogies are not really the way. The misleading thing about analogies is that it really is "as above, so below." By the way, that's one of the things I was taught before I could speak, so I used to think about it all the time. My sense of it is that, if it's happening here it's happening there; if it's happening in the dream it's happening in the poem; it's happening in your life, and if you don't recognize it, now you do have the difficulty that you are not recognizing something that goes on and it withers, or it can sour, or it can disappear and you get disjointed relations of different realms.

Realms of being seem necessary to pose in order to give things their just place. In order not to have, for instance, a dream as a half-assed kind of poem—they aren't the same at all. Sometimes things in dreams insist that they be used in poems, and the poem will take hold so that happens and in the early years, I recorded dreams as well as writing poems just to see how far I could go in recording dreams. But my dream world is considerably impoverished compared to my poetic world.

III. Jacob and the Angel Syntax

RK: What happened with Emmanuel Levinas in Paris last summer? [Levinas is a French phenomenologist who studies Talmudic texts.]

RD: I just heard his sermon and met him. The whole company was extraordinary. We're in a synagogue in Paris, where, after all, all of them had been in some form or other through the Nazi occupation; I mean, they're just shopkeepers and butchers and that's what he was addressing. There was a bar mitzvah, and they were all back at their bar mitzvah age so you had a seventy-year-old man as if he were fourteen or whatever. Is it fourteen or thirteen?

RK: Thirteen. You mentioned that he discoursed on the butcher's just weight and the tailor's fair measure.

RD: What interested me was that these are values that are absolute in the poem, and they're not much understood today because the content and the importance of a poem is what we go by and not how well it is made. So we've got poems that are very poorly dished out, as we would say.

It's also the change at the cash register, because the exactness of the change and the exchange is really made before God and not before the customer. It's not because the customer or God is going to say it's right or wrong. It's because you are practicing—practicing being a Jew at the cash register.

The practice of being a poet during the day is a very different relation to everything that happens than the practice of one who is not a poet. So the poets' reading of what is happening, their attention to and care for what is happening may be for other people's opinions, but that is not the same as in the devotion of the poem.

It seems to me that poetry appears and becomes stronger and stronger as men are no longer religious, although they may be going to church. Donne, after all, is giving sermons forth within a church, but even that church served his poetry. We've got borderlines so we don't have to make either/or. We've got poets who are saints, and we've got writers like Kierkegaard where it would be hard to decide whether the writing is serving the religion or the religion the writing. The writing and the religion meet each other's perplexity, because the same devotion is given to them and they are not the same. Especially with the advent of the idea of the imagination.

RK: But in Judaism, if you abandon the religious law, you no longer have the butcher's just weight.

RD: In my poetry there is no way to abandon the law. The adherence to the law is the art. You can't abandon it, any more than you can abandon gravity. Law for me is either that—or what? "The Law I Love Is Major Mover" [*The Opening of the Field*] comes out of John Adams; that is, the superiority of "the law" to the written law in John Adams.

RK: In Judaism we have the contrast between the oral law and the written law.

RD: But Jefferson and Adams are absolutely opposed to the written law. They're writing in dismay back and forth to each other about: Why did they write the Bill of Rights, since rights are not a bill? They are a reality, and men have to fight for them over and over again, regardless of how they get written down. On the other hand, we cling to this Bill of Rights, and we've gotten to the place where we can have practically a Roman emperor ruling us under the superstition that we've got the Bill of Rights.

RK: I'm interested in the image of Jacob wrestling with an angel in "The Structure of Rime" and the angel being identified with Syntax, the law of the organization of sentences. The wrestling is a kind of defiance. Also, Jacob is a dual figure. In another poem you talk about Jacob cheating Esau, so that the law of righteousness comes from a cheat. But in the "Structures of Rime," you have Jacob wrestling the Angel Syntax; he's almost like the poet who wrestles the angel. . . .

RD: Who also may be the deceiver, by the way.

RK: Sure.

RD: Jacob as the deceiver and the Jacob-Esau thing is in more than one place in my poetry. My mind goes back to it again and again. In the first place, I take it as a fundamental story and one in which we see the same principle as my observing that play is the law, not the law is within the play. Oedipus breaks the law, but that law, "the law," is an obstacle within the play that must be played, and the play is the law that everything is obedient to. Perfectly apparent, since Oedipus can break the law of incest, and break the law of murder of his father, but the play demands consciousness, and contains those laws, and demands the breaking of those laws for consciousness to emerge.

Jacob wrestling with the angel is consciousness. His name changes from Jacob to Israel and a new consciousness emerges, and that is why we went back to, Why is a poem like the Jews for me? First, the whole Judaic tradition is one of the three great strands of myth out of which my own consciousness comes—and they are what I call the European mind—which is the Jewish mythology, the Celto-Germanic mythology, and the Greco-Roman mythology. I don't see any of those in separation. I remember we got into a discussion, at one point, Was the Jewish more ethical? But the view I still would have is, there are no ethics but that one we have to be obedient to and have to have faith in as a matter of fact because we aren't at seat [?]. Yet all of our ethics are a practice of what we truly believe that to be.

RK: We aren't at seat?

RD: We aren't at seat, no, and there's a kind of obedience. Now we have much larger obediences than the European mind proposed, because, by the time it was thoroughly recognized that the European mind was the Jewish, and the German, and the Greco-Roman, we're in the full catastrophic rage of the '20s, '30s, and '40s. The old way of coexisting was through the pieties of being Christian, or the pieties of being Jewish, or the pieties of being German, and the others were thought of as others. But biologically that idea disappeared completely the century before. We catch up much later in our general feel of things. And they all coexist. One thing I still—I think maybe I put it in only once but it could go in a hundred times—was Philo's "God does all things simultaneously." The meaning is in a beyond, and we aren't simultaneous—we're chronological. We're also simultaneous, of course. We've got that character; the minute we speak of the simultaneous, there we are, the simultaneous.

And the warning I guess I keep [is it's] very hard for me to take hold of the principle of evil, so the serpent in the garden is devious like Jacob or Loki, but he's not more than human, and the little story is in itself ludicrous. These things go together in a haunting sort of way. The naïveté when we reenact them over and over again is part of the force of it. So I'm not talking about some particular subtlety, but my own bent of mind is that everybody is eventually to be made good. "Making good" is an important phrase that comes over and over again. Buddhists have something like that with thousands and thousands of reincarnations, and making good is realizing what they are. Like the problem with Nixon was not, Was he a baddie and should be punished? But the main thing was, How many reincarnations would there have to be before Nixon would realize what he was?—which he showed no sign of a possibility of realizing. And if he isn't realizing what he is, if you burn him up or do anything to him, you haven't done anything.

RK: Let's go back to the problem of the written law. The Talmudic insistence is: Let's write it down and return to it, and if it needs to be reinterpreted, so be it, but let's not forsake the law, because if we do that, all hell will break loose.

RD: I wonder if I think exactly that. In relation to the poem, I return to the tradition of the poem. And yet it's a very personal recognition of what I think are poems among after all masses of poems, some of which lead to very different things. What if I picked up [John] Dryden or something? I would have ended up like W. H. Auden.

The law we spoke of first is not written down, and is not, in fact, spoken, because it is not known. But it is immediately felt if you start wrestling with it. Your experience of the law is wrestling with it, or else it isn't there. That's what I mean by the syntax. Such writing is wrestling with its own structure, so it's felt throughout, and that structure is not only a structure of the way language culture itself builds a sentence, but in pun, of course, the sentence is the sentence at the end of the law. When you finish the sentence, that is the sentence, and not some other one. You don't rewrite it. Then you have to undergo it and find out what are its consequences, because it's already been conceived in this wrestling with the law. Yet if you think about my poetry, we are speaking of those times that are invaluable in which I wrestled with the very line you're reading, but most of the time I'm not wrestling with the line at all; I'm riding the wave of it and a whole series of other things that are nonwrestling. But neither did Jacob after all do any more wrestling than with the angel.

RK: You're wrestling with it when you are writing the "Structures of Rime"?

RD: Well, I was trying to confront it in the "Structures of Rime." "Structures of Rime" are a recognition that rimes were present throughout. It's really a doctrine of correspondences I was in, so that not only does "The Structure of Rime" address sound rimes, which we're used to thinking of as rimes, but it addresses metaphors as kinds of rime, and it addresses beings in one world and beings in another world as rimes.

RK: As above, below...

RD: In fact, that gives us another key as to why riming is serious. And that means a designed or lawfully structured reality, but still not teleological. It sounds impossible for it not to be, but while simultaneously it has pattern and so forth, chronology remains and that's a wrestle between both of them, because if there's a teleology, the end is present; then I'm just next door with Eliot, "My end is my beginning" and so forth, because the end is beyond. The law is always present, so you are never breaking it. What happens when you break a law is you prove *that* was not the law. Science is quite right. Once you find a law that unites, you can't go back on it. You look for new things that can't be included in that law, and then the imagination comes to higher laws and they all unite by the time they get there.

RK: These terms in your poetry, of, on the one hand, "obedience," and on the other hand, "need" or "permission," go back and forth, because you assert that one must be obedient, but obviously "obedient" to a law that is not preordained but occurs even in the act of breaking the preordained law.

RD: That is only experienced in this wrestling or this breaking...

RK: You get very close to Sabbatai Zevi or Jacob Frank. [*These were false messiahs whose followers practiced deliberate violations of Jewish law in order to hasten the time of redemption.]*

RD: Sure.

RK: They deliberately violate the laws in order to bring on the Messiah. By the way, Reform Judaism, some scholars think, came from the disillusioned followers of Jacob Frank in Germany, who then said, We'll loosen the law. Of course, you have your own term of "loosening" in the poetry.

RD: Loosening the binds all the way through. But these are parallels. In all of these, the one thing that's clear is that Judaism gave me a purer case than Christianity.

RK: Purer case of what?

RD: Purer case of a completely closed system that presents its predicament. And then the important thing to me, much more restrictive peoples than I see the Jews at being, are the Santo Domingo Indians, where their entire religion is only the valley they're in. And yet my thrill when I saw they were still dancing. I said, "Gee, if they can still dance we can still write poetry." There's a kind of stubbornness.

Because the other thing I highly value is the individuation. That's what Jacob wrestling is, the individuation. But even the hatred: I've got Jacob not only hating Esau, but I've got Blake hating Rubens, where again hatred struck me; and while it's a mark of the fanaticism and shocking as it comes, it still is an ultimate self-isolating gesture of "I will be this and not that." Not like he, I am not his kind.

RK: Yet I see in your poetry that you contest the idea of chosenness and exclusivity. In "Before the Judgment" you write, "The Jews use the term *Israel* / you use the name *America* or the name *Man,* as if for a chosen tribe."

RD: The species . . .

RK: "As if for a nation, or for one animal species the Grand Design labord." Obviously we get here an objection to Judaism in its exclusivity.
. . .

RD: And the larger one to anthropomorphism in general and nationalism. That's in the word of our suddenly discovering that the one thing we all are is the DNA and there's not a life-form that isn't the DNA, so all the time all those other divisions that have been felt, fought, are wrong.

RK: Many poets today simply turn their back on the law.

RD: Writing as if there were no question of the law.

RK: As if there is no law, no difference between prose and poetry.

RD: And still it's a pluralistic universe, so that takes place. In this of course, it's no wonder that the Jew fascinates me, because at its most discourteous you feel that the others are all wrong and they just become "the others." In order to intensify your—and let's say—drive deep what it is you are doing in an art, you do a series of things that are the same [as the Jews]. You divide yourself off from others because you cease to read in the same way. My readings in poetry are exceedingly fanatical. If I put on a tolerant mood, that's because I cease to wrestle with what I'm reading; I don't do it at all; I just allow its existence. And that's not the same at all as suffering its existence. Because now we are talking about those poems that we experience as lawless, as doing anything, as coming from an entirely different world-feeling. . . . Allen Ginsberg is Allen Ginsberg by how very little indeed he is anything like Robert Duncan.

RK: So he's still wrestling with you?

RD: He doesn't have to wrestle with me. I wasn't on site. He didn't design the thing to wrestle with me. And if we think of some of the terms that come in the Old Testament like "abomination" and so forth, that's how I experienced a good deal of Allen Ginsberg; but when I said I wasn't central, I wasn't Jehovah so I didn't have, let's say, the strength of my abominations. The abomination means: I will not be like this. They should be expressed, because they should be out there where you see them at times, once in a while decently, or else we'll all be little hypocrites. The cost of the abominations when they're expressed is that it becomes clearer and clearer how infinitesimal we are with equal powers. There's no doubt that Allen Ginsberg is as intensely Allen

Ginsberg as I am me, and this is what I see as the one thing each poet has to do. The uniqueness is the poet has only himself to be. He can't borrow models, because the cues are in his own life. His attentions have to be on everything in his own experience. And that's the same kind of attention: You have only one way to be a Jew, and that is the way you have to be a Jew. As a matter of fact, if you start trying to go back and convert to a Hasidic hairdo, that's a costume, and it has something of the same weird—I don't know where it puts you but many a poet has done it too. Everson *[Poet William Everson, a contemporary of Duncan's. He wrote also under the name Brother Antoninus.]* with his Walt Whitman hair and beard and so forth is living that way. Now that's an intensification and at the same time a terrific separation of himself from the people around him. It's sort of the hermit direction of it.

RK: In talking about Allen Ginsberg, it seems he's tried everything but Judaism.

RD: I think Allen Ginsberg is avoiding Judaism and like Gary Snyder is ignorant of the Judeo-Christian tradition, ignoring in the French sense. Buddhism is his rescue, and he has scorn for other religions; it's superior to other religions. My parents' post-Blavatskian Hermeticism has a new influx of influence from Buddhism, yet I myself avoid Buddhism and dislike it, perhaps because of its redundancies.

RK: What do you mean by redundancies?

RD: Well, because after all I've struggled to turn my own thought into feeling and if there are too many congratulatory messages coming through . . . I feel . . . this is the nonwrestled-with above-and-beyond. The kind that comes in pieties. Pieties are the worst things of all. That was the trouble with the *Zohar* that Marc Lieberman brought me—that it was a whole series of pieties, and Buddhist books are miles of pieties. *[Duncan refers to a recent translation of portions of the* Zohar, *by Daniel Matt, published by the Paulist Press.]* It's hard to find experience within it.

RK: The pieties are after the wrestling's over and the sheets have been smoothed over.

RD: I don't know exactly when the pieties come along. The pieties may have been why the wrestling took place in the first place.

RK: To disrupt them?

RD: An angel would lose his temper with some of these pieties going on.

RK: I am interested in your phrase "symposium of the whole," used as a title for the recent Jerome Rothenberg anthology. It seems to suggest that the poet seeks knowledge of the whole, to put the whole into his work. Whereas everyone else becomes a specialist.

RD: I'd certainly hold that up. But, it would be something worse than arrogance, and a good deal of foolishness, to talk about the knowledge of the whole. "Who acknowledges the whole" is very different. The knowledge that it's there. Science's proposition of law is to me the most satisfactory, and that is, if there's a fact that won't fit, the thing you've been calling the law is not the law. You must arrive at another one, but you can't just make it up. And yet in the phenomenon of it they have frequently posed laws entirely from the world of mind that suddenly their facts fit, and new facts didn't, for some time, contradict. But they're never in possession of the law. *So,* in [A. N.] Whitehead's *Process and Reality* we think in propositions. In Dante, it's at the same level—we haven't had many at that level—[*he*] says the proper intelligence is potential, and speculative. It isn't there yet; you inhabit its potentiality, and it is speculative of what it might be. We still don't know what it is.

RK: So you can't make a mistake in poetry, because then the mistake has to be examined to see if it's a violation or a recognition of a new law.

RD: Right, that's very much there, but I strongly got that out of Freud. That, what is language? Language is never a mistake—your wanting it to be a mistake is covering up the thing you're about to say. And the real concern in the writing is not what you mean but what *it* means, so you work with it. That, in my poetry, there is no concept of correction, because the so-called mistake belongs to the poem and not to me.

RK: Aren't we caught in a paradox, where we write poetry to acknowledge the whole, but it's not read by the whole, but by the fraction who are interested in poetry?

RD: Oh, you're thinking of the whole people, but I'm not. This is again, at the change counter; you are not justifying to the customer and you're not justifying yourself to yourself, nor are you justifying yourself to God; you're practicing justice.

RK: So, you do it whether someone is going to read it or not?

RD: Right, you practice justice in the line. That's where the art is. The art is doing, and the concept of the whole doesn't make the poem better than if I had a concept of the half or a concept of multi-universes. There are points where I've entertained multi-universes; however, they aren't that imperative to me.

So we have another little case in our grammar of the imperative. The imperative is felt as such in the poem, and that's part of what's obeyed. Sometimes we understand what's back of the imperative; we feel this case of working with what comes, right away grabbing the attention. I was revolted when "Mao's mountain of murdered men" came ["Passages 26: The Soldiers," in *Bending the Bow*]—the alliteration of m's like, okay, that immediate consciousness of bringing it right forward so the reader's in it, too—of what's there, not of what I meant. In some ways it doesn't have to do with what I think. The poem is constantly extending and making various the things that I can think.

Another thing that would have me explore or be fascinated by the Jewish tradition began with Scholem's book. It comes during the time I'm writing *Letters*. It's that history for the Jews is a text of God's intentions. There's nothing that happens in history that is not significant, and that is the way I read history, too. I don't read it with the same set of significances though. And, through that, one sees themes moving—there's also thematic coherence. But I keep trying to break it, because the themes are the past. The themes and the significances are the past. Olson wanted to do away with the word "history." I had no trouble with it, because I didn't think of it as covering everything there was.

RK: You have a concept of circulation so that . . .

RD: It comes around again. That's the deeper. You always discover when you think you're about to die, that's when you know what your religion is. You haven't got anything else to think about at a moment like that. Reincarnation—not reincarnation of personality—I haven't even bothered to try and figure out am I still the "young Robert Duncan." [*At the time of our interview, Ekbert Faas's biography,* Young Robert Duncan, *had just appeared.*] I can hand that one away already. I think the spirit, at the present time at least, I think the spirit is what's "in" work and consequent [*of its*] also being mortal. It can be destroyed. A book can be burned and a clay tablet broken.

Sagetrieb Interview
(with Michael André Bernstein and Burton Hatlen, 1985)

This comprehensive discussion with Professor Michael André Bern-
stein and the late poet and teacher Burton Hatlen appeared in the Fall
and Winter 1985 issue of Sagetrieb, *a journal devoted to poets in the*
Pound-H.D.-Williams tradition. Here Duncan restates in a fresh way
some of what he has elaborated on in previous interviews. He throws
new light on his reading of Pound's Cantos, *Gertrude Stein, Milton,*
Freud, H.D., Hart Crane, and Homer. He also gives his view of English
department reading lists, the elements of line, enjambment, dream, and
humor in poetry, and his character as a humanist poet. His own delight-
ful humor is apparent throughout.

—Ed.

Michael André Bernstein and I interviewed Robert Duncan on his sixty-sixth
birthday, January 7, 1985. Duncan's face clearly revealed the effects of the
severe kidney collapse which he had experienced in 1984. Yet when he began
to talk, his voice soared as freely as ever, for a full three hours. What follows is
a virtually complete transcription of that three hours of talk: I have edited out
some hesitations and repetitions, and I have rearranged a few sentences for clar-
ity. Otherwise, it is all here. In the text of the interview, the three participants
are identified as BH (Burton Hatlen), MB (Michael André Bernstein), and RD
(Robert Duncan).

—Burton Hatlen

MICHAEL BERNSTEIN: You've done interviews before.

BURTON HATLEN: I have, but I'm not sure how to do this one.

ROBERT DUNCAN: Did you have an idea where you wanted to go?

BH: Well, we were talking earlier about your sense of your relationship
to other poets of the twentieth century.

RD: Yes, and I think that in the framework of *Sagetrieb,* I have some grave questions about some of the presuppositions of *Sagetrieb.* The force of my objections to the proposition of *Sagetrieb* is the woolly wide definition of the followers of Pound and Williams. There are patterns in which you went astray. One is, typically, that very few people have looked into why—and yet the correspondence would tell it right away—all of us left *Origin* within the first series and then were never interested again for other than a performance interest. By the second series, [Cid] Corman had been powerfully rejected by [Charles] Olson, read off completely. Then Olson asked me to be in *Origin,* this new magazine he was starting. I waited until issue number 4, and yet I was certainly tempted, because there was everybody that I wanted to be in a book with, and we all were waiting for something in which we could be together, and there was Olson and Denise Levertov and Larry Eigner and [Robert] Creeley, who all meant a lot to me. And it meant a lot to me, for instance, when I went to Majorca, to get across to Creeley the existence of [Louis] Zukofsky. But before Corman hit Zukofsky, he proposed that Williams was more important. This is all a very distorted picture, because all of us as a matter of fact were overwhelmed by Williams's later work. But Corman's was a view of Williams that would not understand how important the D. H. Lawrence / Williams combination is, and if there was anything in which Creeley and Denise Levertov and Olson and I all concurred it was in this conjunction of Williams and Lawrence. With the proviso that Olson wanted *Maximus* to supplant *Paterson* and supplant *The Cantos,* so he had already a good percent of arguments against Pound and Williams going on. But in Corman it was a simple this-was-a-poem-about-plums Williams—and this is not the way I read my Williams. There's nothing like two people reading the same poem with entirely different worlds coming up to it. But the issue came out featuring my work but also with "The Desert Music" in it—imagine finding a combination like that.

The first group that were in *Origin* were poems that had been written before I really sat myself down to realign my own poetry, so they were very curious in relation to being *new* in the sense that Olson was or Creeley. But I thought, well, I've got to get these poems printed. I think I've always made choices about my identity preceding the part that people are interested in. I mean, when Creeley was going to do a book in Majorca and I decided I'd go ahead with *Caesar's Gate* though it was 1949 [poetry], and I was very embarrassed and suspicious of the emotional tone of a lot of those poems and particularly in the long poem, and yet I went ahead, and I've always been glad that I did, but it got considerably edited, but edited not by things being taken out but by things being added to it, by the collagist method. The collagist method is not to correct but to refocus, and that's a great misunderstanding about the collage. The collage world keeps all its references and doesn't improve anywhere, but it knows that if you get a finer construction, more details—*then* you've got something. Because the imagination is leaping to find something that holds all that together. Correcting is to surrender to an earlier picture in which things hold together, by eliminating new things that were impossible.

MB: How central was the concept of the collage method to you before you met Jess?

RD: All this is post-Jess. 1951 is when we . . . this is our thirty-fifth year . . . our anniversary is the first of the year, so it is very easy to remember.

MB: But were you interested in collage before then?

RD: Oh yes, I was. Certainly the collage method is how I saw Pound. Well, when I say "certainly," I think Pound didn't see himself using the collage method. There is a good deal of the reincarnation method in *The Cantos.* Collage is not reincarnation: it is the fact that everything is in the universe, so you know that way out beyond your understanding of it everything has a harmony and I don't think that is something Pound ever . . . nor do I, either, surely none of us do, have a full picture at the present time. Well, that essay of mine on "Man's Fulfillment in Order and Strife," it just opens up that I have to do another essay on war, because war is not a simple big thing, so you've got phony wars, wars like art, etc., so that the word doesn't tell us anything about what our more intense feelings are. Well, there are intense feelings in that period. Denise for one and Corman had quite a lot of rejection, real rejection, because as a personality, well, he was obtuse. And at the point when he did that *H.D. Book* section we had not corresponded at all, and he was here in San Francisco two or three weeks on his way to Japan. And he said could he have something from *The H.D. Book,* and I realized he was also saying, "Are you speaking to me or do you really hate me?" and so I said, "Why don't you take the whole thing and take what interests you and make it selective?" Of course, everybody thought I'd selected the selections but it was as a matter of fact what interested him. He had the whole manuscript done at that time—the first draft, of course, but substantially it was the same draft we were dealing with. Also I wanted to find out what he would do, because that book is *always* in a territory that Corman himself had disallowed. When he came to Don Allen's anthology, now we're the other side of that. . . . Corman was the one person who was asked to contribute to Don Allen's anthology who said, no, he didn't belong. And as a matter of fact, he was quite right. Because really *Origin* had redirected itself and didn't want to get in contact with the movement again, because the movement had not been in Corman's hands. There's a lot of that entrepreneur in Corman. The same thing is true of Jonathan Williams, who felt he owned us all, and so when we began to be known it was as if we had cheated on him. He liked his lonely solitaries who were not appreciated.

BH: You don't feel that way about Don Allen?

RD: Well, Don Allen never even had a pretense. . . . But Don Allen's anthology when it came out was a great surprise to us, because I didn't know anything of the New York school; that was the first place I'd ever read them. It wasn't followers of Pound and Williams, which is how I would have seen it with my own anomaly of H.D. The picture is always more complex with me. And I think Lawrence is a hidden integer in there, the estimate of Lawrence. But Don Allen just had a sense of what was going on in the scene. It was done by correspondence with the various poets who were active, and he did get almost everybody. [Gael] Turnbull was one of the main ones that interested me and still does, but he was Canadian and then English so he was not included. Anyway, Don was not interested at all in Turnbull's work. Then the other one I lay claim to over and over again is that Don wouldn't put Larry

Eigner in, he couldn't see anything in it, and I made a simple blackmail proposition: I said he could print me if he printed Eigner and otherwise no. Or else he would have brought out that anthology without Eigner, which is unbelievable. Which shows how much that anthology had to do with sociability.

BH: So for you a key distinction is the question of the image and the sense of the image. And a purely descriptive sense of the image is what you're sensing in Corman.

RD: Yes, that's it, and in that I find a fault. Let's say we've got a photographic level, which is always very important, but I think that photographic level leads to other levels of the spirit. In Corman's place there's an exclusion, there's a commonsensicalness, and that by the way led him to read Zukofsky in a reductive manner. And I always found his comments on poetics baffling. Yet on the other hand the second series still had things that interested me, like Jonathan Greene. Young people who were not taken care of in any way in Don Allen's anthology and who write extremely well. Corman's often had an eye for that, but he's also had an eye for lots of dullards who write extremely well.

MB: What's fascinating in those anthologies, and one of the things that struck me so greatly when I read your work, is how you don't operate by negative lists and exclusions. . . .

RD: I've got them all right. That's why I started there. It shows that there were very strong negations and made not by Corman toward us but by us. An "us" appeared. It was almost as if we were in concert to drop *Origin,* and that was the proposition that you have to have *Black Mountain Review.* Now that didn't mean that I had carte blanche to publish anything at all. The difference between the two was that every single thing I ever sent Corman went into print. In the case of Creeley I'd send him fifty poems . . . that was a very productive period, and I think he found uh . . . one for four issues. But you know that *Black Mountain Review* was not presenting the "best writing" or something; it was a collage, suddenly it was a magazine composed like a collage.

414

MB: But you know what I keep thinking of, when I read Olson's prose or Pound's prose . . .

RD: Both of them were very annoying indeed. I'm teaching the poetics of Pound and Williams this coming term, and having been through every page of *Pound on Music*, I keep thinking that on every level he's got aesthetics that are just as shoddy as the politics. Now for instance where he strikes, like the [George] Antheil, I'm very glad indeed he did, because I don't think anybody would have resurrected Antheil. Antheil became converted to the Stalinist line of music and is a third-class [Sergei] Prokofiev in his last period, but the early music was interesting, and Pound's music is even more interesting. The violin sonatas I think are beautiful. But along with that, the thing that makes *The Cantos* so impressive is that the feel of the line is absolute and firm and cut with an edge with no compromise. And meanwhile in contrast here I am. When I sent *Heavenly City, Earthly City* to Pound, he wrote back and said, "Why do you still have to go through that? I thought I went through all that, and you would never have to do it." And yet in my talks with Pound, the one thing I wanted to test him on . . . I knew that he had rejected *Finnegans Wake* with disgust, absolute disgust, and I knew why but I wanted to ferret it out. Because where Pound has an uncompromising line, I have a constantly compromised line and finally break syntax so that there's not even a commitment to syntax, and that means every phrase can be compromised by the coexistence of other phrases. In *The Cantos* it's so extreme that Pound really doesn't remember what's going on in that poem. In response to "The Venice Poem," he had said, "You should have had a plan." Well, a plan, a preplan—that's the only alternative if you can't remember what's going on in the poem. Because it's always going on there in the poem and I find a preplan—since I don't believe that a preplan does more than alleviate your judgment or something—I find it would present the same problem. Because now that you've made that line, hasn't it changed everything around it? And in Pound by forcing those lines . . . that's what made for a collage, the shock of the collage.

Remember when the collage starts in *The Cantos*, it doesn't mean a shift from line to line, but it means you might go for five cantos of slowly moving Chinese chronicles. This is a purely aesthetic choice. "I needed to go this sluggish; through this whole thing, it's got to go as slow as Chinese history goes." And then, there's a mimesis which the poem imitates all the time. And you're caught in the imitative if you're not working with what happens as material. So if we go back to description, *if* the wheelbarrow is just descriptive (but it isn't in its movement from line to line), if its interest is only descriptive, take another look at it, the wheelbarrow came forward and the chickens got dropped, and the rain is sort of thrown away—all of the things there are what so much depends on, but more than that, the poem was in a long poem, an articulated long poem, so we know it coexists and so did Williams coexist with the parts of that long poem; that's what was astounding about *Spring and All,* and *The Descent of Winter.* I mean, no one was prepared for that.... It did not have a preplan or only the roughest of all preplans. In *Paterson,* where he did have a preplan, the plan itself suffers from having been lifted from *Finnegans Wake. Finnegans Wake* doesn't suffer, 'cause Joyce never imagined anything that wasn't preplanned. You fill in the plot after you've got the plot all going. And the plan of *Finnegans Wake* is very simpleminded. Williams was fascinated by *Finnegan,* mainly because it stood for the breakdown of language, but we find out that he got steeped in this idea that *Paterson* was going to have the same format that *Finnegan* had.... Both the river and the hill and the time format of summer, spring, and old age and so forth—that classical four ages, and then you illustrate within it.

And my response to Pound was that it had too much plan, I mean "The Venice Poem," because I had really divided it up; I had divided it up into three movements, and each of them into two, and had a work of art for each one and had certain centers like the appearance of Venus for instance, the whole section is dominated by that, by themes of bad women for instance. So that's exactly what you do when you do a plan; the whole thing illustrates itself continuously. In Williams's case everything appears as an epiphany to him. That's where we have our tie to Williams. This is the non-Corman Williams. Williams is not a camera; things came to him, so the poems are always mystical. It's impossible to explain why they have this numinous quality. Williams is very much like [Marcel]

416

Duchamp. He realized that as a matter of fact the crucial experience in art is coming upon something, which is why the preplanned won't do at all. Coming upon something *is* a mystical experience and is not the same as a camera. And yet, there are moments in which the camera comes upon something, like the Wallace Berman photographs; they're surely wonderful. So the photographers recognize that they can come upon something, and for Williams things were coming to him that way, and yet when he came to *Paterson,* because he thought of it as being a big poem, and the question was still there about writing a great or a big poem, he organized it and I think that a lot of it suffered. Once he was done, though, that was his chore, he was suddenly relieved of everything.

Breakthroughs, there are major breakthroughs in *Paterson,* and for all the rest of us. When the first volume of *Paterson* came out, for two years it was only Robin Blaser and myself and Jack Spicer who were reading *Paterson* at all. We had been terrifically excited about the book coming out, and the Campus Bookshop was the only one that stocked *Paterson,* and it stocked five copies and we consumed them, but no one on the English faculty at all bought it. We had some debates that were very interesting in that period about whether the *Four Quartets* or *Paterson* were . . . This is a bore, really. Only now have I returned to reading Eliot with something like pleasure, because there were these simply awful bullying sessions in which we were challenged to show that *Paterson* was important. And of course you cheated on *Paterson,* talking about it as being on the same order as the *Four Quartets.* [*laughs*] And the same thing in Pound. I always took it that there were mysterious reasons at work, beyond the poet's recognitions, that would lead to his bogging down in economics and so forth. That there must be hidden metaphor. But now I keep wondering because when I was briefly reading Adams, I read through the Adams/Jefferson letters and I realized that, goodness, Pound went into a gold mine and came up with all the chunks of nongold, came up with the few little bits of fool's gold that were around.

BH: Would it be correct to say that you see both *Paterson* and *The Cantos* as succeeding in spite of the plan? Or that something in the poetry subverts the plan?

RD: Well, it's a different question. In the case of *The Cantos*, the poem starts out...Well, let's say my reading starts out, and my reading started out when I was seventeen in 1936, and I started with *The Cantos*, as a matter of fact with the first line of *The Cantos*, "And then went down to the ship," and it was too overbearing. I was overwhelmed. It was like the first page of *The Waves* by Virginia Woolf. I thought, "Oh, God, I'll never recover from this." And I sort of knew, faithfully, I was not going to recover. I understood the poem as cohering and even promising all of its possible readings from a Theosophical background...and a lot of that is in that poem, 'cause Yeats had certainly brainwashed Pound. And elements stayed all the way through *The Cantos*. The Neoplatonism is not philosophical but theophanic at the end of *The Cantos*, too. There were two things that were very close to the tradition I had come from— one was belief in reincarnation and...oh, three, because the poem started out proposing it was a séance. It took me a long time, not until I gave the lectures on Browning's *Sordello*, that I realized there hadn't been anything written yet on the presence of Sordello at the beginning of that poem. *Sordello* would be a very good example of a poem without a plan. It doesn't have to conform to anything, and it doesn't have to carry out a project.... Pound is in despair because he didn't carry out a project, or he failed in the carrying out of the project. And Williams is carrying out a project in *Paterson*, and then with great relief, after having said "The End," and having as neat an illustration at the end as you could have, he found he was there with a fifth book, and as a matter of fact that he was going to have unicorns in it, and various things that were not in the original project. So he was freed of the project; the fifth book of *Paterson* frees him from the project. But he's also free in those long poems at the end.

One thing I do know is that Williams's language had become by *The Desert Music* so immediate that I couldn't make a literary judgment of it. It surpassed like passages of Wordsworth the business of making sense.... Pound always leaves you with the feeling that he has secured something aesthetic, and Williams is too human. I mean, there is a certain inbuilt antagonism...Now we see in the extreme right the rejection of humanism, and although in Renaissance studies we had a picture of what humanism was doing, and how profound its transformation was, it still has been derooted, because not only are the humanities under attack, but the humanities themselves have no courage, because they don't come from that; they come from people who are in a thing called humanities, and thinking about their salaries, ha ha ha. Like liberalism. Both of those lost a lot of their meaning. But the *humanitas* is very strong in Williams. In Pound aesthetics takes the place of *humanitas*. When we're called upon to make aesthetic judgment, when we feel the aesthetic judgment, that usually seems to me to disallow *humanitas*. Humanism presented problems for the aesthetic. And Pound's abhorrence of the Renaissance is, I think, the actual abhorrence of humanism, but he never saw where he was; he skipped the sixteenth, seventeenth, eighteenth centuries. In many things, he's very much a person of the Enlightenment. My lines really mean a compromise all the way through, and the Renaissance is a compromise. When you read Blake ranting against the Renaissance, and Pound ranting against the Renaissance, for them chiaroscuro is a kind of blasphemy, and "drawing the line" is what you're doing when you're writing a line. Now my line was being built up from Williams, largely, but from Eigner too—he was a major influence on the line of "Passages," because he was producing poems in which each line had a different margin, and that meant that he had one-line stanzas which suddenly made lines move in an entirely different way. Whereas in Williams the lines are grouped in these little tercets, and if that's kept invariably, as if it were a plan, then you do get a lack of decisions made within the poem, of being right at the point of decision. But we all do this, I mean, I've got individual forms that I ride. . . .

MB: But, your line is more tolerant of polyphony. . . .

RD: Oh, not only tolerant but open to . . . absolutely; it's a line with increased vulnerability, and my complicated syntax comes from an overarticulation, an overcoding of the syntax, not from a nonsyntactical method.

MB: Pound is so rarely willing to violate his sense of the autonomy of the line. Even enjambment—he dreads that. . . .

RD: But I think there are poets by temperament who enjamb and poets who . . . Creeley enjambs and Olson doesn't, Ginsberg doesn't enjamb, Pound doesn't enjamb; I love the list of them. [Alexander] Pope doesn't enjamb. Shakespeare, he enjambs all the time, and [Ben] Jonson doesn't enjamb, and Jonson really isn't so hot about writing song lyrics. But enjambing means things coexist, and it means also you have to hear all the echoes, and listen for the resonances. Oh, just look at Pound's and Eliot's (Eliot's another one who doesn't enjamb) approach to the French—they really can't possibly be reading Baudelaire, because Baudelaire enjambs all the time, and more than that, he has an absolute field of rhymes that are going on; he's the peak of that in French.

BH: A name you didn't mention—and I'm curious, really, where you would put him here—is Milton.

RD: Well, last summer [at New College] we read through *Paradise Lost*, and we had a sort of a seminar, it wasn't a class, but we met together and read together, and that would be a poem that absolutely gets dropped out of its poetry because of its plan. Its purpose is stated in its opening passages, and the purpose is a bore, and becomes increasingly a bore. Yet *Paterson* came dangerously near that: if the woman's a river, and the man's a mountain, and he's got woman and man here, we're almost right down to Adam and Eve, like they are without any depth at all. Pound's more distanced; you see these figures at least as figures, and the puzzles are at a different level. But in Milton there are glorious passages, and you can't deracinate the passages, because they almost come from the fact that this poet has to burst out of this self-enforced theological scheme— the theology is not coherent, the theology is not the poetics; and this is something that I think maybe happens in the Baroque, that part of the strangeness of Baroque architecture and everything is that it's inhabiting now an iconography that it is destroying as it inhabits it, because the space no longer means anything. But the space is not meaningless in the Baroque; it's a new space that bursts out, and truly looks monstrous. Milton's the nearest to the development of a Baroque in English. Shakespeare shows it could have gone much further. But when you've made a choice, when you've chosen sides already . . . I think *The Shakespearean Moment* tells us a lot about that, by [Patrick] Cruttwell.... The formulation that he got that I thought was quite keen was that for Donne and Shakespeare the paradox charged them with energy and so the tension was what they could work with. Well, in Milton the decision had already been made that broke that tension, and consequently we've got lots of perfunctory jobs carried out: "I have to paraphrase the Bible"—of all things to be doing. And it's disheartening at the last; we weren't wrong about that when we were kids. And yet it's striking... the problems of a poet who has got the powers that Milton has, that are absolutely impressive, and hasn't found the architecture. The poem got misled on its architecture, I think in part because it's still inhabiting the architecture of a masque; it's most understandable as Jonson's masques become Puritan theology, and Jonson himself would have found that abhorrent. But Milton is theatrical, at the same time wearing Puritan britches that disapproved of the theater.

BH: The link I was trying to make was to enjambment.

RD: Oh, enjambing, yes, well, Milton enjambs, and as a matter of fact truly enjambs, because there are places where the meaning shifts and changes because of the interrelation of lines. It still won't redeem what happens in the perfunctory carrying out of the plot, but I learned a lot of rhyme in the very early years from Milton's ode on the Nativity, and I was sure that Milton learned his rhymes doing that poem, and it was useful to find a poet who was that strong; I guess I wouldn't then have recognized in Shakespeare ... certainly the deeper affinities lay there in Shakespeare when I came to find them, but Milton was juvenile enough in that poem to be just ...

MB: The thing that got me interested was what you were saying about the willingness to have different voices and the line and ...

RD: That's what I thought was there in Pound, you're right.

MB: But it seems that the other thing that was linked with it was not just an openness to different voices, different lines, different forces running through, but there's no self-protection, there's no fear of embarrassment, whereas Pound is always trying to cover...

RD: I think this is true. Eliot delighted in voices after all, and *The Waste Land* is partly voices, and still it's a poem of considerable personal depth, so that we are aware that Eliot was aware that that poem was a psychic struggle. In 1936, reading Freud had as much to do with my world as reading Pound, and out of Freud—I loved [him], since I had got not one of the cleanest minds in the world, and I loved the fact Freud made for lots of impish observations—but I started out with Eros and Thanatos; I didn't start out with *The Interpretation of Dreams.* So the great invitation of Freud was the sense of multi-layeredness. And the other one was that there was an interchange, so that the world that we thought of as objective was a picture of ourselves, and at the same time our selves were mirroring the world. We knew the world because we were the mirror of the world. You think of the "African Elegy," where my jealousy appeared as Othello, but then he is "I, I, I." There was almost an agony of realization that what was in my poetry was always going to be like what was in my dreams, right along with Emerson's—you know, "You'll never see anything more dreadful in your dreams than yourselves"—that's the opening of Emerson's essay on dreams. So dream in poetry was still a line of thought that seems to me fruitful, but in the very beginning there was lots of puzzling out about how close were dream and poetry. In *The Interpretation of Dreams,* in chapter six, when Freud comes upon the idea of where the dream originates, you find out that he thinks he's found the origin of poetry; as a matter of fact, he isn't even talking about the origin of dreams. He says, "Ah, but I started on the origin of dreams and I found the origin of poetry." And then you get the description of the displacement and so on, and all of those would be memorized over and over again. The years 1936 and '37 were the years of my finding a basis for psychology in William James's two volumes on psychology, and in beginning to read Freud. Then on the other hand, the cheery nature of the Freudians's quirky thought carried me into their curious world. It was not the same as Freud himself, who was much deeper. But Melanie Klein in her description of children as formed by ideas of language . . . Yet it didn't make the Freudian level. The Freudian level is the opposite of Freudian reductionism. I had a sort of a Freudian projectivism. And Olson read *Maximus* as a psychic revelation. That's what Pound wouldn't accept, that *The Cantos* are a psychic revelation; he didn't want to deal with the psyche at all, and it is striking how he turns away from it at any place he comes in contact with it; he immediately has real difficulties.

MB: It's censored out . . .

RD: No, it's censored out, it's censored in, or something, because it isn't incidental that by the time he's screaming "Kike" in that poem, the Jews are Marx and Freud. Because it's perfectly conceivable to me to press a button on five million people. I mean, I feel like Gertrude Stein on that point; she's not interested. But what's not conceivable to me at all is to try to have a mind in the twentieth century without encountering Freud or Marx.

MB: Olson's choice of Jung always seemed most curious, his ill-ease with Freud.

RD: Well, I think to a good degree the Jung came at a time when he could be receptive, and he faced Freudians in a period when he couldn't be. I think that he would have experienced Freud as reductionist. Olson, after all, wanted to be Maximus. One thing I don't need to do is go cultivate big dreams.

BH: You mentioned Gertrude Stein, and I wanted to pick up on that.

RD: Yes, that also was my freshman year [at UC]. I was on the staff of the *Occident,* a freshman on the staff of the *Occident.* I observed that everybody on the staff would vote "no" on something and I would vote "yes," and then if I voted "no," everybody would vote "yes," so I thought, "Gee, at least the score seems to be 100 percent." And a poem came in that delighted me. I was utterly unsophisticated about modern poetry. I wasn't aware of what lay out there. Especially territories like Stein and Sitwell dropped in completely out of the blue. I asked if I could return this manuscript to the author, and then I left a note at the International House, saying that I would like to meet her—this was Louise Antoinette Krause. So she said, "Come to tea," and it was just exactly that formal. It was Robert [Bartlett] Haas and Louise Antoinette, and as we descended from I-House down Bancroft, he said—he was sort of her lapdog—he said, "Should he read Eliot?" and she said, "No, he's too lurid already; he should read Pound." And that's what sent me rushing to the bookstore, to open *XXX Cantos* and see the first line and know it was unbearable. Robert Haas was doing his PhD at Cal, on Stein, and was in correspondence with Gertrude Stein. So one afternoon he played me the records of Gertrude Stein reading, and loaded me with Stein to read, and my immediate response was to start writing in a Steinian manner. It made it possible for me to write about being in love when it was impossible to write any other way... that's one of the first things that Stein provided. It was still so painful to me, because I could see in every direction rejections of homosexual feelings. And the letter would bypass the question of gender, so that you were really writing about the love that you felt, or your desire. Stein immediately wanted me to write to her. She wanted to eat me up. I never did write. More than that, I knew that when you wrote, she would send you everything she ever published, because, still, if anyone ever showed any interest in her work, she would send you a footlocker in those days ... with everything I mean. That's what she got her things published for, to get herself read by a little club of Stein readers, and here she knew she had a Stein reader, but not in her mitts. Well, but her mitts meant baby-talk and all sorts of things that are already there. Haas is an idiot—he's the head, but he must be retired by now, of the Extension Division at UCLA, and he still has some interest in Stein, but his mind is ... He wrote on Stein and Whitehead—not that I could understand his thesis at all. I mean, I read it at that period, but I wasn't thinking about Stein in relation to "what did it mean?"

It was a shock, years and years later when the records came out of *Four Saints in Three Acts*, to realize it was perfectly meaningful all the way through, because I'd been all through medieval studies and never listened to it that way. I had an appetite for writing to be strange. [Roman] Jakobson comments that there is a criterion in Russian poetry that a poem must be strange, that it must be bizarre and that's what the imagination produces, and it's absolutely expected. And it's something that we do not propose: we've proposed it at times and thrown it down. Poe proposes it, and the French propose it, Baudelaire especially proposes it, and yet . . . But not alienation, like [Arthur] Rimbaud says, that's just a sociological concept. I mean, STRANGE. [*chuckles*] That's what I always wanted; I wanted a magic sort of language. I read *Finnegans Wake* for a long time, and the *Skeleton Key* to *Finnegan* came out, and it was sort of horrible. The plan was not interesting. What I wanted to know is why does it still present what it does in every immediate area? The double take in *Finnegan* is that if you're in the large area the plan is perfectly clear, but when you go up to look at the detail it's got something else there, that doesn't conform. Well, in *The Cantos* it really was an adventure, pure adventure for me, and I think it was for Pound. He didn't want *that* pure an adventure; I wanted an adventure in which actually everything *did* take place, meaning it was there, and I think Pound lost track of things in *The Cantos*. The poem was longer than he could entertain. He keeps expressing his difficulties as he goes along. But he wanted a totalitarian view, and keeps announcing he's got a totalitarian view, but he doesn't have one. *The Cantos* would have been, after all, a public poem as tedious as the buildings that were made for Mussolini, if it had been an official totalitarian poem. I mean, that side of Jefferson that could be a totalitarian is there in Monticello, and, boy, that is not what any poem in our time could be. I mean, if something came up like that, you'd say, "Archibald MacLeish dropped this behavior—get to the real thing. . . ."

MB: I'm curious too about H.D.—how central for you so much of her work has been, her writing, what she means, and, in a way, her neglect or the easy way she's been read by so many people.

RD: Now we're suffering from the easy way she's read. . . . I really think we are, because it becomes too available. When I started writing on it I wondered why she wasn't available. So I should have thought about that, maybe. I mean, what would happen if it were available? I mean, that isn't what you really want, is it?

MB: Was anybody reading her when you started?

RD: Oh, it's a perfect example of how chicken everybody was. [Robert] Lowell in Washington, DC, said—I had started writing H.D. things—and he said how he greatly admired her, and I said, "Why don't you speak up? All your pals were scorning that book [*Trilogy*]." But you know, he didn't have the courage. So there were readers drawn to it. . . . Auden was drawn to it. . . . I think that was [Norman Holmes] Pearson, maybe, shoving Auden onto it. That's an interesting series, the intention in Pearson and Auden doing that anthology all the way through, and when you go back to the volume I've especially used on the sixteenth and seventeenth century, the mystery poems are all there, that's the choice they make, and so there was maybe a cult of poetry back of Pearson's speculations, but I think that it was also just his instinct and his sense of powers. But because of the tradition in my family—although by the time I was in college, I understood that these traditions didn't go back as far as the family assumed they did, I mean, the traditions themselves didn't go back that far, and they didn't go back that far in the family for sure—I still respond to poetry as if it too were, as the Hermetic world is, a series of epiphanies that are then discovered, and so a way is discovered—that is, a Blake *is* going to find a Swedenborg, *is* going to find a Paracelsus, and so on. Which is the background of our Poetics Program [at New College]. Now the redundancy in this is that you then begin to have a new set of authorities, and while at the beginning the authorities seem to expand your sense of what's possible, they also cause a kind of reading in which if the authorities aren't present you can't deal with what's present at all, you think it's not worth much.

MB: But the people you knew who were interested in your work . . .

RD: If you look at the people who are constantly interested in my work, most of them are not very constant. By the time I was at work on *Ground Work*, [Tom] Parkinson was so out of the contemporary currents that he would ask me what am I doing and not be aware that he hadn't been to any readings, that he wasn't in the poetry business; I mean, he wasn't in there in all the currents. It's important to me that I coexist with currents, some of which I despise aside from prices, but I've come to a place where I'm truly not interested in currency, so I more than understand what happens when you stop being interested in mere currency. But when I wrote "The Venice Poem," that's when Parkinson dropped me, and quite a number of my readers did. And [Jack] Spicer. I needed to have an important person drop "The Venice Poem." Spicer challenged it when it was first written, but I have letters from Spicer, within six months or so, asking *why* he had challenged it, asking *me* why he had challenged . . . and was overwhelmed by the poem as a totality, taking it already as a sort of center. And I wouldn't allow it, I wouldn't allow that Spicer could be a reader; he had to be an anti-reader. But the nonreaders are very different; they fade, they are no longer in your audiences. They have a spell of reading your poetry. And after all, John Donne's not gonna come around and haunt me because I'm not reading him this week, but we hate it as if we've got this faithful reader somewhere. By the time I was writing *Letters,* my ideal reader was that nice fat woman that sits by the stream and reads—not in the literary world at all, but reads me secretly so I don't get to know it.

MB: I'm remembering what you said at the beginning of the reading at Berkeley, just before the new year, when you said that the audience was going to be shocked because you were a thoroughly Romantic imagination . . . and that they wanted some Modernist, and that you thought Modernism was just a continuation of Romanticism, for your imagination anyway. And I remember looking around the audience, feeling distinctly uncomfortable, and not knowing exactly how to take that.

BH: But if you remove the categories, how ill at ease . . .

RD: But in the '30s—and it went on through the '40s, to the place where I soured on Josephine Miles entirely—our discussions among Miles and Parkinson and all the people who were in the English Department would be asking about whether it was a major or a minor poem. This left us with a kind of marketeering. I remember sitting in the john in somebody's apartment and picking up a collection of short stories, and finding that they were all marked B+, A−, and so forth. This is exactly the way their minds were working at that time. I mean, it was absolutely a betrayal—and Spicer and Robin Blaser and I felt it intensely—a betrayal of what a poem really was, as it was turned into "Will it be on a reading list? or should it be on a reading list?" And yet I have a very firm reading list. At one point my biographer, [Ekbert] Faas, talks about my fickleness, because I dropped Anaïs Nin and I dropped [Kenneth] Patchen . . . but I dropped them with a fury, because their writing was self-indulgent, and didn't measure up. Stein and Pound I stayed with from my adolescence, and never swerved. Williams I didn't really discover until *The Wedge*. In the superstition of Pound's having Williams so central on his list, or my own feel about this—that if I could only get this it would be very important—I was buying early Williams volumes, but not really knowing, and puzzled all the time. What is it? Part of it was not, What is it that Ezra thinks he sees? but also, What do I think I see here? But *The Wedge* opened up the terms of the metaphor, and metaphor is what I had not even imagined in *Spring and All* and in *Descent of Winter*.

BH: Do you think that the problem was that these lists you were rejecting were official lists; that is, they were institutionalized within the academy?

RD: Well, it helped a lot that in those years Stein and Pound were absolutely off the list; they were personal discoveries. Eliot and Auden both raised the question about teaching anybody who's alive, because that sort of contemporary experience should not be directed or given qualities or so forth, and the teacher should not be making decisions about that list. But it was a step too when I realized, "No, I'm not a culture hero." Pound had proposed, out of Carlyle, that there was a heroism involved in being a poet, and Eliot and Pound together made that seem to be a culture hero, especially they were going to rescue the culture. But I didn't grow up in a culture. I mean, I looked around and whatever I was in I was not worried about was it or why wasn't it a culture. I studied the Middle Ages, but it never looked like a culture to me. But culture still is an interesting term, because culture meant like in a biology class, you get a good culture, and all sorts of things can develop it. That would be a fruitful enough meaning. In the book [*Guide to*] *Kulchur,* Pound makes just such a mulch, throwing everything together to see what will happen in it. Only the man doesn't want to look at what does happen in it.

BH: Then as you were growing up in Bakersfield . . .

RD: Oh, you mean, I don't have a culture to turn to; that's quite true. That's part of Olson's bitterness at Pound, was Pound's not imagining that Olson came from an immigrant culture. Of course, I didn't come from an immigrant culture; in fact I came from the full WASP picture that Pound did, but I didn't feel that you needed more of it.

MB: There's a curious kind of tension between the imagination and the freedom that it gives and more traditional notions of "culture." I think that tension is one of the reasons a work like *Finnegans Wake* made Pound so uncomfortable.

RD: Because the work of art itself becomes a threat, about what is it going to do to culture. . . . Fiendish as Joyce is, he doesn't really write all of *Finnegans Wake* to undo a culture.

MB: But if you think how strange it is that in poems as long as some of the big Modernist ones, *The Cantos* included, how rarely they'll allow the free-play of laughter that Joyce is saturated in. . . .

RD: Well, I don't know that there's lots of free-play of laughter in my work either. Williams does have it, in *Paterson,* and a matter of fact has various places where it's got to be, and has that as an image of what the poem is, although that's not what happens finally in the poem. There's a joyousness that goes on in Williams. . . . Contrasting those two works of Milton and Joyce—both of them blind—Milton has built a cathedral that if you giggled it would collapse . . . and Joyce has built a giggle on a cathedral scale. . . .

MB: It isn't so much actual laughter, but what I find in your work is a sense of a nonfear of laughter, a welcoming of it.

RD: You mean I want to find out, will it hurt me? Or trying to dare it, I think. But I notice I never went back to *Faust Foutu,* which is the only one in which the burlesque things appear that are very important in our daily life. My students know in any three-hour lecture they've got a lot of *Faust Foutu* going on all along with everything else. And "Passages" should have allowed for any kind of voice, but it does quite the contrary; it highly censors ribald areas and so forth. At the beginning of the gay liberation readings, Thom Gunn and I were sitting there, and the new writers were reading poems that were hair-raising; and Thom said, "I feel so old-fashioned and embarrassed; I don't mention anything but love." We just belong to the shy generation. [*pause*] With Williams I think I came up against his whole phobia. Reading the biography of Williams, it seems to have been very easy to activate. In relation to Hart Crane, I was shocked at the actual malice of Williams in trying to see that Crane wasn't read, and wasn't valued. I couldn't pursue it very far, because most Crane readers aren't Williams readers, to that extent; they're just [Yvor] Winters readers.

MB: Was Crane an important figure? Because you don't talk about him.

RD: Well, in high school. [Philip] Horton's biography of Crane came out in '36, and it was the first biography of any homosexual poet, or maybe of any homosexual as such. In high school I had already read Crane, and my very first poems, which are lost, are mixtures of *The Bridge* and *The Cantos*. It wasn't so hard to do, because both of them have an underlying idea that you inhabit a mystery, that history itself is a mystery, and so the poem reveals the key things—not just lists of key poets, but lists of the key events for such people. Well, Williams will sit down and write *In the American Grain,* and he defines and projects the American grain that he will belong to. And that is definitely what Hart Crane was doing; and what drew me in at first was the emotional language in the allusive homosexual poems, because the pathos was very much like what we feel in high school. But in time I turned against *The Bridge*—not because there was a plan in *The Bridge,* because as a matter of fact there gloriously is not a plan, it's sort of a Cubist picture of a bridge—but because I can't see immediate language anywhere, because of the way Crane used words to give a strange atmosphere, without the words themselves being anything, so that when you looked at [them] you found out you didn't have anything. And I was already deciding in that period, not to have the line interesting, curious in and of itself. Again this is breaking down the idea that the line exists in and of itself. Crane would produce lines in and of themselves; he is [Christopher] Marlowe-centered, and that makes him another enjamber.

BH: Could we steer back toward your critique of *Sagetrieb*?

RD: Yeah, well, the proposition that a magazine would present the tradition of Pound and Williams and H.D. might go far, but I really have a question about some of the associates. Some don't really seem responsible in relation to Pound and Williams. . . .

BH: So in some ways you're saying that *Sagetrieb* has defined the tradition too loosely.

RD: Well, it actually could be called the tradition of Don Allen's anthology, and that's where it started being on a wobbly pivot.

BH: Do I understand you to say that you do see a coherent Pound-Williams-H.D. tradition leading directly to your work?

RD: Oh, yes, indeed, yes, and I've never experienced an incoherence there. . . .

BH: But then, it seems to me, Lawrence and Freud perhaps, on one side, and Stein on another side, are also very important to your work.

RD: Well, I think there's no need at all to pitch Lawrence and Freud against the Pound and Williams tradition—it's Williams who understands how much that goes together. And if we add—Wallace Stevens is also awfully important, but not in the line, because it's always ameliorating—that's the difficulty about Stevens—and so it's acceptable. But there's a drive in Pound and Williams and a drive again in H.D. not just toward the Modernist poem, but all three and Lawrence too—and so does Freud—believe, in the first place, in states of mind, of the divine. It's no longer supernatural; the gods are states of mind, and that's certainly where H.D. is. By talking about fictive certainties, Wallace Stevens had avoided the real question, because these were not fictive to Pound and Williams and H.D., who are all now actual heroes because they suffer in the error of their ways, but there's no possibility of an error of your way if you're a [George] Santayana philosophizing while it's going on. In the late Stevens we feel the pressure of immediacy and of experience, but it has so many answers for itself—here we're giving answers for itself, so we better not, better not dig in too deep. In my mind there is a line of affinities. . . . Rexroth always said it comes together in Yeats, and you should not pay attention to Pound, and so forth; the real place where the whole thing is is Yeats. Rexroth would have been in lots of ways a root. I've just been reading Bradford Morrow's selections from Rexroth. Rexroth pointed out the importance of my parents' Hermeticism—I could read too, I didn't have to be an initiate, and there was a series of actual books. And Rexroth pointed out [Jacob] Boehme to me, which was an absolute revelation. I mean, he had an intuition—Olson could do that too—about what would be a central book that would change the soul. If you go back to that question, that's exactly where I find mere literariness disturbing: no soul.

BH: You were talking earlier about humanism, and about Pound as an anti-humanist.

RD: Yes, and that's a flaw, to put it mildly. It's hard for a humanist to account for an outbreak like "Kike, Marx, and Freud" as anything other than as an absolutely demented state. There's no critique of Marx in Pound. In the *ABC of Economics* there's a kind of critique, but it's obviously almost impertinent. You can use Marx, let's say, or Freudianism, because both of them kind of represent "isms," but that's entirely separate from their speculations. Marx's great contribution is economic analysis, which he had a genius for, when you compare him with [Max] Weber—not until you get to Weber do you have anything like it again. Pound was not sitting around reading Marx—he was responding to the kind of Marxism that he met. In our Homer Club, we're now in book seventeen of *The Iliad*, and I'm convinced that, when Pound says, "When I read Homer," he went and read for half an hour and probably read the same passages over and over. Whereas, as I read Homer, we read him in depth all the way, the way we read through Milton. And Milton in depth does not yield anything, whereas *The Iliad* is indeed a wisdom text, it's amazing, it's a revelation at every level.

MB: I often doubt, as you said, that Pound had ever read that much Homer in the original, and I think it likely that he had read almost no Marx or Freud in any language. It was Freudian*ism* and Marx*ism* he reacted against, but I don't think he ever sat down and seriously read either man. All he'd have had to do is read a little of *The Psychopathology of Everyday Life,* and he would have found crucial elements of his own biography!

BH: Well, would you identify yourself with that word "humanism"?

RD: Yes. Olson was the first one who said I was a humanist, and can be read as a humanist, and I thought at that time, "Wow." And in reading for the Pound part of the course I'm teaching, I thought if there were a cleavage this is it—and, as a matter of fact, how rightly I could be read with a humanist base, for I do not reject the Renaissance, and I'm fascinated by it in every angle. And I love chiaroscuro and the richness of the painting that Blake and Pound so hate.

BH: Then would it be correct to say that you define yourself, in contrast to Ginsberg here, in that Ginsberg has really rooted himself in a religion?

RD: Yes. And my profound humanism explains indeed why I am everywhere involved in religion, but nowhere does my involvement produce a church. Because it's always in question, and because I've always got the condition of Man as a deeper mystery than any religion proposes, so I go to religions to find out the condition of Man, and I'm not ever into a theology....

BH: But isn't it true, with Pound, that even though in a sense he is anti-humanist, he too never really commits himself to a transcendental dogma?

RD: Oh no, you're quite right. We can't stick him with it; we can't even do a duality if we're tempted to, by talking Pound versus Williams. It really *is* a great relief that Pound's anti-Semitism is incoherent. What in the hell if it had been coherent? I mean, and the poem is so much deeper. Anti-Semitism is, I think, the beginning experience of Jews—of Jews of Jews, and everybody else of Jews—at least it shows that they're actually being thought about. The period when there's no anti-Semitism and there's just the good old formulation of where people are—like, "I'm not really Irish," you say—is one which I think would be much more fatal, and so do the Jews today. Yet they make it that you have to have a Holocaust in order for them to exist—that tells a lot, as if their suffering didn't exist until the Holocaust. But Pound is the beginning of Jews entering American poetry. I was struck by that when I read Jerry Rothenberg's *Poland/1931*. My goodness, here in *The Cantos* we've got Jews actually being part of a big poem that proposes history—and even negatively being part of a history of the United States, because mostly they weren't in the history of the United States any more than blacks were, and blacks were dramatized by the Civil War, so that they began to enter there. But now we've got Jews actually *there*, as a good part of the culture.

MB: Isn't there one difference though. . . . There clearly are Poundians, you know, we've had them, I don't just mean critics, but little people running around, running their lives by Pound's reading list. . . .

RD: Oh, yes. . . .

MB: There are Olsonians, too.

RD: Oh, yeah . . . I mean, God, I mean, that's even closer clipped to the nail.

MB: Whereas I can't imagine what kind of a strange beast a Duncanian would be. . . .

RD: Oh, yeah, I defuse the fuses while they're going along, if that's what they want. I never became a Poundian in the sense of ever adhering to a line. After all, I was discovering Milton at the same time I was discovering *The Cantos*, and discovering the impact of Pound's bad temper even in his criticism. . . .

MB: When I think of Pound's criticism, which I've admired and learned a lot from, what I also think of right away is "A Few Don'ts. . . ." You know, always a list: "you are not allowed to read these people." It's not just "read these," but "these are the ones that you're not allowed to read," whereas when I read through your prose what I'm always hearing is "read this," "this is fun," "try this." I haven't come across once, at least in the prose of yours I've seen, anything resembling "Not to be read, colon." Whereas Olson's full of that sort of thing too.

RD: Oh, yeah, there were lots of things that were really on the index at Black Mountain [College], absolutely on the index. When I arrived at Black Mountain, the very first night I was there I started a series of *Finnegans Wake* readings, 'cause I knew that was heretical. I didn't really know what might happen. Three people turned up, and they were looking around like you're having a meeting underground in Moscow to read Trotsky. And *Ulysses* was off the map. I always thought that *Ulysses* was off the map, because a good bit of the quality of *Maximus* was learned—Olson's a great denier of his sources—in the impact of *Ulysses*. Then I discovered that Emerson was off the map. These were the big no-no's, and students wouldn't read them at all. Olson had pitched everybody [up] against Melville, so that even to have an appreciation of Hawthorne was [hard]. I was amazed that Creeley didn't know Hawthorne, 'cause it seemed that temperamentally they were very close together, and yet, he had been . . . He's a very dutiful post-Olson reader of things—he can feel that disapproval. I never paid attention to the disapproval. Before I taught there, we were on our way to Europe, and I wanted to see Charles before we left, so we swung around in the middle of the winter, and went to Asheville, North Carolina, before coming up to New York, where we got the boat, and that first night, Charles . . . we really wanted to talk all night, and I'm not sure we didn't, and I said, "I'm taking only twenty books with me to Europe, and only two are by the same author.". . . [*gap here*] Looking at the lists in *ABC of Reading* and so forth, I said what, no Marlowe? What, no Shelley? What, no Coleridge? It did look like an English department reading list. But in 1936–37, *The Waste Land* and *The Cantos* opened up the most of what seemed to be a very exciting adventure in poetry, and an adventure in reading—it's always going to be an adventure in reading. When I went line by line through *The Cantos*, the one passage I can't take at all is the one about the beaneries and the kikes and so forth, applying the word "kike" to Freud and Marx—it's so demeaning—I mean, to Pound, not them. But when you go line by line you can't dodge things like that, so you know how few lines there are in there like that. . . .

BH: Olson's reaction to your reading Stein also seems to me significant.

RD: Oh yes, phobic, absolutely phobic. And all the way through, by the way, ranting letters from Denise Levertov... I'm the only one who reads Edith Sitwell and has a high regard for her. It's easier to announce that you're a homosexual than to say that you read Edith Sitwell. At the [Richard] Wilburs, in very early days when there was some ambiguity about where they were going to place my poetry, when I named Edith Sitwell they were absolutely, absolutely offended. The whole room was offended; they all got up and moved to the other end, as I remember, like a pig had just appeared. As for Denise, part of it is her feelings about the English genteel writer, the presumption of the Sitwells, so verifiably non–middle class, to be writing poetry, that was more than she could bear, and then Edith didn't cool it at all.

BH: Now Pound had a reaction to Stein that was very similar to Olson's. . . .

RD: No, Pound is very interesting. In my talks with Pound at St. Elizabeths he said something about how he always thought that Stein gave balance to a magazine. You know, gave contrast and balance. 'Cause his principle of a magazine, by the way, was the collagist again. You should always have elements that are "nutty." It was almost a Poundian formula for a magazine, that you had to have strange things. The magazine was not a movement. Though *transition* was; *transition* was going more and more toward a "language of the night" proposition when it disappeared.

BH: But it would seem to me that your engagement with Stein and Olson's lack of interest in Stein points toward some difference between your work and Olson's work, right?

RD: Well, for instance, my work always does get to play, and Olson . . . *O'Ryan* is an example of Olson at play, I guess, but playfulness is not exactly Olson's home ground.

BH: And the play in language . . .

RD: Yes, right, and very early. In "An Owl Is an Only Bird of Poetry" I think, or is it in *Letters,* I have a list of what's in the coffeepot. That coffeepot is a fairly thoughtful coffeepot. So I did mean something brewing. As these things come back to me it never bothered me that they themselves might within themselves be intolerant of one another, because my imagination was to see how it all went together. Not necessarily to be able to see how—I mean, I'm perfectly willing to grant that I wouldn't be able to see how it all went together, but I had an underlying faith that it does, that it coexists, and the simple faith that since Milton had power and so did Pound they must be united in some way. Milton has really put over his show pretty good. In the early years of the war we pursued the whole Protestant dissenting world, which I still think . . . My parents, when I look back at their Hermeticism, were Calvinists, and all the Protestantisms interested me as if they presented a problem-world of itself, just a simple riddle, a kind of riddle of the intense reality of things. Now when we went back this time to *Paradise Lost,* it had lost a lot of that intense reality. It seemed so purposive toward the end. I saw him as merely carrying out this chore and being as disheartened as I was as I was reading it.

BH: I'm concerned that *Sagetrieb* in a sense may confine the tradition too narrowly. Are you familiar with [Laszlo] Gefin's *Ideogram*?

RD: Oh, remember when I was in your office I was looking at *Ideogram*. I never did get to see a copy of that.

BH: Well, it defines a single line of filiation from Pound to Williams to you, among other people. When I reviewed the book, I objected to it precisely on the grounds that I don't think one can understand your work except in relationship to Stein. . . .

RD: No, I coexist with the world. I mean, that's why Don Allen's anthology does . . . We discovered our work as coexisting and coexisting with poets we hadn't read at all and didn't know of. And there was a lot of festering along lines of the fact that you were one, that you did inhabit one ecology. There's a real question here, the basic point (I've used it over and over again) is the difference between a zoo that arranges you by alphabet, so if you're a polar bear you're next to a polecat and give no more explanation, or a zoo that arranges you by when you were born, or a zoo that arranges you according to a zoology, as it used to be, where you could be shown by species, and the modern ecological zoo that shows the creature in habitat. So one of the real lines of conflict were lines of habitat. At the point of Don Allen's anthology he was both in San Francisco and in New York, and he was aware that these two habitats overlapped, and that gave him his real clue. The middle of the country dropped out, but it wasn't even in there yet. It was just that people were hitchhiking between New York and San Francisco—not between New York and Chicago. And that was Allen Ginsberg's generation as they went back and forth between the two cultures, the two cities; and more than that—let's forget the poets—San Francisco in the same period was being Manhattanized. Manhattan was spreading over the whole world. So that was the recognition that was in that anthology: that the trouble with English literature was the design of the zoo and that it had no habitat except the English departments. "English literature" was those poets who might come and lecture at your university, but think how puzzled Shelley would look if you said to him how wonderful you are, you can come and lecture at our university.

BH: Wasn't the middle of the country Robert Bly and . . .

RD: But they came up later, remember; they came in response to that anthology, finding themselves left out. But Robert Bly was just beginning then, so he begins as being one of the out ones, so he begins in challenge. Paul Carroll had been in the first series of *Origin* and then drops out. But he had already dropped out in his own work.

MB: With reference to what Burt was saying, when people make these imaginary lineages, what they don't understand is that there is a huge difference between a collage principle and an ideogram principle. The ideogram principle, if you think through it, doesn't allow for interferences. It can take different elements, but it always has to blend them into a unity, whereas in a collage . . .

RD: As a matter of fact it's an immense difference in thinking about what a society is. And here Pound really is a noncollagist. When he is faced with the problem of society, he sees it *contaminated* with other elements. And the people who feel that—and they certainly are to be found in the dominant, ruling majority and in lots of little minorities—want authenticity within their group, and then everybody else is experienced as corrupting. For instance that's what my experience of Ginsberg was.

MB: That's why Olson isn't a collagist.

RD: No, he isn't a collagist; he is a New England town. Right. And ultimately the division between my household and the outside world is at the point where Ginsberg came screaming into the house to borrow a cup of sugar or something. Jess was home but I wasn't, but I certainly would have been backing it up. The embarrassed nondemocrat when the democrats come streaming in. The problem is not democracy but plurality, and the temperament of plurality is not just a temperament for some virtue or a belief that it's nice manners to be pluralistic and bad manners to be dualistic. It's simply that the pluralist finds things more vivid when they are seen as new elements, elements that challenge the mind to imagine how they all go together. One feels a challenge and wants it to be eliminated. Those things are there to be eliminated. Or not even thought of, which is the worst pattern of all—which is where Pound is.

MB: That's the totalitarian . . .

RD: Well, Dante's is a totalitarian mind, but on the other hand so is Whitman's, the totalitarian Democratic mind. Whitman's got a lot of no-no's, and then he breaks his own no-no's, and recognizes it. The thing about Whitman is that in *Leaves of Grass* every line *does* know what every other line said. So it gets to be quite a crowd. And in *The Cantos* that never happens. It isn't just that Whitman can contradict himself, but he doesn't mean to correct himself at all, and the two things stand there and then he deals with them, and then out of their conjunction come the leaps. So that if you're reading *Leaves of Grass* you want every edition, because every edition is finally changed by these leaps that take place. Whitman read himself until he died, so he was never a non–self-reader.

BH: Are you identifying with that as a pattern for yourself?

RD: I did indeed when I did the essays on Whitman. I felt very strongly and stated this strongly in the first essay that Whitman's command of the poem was superior to Pound's or Williams's. Williams gets baffled. He reads his poems over and over again and is baffled by them. Pound just doesn't really read 'em ever, doesn't go into 'em. In the case of Whitman ... *Democratic Vistas* is a picture of a nontotalitarian ... but the totalitarian character of Whitman's mind is cosmic—you have one cosmos—so there is a totalitarian picture. I'm particularly fascinated by that, because once I began to spot that in my work I erased the picture of empire and king. Already by the Venice poems the emperor stands for the person in command of the whole poem, and yet that emperor is not central. For one thing the court jester [*laughter*] points out various details whenever the emperor would tell him too much.

BH: Is this why Whitman couldn't admit his homosexuality into his poetry?

RD: Oh no, I think the homosexuality is as freely admitted as possible, and it is very likely that Whitman's sexuality didn't go much beyond onanism, as far as conscious sexuality goes. He has one map that's quite destructive—that's his totalitarianism. Because he's supposed to be the Adam—the same trouble Ginsberg has. The Adam is bisexual, so he's got to be bisexual. After reading Freud's essays on sexuality, I would have said yes, we're bisexual and so forth and so on. So what? But then I would want to think about it—which ways was I bisexual, and then when you know some bisexuals you realize, no you're not really caught in the trap they're caught in. But all that was this Adam Kadmon, who was both male and female. By the time propositions like that come up in my poems, I'm looking at them. They come up all right, vehemently; but then it becomes my business to go into the lore first, research the lore of the thing that looks dangerous or looks wrong or whatever or even right, and it's at that point that I make my detailed observations, because I don't start out in a world of observations. In *Heavenly City, Earthly City,* I wanted to give a portrait of what it was like to live in San Francisco. Well, anybody could tell by the time I was a hundred lines in that I wasn't doing that. Where's San Francisco? Here's this address, but is this the hat I live in? It was the hat I lived in in those days.

BH: You came to Orono in 1972. I remember a statement you made during the reading. You had just come from Kent State, the memorial reading there. You said, "Again and again the world divides between the crucified and the crucifier, and every one of us must choose."

RD: I wish we could.

BH: It seemed to me a prophetic statement.

RD: Yes, but it's also a totalitarian statement. Jess says that the wickedest thing ever said was Christ's statement, "If you are not with me you are against me." I remember Patchen at one point drawing a line and saying, "Are you on the side of the angels?" And I said, "When you draw a line I'm on the other side, Kenneth." That happens a lot in my reading. I'll read deep in Stein until she draws a line, and then I'll find that all the time I have been becoming more and more definitely *not* Stein. Even undergoing conversions like the Olson one, and the effect of that was certainly to convert my mind.... And so are the Stein imitations. I just wanted blindly to find out, "Since this is so attractive I've got to go into it 100 percent, and I'm not going to go into it in order to argue about it. But I know that I will exhaust it and it will still be me writing." It took about a year or a year and a half.

MB: Wasn't that one of the things that Olson keeps hammering into you in essays like "Against Wisdom as Such"? I mean, his anger at pluralism . . .

RD: Oh yes, he never accepted pluralism.

BH: At what point does Stein become totalitarian? Or does she?

RD: She's just one large totalitarian mind. You know the characteristic of the totalitarian is they can't repropose themselves. Stein does quite a good job, but . . . the nontotalitarian is Joyce. Although the work will be quite whole—so it isn't whether you make a monument or not but the fact that he would write *Ulysses,* which is the sanest book of the day, or maybe ever written, and then write the book of the nightmare in an entirely other language. Of course, he exhausted his transformational powers. It's clear that there is a sort of misery after he finished *Finnegans Wake,* and he gave *Finnegan* twenty years.

BH: But whenever someone is excluded or an outsider your imagination seems . . .

RD: To leap to them. Exactly. But plenty of times not. Now let's cool this. Somebody who has been excluded from any world that I was ever in and no one ever mentioned was Conrad Aiken. And so my impulse was to look into Conrad Aiken, but then I didn't find anything. I mean, it was like reading an empty sieve, so I was not going to worry about it.

MB: But the difference is you did go and look. You were curious.

RD: Yes, and now when I say I'm no longer interested in currencies, I can tell if it's not *really* my business, and yet the poems that I find most distinctive and enjoy at the present time are puzzling from any angle of my own work, like [John] Taggart's. Or [Gustaf] Sobin. These are pure pleasures of poetry, because they are not at all filled with the promise of being sources. I don't like the things that have been influenced by me. [Robert] Kelly bored me. I have to sort of sit myself down with more and more respect for [Kenneth] Irby and read it, but it isn't in this category of freebies. Susan Howe is a person whose poetry I keep contemplating and wondering could I gobble this up, could this be built into the range of "Structures of Rime" and "Passages"? But I have less and less sense of that. Most contemporary poetry doesn't seem very contemporary. The real feeling of being contemporary was when Charles was alive and I could be a heretic. I haven't found anybody to be a heretic to.

BH: What about George Oppen? Do you have any, any . . .

RD: I never read him until he was dead, because I loved Mary and George, and that was stretching the rubber band enough, because they had been Stalinists. And then George died and I was to give a reading at the memorial we held here and I read through his poetry and I was overwhelmed. I didn't realize how close he was to my work, and it's a damn good thing that I didn't read it before, because it would have been confusing. But I found it extraordinary. Just very, very moving. Whereas Carl [Rakosi] . . . I don't know what Carl's about, and he doesn't know what I'm about. In general, I've met some poets whom I just adored, and where I mistrusted what might be going on in the poetry. In back of Oppen's negatives there's a lot that I wouldn't agree with at all, and that was always there as we were talking about anything. . . . Yet the poetry was always deeper, always originating deeper, going deeper but also originating deeper. In the case of Elizabeth Bishop, I adored her and I've never read her, because I had early heard a couple of her poems and we made fun of them, which is disastrous anyway. Spicer used to be very great and so was I at making fun of poems, driving poets out of existence by doing a monkey job on them. But yet I hear rumors, and I might eventually read a little bit of Bishop. There was nothing in our friendship that would tell me that we would have great rapport, however. Lowell's the only one that had the imprimatur of Pound and Eliot and Williams (all three), and I read Lowell until the volume of *Imitations*, and then when Robin Blaser said the new one was a great lapse, I said I don't want to get data on the collapse of this poet. But there were lots of interesting lines of affinity between us. He was only two years older than I am. At the time that the *Land of Unlikeness* came out I was one of the 250 subscribers, and anybody looking at *Medieval Scenes* would see why, because there was a lot of similarity between the two. In structure, and Lowell also enjambs. I was always responsive to the metaphorical level in Lowell. I remember the "paths snaking up the hill," in *Mills of the Kavanaughs*. Because it was charged with more than immediate metaphor. If his world was haunted by the devil I could imagine the devil. It is always the imagination of gods and states of mind that I think are telling in the poem. That's the trouble Milton has. Since the theology is real, he isn't imagining it. That's the curb on the imagination. And the proposition of a poem with history in it would be a reimagination of history, which is not one any of them have the courage to take. Olson

With George Oppen, San Francisco, 1970s

always has to be throwing up the illusion that he's got history right finally, and that's the block to the imagination in *Maximus*. Because the great moments in *Maximus* don't pay any attention to getting history right at all, or geology right. And yet the offspring from it . . . [?] and so forth at Cambridge—that whole group. I came back and said I discovered in England that their response to *Maximus* is that they now test how good a poem is by how much of the encyclopedia it has in it. Literally, like square foot and do they have their facts right about geology?

MB: I remember you said that you kept up with [John] Ashbery and were interested in his poetry.

RD: Yes, and off and on the poems have seemed overwhelming to me, like "The New Spirit" in the *Three Poems* and "Self-Portrait in a Convex Mirror." Both of those were really marvelous poems. When I'm not making it the poems seem trivial, belonging to a different realm. Again I think habitat is here. That's a different habitat and one thing I am not is East Hampton.

MB: What about [Frank] O'Hara?

RD: Initially when O'Hara wrote the *Meditations in an Emergency* I wrote a long letter. I still think this was more in the spirit of Whitman than anything else going. I don't know what was in that long letter but from there on he revealed a real hostility. Once LeRoi Jones wrote and asked if I had a play for the drama issue of *Kulchur* and I sent *Adam's Way*. And then O'Hara and that entire group said that if *Kulchur* published anything by me they would walk off the magazine. Ashbery was in Paris at that time, so he wasn't on top of whatever it was in New York that was brewing, and I never fathomed exactly...

MB: Strange that he would react like that, because here is somebody who clearly isn't a totalitarian. O'Hara seems open to lots of possibilities.

RD: Oh no. As a matter of fact the entire work was overwhelming when it was there all together. Talk about being able to reorient one's place and position, and not get stuck with the Maximus.

BH: Michael and I were talking earlier about this whole issue of traditions and schools and so on. And I think the problem I've always had with Ashbery is that, while he's open to a lot of different voices, the dominant tonality seems to be ironic. And I guess I don't read your poetry as ironic.

RD: No, as a matter of fact, to Olson irony was an absolute darkest sin. In a nice balance I think he keeps Creeley from thinking whether he is ever ironic.

BH: Which he is all the time.

RD: Well, he certainly doesn't want to admit to it, because Papa Olson would disapprove. Mama don't want no irony in here. The letters on irony between Olson and Creeley took place over [e. e.] cummings. They are about the privileged position in which cummings placed himself in relation to the poem. And I think there is a privileged position question in Ashbery. The problem is its sophistication: the poetry is sophisticated in relation to its own condition. That's more serious than is there irony here. When I'm doing a reading I often am amused by the irony of the line that I've just given and wonder whether the audience observes this. Meanwhile the important thing—that early definition of responsibilities—is to keep the ability to respond. So you don't disallow, you don't distance—distancing is something I don't do, although I can. But certainly not sophistication. What we call the Academic poem is actually the sophisticated poem. One that knows whatever happens in the poem. Although you may surrender to the poem, and the term of what you do when you surrender is still a large term with me. Ashbery's "The New Spirit" was a poem of surrendering *to* things. How strong it was of the poet to be sophisticated and to write a poem in which . . . Auden never surrendered. Yes, Ashbery accepts his unhappiness and doesn't go into a deep quarrel with it, and yet he does somewhere, because it bursts out in him. But I still have my self-definition as coexisting with the master generation, as I call them, which includes Pound and Williams and H.D. and Stevens.

BH: What about Zukofsky in relationship to that group?

RD: Well, Zukofsky like Rexroth gets isolated out as a loner. And Zukofsky thought himself as a master in relationship to students, and so when I turned up, there's a letter in which Zukofsky says a disciple has turned up. And he was always puzzled about what this disciple was. But on the other hand I was the only reader at that time, so I had this very singular magic quality. Yes, I think that in some sense Zukofsky always thought of himself as a disciple of Pound, having learned his craft and then setting about "A." But "A" was not a continuation of *The Cantos* or of its problems at all. "A" is a philosophical poem. And Zukofsky's psychology is simplified Spinoza. It really is a philosophical rather than a psychological bias. Whereas in my work there is a psychological bias.

BH: Is Zukofsky still a source for you, though, in some sense?

RD: Well, he always is a source of discipline, because we are so very different. That's the part that he didn't understand either. While I was different enough from Pound, and Pound would be puzzled over that first volume, I also at that very same time was doing disciplined work where Pound could keep the sense of where I would get with the divided line, the propositional line. In the poet who doesn't enjamb, every line is a statement—it might not be a sentence but it is a completed statement. So he can't linger other places, and if there is rhyme it's usually a formality; I mean, it's usually a manner, not an inner rhyme like it is in Shakespeare. The one thing in Pound that gives a hint that he also was an enjamber is that in order for him to keep that clean line, you see him breaking the line off. And he prevents himself from having reference back to it, so he short-circuits it all the time. He short-circuits his own thought, and yet that doesn't mean that he makes a loop. Nor even if he makes a loop the inbetween matter doesn't—he keeps one distinct from the other. Where in actual enjambment we recognize how much everything is blended, how much chiaroscuro is going on, so that the *thing* that you're most positive about, you will immediately see that that was a proposition of a negative. And Olson isn't going to see his negatives, because he doesn't want to see his positives. Jess said, "If you read Olson just for his positives and don't pay any attention to his negatives at all . . ." And then I said, "But you know his negatives are accusations. They're accusatory, and he's the one who brought up the subject, so we had better think about them." And yet Jess didn't read very far in Olson, and I always felt enough that Olson was accusing me for it to be interesting. I could stand up to it at every point. I've overused "Against Wisdom as Such," because that was a rather foolish remark of his, but there are other things too. There's a way in which from the very beginning Olson doubted me— that's putting it mildly. And he also, however, believed in me, which is the strongest belief I think I've ever had in my life, because it was over his own doubts. But Creeley didn't want me at all in the *Black Mountain Review.* The Creeley-Olson correspondence in relation to me in the early years is exceedingly homophobic, but Olson is most insistent upon his absolute feel that I was a major poet and that I had to be on that football team, for his putsch.

BH: It seems to me that Zukofsky's work really goes into the Language poets.

RD: Yes, well, they're the ones who've made the richest use of it to date.

And Creeley's quatrains were of such extraordinary quality that I was sure he had read Coleridge and I was sure he had read Zukofsky and I was sure he had read H.D., and he hadn't read any of the three. When I read those three aloud to Creeley he was *really* charged. I should have done the reverse, because he has been in quatrains forever, but it showed him that there are other masters.

BH: He had been reading Emily Dickinson?

RD: Yes, he had.

BH: Are you interested in the Language people at all?

RD: As a phenomenon in relation to this. They're like a crowd of mosquitoes off there in somebody else's swamp. The students in *our* program really come in reaction to the Language poets' program. I find their poetics reductionist. I have absolutely no use for minimalism in art. They don't carry the responsibility through, and philosophically I don't know where in the hell they get it . . . from a linguistic basis most of them I know and they don't reach back. Once we had logical positivism, and now we have illogical negativism, which is the next step in reductionism.

MB: It is a shame that when one thinks of Zukofsky now, one so often thinks of that particular set of responses.

RD: And they were usurping it, so the beauty of Zukofsky is lost completely in that transaction. That isn't what they look for. And Zukofsky has a Lewis Carroll–like humor, while the Language poets have no humor about it at all. It's like *seeing* how humorous Calvinism is. Louis Zukofsky tells us that Lewis Carroll is where you've gotta look. There's a delight in nonsense in Zukofsky and a play within the content. I have no trouble with that in *"A,"* because again like *Finnegans Wake* it illuminates itself but not some other text. By the way, it's clear in the big work on Shakespeare, *Bottom: On Shakespeare,* that he consciously proposed it as a collage. He didn't at the beginning of *"A"* propose that poem as a collage, but by the time he's working on *Bottom: On Shakespeare,* that's a massive proposition in collage and stands in contrast with *Guide to*

Kulchur. In *"A"* you see Louis knows what he is doing, and as a matter of fact he's doing it and constantly thinking about it. Whereas in *Kulchur* Pound is sort of a victim of opinion by that time. Louis can ponder. So I turned to that poem for two things. One is a discipline against my own tendencies which would be not like Louis's. In my first correspondence with Louis, I sent him a poem that I had never brought into print and he blue-penciled it and sent it back, so I know what he was doing—he was doing like Pound did. I mean, this is what you do with a disciple. And I typed out all the lines that he had crossed out and all the lines he hadn't crossed out and looked at the two poems and saw that there was something here and something there too. I sometimes wondered, Does Louis read me? Because while *Letters* could still be in Louis's line, by the time of *The Opening of the Field* there's lots of it that's not Louis. Louis had a certain narrow view of what he would read. We found little lists of "what I must not read" in the index. Does he have an index for . . . I think he does.

BH: For *"A"*? Yes.

RD: Yes. I was thinking of an index like the Catholic Church has an index, lists of corrupting texts. [*gap here, to turn over tape*]

MB: To what extent is that emphasis now a partial response as well to the immediate political situation? I mean, that sense of the necessity to reaffirm some kind of humanist values in the face of the onslaught.

RD: It goes beyond that. And also I'm beginning to realize that when we're talking about humanism in the Renaissance we are talking about an embattled small group of intellectuals in a society that was not humanistic at all—far from it; and a group that managed a kind of habitat for itself. After the Second World War the question became lifestyle instead of tradition, and as a matter of fact I have a lifestyle now, not a tradition. A lifestyle that draws upon those elements in my parents' traditions that I found fascinating and drops like a hot potato the ones that I didn't, the ones that I found fundamentalist. And fundamentalist occultism and Hermeticism is as much a bore as any kind of fundamentalism. But what's interesting to me is I think it's always been the same. The

Pre-Raphaelite group become interesting because they did make a habitat for themselves in an entirely foreign place. Everybody else was a Philistine—that was their sense of it. And yet there was a kind of humor in their position, because it was theatrical. But Pound isn't able to take that aesthetic position, so then he has to have the aesthetic himself.

MB: I have a sense—not just because *Ground Work* is largely composed of poems that were written almost a decade earlier . . .

RD: Yes, yes . . .

MB: But in your readings there's a great deal of emphasis on the political situation in America today.

RD: Well, it hasn't changed at all. I get so tired of hating Presidents; I've been hating Presidents consistently from . . . I started out hating Roosevelt, so I'm really good at it. Eisenhower was the only one that I really didn't bother hating very much, since he was so incompetent that he made jokes about it. The rest of them were quite a lot.

MB: Because I find that the interest in Dante, both the political and linguistic interest that you talk about in the *Dante Études*, goes right into the poems that have an immediate political reference.

RD: Oh yes, yes. In the *Dante Études* I felt I did get at what it was like to live in the city. I realized it as I was going along. There were a lot of things I was drawing from, the *De Monarchia*, for instance. But while Dante was talking about principles or something, I was really seeing streets. I realized how much it seems to me that life in America is liberated with the appearance of the boutiques and that kind of gentrification of the city, and the opening up of a city of pleasures—all this is very much what goes on in San Francisco, like the 24th Street district with its coffeehouses, etc. You *stroll* through the streets. That was really the experience I have of walking around and of living in a city which is not the city itself. The city itself in those same poems is as reprehensible as Florence—ten times over. If I were to think of it, Mayor Feinstein would be enough to have me committing assassinations.

MB: But there's something else that makes me wonder about political poetry, I mean like the poem about Alioto in *Ground Work*....

RD: Yes, and even the poem says and who is he?

MB: And yet you've given his name.

RD: Yes.

MB: I wonder what happens for all the people who don't know...

RD: You know there's an interesting case out of Dante for this. I just got a book on homosexuality in the Middle Ages. Brunetto Latini wasn't homosexual at all. Dante just took all the opposite political party in Florence and labeled them homosexuals and put them in that Sodomite circle.

MB: What a sly guy.

RD: And they can't find any evidence . . . you know, they research, they look for letters, look for any hint . . . and known homosexuals were *known* in those days and could get into trouble. So you have to presume that this was a closeted circle or something, but it still won't work. It won't stand for a moral example, 'cause there is no substance back of it. And yet this is exactly like Richard III with the hump on his back, because the figure of Brunetto Latini is so strong that we don't care if Latini himself wasn't a homosexual. But this is a slander as a matter of fact—everyone who is named in that section is placed there with a slanderous intent—not as a serious description of their own sexuality.

MB: Maybe that's why it gives such a gorgeous image at the end. "Like somebody who wins the race, not somebody who loses it." But if you think about it, that's the only poem that I can imagine reading in which Joseph Alioto's name is going to be . . .

RD: Oh yes, immortalized. But more than that it ends up with [Jerry] Rubin, the clown on the other side. Originally he hadn't been on that list. And then Rubin suddenly showed up and I thought, "Well, gee, since the whole theme in this is liars, I've got to put this liar in—this lying is supposed to be on our side but it is still a lie."

MB: To continue with the political theme, one of the things that has always made the kind of anarchism and the pacifism you've talked about so powerful, although I can't say that I'm either of those two, but what makes it so powerful is that I think in your writing it comes not out of a denial of your own imaginative capacity for angers, hatreds, violence, but from an open recognition of them.

RD: Oh yes. When I show my Freudian disposition in the poem it's most powerfully in me and who else?

MB: Is that part of the reason for your quarrel with Levertov?

RD: Yes, well, the quarrel with Denise... By the time you have chopped-up bodies, you're the one who is doing it, the poem—not whatever your source was; and she didn't even have a source for that. And still, and it made it even worse, let's say you don't have a source in that case; it really is just that you have that on your mind, and *that* must be the subject of the poem. I didn't say it was wrong for her to have it on her mind, but I said if it's on your mind the poem had better go into that, because that's its real ground—how come these things are here?

MB: Surprising she denied it so much, because in the early poetry some of the best lines are those very violent...

RD: Ohhh, I don't know what that correspondence will look like when it's dug up. I know I was so insulting by the time it ended, she didn't want to hear of me again.

MB: But so much of your own writing talks about the notion of the *polemos* and the struggle of the war and the violence.

RD: Well, I keep trying to locate them. I'm going over "Man's Fulfillment in Order and Strife." For the second volume, I am going to be doing an essay on war again, because I saw that peace isn't an opposite of this, and that order and strife are not peace and war, and we're often opposed to a war because it is a false one and so that there's more than one war—there are different kinds of wars, and our period is one in which the symptoms of war at every level show that the Hydra of The War is beginning to appear and take over. And especially alarming is of course that [people] only have one wish and that is a fear which is atomic war. They can't think of any other possible conclusion. Well, they have another one, but they don't want to think about it and that's overpopulation and if you follow through the pages of *Scientific American* you can find that the scientists think we'll be extinct from overpopulation. And that is a grimmer picture yet, if you think of the thousands, even millions of years of human endeavor to try to populate the world.

MB: Has the reading of your Homer group and your working through of *The Iliad* fed into your notion of The War?

RD: In the second volume [of *Ground Work*] some things appear directly out of Homer. Well, there is a Hesiod passage in *Ground Work*. I wanted to pervert the Hesiod, so I had to go back and work the Greek to do that. And then I translated and translated and translated the Pindar with no proposition of making a poem of it, but I thought I would get past any possible reference to it and then it would burst out. I thought it would come in a dream. I knew it would come transformed. And I was making notes—as a matter of fact making notes on the *Theogeny*—for my morning class in Inverness, and I was up about six o'clock writing and began writing—something I *don't* do—but there I was pouring forth the kind of associative writing that I curbed very early and in the midst of all that afterbirth there it was, a very recognizable poem. I lifted it right out just like that—prfft. That's the one that dated the point at which the book was finished. It was ten years ago. Yes, I was well along. At the present time after all I'm fairly well along on the second volume, so I don't have to worry about it, and yet I've gone three years with only the beginning poem.

BH: Volume one of *Ground Work* is *Before the War*.

RD: Yeah, and then *In the Dark*.

BH: One thing I find myself puzzled about is the sense in which this is "before" the war.

RD: Well, standing before the war is like standing before . . . In the first place, like I said to Denise, you can't scold an earthquake, and you can't scold a war. A war is a real state. In this I would be like Homer. Homer doesn't praise war or disparise it. It isn't a moral question at all. It is a catastrophe. You realize as you read *The Iliad* that they can only fight by going out of their minds, by building themselves up and going berserk. Otherwise they want to go home. They have to be incited and work themselves up. Achilles's wrath is identical with the only moving force there is anyway, because everybody moves only in wrath: Hector is not a hero when he comes sweeping down, any more than Diomedes. Diomedes is almost Homer's caricature of this factor in the hero. They are compared with firestorms, with lions cornered by hunters, with earthquakes. They are a natural force. They are no longer human at all. War to them is like nemesis. It doesn't come from what they have been doing. It *seems* to come from what they've been doing, but they feel that it overtakes them and that once they're in it they're helpless. They can't manage to turn around and go back. And in Homer, Zeus's plan is the whole war itself, so that there is an organum in back of the thing, a hidden plan. And Zeus is the great liar who manipulates everything. But the human beings don't have a plan. They're caught in it.

MB: Outside of your work, do we have any other modern poems that really take the issue of the war as not just a local phenomenon but a much larger, a central . . .

RD: The haunting thing about it is that our time is really fixated on that war. It's just like Hitler. Hitler terrorized the world. Why were they giving in to that terror? He was a nightmare figure before he started carrying it out. It's not an empty threat at all—the threat will be carried out, but there's this downward current in which nobody can think of any alternative. That they could invent a bomb with atoms and they can make machines that radiate poison. And then they've never been able to do another fucking thing with the split atom. All the promises, the great buildup, the lies that you are going to be able to ride around the world on a single atom and you will have electricity forever and it will be cheap and will only cost you about $2 a year. Every one of those was a lie. And not only does it cost twenty million times more than they ever said, but they are also poisoning and polluting the environment, as if they won't let go until the whole thing is . . . So I've got a very negative picture about what is at work in humanity. In every dimension. And the fact that the very ones who are suffering the most from the overpopulation have inbuilt nonregulation so that they are indeed choking themselves and screaming to the rest of the world for food, and soon they are not going to be getting the food.

MB: If you look back at the various political poems written in English from around the time of Korea through Vietnam, don't you think that one of the things that distinguishes your poems is the taking of responsibility for the imagination?

RD: Oh yes. And also in some way which I find questionable—is it a sentiment?—that I can't separate myself from the doing of these things. And they aren't anything I *could* do, much less would, in fact literally *couldn't* do. And yet I can't separate myself; I can't take a moral stand against them, because I feel entirely part of it. That's again the sense I think of habitat in part. It's my habitat too if they ruin it. Asking the question of good and evil that underlies the Gnostic sensibility which fascinated me, though I never have been won to it even when I was following it with absolute fascination. I early thought, "Well, how do I feel about good and evil?" And, then I'd realize that I thought you did good as good, not because it was going to win. I made something beautiful in order that something beautiful exist. Whereas let's say a Jonathan Williams will accuse the world of not reading . . . let's say they accuse the world of not reading Olson. Okay. And meanwhile they pay no attention to the ones who do. All the ones who don't read Olson. It's like grabbing the bus driver and saying you aren't holding up culture, or something like this. This is one I never accepted at all. It's like educating your parents—although I certainly did in high school. I was in open war, because of the shock to me when I saw that my parents' culture world was not going to extend to include the *Ulysses* that I was reading. Nothing has ever given me such a shock and shiver. Mommy used to read to us, but now you know she isn't going to read that same thing that you read at all. She's already looking angry and bewildered. She belonged to a group that got together to read *Conversation at Midnight* to figure out what Edna St. Vincent Millay was talking about. God. With a vengeance I wrote a poetry to get even with that. But I think the illusion you get into . . . because the poem is central to my life and takes over my imagination completely, I have to realize all the time that's a kind of dementia, since that poem isn't taking over for instance Olson's mind and isn't the center for reading *Maximus*. If you can't shift gears, you can't go from one to the other. In relation to my own work I'm always trying to see if I can't find a gearshift that will leave it not totally self-absorbed. It's *always* got a tendency for selfabsorption—I don't have to worry about that. I'm not the one who has to be sure that I remember all the lines present—I'm haunted by them. So I have to in a sense exorcise the contents, and for that reason I go into other particulars or try and find out what a thing is. Like still thinking about war—can't I think of it in a different way? That's certainly one of the squirrel cages that I've got in my mind. And yet when a poet refuses to have anything to do with the war, like Ashbery, I find it very unreal at this level. I don't *believe* you can walk around. . . . And yet they *do,* so, okay, that's where they are walking.

MB: It's a different habitat?

RD: Yeah.

MB: I think they don't have a habitat.

RD: And that is, I think, already showing up in [Frank] O'Hara, because the point at which O'Hara broke with my poetry was one at which he is in his habitat and speaking from it and not allowing at all that you might get fussy about . . . But if you look at the later poems . . . I'm still convinced he was killed mid- . . . If we imagine him living longer, we would have had a constantly developing poetry, because that's what was going on here. He has a true dialectic in his poetry. But the interesting earmark would be that the followers of O'Hara already were ironic in relation to the war. [pause] I guess we should be. That movie star Reagan for president. Think what we would get if we took him seriously.

BH: Well, it's four o'clock and we should . . .

RD: Yes, I have to rest before I do my dialysis.

BH: Thank you very much for . . .

RD: Oh, jabber, jabber, jabber!

An Interview with the BBC

(1985, excerpts)

The following is added here for its illuminating observations, both Robert Duncan's and his interviewer's. Duncan's files, where this discussion was found, included no information about the specific source of this interview or the interviewer. This brief exchange, a fitting end to this volume, was apparently unpublished.

—Ed.

ROBERT DUNCAN: I have absolute recognition when I was about sixteen or seventeen that I was a poet. Hopeless. My father was an architect, and I was in line to inherit the firm. And I was interested in architecture and geometry. And suddenly, in a real conversion experience, a little voice tells you you're a poet. And then I went—very practical, it's the middle of the Depression, it's [1935] or so—I went to the library and read and found out that the most any poet had made that year was $400, and that was Ogden Nash. And I knew he had a poem every single week in *The Saturday Evening Post*. I didn't even have any ambition in that direction. But I did know it was beyond my wildest hope, that I couldn't go home and propose that I was going to be a poet instead of an architect. Luckily my mother was absolutely ignorant about contemporary poetry, and I was happily innocently ignorant too. So in our controversy she said I could be an architect and a poet, too. And I said . . . well, to tell you the truth, it would be impossible for me.

BBC: "I had committed myself to poetry, as if to a madhouse or religion," Robert Duncan wrote later. And his single-minded dedication to poetry has continued for more than fifty years. When I arrived at his home in San Francisco's Mission District, I was led up a steep staircase and shown into his bedroom, which was filled with collages, books, and the good kind of clutter that means home. Robert was resting after his morning dialysis session, his left arm in a cast after a recent fall. Beside him in bed, his companion, Jess Collins, propped up his ankle, which was cased in plaster. We made some jokes about couples who fracture together stay together. For in fact they've lived with each for the last thirty-five years. For me one poem, "Circulations of the Song," sums up Duncan's work. He based it on translations of the Sufi poet Rumi.

RD: Very early I was reading Rumi, because there were only a handful of poets who we knew were homosexual and that as a matter of fact speak for that condition. And all of that Persian poetry is written with a male object. So it was a genre in which you could write... I'd read Rumi, and I was never able to key into it. I always thought it was Professor Arberry's, a professor translating and not really giving me Rumi. And I had all the translations I could get of Rumi. I knew the philosophy, and it isn't the philosophy you get from a poet. And Rumi was like a *Leaves of Grass*, a bedside book. I'd read him really to comfort my soul, and when I was troubled. That's a very important role of poetry for me; I turn to it then. And the rest of the time I wonder why do I ever read that stuff. So that Rumi is sort of a presence. ["Circulations of the Song"] isn't addressed to Rumi, although it addresses Rumi directly as a lover several times in the course of the poem. In the poem, of course, I really seem to be in an inner dialogue of the soul, and Rumi is so close to that. But I had been reading Rumi over and over again, and I wasn't copying him at all; it's just that a song began in me.

BBC reader:

> If I do not know where He is
> He is in the very place of my not knowing.
> If I do not know who He is
> He is the very person of my not knowing.
> His is the Shining Forth I know not.
> My heart leaps forward   past knowing.
> . . .

BBC: When he was thirty-five Duncan had a sudden release of creative energy that led to his mature work in *The Opening of the Field* and the two books which followed. This new freedom seemed to be linked to his particular use of the word "permission."

RD: Permission is one of the most powerful terms [for me]. That came in the "Often I Am Permitted to Return to a Meadow" that began that volume. And I was distressed I think even to the middle of the next volume by did I *have* any permission? And in back of that was, Did I have any permission for the things that were most important in my life, I mean to relate to God? And the Sufi God is the nearest I would accept for a God. But I'm a pluralist as far as gods go, and some of them are really bad.

. . .

The universe is living for me throughout, and generative. I'm Darwinian in my persuasion, and evolution makes a higher sense to the imagination than previous propositions. I always had great scorn even as a child for the Bible account of God's creations, because that's like children creating in a sandbox. And Darwin proposed a universe something like Heraclitus did, that the universe is constantly creative of itself, and that really stirs the imagination for me.

. . .

You recognize in the human beloved that there really is a divine Beloved.

. . .

Much of the material in my poetry is nursery material. I love it when they say I am erudite and then they say "Apollo," and I say, "Well, I think that was a nursery-rhyme once." [*laughter*] The Duncan ancestor came from Aberdeen, and the tradition was that the Duncans were storytellers. You know, no radio, no TV, then you do need somebody who will talk all night while the others fall asleep.

BBC: . . . and who knows the sagas and the myths.

RD: Yeah, right, and they're always immediate, you know, you're telling it for the first time. That's an experience I learned as a child. That when you start telling these stories you're *in* them, so that they're not just being retold.

. . .

But also I'm permitted to return to some source, and it seems to be outside me.

. . .

BBC: It was time for Robert to rest. His methods in "Circulations of the Song" are those of the alchemist he refers to. He dissolves ordinary experience, mixes diverse images, precipitates sudden radiance. Mysteries engage him. How did the world begin? What becomes of us after death? Although he writes about transcendental subjects, he still celebrates the physical beauty of this mortal world. And Duncan's search, through human love, for divine love, links him with Dante and with Rumi. He has returned to these sources by becoming a vessel, a song outside of time. So as I left his bedside, I felt that the song which had welled up in him so strongly was still circulating.

Permissions and Copyrights

A Conversation about Poetry and Painting: permission granted by Kevin Power.

boundary 2 Interview: © 1980, Duke University Press, all rights reserved. Reprinted by permission of the publisher.

"Nematodes! Nematodes!" (original title "In Interview"): permission granted by Michael McClure.

"Realms of Being": permission granted by Rodger Kamenetz.

Sagetrieb Interview: permission granted by Michael André Bernstein.

Cover photograph of Robert Duncan: permission granted by Mrs. Violet Redl, for the Estate of Harry Redl.

Pages 16 and 76–77, photographs of Robert Duncan in Berkeley in the 1940s: courtesy of Becky Brockway and the late Lyn Brockway.

Page 62, photograph by Wallace Berman of Robert Duncan writing: copyright by and with the permission of the Wallace Berman Estate. Courtesy of Kristine McKenna.

Page 181, photograph of Robert Duncan in New York circa 1940: courtesy of the Poetry Collection, University at Buffalo.

Pages 216 and 253, photographs of Charles Olson and Robert Duncan: courtesy of Stephen Witt-Diamant.

Page 229, photograph of Jaime de Angulo: permission granted by Gui Mayo.

Page 241, photograph of Robert Duncan and Jess at Black Mountain College: courtesy of Joanna McClure.

Page 380, photograph of Michael McClure and Robert Duncan: permission granted by Joanna McClure. Courtesy of the Poetry Collection, University at Buffalo.

Other photos of Robert Duncan and Jess: courtesy of the Jess Collins Trust; all interview material by Robert Duncan: copyright by the Trust and reproduced by permission.

Every effort has been made by the editor to secure written permissions for each interview reproduced in this book. He sincerely apologizes to anyone whose material is included and who has not been contacted, and he hopes that you will inform the publisher and editor of your current address. To all those who gave permission to publish material, warm thanks for your generosity.